A Traveler's Highway to Heaven
to Heaven
History on the Hoof

Exploring the History and Culture
of Northern Spain on El Camino de Santiago

2nd Edition

William J. Bonville

Bonville, William J.
ISBN: 978-0-7443-2082-4
Traveler's Highway to Heaven, A – *History on the Hoof:*
Exploring the History and Culture of Northern Spain on El
Camino de Santiago – 2nd ed.

SynergEbooks
948 New Highway 7
Columbia TN 38401
www.synergebooks.com

Front Cover photo: The Cathedral of St. James,
Santiago de Compostela, by A. Korzekwa
Back cover photo: Hoofing the Highway to Heaven, by Sarah Nicholl

Cover art by William Jesse Griffith – www.tivmonkey.com
Contact the author via email at bonville@q.com

Printed in the USA

A Traveler's Highway to Heaven

TABLE OF CONTENTS

LIST OF ILLUSTRATIONS

The Monastery of San Salvador at Leyre
Gothic Portal, Santa Maria la Real
Santa Maria de Eunate
Roman Road at Cirauqui
Iglesia del Santo Sepulcro
The Apse of the Church Built by San Juan Ortega
El Sarmental, The Pilgrims' Portal
The Church of Our Lady of the Apple Tree
The Church of San Martin de Fromista
The San Tirso Church Tower
Covadonga, The Sacred Cave
The Monastic Church of San Pedro
Santullano
Santa Maria del Narranco
San Miguel de Escalada
Santa Maria la Real, Cebrero

PREFACE TO THE SECOND EDITION

This book is intended for travelers who have a taste for history and an interest in how the things they see got to be the way they are. I call it history on the hoof

What the book is about is an exploration of what some call the Highway to Heaven, El Camino de Santiago, The Way of St. James. These pages describe a motor-walking junket that courses that highway, end to end, through Northern Spain. Pilgrims afoot have plodded its length for more than a thousand years, believing it to be a sure route to Heaven.

Travels described in this book were undertaken a decade ago. Learning that a thousand-year-old abandoned monastery had been reborn recently as a plush parador, meanwhile preserving rare features of Asturian Pre-Romanesque art and history that we admired, prompted a fresh look at the Camino. Out of that came this new edition of *A Traveler's Highway to Heaven*.

A detailed itinerary, which may be used as a model for personal planning, is presented at the back of the book. The itinerary is designed for the time-limited working person taking a three-week holiday using a rental car and shank's mare. Nonetheless, a large part of the book's audience has been drawn from that company of dedicated footsloggers hiking (or who have hiked) El Camino to its sacred destination. From them I learned that *A Traveler's Highway to Heaven* became favored by these foot travelers mainly because of the historical and cultural spice with which it flavors their "El Camino experience."

What the author wished to craft was a guidebook that would enable nuances of that Camino experience to be accessible to travelers who – whether from age or infirmities, or perhaps with young children in tow – were physically incapable of walking the hundreds of kilometers of the Camino. There was nothing hollow about that intent. Following the plan of this

1

book, the author unexpectedly discovered a taste of the pilgrim's experience himself.

There are competing opinions as to the nature of the "El Camino experience" that the hiker cum pilgrim ordinarily claims all for himself. Some say it is a psychological "high" that comes of the weeks-long regimen of the walk itself. There is respectable research, reported in *Venture Inward*, that supports that idea. On the other hand, those sharing the mindset of the pilgrims who have trod the Way for more than a millennium are of a different mind. They say the kernel of the experience is religious or spiritual in nature. What adherents to both points of view agree upon is that there is a convivial social element in the experience. It comes of days spent putting one foot ahead of the other, and settling down in the evenings for socializing with one's fellows and recuperating together from the physical stresses of each day on the Way.

Regardless of all that, a traveler may seek nothing more in Northern Spain than a pleasant holiday. There is real pleasure to be found browsing through this colorful, historic land, meeting the people, enjoying their mountainous countryside and picturesque towns and villages. Stroll through old cities teeming with the business of today alongside the residue of centuries past. El Camino offers all that amidst a fabulous historical record of a unique culture that gave birth to a nation, Spain, where none had been before.

The detailed itinerary, presented at the back of the book, follows the travel sequence provided in the pages which follow. The author went there, did that and came home, just as described, verifying it could be done as advertised. Moreover, he had a wife with him who made sure it was done enjoyably without hectic dashing around and sacrifice of creature comforts.

Would a longer trip be worthwhile? Are there other things to see?

You bet.

Can you modify that itinerary to suit your own taste?

Certainly. It also adapts to the needs and whims of free

spenders or folks on a budget. Back pack it or make it a luxurious grand tour. Have the time and the legs for it? Then don your hiking boots and join the files of pilgrims and backpackers on the Way.

Can it be adapted for someone only able to allow two weeks for the trip? Of course. Better just two weeks than nothing at all. Simply review the book, decide what you think is appropriate to skip or cut short, and plan accordingly. Suggestions are given at the end of the listed itinerary.

Been there and done that?

Read on and find out what you missed seeing or knowing about what you saw.

Finally, since this history deals with a cultural milieu unfamiliar for many travelers, a glossary is appended to the book. It clarifies repetitive uses of terminology peculiar to the region and its history, and provides brief summaries of detailed descriptions provided but once in the text where applicable, and not repeated where the terms are used elsewhere.

INTRODUCTION

Our destination is set in Northern Spain. There we travel a very special route: the historic pilgrimage road, El Camino de Santiago, The Way of St. James.

For the faithful it is a Highway to Heaven. For anyone else it is a fascinating junket through a region awesome not only in its extremes of topography and climate, but also for its people. Their history and physical record are the mirror of their land. Awesome.

Yes, the land and its people.

Northern Spain is turned sparkling green by moist Atlantic air currents that leave its mountains awash in violent storms. Down between the stolid, gray peaks are a host of narrow, intimate valleys made lush and fertile from the runoff. The tallest mounts rise above 3000 meters. Their verdant timbered flanks and towering crags sustain a wild remoteness, replete with packs of wolves and companion wild things that most of Europe has not seen since the Middle Ages.

This rugged, unforgiving land has been home since prehistory for clans of tough, independent-minded Celts, Iberians and Vascons (Basques). These feisty peoples and their mountains made Northern Spain the last frontier for every alien civilization that sought to invade and dominate the Iberian Peninsula, whether Carthaginian, Greek, Roman, Vandal, Goth or Arab. Only the Romans were able to conquer and marginally pacify these mountain folk.

Although the Romans ruled Spain for half a millennium, this northern region never was more than superficially Romanized. Even today the region retains its frontier flavor and in the hinterlands its people maintain traditions and ways of life that predate the coming of the Caesars. Nor have their sentiments for independent thinking been dulled. Northern Spain remains a perennial thorn in the side of the central government in Madrid.

The history of these people is even more interesting than their mountains. After more than a thousand years fending off invasions from Southern Spain, these northern peoples burst down from their mountain strongholds and turned history upside down. They conquered the south during a centuries-long duel with the armies of Islam. More than achieving mere victory, they created a nation, Spain, where none had been before. They carried down from their mountains the core of a new culture and the seeds for a new language, plus a brooding, fatalistic, aggressive spirit that became forever imprinted upon the Spanish national character.

That psychic gift to generations of Spaniards is what Jung called a collective unconscious, though here it assumes a narrower, almost tribal character. History buffs will remember that for a while during later centuries, that dour, doggedly aggressive psychic heritage made the Spanish nation the Western superpower, dominating Europe and the world. What else could explain the victories of Cortez in Mexico, Pizarro in Peru, and Alfonso in Italy?

These are the Spanish roots. They spring from a psychic character born of endless battle against the adversities of a harsh environment and centuries of life or death defense of their beleaguered mountain retreats, fending off a succession of foreign invaders. For these mountain folk it was a millennium-long experience of "enslave or be enslaved, kill or be killed, destroy or be destroyed." Cruelty was as natural as loving kindness and all was fair in war against stubborn adversaries who possessed every advantage given by superior numbers, wealth and armaments.

Spain for Travelers

The birth of modern Spain thus was midwifed in the violence of pitched battle high amongst the gray cliffs and jagged peaks of Asturias. It came of age as the mountain folk fought their way down into the fertile valley of the Ebro and onto the high plateau, the dry Meseta of bieges and browns, that is the dominant geographical feature of central Spain. There, at the expense of the Muslims, the mountain people hacked out the kingdoms of Navarra and León and the turbulent County of Castile. Full maturity as a nation came only after seven centuries of virtually constant warfare, a bitter struggle the Spaniards call the Reconquista, the reconquest of Spain from the Arabs and their Moorish minions. For only after that bloody, centuries-long campaign could Isabella – in whose veins still flowed the blood of the hill peoples of the north – join with Ferdinand of Aragon to expel the last Muslim kings and unify Spain under one flag, one religion, and one civilization, all of which looked to these northern mountains for their cultural origins.

No matter all that, a traveler's visit to Northern Spain need be nothing more than a pleasant holiday spent meeting the people and enjoying their mountainous countryside. The experience is especially attractive because it escapes the beaten and crowded paths most tourists follow. Hardly any tourists pass this way except to visit the few major cities. They congregate in Pamplona in July for the world-famous fiesta and running of the bulls. In season the tour buses trundle through Santiago and Burgos to visit their world-renowned cathedrals and landmarks recalling the legendary escapades of Santiago Matamoros and El Cid. But such a visit, whether by a traveler or tourist, pleasing though it may be, misses one of the most remarkable experiences that one may enjoy in a lifetime of travel.

For a thousand years the principal reason outsiders ventured into Northern Spain was to obtain the spiritual benefits of a sacred pilgrimage. They came from all corners of Christendom. Their destination was the sepulcher of an Apostle of Jesus, known in New Testament history as James the Greater. In Faith, they trod what they believed to be a sure route to Heaven. That was the promise of the pilgrimage. It remains so today.

El Camino de Santiago, the Way of St. James, is the ancient

route of the pilgrims. Originating in France, in Spain the pilgrim Way extends some eight hundred kilometers from Roncesvalles, high in the Pyrenees, to the holy city of Santiago de Compostela, a few steps from land's end at the Atlantic Ocean. It followed old Roman roads that snaked through the mountains and drove straight across the hot, dull boredom of the Meseta. Pilgrims still course the route by thousands every year. In centuries past they came by the tens and hundreds of thousands.

As travelers we follow the pilgrim Way because a full millennium of pilgrimage produced an astonishing wealth of historic and cultural artifacts. Add the evidences of earlier Roman, Visigoth and Arab conquests, coupled with the Christian Reconquista, and one discovers a fascinating physical record of the birth of modern Spain. Clearly chronicled in the art, architecture and artifacts of the region is a battered, isolated civilization overwhelmed by invaders and reduced to ruins. Over a span of centuries we see it recovering, finding new cultural sharings with friends and foes alike, and flourishing anew.

The cultural agonies and achievements of that history are preserved in imposing landmarks as well as fabulous artistic shapes and forms reflecting the experience of a birthing civilization rising Phoenix-like out of the ashes of its past. We trace it from initial destruction and cultural isolation to the cosmopolitan sharings that evolved into a new expression of Western civilization during the violent storms of the Reconquista.

This newborn Spain erupted like an angry spirit out of primitive mountain shelters and caves where the nascent Christian Reconquista found safe sanctuary. That spirit appears only half soothed when, along the Way of St. James, it created a host of world-famous cultural treasures celebrating the victories of Christ, His warrior saints and the kings of the Reconquista.

An exaggeration? Consult Arthur K. Porter's, *Romanesque Sculpture of the Pilgrimage Roads,* published some eighty years ago. Note that Porter dealt only with Romanesque sculpture, pointedly ignoring Gothic, Mozarabic, Mudéjar, Baroque and all the rest, not to speak of the architectural gems with which each style is associated, and the priceless documents and other artifacts that come down to us from those tumultuous times. Nevertheless, despite the narrow limits of his topic, Porter required ten stout volumes to report his study. Admittedly, Porter wrote in fine detail for specialists in the arts and their history, yet the scope of his work implies the richness of the cultural heritage a traveler encounters along the road between Roncesvalles and Santiago de Compostela.

Preceding Porter's work by eight hundred years, a French priest, Aymery Picaud, in 1140 wrote a guidebook for pilgrims who dared face the deadly perils of the journey. His motives were purely religious as he described both the hazards and the spiritual pleasures he himself found along the pilgrim's route to the shrine of St. James when he came this way in 1130. Here was the first record of that "something more" tied to the Camino experience.

Mention of Picaud's guidebook suggests that a modern traveler might indeed consider this junket through Northern Spain to be something more than a pleasant holiday. Please observe: With a slight change of mindset, you might become a pilgrim. The fact remains that our path does follow El Camino de Santiago – with a few side trips to special places such as the sacred cave where the Reconquista was born. Thus with little further ado you also may opt to win the spiritual advantages that accrue from a pilgrimage. More about that in a moment. For now the place and its peoples remain at the heart of what this book is about.

Geographically, Northern Spain is dominated by the Pyrenees and the Cantabrian Cordillera. The one is a massive range of high mountains that effectively block off the Iberian Peninsula from the remainder of Europe. The other, the Cantabrian westward extension of those peaks, separates the stormy Atlantic from the high, dry central plateau of the Iberian interior, the Meseta. These mountains dominated and totally shaped the destiny of the peoples of Northern Spain throughout history. The high passes are easily defended by a few determined fighters. This meant that conquest from the outside was rarely worth the price. Only the methodical Romans with the resources of empire were able to accomplish the feat.

With conquerors generally excluded except for punitive raids or hit-and-run plundering expeditions (the most famous of which was conducted by Julius Caesar), the ancient cultures of these peoples tended to be change resistant. Old ways persisted with extraordinarily little outside influence even into modern times. Meanwhile, the tiny valleys and high meadows could never support the population explosion when throngs of flatlanders fled to the mountains to escape the eighth century Arab invasion. In consequence, the ethnic sentiments motivating the Reconquista were reinforced by burgeoning highland populations that inevitably had to drive down out of the mountains in search of living room, taken at the expense of their Muslim neighbors.

If you detect a mood of violence and a fundamental theme of cultural conflict in what is related here, you have gained an intellectual close encounter with the history of Northern Spain. Not only the Christian Reconquista set its roots into these mountains. The same was true of the Carlist revolts of the nineteenth century, the Nationalist victory in the civil war of the twentieth, and the Catalonian, Basque and Cantabrian moves for autonomy that seem presaged for the twenty first.

Spain for Pilgrims

In one sense the pilgrimages of a thousand years had little to do with the people and their mountains that we have just described. Pilgrims came in spite of those bellicose mountain folk. Indeed, early chroniclers railed against the rude mannered bandits who preyed on defenseless pilgrims. Robbing pilgrims, extortion of money for unhindered passage, or ransom for the very rich, became a sort of cottage industry during the early years of the pilgrimages.

In another sense, the pilgrimage road had everything to do with the history of Northern Spain during the past millennium. In the early Reconquest, once the kings of Asturias and Navarra had moved down from the mountains and made secure what became the Way of St. James, hundreds of thousands of pilgrims came each year from the French side of the Pyrenees. Because of them the Way of St. James became known as the "French Road."

At the peak of the vogue of pilgrimage, in the eleventh and twelfth centuries, Pilgrims came in astonishing numbers, at times more than a million strong in a single year. This occurred during a period when the entire population of Western Europe probably was comprised of fewer than fifty million souls. That massive influx of travelers from across Europe poured tremendous wealth into the region, wealth that found its way into royal treasuries and helped finance the centuries-long campaign of castle building and warfare that expelled the Moors from the peninsula.

Much of that pilgrim wealth also found its way into the hands of the Church. It was invested in great cathedrals and humble parish churches, hospices for tired and needy pilgrims, shrines to honor the saints, hospitals for the sick, plus funerary chapels and consecrated ground for the unfortunates who failed to survive the rigors of the journey.

Most of those creations were built to last. Many survive more or less intact, including a pair of cathedrals that easily make everyone's list of the top twenty in the Western world. So much is preserved that at times along the pilgrim trail you need little imagination to feel a sense of that yesterday when the Way overflowed with long files of plodding pilgrims stoically embarked on their search for eternal salvation. There was no doubt in their minds: This was their highway to heaven.

Many of those pilgrims decided to resettle along the Way, finding new earthly lives as well as spiritual rejuvenation. Landless knights from Germany, France and Normandy offered the service of their swords to Spanish lords and kings. They were granted honors and fiefs in exchange for their prowess at arms during the interminable wars against the Moors. Merchants and craftsmen discovered economic opportunities and stayed to ply their trades and conduct commerce along the pilgrim's path. Whole new districts of existing cities were created to house these newcomers. Elsewhere, entire towns were created and settled by these mostly Frankish immigrants.

Others arrived who were not on pilgrimage. They were recruited by agents of the Spanish kings, promised land and opportunity simply to help repopulate a territory swept nearly barren of human inhabitants during centuries of Moorish conquest and occupation. The names given those places settled by the immigrants, known as Villa Franca this or that in recognition of their French origins, persist to this day, no matter how completely the descendants of those immigrants have been absorbed into the cultural melting pot. The family name of Francisco Franco himself betrays his ties to the medieval migrations of Frenchmen into the region where the Caudillo was born a thousand years later.

The Christian kings of Castile, León and Navarra in the eleventh century also cooperated to improve the Way of St. James so that immigration as well as passage of pilgrims would be less daunting. With the assistance of local monks, hermits and townsmen, bridges were erected over rivers, causeways built across swamps and bogs, and the road refurbished to a condition that it had not seen since the glory days of Rome. The kings also encouraged the work of Augustinian, Cistercian and Benedictine monastic orders, who constructed hospitals and hostels as adjuncts to their monasteries along the route.

Physical security also was addressed by both civil and church authorities. Beginning late in the eleventh century, military orders of monks were established to cope with brigands who harassed pilgrims along the Way. By the twelfth century these fighting monks included well-organized commanderies of Knights Templars, the Hospitallers of St. John and the Order of St. James, replete with their own castles, hospitals and hostels for protection and care of pilgrims.

To comprehend the centuries of pilgrimage, one must understand the world out of which the practice sprang. It was a world in which God was in complete charge of everything, except that the Devil was everywhere, in many guises, setting his evil snares to trap men's souls for eternal damnation.

The saints were regarded as potent allies in the battle against evil. Their relics were cherished as reminders of the saints' personal victories over the powers of the Devil, as often as not won by martyrdom. More than that, prayer had the power to gain intercession by the saints in favor of the supplicant. Such was the position of the Church.

The beliefs of ordinary people went beyond the devotional limits of the abstract religious ideas fostered by the Church. The common folk believed the saint was spiritually present with his physical relics. This led inevitably to veneration of those relics, which lay people believed to hold miraculous powers, such as healing the sick and granting special favors. All the supplicant needed to do was to gain the attention and approval of the saint by means of prayers and devotions that would move the saint to intercede in one's behalf.

Nothing demonstrated deservedness more than a long, tedious and even dangerous pilgrimage to the relics of a powerful saint. None was more powerful than St. James the Greater, Apostle of Christ, Champion of the Reconquista, whose remains were said by legend and Church authority to be enshrined at Santiago de Compostela.

At best the effort of a pilgrimage could work major miracles. At least it would win favors freeing the penitent from suffering punishment in the afterlife. For while the Sacrament of Confession certainly gained absolution for one's sins, a sinner didn't get off scot-free. There was still time to be served in Purgatory. But with the saint's intercession a pilgrim could gain a plenary indulgence. It granted no less than remission, that is, pardon for past sins, and thus one might escape the awful consequence of Purgatorial suffering. In effect, the reward of this pilgrimage is a guarantee of salvation from all that, an immediate ticket into Heaven. El Camino de Santiago is, in short, a highway leading directly to the Pearly Gates, which are seen by the pilgrim at Santiago as the Pórtico de la Gloria, presided over by St. James himself.

Yet when the truth be known, there was more than eternal salvation motivating many pilgrims. For some it was simply an excuse to travel and get away from the affairs of ordinary life. For others the pilgrimage was ordered either by church or civil authorities as a penance for some terrible wrong or simply as a means to rehabilitate a life wasted on evil. And for anyone filled with the fear of God's wrath, but still with no stomach for having his local confessor discover his most private sins, pilgrimage was an excuse to find a foreign priest and unload sins he could never admit to his personal confessor – and escape Purgatory besides.

By the thirteenth century the dress of the pilgrim achieved virtually the character of a uniform: a heavy, flowing tunic that reached down to the ankles as protection from the weather and the chill of nights spent in the open along the way; a walking staff; a broad-brimmed hat turned up in front where a scallop shell was pinned as the badge of the pilgrim; plus a pouch (scrip, or wallet) secured at the waist for carrying a few personal belongings and the all-important tokens obtained at various shrines along the way. For those tokens were proof-positive of his journey.

The pilgrim of centuries past went afoot for the eight hundred kilometers of the Way of St. James between the French border and Santiago de Compostela. A gentleman of means, or a knight, made his way on horseback. There are purists who insist that those ancient means of transport are still the only acceptable modes of travel for a pilgrim. But times change.

Walkers by the thousands still plod each year along the ancient route to Santiago. Yet if one holds that the spirit of pilgrimage rather than the method of transport is the crucial factor deciding the issue, then a bicycle, motorcycle, jeep or even public transport is allowed. Even the Church accepts this point of view. Yet Church authorities still expect modern pilgrims to course at least a hundred kilometers of the Way afoot, and to prove their pilgrimage by visits to the shrines along the Way, just as their predecessors have done for a thousand years.

Our approach to the Way of St. James, even as a pilgrim, thus may involve modern transportation. We used a rental car. As for the hundred kilometers afoot, the walks we describe following the Way through the towns, villages and cities along the Camino do not qualify for it. The very last hundred kilometers of the Way, Sarria to Santiago de Compostela, must be navigated afoot. It is acceptable for your car to be used as a carryall with a "designated driver," while you walk. That walk, plus your stamped pilgrim's "passport," or pilgrim's credential, will be proof enough for the churchmen. To gain official recognition as a pilgrim, obtain the "passport" at the monastic church at Roncesvalles. Then, at shrines and churches along the way, obtain the required rubber stamp imprints on the passport to validate your personal record of pilgrimage. To have gained those stamps it is assumed that one has experienced the special spirituality of each of those shrines, and meditated for a moment on the model life, or the acts, of the saints honored at those holy places. Finally, at Santiago de Compostela, with the last stamp in place, the Cathedral Secretariat awards the badge of the cockle shell (most call it a scallop shell) and the certificate – the Compostelana – that announce to one and all the pilgrim's achievement of special favor in the eyes of St. James. The certificate also gains a pilgrim the traditional free repast across the square at the Hostal de los Reyes Católicos – but do not expect to order from the regular menu or to dine cheek by jowl with the paying guests. That grand and gracious hostelry – an architectural wonder in its own right – was built at the order of Ferdinand and Isabella in the fifteenth century. For centuries thereafter it was a refuge for pilgrims. Now it is a five-star parador operated by the Spanish government for pilgrims and travelers with deep pockets.

The "How to" of Things

Pilgrimage lore not withstanding, this book is intended for travelers with a taste for history. On these pages you learn what highways to drive along, where to get out on foot for a better view of things, and all about sights you won't want to miss. It is full of "Walk left at the corner and after fifty meters you will see...." Or, "Drive down Calle XYZ and, just before it dead ends, look to your left where stands...."

Such directions are only a minor part of our story, necessary though they may be for facilitating your travels. What we have here is essentially a history book. I like to call it history on the hoof, where the story of people and events is told in the exact places where history was made. Such history thus escapes the impersonal recounting of dates and happenings, or vague pointings and seeings. Instead, you can picture things as they happened, whether ten or a hundred or a thousand years ago as we make our way along El Camino de Santiago.

The modern roads accessible to our rental car often merely approximate the ancient Way of St. James. The pilgrimage route followed old Roman roads, with detours to special shrines or fortified towns and monasteries that offered safety and sustenance along the way. At times the old walking route becomes the road you drive, or runs alongside. More often than not it strays anywhere from a few meters to a kilometer and more distant, joining the modern road again near cities and villages further along the route. So do not expect to see pilgrims afoot along every kilometer of the roads you drive.

Auto roads are well marked by the assigned numbers for Spanish highways and by signs pointing the way to the next towns and cities. No matter that and the directions given here, never venture far without the latest map of the highways or of the street plans when in the larger cities. Sometimes I think that the government changes the highway route numbers just for the sake of complexity. On the highways you will often notice prominent blue and yellow signs posted along the route. These announce the "Camino de Santiago," and display a sunburst shaped like a scallop shell.

For hikers, the walking route is indicated by painted yellow arrows that a driver occasionally sees alongside a roadway when it and the walking route coincide, or by blue and yellow signs depicting a hiker with his walking staff, warning where the pilgrims' path crosses or uses the highway.

Our initial explorations of the route depart from Pamplona, where we set up our travel "headquarters" for the first couple of days. Initially we climb the Pyrenees to Roncesvalles, only fifty kilometers distant. There we survey the pilgrims' gateway into Spain, which was also the route of Charlemagne and other conquerors who passed that way throughout the centuries. And, as noted, it could as well become the beginning of your personal pilgrimage to Santiago de Compostela. If so, you may wish to put up overnight in Burguete, just below Roncesvalles, convenient so that you may attend the pilgrims' early morning Mass at the Royal Collegiate Church and obtain both your passport and the priest's blessing as you embark upon your journey.

After exploring Pamplona itself, our next sortie leads southeast along another route of the pilgrimage trail. There were, you see, two principal tracks for pilgrims crossing the Pyrenees. The pass at Roncesvalles was the easiest, lowest in altitude at slightly more than 1000 meters. It was also the most direct way from the greater part of France and points north, and thus the principal route. The pilgrims called this the Navarran Road.

The other pass was at Somport. There the road crosses at 1600 meters. At those elevations, Winter comes early and stays late, with all the weather-borne adversities that the Winter season entails. Nevertheless, for pilgrims coming from the Cote de Azur, Italy and other regions of the south of Europe, the pass at Somport was preferred as the most direct route. It was known as the Aragonese Road.

We do not propose to explore all the way up to Somport. Rather we plan an excursion from Pamplona that leads out on route N240 some fifty kilometers. There we find the San

Salvador Monastery at Leyre, in the hills above the modern Yesa Reservoir. Leyre was not only a major stop along the Aragonese Road. It was regarded by the Navarrans as the spiritual cradle of their land and the sacred seat of their success in the Reconquista. From there we follow the pilgrim track westward to a town called Puente de la Reina, Queen's Bridge. There the Navarran and Aragonese roads join on the Way to Santiago de Compostela.

Going by automobile, best practice often is to stay at hotels outside the large cities because of parking difficulties associated with city-center hotels. Valet service at the four and five-star hotels precludes that sort of problem if your budget can afford the tariffs. When staying outside a city, obtain a map (plano) of the city from your reception clerk, locate the inevitable public parking lot (often underground beneath a central plaza) in the vicinity of your in-city walking tour, and proceed with your explorations from there.

Should you desire to walk or go by horseback or trail bike along the ancient pilgrimage trail, there are many sources providing more or less reliable instructions. Granddaddy of them all is *The Pilgrim Route to Compostela*, written originally by Abbé Georgés Bernés for the Editiones Randonnés Pyrénéennes. It is still available in a revised, updated English-language edition published in England by Robertson McCarta. It provides step by step instructions to the walker all the way from St. Jean Pied de Port at the French border. Many changes in the path have been made since publication of the book, but the yellow arrow markers and blue and yellow signs compensate for that. Still, there are more up to date guides available. Check with your favorite bookseller.

Of interest to the horsey set is *Spanish Pilgrimage: A Canter to St. James,* by Robin Hanbury-Tenison, published in England by Hutchinson. It is the day-by-day journal of the problems and solutions found by a pair of riders who offer advice and share the experience of their adventure. Much less detailed as to the route than a hiker's guide, a horseman ought to have both books in hand so as not to suffer a mistaken way.

17

The emphasis of both those types of books is on providing directions and information about the way traveled rather than giving detailed data and descriptions concerning historical and cultural points of interest. For that you need this book. There is no other like it.

For pilgrims, best current practical information may be obtained by contacting the Asociacion de Amigos de los Caminos, Calle Carretas 14, 28012 Madrid, Spain. Also, at the very beginning of your journey, visit the Oficina de Informacion al Peregrino, at Roncesvalles, located nearby the collegiate church. You may also write to that office in advance, addressing your letter to the Oficina de Informacion al Peregrino, Real Collegiata de Roncesvalles, 31650 Roncesvalles, Navarra, Spain.

Best time to go: May or September. The Meseta is an oven and Santiago de Compostela is crowded with tourists in Summer, while some of the mountain facilities begin to close in October. Snow-blocked roads in the high passes are also a possibility at any time between mid-October and April.

Whenever you go, however you go, heed the basic dictum of experienced travelers: Always have a good map in your hand. Your rental car company will provide road maps and your hotel usually will provide a good town or city map at the places you visit. Otherwise, locate the local tourist information office or try a bookstore.

A suggested itinerary may be found in the final chapter of this book. Note the recommendation that one ought to stay in or near Pamplona at the outset of the trip. There are suitable accommodations at Burguete near Roncesvalles, but it is more convenient to use Pamplona as a travel base during your initial explorations.

How you get to Pamplona is a matter of personal choice. The airport is without international connections and local connections leave much to be desired. Train service is no better. Our decision was to get there by rental car from Madrid. It is possible to head home using air connections out of Santiago de Compostela or Madrid..

The roads for the entire junket are excellent. Roadside services are generally available. However, best to always gas up before you venture too far from the cities along rural roads, and carry a jug of water for the radiator and a couple of quarts of oil for the engine. For the record: We found no need for making use of such precautions, but we take them anyway.

Rental car pickup may be made in Madrid or Pamplona, with no penalties for drop-off in Santiago de Compostela. We found that in September or May there is no need for air conditioning in the car except for a couple of days out on the Meseta. Those were days when we were out of the car on foot much of the time anyhow, so air conditioning is an unnecessary expense for the frugal traveler. During the height of Summer that would be a different story.

Finally, note that many of these explorations take us out into the countryside and lunchtime often finds us far from any likely sources of a meal. Our solution, learned years earlier on travels in Greece and Italy, was to visit a village (or town) mom and pop store and purchase some locally baked bread, cheese, a couple of slices of meat and a bottle of the local wine. With that, when the time for lunch arrived, we invariably have been able to find a nice place to pause and picnic. Indeed, many such pauses were memorable for their ambience.

That said, let's begin our exploration of the Highway to Heaven, El Camino de Santiago.

THE BASQUE COUNTRY

Basque, Castilian and French cultures meet, albeit with an almost palpable tension, in Navarra. The predominantly Basque people of this mountainous region are very Catholic, very conservative, very independent of mind.

Beginning in times before history, the Vascon ancestors of the modern Basques moved restlessly down into the foothills below their snow-capped mountains. In time they spread out further onto the Spanish and French coasts of the Bay of Biscay, and southward onto the fertile banks of the Ebro River. This is the land the Basques know as Euzkadi, the Basque Homeland. A thousand years ago it became the heart of the Basque kingdom of Navarra.

The modern Euzkadi, the "Basque Provinces" of modern Spain, extends from the crest of the Pyrenees and Bidasoa River, which form the border with France, to the Ebro on the south and westward into the Cantabrian Cordillera and beyond to the Bay of Biscay. The Euzkadi contains the provinces of Navarra, Alava, Vizcaya and Guipuzcoa, containing in all about 17,000 square kilometers. The French portion of the Euzkadi, of course, occupies the southern border provinces of France.

From their mountain redoubts the Vascons of old challenged all comers whether Carthaginians or Romans, Vandals or Visigoths, Franks under Charlemagne, and Arabs under a succession of powerful leaders from the initial conquests to the time of the Almohades. Carthaginians under Hannibal were stopped at the Ebro (Iberus, to the Romans), but not so with the Roman legions. The Romans pacified the Vascons and founded the city of Pompaelo, now Pamplona, to govern the district. The name honors a Roman administrator of the region, Pompey, later one of the triumvirate of consuls, including Julius Caesar, who governed the empire.

When the Roman Empire dissolved and barbarian tribes

swept down through the former provinces of Rome in 409 AD, Spain was the target first of the Vandals, then of the Goths. The Vandals moved on to North Africa, but the Goths remained and in 419 set themselves up as a kingdom as well as a governing aristocracy occupying the place of the former Roman overseers. Familiar with the ways of the Romans, the Goths largely retained the Roman administrative infrastructure.

The Goths encountered little resistance in Southern Spain and the Eastern coastal regions, mostly because the indigenous peoples were fed up with Roman tax collectors and welcomed a change of overlords. But the Basques and the Cantabrian tribes were a different matter. They fought the Goths to a standstill throughout all three hundred years of Gothic rule. King Roderick in fact was campaigning against the Basques in 711 when the Arabs landed in the south to commence their conquest of Spain.

The Franks maintained a loose hegemony in the Basque region from about the seventh century, supporting the Vascons against the Goths. This situation was a constant irritant to the Visigoth regime headquartered in Toledo. But that mattered nought once the Islamic wave of conquest struck the south coast in the eighth century. Islam swiftly inundated all of Spain and Southern France, but the wave broke and fell back when it came to the Pyrenees and the Cantabrian Cordillera.

Although Pamplona eventually fell to Moorish attacks, the conquerors never could do more than raid into the mountains. With the help of the Franks, Pamplona threw out the Moors in 750 after only 12 years of occupation. The French helped because they wanted Navarra as a buffer between France and the Moorish territories to the south. Yet as events surrounding the Carolingian thrust across the Pyrenees in 778 demonstrated, as a buffer Navarra was not necessarily either friendly or peaceable. The result was a military catastrophe inflicted upon the army of Charlemagne by the Basques high in the Pyrenees near the village known as Roncesvalles (Roncevaux).

Our first day exploring Northern Spain takes us to Roncesvalles. There El Camino de Santiago descends from the high pass through which the great King Charles led his army back to France. It was there that his nephew and champion, Roland, gave his life in defense of the king's rear guard. In memory of that heroic sacrifice, Roncesvalles was made forever famous by the immortal *Song of Roland.* Yet, historical truth be told, it is an epic that sings more poetically than accurately of Roland's valiant death and Charlemagne's military misfortune.

The Way to Roncesvalles

Depart Pamplona driving east on the broad Avenida de la Baja Navarra, route N121. Before you are out of the city, watch for a right turn onto route N135, which leads to the French border at St. Jean Pied de Port via Roncesvalles (Valley of Thorns).

The modern road turns and twists through the foothills, now rerouted around most of the ancient villages on El Camino de Santiago. Despite lots of ups and downs, by the halfway mark at Zubiri you are still at the elevation of Pamplona, slightly more than 500 meters. From there the real climb begins.

Just prior to Zubiri is Larrasoaña, which the highway bypasses. Larrasoaña is notable historically as where a French king of Navarra, Philip III of Evreux, gathered the Cortez (parliament) of Navarra in 1329 to take his regal oath.

Now you are more and more in traditional Basque country, full of well-tended farms with neat white farmhouses decorated with red roofs, shutters and doors. These are the marks of a proud people, well satisfied with what they are, and forever willing to contest the outsider who would make of their land or themselves something different.

Navarra, geographically the largest of the Basque provinces, contains only about eighteen percent of the Basque population of Spain. Yet eighty percent of its people are Basque. What this tells you in numbers is what you have no doubt already observed: Navarra, except for Pamplona, is thinly populated. It

is a region of farms, small towns and vil
expanses of rocky foothills and steep mountai
thrifty Basques are unable to make productive.

Linguists find the Basque language somethin
relates to no other tongue and thus is unique. Ignatius Donnelly
came to believe that this distinctive language, coupled with
other evidence he obtained from a study of the legends of many
peoples, indicated that the Basques were survivors of the
legendary Atlantean peoples who inhabited the now submerged
land west of the Pillars of Hercules.

The Basques call their language Euskera. Its use has
persisted in spite of the opposition of church and state. Under
the fascist regime of Francisco Franco it was forbidden to be
taught in schools. Until the past century the Church regarded it
as a pagan tongue, proscribed to such an extent that children
could not even be baptized with Basque names.

At Zubiri, which in Basque means "village of the bridge,"
the Navarran Road of the pilgrims passes a thirteenth century
church with a Romanesque tower. The main structure of the
church is a not overly pleasing mix of Romanesque and Gothic.
There was a monastery here in the early tenth century, but there
is no trace of it now.

The medieval **bridge** from which the town gained its name
still stands and serves the townspeople. Its twin spans are
found about a hundred meters off the main street. Watch for the
sign pointing the way off to the right. Follow that street to
where it turns right between a row of modern houses, park
where that street ends, and walk twenty meters to the stream
where the picturesque bridge is located a stone's throw to your
right.

Viscarret, about ten kilometers further along and two
hundred meters higher in elevation, was another monastic
center devoted to pilgrim care. Nothing is left to remind us of
its former importance.

Still climbing, the road passes through the village of Espinal
and, a couple of kilometers later, you reach Burguete, known to
Hemingway enthusiasts as the place where, in *The Sun Also*

Rises, his characters spent several days fishing in a nearby stream.

Burguete, just below Roncesvalles, is both modern and ancient. It boasts of several small, antiquated but comfortable hotels and restaurants along its narrow main street, the millennium-old footpath of pilgrims. It is still lined with fine old **houses** sporting fancy facades bearing the coats of arms of their Medieval and Renaissance tenants. An unprepossessing inn on the left near the far side of town served us a delicious noontime meal.

A Walk with the Pilgrims

Our sightseeing plan is to continue along N135 all the way up to the pass at Puerto Ibañeta, gaining insight into the mountainous lay of the land as we go and, for the moment, bypassing the famous monastery at Roncesvalles. We will explore it at our leisure on the way back down.

The more adventurous traveler will park his car at the monastery and walk the footpath up to the pass and back, better to obtain a sense of the general feel a pilgrim has for the trail. Note that the altitude of Roncesvalles is 925 meters, while Puerto Ibañeta stands at 1057 meters.

Reaching the pass, whether by automobile or afoot, you have attained the divide between the Atlantic and the Mediterranean. A few feet off the road on the right, prominent as you approach the pass, is the tiny **chapel** of San Salvador de Ibañeta. The chapel is located on the site of the one-time monastery of San Salvador, a large institution which served pilgrims from the early eleventh century to the seventeenth. Old histories tell of its bell, which tolled during the early darkness of evening, or when the mountains were socked in by clouds, in order to guide pilgrims to safety and shelter at the monastery. A similar bell now hangs in a tiny campanile beside the chapel.

Some say the modern chapel marks the site of the tomb in

which Charlemagne interred the body of his fallen nephew, Roland. Nearby, on the peak of the hill, is a stone monument displaying the dates, 778-1967. Upon its face is a wrought iron replica of Roland's famous sword, Durandel, with a pair of chain maces crossed above it. To prevent his sword from falling into the hands of his enemies, Roland supposedly threw the sword into a nearby stream before he died.

Another stone monument beside the chapel contains an inscription in Basque, Spanish and French, asking pilgrims to offer a prayer to Our Lady of Roncesvalles, whom we shall meet after we descend from the pass.

Now walk into the open ground beyond the chapel so as to gain the best impression of the defile where the historic ambush of Charlemagne's rear guard took place. The heights of the Astobizcar shoot virtually straight up for five hundred meters, and the pass narrows to little more than the width of the road. It is a spot ideally suited for the ambuscade recalled in the Chanson de Roland.

For the most lucid account of the actual historical events surrounding the Song of Roland, consult Dorothy Sayers' introduction to her translation of the epic poem. Her work is both accurate and eminently readable for a modern audience. Note, too, that her literary credentials in this instance have little to do with her fame as a mystery novelist. She was, before that, an Oxford-trained medieval scholar and linguist.

Briefly, the story comes down to this: In 777 a delegation from the Arab king of Saragossa petitioned Charlemagne to aid in overcoming other, less friendly Arab potentates in the north of Spain. The benefit to the Frankish king would be a passel of friendly tributary states on his southern border. Charlemagne rose to the offer. It promised one less frontier to worry about while he engaged in his lifelong campaign to expand his kingdom into an empire rivaling what once was Rome's. So in 778 he moved his army south in two columns. One drove along the coast to capture Girona, while he personally led a second force over the pass here at Roncesvalles to secure Pamplona before reuniting his army for the main attack on Saragossa, which the Arab king promised would be easy pickings.

As often happens in matters of war, the campaign failed to work out as planned.

Pamplona welcomed Charlemagne with open arms and gates, greeting him as welcome relief from their tributary status to Arab overlords, who fled the city as the French approached. Girona also fell with little effort. At Saragossa, however, a dissident faction within the city staged a coup and rallied the people to defend the walls. Lacking the quick and easy victory he was promised, and faced by a Saxon uprising in the north, Charlemagne elected to abandon the enterprise and head for home. Before leaving, however, he leveled the walls of Pamplona so as to leave one less fortified stronghold available to the Arabs adjacent to his southern borders.

The Basques of Pamplona were furious. The flattened walls left them defenseless against the return of Arab rule and certain punishment for having welcomed and aided Charlemagne. For revenge, they set an ambush at the pass above Roncesvalles. The main body of French troops was allowed to pass unhindered, but the rear guard and baggage column were halted and dispersed by boulders cast down the steep sides of the ravine. Thereupon the French rear was overwhelmed and slaughtered to the last man, while the baggage train was looted and destroyed. Among the dead was Roland, nephew and favorite of the king, along with other notables including the king's seneschal, chief of his entire army. The date was August 15, 778.

Looking at the steep sides of the pass to the pinnacles far above, you wonder what Charlemagne was thinking to have allowed his army to be exposed to such a threat in a place so ideally suited for an ambush. As for the poem itself, Sayers comments, "In short, beginning with a historical military disaster of a familiar kind and comparatively small importance, we have somehow in the course of two centuries achieved a masterpiece of epic drama; we have arrived at the Song of Roland."

The epic turned Basques into Saracens and the event into

the worst kind of treachery by jealous Frankish nobles and mischievous Arabs alike. But small wonder the change. A new spirit by then was alive in the land. The eleventh century was a time of Christian triumph over Moslems in Italy and Spain, and the whole of Europe was soon to gird itself for deliverance of the Christian holy places in Palestine.

Pamplona was subsequently captured by the Franks in 806, but the effort failed to garner full control of the district. The Franks thus were again crossing the pass in 810, led by Louis the Debonair. He took the precaution of seizing the women and children of the local Basques, and making them accompany his troops through the pass before letting them loose.

The Franks held much of Navarra until 824 when they again were confronted by revolt. They moved an army south through the Pyrenees that year, hoping to punish the Basques and recoup their territories. The Franks once more were met and defeated by the Basques here near Roncesvalles. That defeat more or less ended the Frankish threat to Spain, and the Basques established an independent kingdom in the no-man's land between the Franks and Moors.

The first of the Basque line of Navarran kings was Iñigo Arista (d 851), who sired a dynasty that ruled this mountainous land for four hundred years.

The monastery of San Salvador here in the pass was leveled by fire in 1884. Only fragmentary ruins remain. A few chunks of foundation stones are still visible poking through the grass in the gentle open slope behind the chapel.

The present chapel, built in 1965, marks where the pilgrim, as he reaches the Spanish side of the pass, is expected to set a cross in the ground to mark the beginning of his pilgrimage in the land of Santiago. The French border is but two and a half kilometers down the steep trail to the north.

With cross implanted, the pilgrim then kneels to make his first prayer (in Spain) to St. James. Behind the chapel you thus find a small mound some ten meters in diameter and a couple of meters tall on which a forest of crude crosses have been set in place by recent pilgrims. Most of these crosses are fragile and rather nondescript assemblies of twigs and branches. The expression is what is important, you see.

The monumental stone cross you see by the road is modern, memorializing the king-sized cross supposedly planted by Charlemagne as he passed this way and appealed for the aid of St. James. That cross was destroyed by the French revolutionary army as they passed here in 1794. Among others who came this way was the English Black Prince. He brought his army south in 1367 to help Pedro the Cruel regain the crown of Castile at the Battle of Nájera (Navarrete), a site on our route a few days down the road.

In 1813, Marshal Soult came this way in his unsuccessful attempt to launch a surprise attack on Wellington and save Pamplona during the Napoleonic Wars. Some still refer to the route as Napoleon's Road, heavily traveled as it was by French armies during the years when Napoleon fought to bring Spain into his empire.

Our Lady of Roncesvalles

Retrace your way to Roncesvalles by car or afoot, descending the pilgrim trail through the silent forest that arches above both road and track. The return trip to the monastery seems to course much swifter, now that the way is all downhill. So, perhaps sooner than we expect, we arrive at the monastic compound (open 8 to 8).

Staffed by Augustinian monks throughout its history, the foundation remains active and still caters to pilgrims. It has also become prominent as a tourist attraction. On a busy day you may have to park precariously along the narrow shoulder of the highway. Otherwise there is ample parking in an area of the compound beside the road.

The monastery was founded by King Alfonso I of Navarra in 1130. Once famous for its Hospitale Rotolandi (Hospital of Roland, built in 1132 by Sancho de La Rosa, Bishop of Pamplona), it is younger by a hundred years or so than was the monastery of San Salvador up at the pass. The monastery has been restored and refurbished countless times over the centuries, and while its modern incarnation is not all that appealing at first glance, you will discover that our first impression of an old barn of a place (with its steep metal roofing and squat walls beneath) will soon be erased by the wonders to be perceived within.

Approach the monastic complex from the parking area through a broad open area on which face the museum, located in the large building on the upper far side, and a pair of small churches on the right. Rising beyond the museum building is the Royal Collegiate Church of Nuestra Señora de Roncesvalles, founded by Sancho VII, the Strong (1154-1234), in 1219. Sancho and his queen, Clemencia, are entombed here in the chapel of St. Augustine, which occupies the one-time chapter house adjacent to the main church.

Set furthest apart from the monastery and thus the first historic structure we encounter, is the Church of the Holy Spirit. This is a Romanesque funerary chapel for unfortunate pilgrims whose dreams of traveling the Highway to Heaven died along with their worn out bodies here at the Hospital of Roland. The bones of many of those pilgrims repose in an ossuary inside the chapel.

The chapel consists of a square central structure surrounded by a broad, covered porch supported by a Romanesque arcade. Within the porch, interred beneath its pavement, are the tombs of monks who served their Lord and tended the pilgrims who passed this way throughout the centuries. Beautifully restored, the chapel was probably built during the eleventh century, but may be older. It is sometimes called the Silo de Carlomagno, honoring the tradition that Charlemagne's slain knights were buried from it. Other traditions say it marks the site of Roland's sepulcher.

Adjacent to the funerary chapel is the tiny, single nave twelfth century pilgrim church of Santiago. It is plain-faced Romanesque, later remodeled with a touch of Gothic often referred to as Cistercian style, which was transitional between the Romanesque and classic Gothic styles. In its belfry is the bell that once rang to signal the pilgrims at the monastery of San Salvador at Puerto Ibañeta. The interior is as Spartan as the exterior, boasting of plain wooden benches facing a small altar. Behind it, posted on a small pillar and framed against a small window in the thick wall, is a dark-hued statue of St. James. To go inside, you must visit the administrative office near the road above the museum building. A tour may be arranged there. Pilgrims may also at the office find information on the pilgrimage route and obtain their "passports."

The museum is located on the ground floor of the building facing you as you leave the church of Santiago. It occupies what once were the monastery's stables. Its entrance is towards the left end of the building. While not large and certainly not outstanding, the museum (open 10 to 2 and 4 to 7) does contain a few choice items worth the price of admission. Among them is a fourteenth century reliquary known as "Charlemagne's chessboard" because of its checkered gold, silver, and enamel squares. Also displayed is an emerald from the turban of the Moorish king, Miramolín, slain by Sancho the Strong in the crucial thirteenth century battle of Las Navas de Tolosa, which sealed the fate of the Muslim kingdoms in Spain, no matter that a few hung on for another two hundred years. Paintings include a Holy Family by Luis de Morales, and a triptych attributed to Hieronymus Bosch.

Exiting the museum, turn left along the face of the building to reach the passageway that leads to a courtyard beyond. There you find the collegiate church and other monastic buildings. A doorway to the right leads through the cloister to the former chapter house, now known as the Chapel of St. Augustine. Both cloister and chapter house date from the fourteenth century.

The cloister is a heavy early Gothic, almost oppressive in mood because of its ponderous construction. Note the small, smooth faced riverbed stones set in the floor as a mosaic design. Although a modern restoration, this is characteristic of the period, and is a style of paving we will see repeated many

30

times as we journey west to Santiago.

The contents of the chapter house are what attract us here. It contains the tomb of Sancho the Strong and his queen, Clemencia. The regal tomb is a thirteenth century construction on a twentieth century base, the latter created when the chapter house was converted into the chapel in 1912, exactly seven hundred years after Sancho's smashing victory over the Moors. The two and a quarter meter length of the sarcophagus, with a similar-sized statue of the king reposing atop, match the actual build of the king, who in life was said to have been no less than seven feet tall, with the strength of several men.

The large stained glass window, installed during the remodeling of 1912, commemorates Sancho's victory at Las Navas de Tolosa in 1212. Displayed in the chapel on a wall plaque are lengths of the chain that held Christian slaves captive in a circle around the tent of Miramolín, the Moorish king who fought the Christians at Las Navas. Sancho is reputed to have broken the chain with his bare hands to free the Christians during the battle. He was not known as Sancho the Strong for nothing.

Outside again, we turn right and approach the Church of Nuestra Señora de Roncesvalles. Its square campanile has a pair of double-arched windows on each face, lending it something of a Byzantine appearance. It is the Royal Collegiate Church of the Augustinians. Constructed between 1195 and 1219 in the Romanesque style, it was said to have been a copy of the Parisian Cathedral of Notre Dame, but certainly not on so grand a scale, I am sure. It was destroyed by fire not long afterwards. Immediately rebuilt in a Gothic design, and much revamped by restorations since, it is regarded historically not only as the first, but one of the finest early Gothic constructions in Spain. Step inside and take a seat on a wooden bench toward the rear of the nave to admire and learn about the edifice that surrounds you.

Gothic is a style of architecture imported from France, not penetrating the remainder of Spain until late in the thirteenth century, several monkish generations after this structure was raised. Compared to the sturdy plainness of the then dominant Romanesque, Gothic is flamboyant and high flying, featuring tall, ribbed vaults. The ribbing reduces the weight of the vaulting, permitting lighter, higher walls and use of relatively tall and thin columns rather than squat, sturdy piers for supports. That lightness also allows the walls to be perforated by windows decorated with stone traceries and stained glass, as you see here in the round openings above both sides of the nave within the side vaulting of the roof.

The dominant effect of Gothic, easily perceived here no matter that this church is minuscule compared to such grand late Gothic structures as the cathedral at Chartres, or what we will find later on this journey at Burgos, is that of vast space within tall elevations. This is achieved by the pointed arch with ribbed vaulting over a single aisle or, as here, with the central nave the dominant space with narrow, but still quite tall, side aisles. Above the side aisles here are ten galleries, each with a rose window containing stained glass. The term, triforium, refers to these upper galleries, the half vaults of which are a design strategy first developed by Romanesque builders to translate the outward thrust of the nave vaulting to the heavy outer walls while providing for interior illumination.

During the fourteenth and fifteenth centuries the Gothic design grew much richer in carved decor, with much more complex window tracery changing from geometric to curvilinear, and much greater flamboyance in both internal and external decoration. We will find the epitome of all that at Burgos, where the ponderous flying arches of early Gothic become a construct of light semi-arches decorated with spires, canopies, statues and miscellaneous bric-a-brac, increasing the appearance of structural lightness even more than you see here in this relatively early development of the style.

As you see from this brief synopsis, the evolution of medieval architecture is a richly detailed and fascinating study. Available with a recent edition is David Watkin's *A History of Western Architecture.* The best introduction to the field, in my opinion, are the chapters dealing with Romanesque and Gothic builders in Talbot Hamlin's *Architecture Through The Ages.* Though first published more than sixty years ago, it remains a classic study in the field. As Hamlin relates, architecture was completely an art and not a science in those days, and the catastrophic collapses of many grand or not so grand structures attempted by second-rate master builders is a fact of history.

How came such talented builders to this out of the way place? Their coming was a product of the monastic system as it existed in the Middle Ages. Given the multitude of monastic establishments (some active and others merely historic in their ruin) that we will see on these travels with St. James, we ought to explain that system now as we sit in this church near the beginning of this journey.

Monastic living began simply as a way for hermits and other ascetics to band together for protection or to create self-sufficient communities during the rough and tumble times of the Dark Ages. As feudalism developed, these communities often allied with each other for protection against powerful secular lords. In a barbarous age dedicated to warfare and little else, many of the best minds were drawn naturally to the often studious and (usually) gentler pursuits of monastic life.

Bequests of land, particularly during the decades of religious fervor leading up the Millennium (when everyone was sure the world would come to an end), eventually made the monastic orders powerful landlords themselves, controlling wealth that permitted the monasteries to become places of learning, teaching and repositories of the arts. In effect, they performed functions we expect of our universities today. Indeed, our university system as we know it developed out of these monastic beginnings.

Among the arts studied and practiced in the medieval monastery was architecture. The monkish builders initially studied ancient Roman forms and techniques as they became masters of the craft. They taught their art to other monks (and also to talented lay artisans) who then carried their learning to other monasteries where there was need of such expertise for glorification of their houses of God and to provide durable shelter for themselves and their sacred work. The Cistercians were particularly noted for fostering the architectural arts and sciences within their order.

Following the master builders came small armies of itinerant stonemasons and sculptors, both monastic and secular, who went from place to place in the practice of their trades. The principal origin of these architectural arts was France, although a native Spanish tradition molded from Roman and Gothic sources had been preserved in culturally isolated Asturias. In Northwest Spain the French influence was at first muted and later embellished by Moorish influences, expressed in the Mudéjar and Mozarabic styles carried north by monks and artisans escaping Islamic persecutions of the ninth and tenth centuries, or remaining in the North once their Arab masters had been expelled. As Hamlin sagely points out, the fact that all Europe visited Spain on pilgrimage resulted in many Spanish architectural innovations (such as star vaulting) being carried back for application elsewhere in Europe.

Now, gazing forward through the nave, we observe the medieval statue of Our Lady of Roncesvalles, the Virgin Mary with her Christ Child, situated beneath a high, gilded canopy and centered upon an arched support above the altar. Made of cedar wood, probably in France during the thirteenth century, it is plated in silver, bejeweled, and stands above a silver tabernacle. Our Lady of Roncesvalles over the centuries is reputed to have worked many miracles for the faithful.

Before walking forward to examine Our Lady in detail, note the sturdy columns along the nave, with capitals that are more Romanesque than Gothic in their carving. The stained glass windows above the pillared openings into the galleries, and the saints glowing in the apertures at the head of the side aisles, are rather standard fare as such artistry goes.

Also within the church, located in a small side chapel to the right rear of the main altar, is a remarkable, emotionally disturbing piece of art said to be the work of Pedro de Mena. It is a terracotta bust of the Virgin, here a grief-stricken lady with wild strands of black hair tossed in bleak disarray. She is

34

known as the Mater Dolorosa. Her tears are simulated by diamonds. Here is a Mother who has lost her beloved Son and made no peace with her emotions.

In this church, every evening, the bell tolls to announce the 8 p.m. Mass for pilgrims. The priests of the order celebrate Holy Mass and bestow a divine blessing upon the attending pilgrims so as to send them on their way in a proper state of Grace.

We conclude our visit to Roncesvalles with a drive back through the whispering pines to Burguete. The town is old, assertively quaint, but well equipped to provide refreshment in a pleasant setting replete with the shades of Hemingway and his aficionados of the bullring and the trout pool.

Now follow the sun and the Way of St. James to Pamplona, the first of the great Spanish cities along the pilgrimage track.

PAMPLONA

Near the Arga River, the pilgrim's track from Roncesvalles intersects route N121, then crosses the river on the fourteenth century Magdalena Bridge (open to foot traffic only). The way climbs through parkland for about 200 meters as it approaches the towering ramparts of the old city wall. There the pilgrim finds a broad gateway, the Portal de Francia, that now funnels motor traffic in and out of the central city. About 300 meters to the right, inside of and almost abutting the city wall, stands Pamplona's cathedral. On the near side of that is the bishop's palace.

Our exploration of Pamplona begins among the arcades surrounding the tree-shaded Plaza del Castillo, for a thousand years and more the center of affairs in Pamplona. More recently, the plaza was a favorite stamping ground for Hemingway and his cronies, fictional and real, with its sidewalk cafes, shops, and the stirring of many people.

Here in early morning the cafes are hardly open, but find a sunny spot to sit for coffee and let me tell you about the history of this place.

Nearly a century was needed for the early kings of Navarra to dispense with the French and Moorish presence in Pamplona and the lands round about. Not until 905 did Sancho I feel secure enough to establish his court at Pamplona. Even that was premature. Near the end of the tenth century, in one final attempt to wipe out the Christian insurgency, the Caliph at Córdoba hurled massive armies north under the command of his vizier, the legendary Al Mansur, known to Christians as the Scourge of God.

In central Spain, León was retaken by the Muslims and Santiago de Compostela was sacked and destroyed in the northwest. Here in Navarra, the Christian king marched his tiny army out to defend his kingdom and met destruction in a fierce battle near Sangüesa. Pamplona was abandoned and soon flattened by the Moors in 997. But the conquerors lacked the power to stay, unable to take and hold the mountain redoubts into which the Christians retreated. Sancho the Great (r 1004-1035) won his appellation by driving the Moors back to their base at Saragossa.

Sancho's achievement was perhaps less grand an accomplishment than appears on the face of it. Certainly the empire created by the Arabs was the greatest of its day. It extended from the Atlantic to Persia and beyond. It gained tremendous wealth and developed an advanced culture that made Europeans of the time appear as little more than rude barbarians. But Islamic regimes then and to this day fostered a fatal flaw: Reliance upon the word of the Prophet for conduct of secular affairs. Abidance by the concepts of world and human relationships contained in the Koran too often made politically incompetent religious leaders the rulers of their lands. Worse, the weakness of secular law tended to produce regimes based on military intimidation of the populace. There were no provisions for orderly development of secular power and transfer of that power from leader to leader. The consequences were palace coups, while Byzantine intrigue was the rule and not the exception of governance in the Islamic world then and throughout the centuries since.

The system worked during the early years of the Islamic conquests as the Arabs and their converts maintained a fierce loyalty to their religion and its leadership, vested in the Caliph at Damascus. Then religious heresies split the formerly monolithic power of Islam. Two and then three competing caliphates were established. The third was founded in Córdoba in 922. But that only certified what was already historical fact: the Emir of Spain had become virtually autonomous a century earlier. Where once the entire Islamic world functioned in unison, now it squabbled with myriad internal dissensions that sapped its economic, political and military power to the extent that Al Mansur's campaigns near the turn of the millennium were virtually the last gasp of the Caliphate at Córdoba. It was overthrown in 1031.

When the Caliphate collapsed, Islamic Spain disintegrated into a covey of major and minor kingdoms known to history as the Taifa (Arabic term meaning "faction") states. These were established by various army chieftains or influential nobles who made their headquarters in leading cities of the south of Spain. They then set out to dominate and/or take over their neighbors. Nearly forty Taifa kingdoms were carved out of Moslem Spain to begin with. By midcentury they had been consolidated by force of arms into fewer than a dozen, of which a half-dozen dominated the remainder.

During this period of Islamic instability the Navarran king, Sancho the Great, won back the Ebro valley and rebuilt Pamplona. He then conquered Aragon and took over Asturian-backed Castile when its count died without a successor. Under his rule, history produced the first truly powerful Christian kingdom in Spain. Unfortunately, custom dictated division of the kingdom among his three sons upon his death. It was a tradition that literally sapped the Christian kingdoms of the potential for final victory until the thirteenth century when the custom was abandoned.

In the latter century, Sancho the Strong of Navarra allied with Alfonso VIII of Castile to defeat the Moors at the battle of Las Navas de Tolosa in the far south in 1212. That victory over the Almohades, an African force that had unified most of Moorish Spain, was the beginning of the end of the Moslem presence on the Iberian Peninsula.

Not long after Las Navas de Tolosa, Sancho the Strong died without an heir (his infant son perished at the hands of a careless nanny). Sancho was succeeded by a nephew, Thibaud I of Champagne. From him issued French dynasties that ruled Navarra for three hundred years until, in 1512, Ferdinand, in his dotage and the widower of Isabella, claimed Navarra for the Spanish crown and evicted the French by force of arms.

Ferdinand's annexation of the Basque provinces achieved peace in the region only by allowing the Basques a level of autonomy and special privileges (fueros) not granted to others. Navarra was allowed self-government, responding to the King of Spain through a viceroy. Indeed, during subsequent centuries successful attempts by various outside factions to eliminate Navarra's privileges and autonomy became the key that turned the sentiments of most Basques against the central government. Such sentiments are common to this day, no matter that the reforms instituted under King Juan Carlos in 1980 have done much to restore regional autonomy.

In the nineteenth century, the Basque provinces figured centrally in the Carlist revolts that unsuccessfully challenged the central government over the issue of monarchial succession. The problem began with the death of King Ferdinand VII in 1833. Virtually on his deathbed, he had restored the right of women to inherit the throne, if for no reason other than to spite his brother. That allowed him to be succeeded by an infant daughter, Isabella II, whose mother, Maria Christina of Naples, ruled as regent. While that was bad enough in the eyes of many Spaniards, Maria infuriated Catholic Spain by initiating a series of anticlerical measures, including widespread confiscation of church property as a means of replenishing the royal treasury to finance her spendthrift ways. That brought the problem of the succession to a boil.

In 1834, supporters of Carlos, the late Ferdinand's brother, headquartered in the Navarran town of Estella, rose in revolt. Their intent was to place Carlos on the throne. This, the so-called First Carlist War, ended five years later in negotiated defeat of the rebels. But the sentiments for Carlos and his heirs did not fade away. A Second Carlist War in favor of Don Carlos' son, Carlos Maria, lasted from 1873-76, with similar results.

Carlist sentiments persisted into the last century as a latent insurgency just beneath the surface of Spanish politics. A principal reason was that the Basques were stripped of their fueros by the central government as part of the settlement forced upon the Carlists. The bureaucrats of Madrid were just begging for trouble, and they got it.

The Carlist militia, the Requetés, headquartered in

39

Pamplona, was reestablished by Church leadership when an anti-clerical Republican government replaced the dictatorship of the 1920s. When General Emilio Mola, in July 1936, led the army-centered opposition to the Republican government in Madrid, the Requetés immediately rallied to Mola's support.

Another militia also had been formed during the early 1930s by the Falangists, led by José Antonio Primo de Rivera, son of the 1920s Spanish dictator. The coupling of the monarchist Carlists with the fascist Falangists and the army led by General Mola, accomplished by General Francisco Franco in the Fall and Winter of 1936 at his headquarters in Burgos, was the political stroke that ultimately awarded military success to the revolt. The role played by Navarran Carlists probably was the deciding factor in the victory won by the Franco regime.

Neither did the Republicans help their own cause. Their massacres of nuns and priests during the early months of the civil war brought all of Catholic Spain into sympathy with the Nationalist movement headed by Franco. And when the Republicans executed de Rivera on November 20, 1936, they removed the only competitor to Franco as leader of the movement. In effect, they made Franco a present of the dictatorship of Spain.

It is proper to note, however, that the Basques were not fully united in their support of Franco. Indeed, the Basque provinces on the northern slope of the Cantabrian Cordillera, promised return of their *fueros* by the Republicans, joined in defense of the Republic. Bilbao, the last stronghold of these northern Basques, was conquered by the nationalists in June, 1937. A part of that campaign saw the bombing of the Basque town of Guernica by German airmen sent to Spain to train for World War II.

The end of the civil war was not the end of the Basque rebellion. Their leaders fled to France while Franco vindictively conducted a campaign of Basque repression that lasted until his death, November 22, 1975. King Juan Carlos then brought democracy back to Spain, dismantled the dictatorship despite army opposition and, in 1979, for the first time since the civil war, the Basques were able to elect municipal and provincial assemblies and regained many of their precious *fueros* in 1980.

Unfortunately, the move was too little, too late for the Basque nationalists of the ETA (Euzkadi ta Askatasuna). Many of the small core of activists who make up the military, or terrorist, wing of the movement are men and women whose entire lives have been devoted to their cause, and whose reputations have been built upon their campaign of violence. Even worse, there are those among the government police and military whose lives have been so badly abused by the terrorists that they are no less intransigent in their hatred for the ETA in particular and the Basques in general.

For the traveler, this persistent political hostility poses no threat. ETA and government forces seek to punish each other, and do not resort to mindless terror directed at innocent bystanders as has been typical of the Palestinian and other Islamic terrorist factions. Moreover, as the old guard on each side dies out, and as the reforms led by King Juan Carlos settle in and are accepted as the normative facts of life in the Basque lands, the level of terrorist activity is receding, and might be expected to die out provided that neither side undertakes some foolish extremist aggravation.

Here in Pamplona we find the residue of all that: The age of the Sanchos and the centuries of rule by French kings (one of whom went on to rule France itself), and then the more recent times of Ferdinand, Franco, the Requetés and the ETA. Pamplona is a place where the past thrives as a sort of a growling undertone in a bright, modern city. It boasts of one of the leading medical schools in Europe, associated with a university whose supporters say is the best in Spain. But most distinctive of everything is the record, inscribed in stone, of Pamplona as a center providing safety and sustenance to throngs of pilgrims making their way along El Camino de Santiago.

The Navarrería

From the Plaza del Castillo, we reach the pilgrim route by walking southeast to the Plaza del Toros, then east on the north side of the bullring, which extends nearly to the Portal de Francia and the pilgrim's way. However, first we plan digressions to see points of interest along the way.

On the south side of the Plaza del Castillo, note a large but not too imposing structure with a classical facade sporting six Greek columns and a pedimental frieze above the name, **Diputación de Navarra.** Sometimes called the Palacio de Navarra, this is the seat of the provincial government. It was constructed in the mid-nineteenth century by José de Nagusía, and contains interesting tapestries and paintings, including a portrait of Ferdinand VII, done in 1814 by Goya.

West from the Palacio, at the corner of the Plaza del Castillo, is the Paseo Sarasate, a favorite for the Pamplonans' evening promenade. It is a broad double-drive with a park-like median containing an array of statues of various national kings and heroes.

In front of the Palacio de Diputación and coursing south into the distance, is the broad, tree lined Avenida de Carlos III. Walk down that avenue for about a hundred meters and take the first right, Calle de los Cortez de Navarra. It is named for the provincial parliament that meets in the building we just passed. The building you walk beside contains the Archivo General, in which are preserved a valuable collection of medieval documents.

Believe it or not, we are walking this way simply to stand at the next corner. There, on the right beyond the archive building, is the **church of San Ignacio,** facing onto the Avenida de San Ignacio. Why go out of our way to come here to this spot? Because it is involved in an episode of history that had repercussions around the world. The church, that is, is built on the spot where Ignatius Loyola is said to have been wounded by an exploding shell during an attempt by the French to retake Pamplona in 1521.

While the church, second-rate Churrigueresque in style, is nothing special to see, the event of St. Ignatius' injury reminds us first of important aspects of Pamplona's history, and then of the impact that injury had upon the man and the world in the centuries since.

As described earlier, the coming of the pilgrims brought tens of thousands of French immigrants into Northern Spain. They not only founded many new towns along the Way, they created new districts in many cities, including Pamplona. Here the area around the cathedral is known as the Spanish Basque section called Navarrería. It was separated from the French sections to the south and west by cross walls within the city. The walls isolated the Basque-dominated Spanish population from the French, between whom there were many violent ethnic episodes over the centuries. One of those walls stood here along what is now the street of the Cortez.

The French population, accustomed to centuries of rule by French dynasties, resented the takeover by Ferdinand in 1512. Thus they conspired with France to reverse history. They failed in the attempt, but they made a tremendous impact on world history if only because of what happened to Ignatius.

Ignatius was born in 1491 at the family castle of Loyola, south of here. He came from a noble family of Basques, and was sent as a boy to serve as a page at the royal court here in Pamplona. Under Ferdinand of Spain he became a soldier, for as the eleventh son of his family, his prospects to inherit were not that promising.

He was twenty-two years old when wounded during the French siege of 1521. The wound required a long convalescence, during which he read extensively to pass the time. Soon his bookish pursuit turned into something else as he pored through books on the Church and religion. His casual interest turned into a religious fervor that dominated his life thereafter.

Ignatius turned first to monasticism, sampling life with the Benedictines, Franciscans and Dominicans, the leading brotherhoods at the time. None satisfied the intensity of his feelings. Hoping to find new inspiration on which to pursue his calling, he went on pilgrimage to Jerusalem, only to become even more disillusioned with his religion by the experience of the petty squabbles of the warring sects in the Holy City (which as late as September 2004 led to a fist fight between priests of different orders in the Church of the Holy Sepulcher in Jerusalem).

Upon his return, disillusionment added flavors to his preaching that the Inquisition, which was sweeping across Spain at the time, found suspect. The threat of imprisonment or worse sent him scurrying across the mountains to safety in France. There he fell under the influence of Francis Xavier, another refugee Basque nobleman from the Navarran town of Javier, who was teaching at Beauvais. Together they created a new religious order, the Society of Jesus.

Known as the Jesuits, the Society of Jesus was conceived as a militant order devoted to propagation of the faith, with emphasis upon education for both the members of the order and the laity. The order won Papal approval by Paul III in 1540, and soon was a worldwide force within the Catholic Church. All that because a soldier, wounded in battle near this church, then overcome by boredom during his convalescence, found religion in his books.

Now walk back towards and across the Avenida de Carlos III. Proceed a block beyond to the Plaza del Toros, where the **bullring** dominates the view on your right. The bullring is a major attraction here, perennially associated with the wild antics of the "running of the bulls" every July 6 to 14 during the Fiestas de San Fermín.

Made famous by Hemingway in *The Sun Also Rises,* the bull fights are preceded each day by the running of that day's card of bulls through the city streets to the ring preceded, escorted, and harassed by the young bloods of the town, a scene we all have viewed many times on TV and movie screens. The "running" is a tradition begun in 1591, simply to move the bulls to the arena. The mixing of spectators into the "running" began during the following century. Otherwise the fiestas are simply a great excuse for everyone to have a good time. Note that Hemingway is honored here by a statue placed near the entrance to the bullring on the Paseo de Hemingway.

Northeast of the bull ring (near the Portal de Francia) on the left across the street, walk up into the Plaza Santa Maria la Real. From there a stairway leads to the top of the **city wall**. These ramparts are of sixteenth century origin, rebuilt from and upon earlier versions.

From the parapet of the main bastion adjacent to the old city gate, gain a fine view of the wooded park below along the Arga River. To your right across the river is a large water sports complex. Mostly obscured behind the foliage of the trees is the pilgrim's crossing at the single-arched Magdalena Bridge. In the distance on a clear day is the picturesque silhouette of the Pyrenees. The park at the foot of the wall is called the Jardines de la Media Luna.

What remains of the city wall extends only a couple of hundred meters south from where you stand. Northward it proceeds to a point just beyond the cathedral, the apse of which stands out against the skyline. Beyond the cathedral the wall turns west for about a kilometer, where it borders the northern extremity of the Jardines de la Taconera and abruptly ends. The walls to the west and south were torn down to make way for expansion of the modern city during the eighteenth and nineteenth centuries.

Walk north toward the cathedral atop the ramparts. If you treasure a good view, or fortifications are your thing, you must pass that way. The views from the wall are incontestably pleasing. On the left as you walk is the rear of the **Bishop's Palace,** and then the cathedral.

After absorbing the view across the valley from the northeast corner bastion, walk down to the cathedral on Calle de Redin, passing beneath the ancient footbridge that spans the narrow street. A turn to the right alongside the cathedral brings you to the tiny square in front. There you will be surprised, possibly struck aghast, at your first view of its eighteenth century neoclassical **facade.**

The design by Ventura Rodrígues is regarded as somewhat of a monstrosity compared to the serene Gothic severity of the fourteenth century structure behind it. What we have here is a Greek-revival portal with double row of columns supporting a classical entablature and gabled roof, situated between twin, square sixty-meter-tall towers, each with fancily appointed cupolas of Spanish Renaissance style. A tower to the right contains the largest bell in Spain, all twelve tons of it.

The cathedral (open 9 to 1:30; 6 to 8) was originally Romanesque, dating from 1023. It replaced an earlier basilican-style structure destroyed by the rampaging army of Abd ar-Rahman III, Caliph of Córdoba, near the turn of the millennium. That early church is believed to have been built on the site of a Roman temple. The later Romanesque church was demolished in the fourteenth century to make way for this Gothic edifice completed in the early fifteenth century by Carlos III, the Noble. Final touches were not applied until 1525, after which it received its unfortunate facade in 1783.

The main gate opens upon a tiny courtyard enclosed by a tall iron-picket fence. Its plan is the typical Latin cross Gothic, relatively plain-faced as early Gothic tends to be, with many side chapels between the interior buttresses, and rising to a groin-vaulted roof. In the right transept, in front of the wrought-iron Renaissance grille, is the **tomb** of the church founder, Carlos III (1387-1425) and his queen, Leonora of Trastámara. Their recumbent figures adorn their sarcophagi. The tomb was carved in alabaster by the Flemish sculptor Jean de Lomme of Tournai. Note the famous "procession of mourners" around the base. The grille of the Capella Mayor was completed in 1517, with choir stalls installed in 1540 by Esteban de Obray. Above the high altar is the Virgen de los Reyes, in front of which the kings of Navarra kept vigil on the night preceding their coronation. The retable dates from 1507.

A quick tour of the **side chapels**, including those around the apse, is recommended. Many are baroque, but early and outstanding are the fifteenth century altarpieces in the chapels of Santa Cristina and San Juan Battista. From the same period is the crucifix that dominates the Capilla del Santo Cruz. The grille before the Capilla de la Santa Cruz is said to have been forged out of the tent chains of the Moorish chieftain, taken during the Battle of Las Navas de Tolosa in 1212. More likely is the story that the grille is made from the chains of ten thousand Christian slaves and captives freed after the battle.

The outstanding artistic feature of the cathedral is the **cloister**, off the south side of which was once the meeting place of the Navarran Cortez. Their meeting room is known as the Sala Preciosa (Beautiful Room). Exit into the cloister from the south transept through a fourteenth century portal. On its exterior pillar between the double door is a rather conventional Virgin and Christ Child, but in the Gothic archway above the portal is a remarkable tympanum portraying the Dormition of the Virgin Mary.

The cloister is regarded by many experts as the finest to be seen in Spain. The north and east galleries were built in the late fourteenth century, followed by the south and west in the early fifteenth. The galleries surround an open court providing an exterior view of stone work across the courtyard that is truly impressive. Each bay contains three slender columns supporting stone tracery rising beneath Gothic arches that extend through more fancy stonework comprising balustrades on the second level of the cloister. Note that the design of the tracery alternates from bay to bay.

Within the galleries of the cloister you find yourself beneath ribbed Gothic vaults lifting high over the square-tiled corridor. Opening toward the inner courtyard is the fancy stone tracery above an iron picket fence, while the inner wall is comprised of plain-faced Gothic blind arches except for a few portals, plus an occasional statue or niche for sculpture.

As you walk through the cloister you find, in the northeast corner, a sculpture of the Adoration of the Magi by Jean Perut, dating from the early fourteenth century. In an adjacent niche is a much earlier depiction of the crucifixion. On the east corridor is the **Barbazán Chapel**, built in the fourteenth century by the bishop of that name to serve as his tomb. Its decor includes his effigy situated on the floor before the altar, above which the Virgin presides. The vaulting therein is spectacular and of a design known as star vaulting, of which we will see even more sensational examples later on our journey. The large stained glass windows are rich in color, but unimaginative in their depiction of the saints. You will note other, less prestigious tombs at various points along the galleries. At the door to the **Sala Preciosa**, on the south gallery, you find another richly carved fourteenth century construction. The tympanum contains scenes from the life of the Virgin. At the sides of the portal are statues of the Virgin and the Angel of the Annunciation.

Still another fine portal leads to the former **refectory**, used by the Augustinian monks until the nineteenth century. Its tympanum displays the Last Supper and the Entrance of Jesus into Jerusalem. The one-time refectory now houses the Diocesan Museum, which is worth a look because of a masterfully done fifteenth century reliquary containing a splinter from the True Cross. Also displayed are sculptures from the thirteenth and fourteenth centuries and a collection of Renaissance paintings, plus the usual church furnishings, statuary and vestments. The museum is open 10 to 7 weekdays, 10 to 2:30 Saturdays; closed Sundays and holidays. Winter hours are 10 to 1:30 and 4 to 7 weekdays, 10 to1:30 on Saturdays.

Adjoining the refectory is a vast old kitchen, square with a fireplace in each wall, covered by a twenty-four meter tall lantern tower admitting light and ventilating heat and kitchen odors through its high-up windows. It dates from 1330. A chef will be fascinated.

The Pilgrim's Pamplona

Leaving the cathedral the pilgrim's way proceeds to the church of San Saturnino, a distance of about four hundred meters. To get there, take Calle Curia, the middle one of three streets leading away from the small plaza in front of the cathedral. It takes you to and along Calle de los Mercaderes to the Plaza Consistorial. There, on the right, is a fancy, three-story facade, which is all that remains of a late seventeenth century city hall, or **Ayuntamiento**. The structure behind it is modern. This Baroque phantasmagoria of architecture has a fancy iron-grilled balcony on each level, supported by pairs of engaged columns: Doric on the first level, Ionic on the second, Corinthian on the third. Pairs of louvered doors open onto the balconies, on the grilles of which are gilded lions in front of each of the three doors per balcony. Above all that is a stone balustrade, fronting a gabled cupola holding a clock and topped by regal lions, bells and a trumpeting statue of Fame. The whole of that is flanked by a pair of club-wielding, rough-clad protectors representing Hercules on one of his many labors. Oh, yes: Another pair of baroque statues, Prudence and Justice, stand to each side of the carved archway of the central portal at street level.

All that describes only the half of it. Baroque designers just never knew when to quit.

The site of the facade is where the old French quarter of San Cernin once began. On the plaza before it, every July 6, a rocket (the chupinazo) is fired skyward to announce the start of the Fiestas de San Fermín, followed by dancing and the parade of the gigantes y cabezudos (giants and bigheads) through the city streets.

Bear right on the far side of the plaza along Calle de San Saturnino. After less than fifty meters and a slight jog to the left, you are at the church of San Saturnino, the oldest church still standing in the city. It was known as the **pilgrim church**, for it stood in the French district of Cernin, where pilgrims, mostly French, found comfort among their countrymen.

San Saturnino (Saturninus) baptized the first Christians in Pamplona. The church marks the spot. A plaque in front of the church indicates where he is supposed to have preached the Gospel. Nearby is the well from which the saint obtained water for the first baptisms.

The church you see dates from the thirteenth century and is the latest of several built on the site. Its fortress-like main structure in part was retained from the twelfth century church and, like the square brick towers, it is Romanesque. The towers once were topped by crenellations instead of the belfries now in place. The Gothic porch is of the same century, but later. The tympanum portrays Christ in Judgment.

Above the north porch is a statue of Saint James with a pilgrim praying at his feet. While the time-weathered saint has lost both arms, note that hanging at his side is his pilgrim's scrip, or purse, its flap sealed by a scallop shell.

Inside you find a single-aisled church with an apse containing a gilt retable more spectacularly ornate than artistic. The rough-hewn and tread-worn wood panels on the floor, each with a number, cover the tombs of the faithful who have been interred here. In the chapel near the main door is a colorful statue of Christ, a Gothic sculpture of the Flemish school. Beside the main structure is the eighteenth century chapel of the Virgen del Camino (seldom open), constructed on the site of the former cloister.

Just past San Saturnino, Calle Mayor (Main Street) begins. It was the path the pilgrims took as they exited Pamplona, and is so labeled on the street signs. Now it is a busy shopping thoroughfare.

About three hundred meters down Calle Mayor, on the left, just short of the Jardines de la Taconera, is the church of **San Lorenzo**, where resides the statue of San Fermín, patron saint of Navarra. The wooden statue, with dark face and decked out in silver vestments, is supposed to be especially protective of those who run with the bulls during his fiesta. It resides in a baroque chapel within this otherwise Neo-Classical structure.

We continue our walk through Pamplona with a visit to the **Navarra Museum.** To get there, retrace your steps to San Saturnino. Across the street from its porch is a stairway down onto Calle de Santo Domingo. There turn left and a stroll of about two hundred meters brings you to the museum, which faces you at the end of the street at the top of a broad ramp.

50

The museum (open 10 to 2, 5 to 7; closed Monday) was built on the site of an old pilgrim hospital of which only the highly decorated Renaissance (1556) portal has been retained. Passing through its Plateresque adornments into the courtyard, in the galleries on the left are Roman-era mosaic pavements and funerary steles. One mosaic depicts the Athenian King Theseus and the Minotaur. Other galleries display capitals and related materials salvaged from the twelfth century Pamplona Cathedral. Best known are the Romanesque carvings of the Passion, Resurrection, and the Story of Job, on the capitals. In the one-time chapel connected to the hospital is an interesting altarpiece by Esteban de Obray.

Also displayed in the museum are respectable collections of Gothic and Renaissance paintings and murals. Obtain a guide pamphlet (available in the language of your choice) at the entrance.

As you leave the museum, walk back along Calle de Santo Domingo to the Ayuntamiento square. There bear left for a few meters to reach Calle Chapitela, which in about seventy meters returns you to the Plaza del Castillo and the refreshment that you so richly deserve. Enjoy it at one of Hemingway's sidewalk cafes.

The Aragonese Road

A second pilgrim track traverses the Pyrenees further east than the Navarran Road via Roncesvalles. This second route, known as the Aragonese Road, was a more direct path to Santiago for pilgrims from lands bordering the Mediterranean. This alternate route crossed the Pyrenees via Somport, descended south to Jaca, and then angled west through the foothills along the southern flank of the mountains.

To investigate the Aragonese Road all the way from Somport would add little to our travel experience other than a pleasant outing amidst another and much wilder section of the Pyrenees, plus a visit to some interesting landmarks in and around Jaca. Make the journey if you wish, but we recommend it only for travelers who have a great deal of time on their hands or who have a special interest in Aragonese history.

Some travelers might take exception to that rather off-hand dismissal of Jaca and its environs. Yet in the final analysis, since time is of the essence for most travelers, a studied opinion holds that to pursue the Aragonese Road east of Leyre adds nothing substantially unique to our journey along El Camino de Santiago.

Today, then, drive east to meet the Aragonese Road and visit the monastery of San Salvador at Leyre, then turn back to follow the Aragonese Road westward to where it meets the Navarran Road at Puente de la Reina. Be on your way early, so as to arrive at Leyre in time for morning services at 9 in the monastic church. Catholic or not, you will be fascinated by the experience.

Leave Pamplona from the traffic circle at the Plaza del Principe de Viana, going south on Avenida de Zaragoza, which is route N121. About five kilometers along, N121 meets A15, the superhighway to Saragossa and Madrid. Pass it by. Proceed another five kilometers on N121, and there take route N240 east.

At first the highway courses through a broad, fertile valley containing mile after mile of wheat fields, with low mountains in the distance. Then the mountains draw closer and higher, pinching the valley nearly shut until the highway twists and climbs through increasingly steeper hills.

About twenty kilometers after Monreal is the Embalse de Yesa (Yesa Reservoir), with the Sierra de Leyre rising sharply on the left. In the gnarled, rocky foothills of those mounts, above the west end of the reservoir and four kilometers off the highway, stands the famous Monastery of San Salvador de Leyre. Watch for the sign pointing left.

San Salvador de Leyre

The road up to the monastery is steep with many sharp turns among out-jutting rocks below ocher-colored cliffs. Up out of the valley, the arid hillsides are covered with brush and a few blades of grass. First view of Leyre sees the monastic church perched on the brow of a hill. We see its western face, with the chapter house extending off to the right. Arriving atop the shoulder on the hill upon which the monastery is situated, park and look down across the rough-cut plateau below, with the man-made reservoir in the foreground and the rock-bound cliffs of parched sierras some distance off on each side. It is a view well worth a pause in the morning sunlight, and a fitting time to introduce you to the background of the place you are about to visit.

The monastery of San Salvador at Leyre is believed to have been established during the time of the Gothic kings. Far north as it is, it continued to thrive during the initial phase of the Arab conquest. St. Eulogius, who served at the monastery for a few years in the mid-ninth century before he was martyred at Córdoba, described the remarkable extensiveness of its library. Eulogius also wrote of the martyrs, Nudilius and Alodia, young sisters from Huesca who about 850 were beheaded as apostates from Islam, as required by Sharia Law. Their remains were brought to Leyre by the wife of Arista, the founding king of Navarra. We will see them memorialized above the church doorway.

In that same century the pantheon of the kings of Navarra was installed in its church. At times the monastery became the seat of the royal court for religious retreat or simply for escape from the affairs of the world. Ever since then it has been regarded as the spiritual heart of the old Basque kingdom that lives on spiritually in the modern province.

In the late tenth century its mountainous redoubt for a while became the sanctuary for the kings and nobles of Navarra seeking shelter from the depredations of the Moslems. However, it too was eventually destroyed by Al Mansur after the defeat of the Christian Army at Sangüesa. Rebuilding began immediately under the auspices of Sancho the Great. The new church, with its famous crypt, was consecrated in 1057. It is regarded as the earliest surviving large-scale example of Spanish pre-Romanesque architecture.

The monastery, under Cluniac (Benedictine) discipline at first and the Cistercians after 1307, has served monks and pilgrims alike for eight hundred years. It was the wellspring of the Cluniac reforms that swept through the Spanish church in the eleventh century.

Disaster struck the place as a result of the Carlist Wars of the nineteenth century.

Government forces, inspired by the anti-clerical bent of their monarch, and recognizing the millennium-old regard for Leyre as the spiritual seat of the heart and soul of the Navarran people supporting the Carlist movement, in 1835 expelled the monks, confiscated their holdings and, after largely wrecking the place, left it desolate and abandoned. Not until 1954, under the Franco regime, was it turned back to the church and reinhabited by a colony of Benedictine monks from Silos. Today, after much refurbishing and rebuilding, the monastery again welcomes pilgrims making their way along El Camino de Santiago. But these modern reconstructions, no matter how welcome and worthy, can never recover everything that was lost.

Certainly the church has been restored, if somewhat clumsily. Its external lines are obscured by near-by modern structures (seventeenth and eighteenth century, recently restored) erected on the foundations of buildings that time erased. The cloisters are now a plot of lawn called the Patio de Hospeteria. Much else remains as bits of foundations amidst the brush and weeds round about. All of which is by way of a warning that, as at Roncesvalles, you should not expect too much at first impression. The Pre-Romanesque and Cistercian survivals within the church are the main features we come to see as we explore this early flowering of authentic Spanish culture. Its most architecturally significant elements are its eleventh century triple apse and the crypt beneath the church. The nave was extended and rebuilt in each of the twelfth through fourteenth centuries by the Cistercians, and topped by a turret and square tower sporting triple windows with a character hearkening back to Visigothic times.

As we proceed here at Leyre, some travelers may become impatient with the extent to which I attend to historical and architectural details peculiar to this place. However, more than the devil is in such details as these, as the saying goes. What we discover here is evidence of a painful reawakening and flowering of a civilization that had been driven to its knees, forced to reinvent a culture that had been virtually lost for generations. We promised an exploration of a culture and its history, and in constructs of stone such as these we may read the record, first hand, as explorers in our own right. Thus, just as we paused at Roncesvalles to become familiar with the character of early Gothic, here we devote more words than usual to these architectural expressions from the Pre-Romanesque followed by the evolution from Romanesque into the Cistercian.

So: First, walk down to the rear of the church to view the semicircular **apses**, all of equal height, that rise upon foundations defining the bounds of the crypt beneath. The tower and its windows are also best observed from this perspective. The building to the left is the new monastic quarters, while to the right is the old monastery, now converted into a hotel and restaurant for pilgrims and visitors to this remote location. Your reservations would be welcomed.

The central or choir apse of the church is eldest of the trio and regarded as architecturally most significant. It represents the earliest Navarran expression of the Spanish Pre-Romanesque, revealed in these apses and no less spectacularly in the crypt beneath the church. As your eye compares them to other French-influenced Romanesque constructions of later date, you will see how these distinctive architectural features, particularly in the crypt, express a primitive Romanesque derived independently from Visigothic sources. Also characteristic of this style of early Spanish Romanesque, and maintained by the later Cistercian renovations, is the plain simplicity of both the interior and exterior, virtually devoid of decoration except at the portals.

The Monastery of San Salvador at Leyre

As the name suggests, Romanesque architecture is based on building concepts of the Romans, particularly on the use of the round arch and barrel vault. As compared to the sophisticated Gothic that we saw at Roncesvalles and Pamplona, or the Cistercian style that we will view here in the vaulted nave, the architectural character of Romanesque is relatively squat and ponderous. And here in its early Spanish manifestation you will discover a primitiveness that speaks of builders and artisans copying from the past, but with tools and skills dulled by disuse for generations.

The crypt is accessible by tour only, through an entrance here by the apse end of the church. Since the tours usually begin in mid-morning (inquire at the hotel), we will visit the church first, since it opens early for services. Perhaps, as we did recently, you will arrive in time to hear the monks sing their morning Mass, to which they invite the attendance of locals and travelers alike. If you enjoy colorful ritual and the male voice chanting the liturgy, seen in a thousand year old church lit by modern electricity and heard with the advantages of a flawless sound system, the experience will be memorable. Their fellow monks from Silos, it is worth remarking, have gained world renown for their recordings of Gregorian chants.

Enter the church by walking all the way around to its west portal. The broad, open space north of the church once held the cloister. The one-time **side portal** into the cloister, far back in the corner of the grassy courtyard, is lightly carved in the Romanesque style characterized by low relief. Note the pilaster-like buttresses in the church walls, designed to support the thrust of the ribbed vaults of Cistercian design that we will find inside above the nave. In the transitional Gothic of the Cistercians the prominent flying buttresses of later Gothic played no role.

We enter the church climbing the steps up to the main portal on the west, known as the **Porta Speciosa**. Before entering, step back, take a seat on the stone railing and devote a few moments to a study of this well-known and architecturally famous doorway. Created in the thirteenth century renovation that extended the nave, it contains a central pillar with three columns at each side, each group supporting three arches, each interval of which contains statuary. The tympanum is believed to have been incorporated from an even earlier entryway.

First, some general remarks about such portals in general, drawing upon what you have already seen at Roncesvalles and Pamplona.

While the style of this pointed arched portal is distinctively Gothic, it is worth reminding ourselves that the concept and character of such portals was a development of the

57

Romanesque period. In Romanesque the archway is round and the carving in much lower relief, as at the cloister door, though not necessarily executed with more primitive skill. The opportunity for the receding arches, narrowing down to the doorway, the archivolts all ornately carved, derived from the tremendous thickness of the walls that Romanesque design techniques required for support of the heavy superstructure, the weight of which not even blind arches could totally relieve. Nor did it take much imagination to decide that beside the portal one should carve pillars (supporting or merely decorative) with fancy capitals placed beneath the respective arches, as you find here. Not that creation of such fancy detail was always the case, as we shall see at a number of Romanesque and Cistercian churches later on.

The tympanum is but a stone facing atop the door lintel and extending upward to fill the space below the arch. It offers a fine surface for the sculptor to decorate. As for the decor chosen, Christ and/or the Virgin Mary are nearly always the dominant figures in the tympanum, cast in various scenes from life and death. Accompanying them you find the Evangelists, the other Apostles, angels and such figures as the Magi depicted in companion scenes evoking their parts in Biblical stories. Remember that the people who passed through these doors were for the most part illiterate, and these carvings made real the stories of Christ the Redeemer, the saints who worked for man's salvation, and the Devil who would frustrate a man's search for goodness and Grace.

Here at Leyre, the **tympanum** contains a Gothic high relief of Christ in the center, with the Virgin Mary and St. Peter on his right, and St. John on his left. Note the secular character of the carving on the arches above, with representations of foliage and assorted monstrosities. These motifs are a holdover from Roman times, part of the heritage that defined Romanesque as a vague cultural recollection of a time more idealized than understood. Above that are images of various saints, the Annunciation, Visitation, and the martyrdoms of the young girls, Sts. Nudilius and Alodia, all of which introduce us to

Gothic tendencies of decor. But the primitiveness of this work, compared to the Gothic or more sophisticated French Romanesque we will see later, is remarkable. Nevertheless, that primitive character detracts not at all from the importance of the work as such in the eyes of the experts in these things.

The **floral carvings** and monstrosities are not unusual, particularly in Romanesque and early Gothic, as we pointed out. The florals are believed to have been copied from old Roman work, while the grotesques and imaginary beasts that often are found interjected into the decor of these churches are a cultural holdover from Gothic and Nordic influences that permeated both France and Spain during an earlier period when Goths and Northmen added the dissonance of violence and pagan myth to the mix of culture coming out of what we call the early Middle Ages. At some sites we even find motifs drawn from classical legends: mermaids, nymphs peeking from behind leafy boughs, and such things as the Greek hound of Hell.

As we described earlier, Satan and his works were real for these people, as real and pervasive as the sun in the sky and the furrow in the plowed earth. What the monks built here was a House of God where Christ is surrounded by his saints and angels, all poised ready to help poor sinners find solace and salvation through Confession and the message of the Gospel spoken in stone upon, and then audibly within, these walls.

The building of a church or a cathedral was thus a very serious business for the time in which these people lived. To understand that seriousness is to understand much of what we will see in these coming days. Do not mistake any of these structures as show-off pieces or mere efforts to keep up with the religious Joneses, even if such motives at times no doubt crept into the thinking of the founders. These places were built for the glory of God and the everlasting salvation of the human soul.

Inside we find that the twelfth and thirteenth century single-aisled **nave** has tall and spacious Gothic ribbed vaults dating from the fourteenth century. These were the work of the

Cistercians and represent a style transitional between Romanesque and Gothic, a style that became identified with their order, and one that we will view many times during our journey to Santiago. Their plain and sturdy Gothic vaults are designed to rise above Romanesque piers and blind arches in the walls on each side, with only minimal external buttressing, as you recall from your view of the exterior.

Note that the entire superstructure, oddly enough, appears to be offset to the right as you stand at the rear of the nave and look forward to the tunnel-like barrel vaults of the Romanesque apses. The eye's first clue to that misalignment is the Romanesque **round window** above the central apse. Its aperture is centered on the ribbed peak of the vaulted nave, and not aligned with the arch defining the choir apse. This seems to devolve from peculiarities of the builder's execution of the original eleventh century plan. Note that the arch of the left side apse is visibly narrower than its companion on the right, while there are distinct irregularities in the vaulting.

No matter that monkish lapse in construction, this structure is esteemed by architectural scholars as a definitive example of the Pre-Romanesque accomplishments of local Spanish builders and stone masons whose skills had been shaped by recollections emanating from their Visigothic ancestral roots. The primitiveness speaks of culture in the process of rebirth after centuries of chaos.

As we see in the construction of the **apses,** the lack of the later Gothic techniques of buttressing, or ribbing designed to reduce the weight and outward thrust of vaulted superstructures, greatly limited attempts to attain height or expanse between supporting walls and piers. The round arches and barrel vaults inherited from Rome thus disallow the broad, high-flying spaces of the Gothic arch or the windowed walls between the Gothic ribs that opened the way to the profusion of stained glass that became a trademark of the Gothic cathedral in its later manifestations.

In Spain, the Romanesque style became the dominant form of Christian church construction in the eleventh and twelfth centuries. The refinement of the style was largely influenced by French Benedictine monks and especially by the monastery at Cluny. The Benedictines popularized the T-cross design (nave and transept) of the Roman basilica style, called the Latin cross, adopted by the early Church. However, they placed the choir at the fore and made it much more elongated than in the early Christian plan. It generally used the three-aisle, three-apse plan except in the smaller parish or monastic churches such as we find here.

Early Romanesque still used the Roman wooden roof, at least over the central nave. No doubt the original incarnations of this church had such a roof. Stone vaulting came later and required heavy buttressing of the piers at the exterior wall. The most outstanding example we will see of this later Romanesque is the cathedral at Santiago de Compostela (1075-1130), which is modeled after St. Cernin of Toulouse in general construction.

Off the north side of the plain-walled nave is a bay-like shrine protected by an iron lattice. This is the **Pantheon** of the early Kings of Navarra. It contains a wooden chest said to hold the bones of ten kings of Navarra whose remains formerly reposed in the crypt. They are said to include the first king of Navarra, Iñigo Jiménez Arista, and others from the ninth to the twelfth centuries. A bronze plaque presents the complete list and their dates.

Behind the main altar a crowned and gilded Virgin and Child sit atop a tall pedestal, glowing in the morning sun that filters through a thin sheet of beige alabaster in the single window of the apse. Again we call your attention to a building technique, this time for interior illumination and weather-proofing, using the **alabaster sheet**. It was invented by the Romans and commonly used throughout the Mediterranean and Middle East.

Otherwise there is nothing fancy about this place. Aside from the sanctuary, there is a dimness surrounded by barriers of stone that lends an almost cave-like character to one's experience. While the tall vaults of the Cistercians relieve this feeling somewhat, there is a special feeling about this place that is peculiar to itself and no doubt speaks of its time.

Now to the crypt, which for architectural scholars is the most fascinating structure of all that the monks built here. It may be reached by a stairway near the right side apse, through a portal with a carving representing the Trinity above it. But that way is forbidden to the public, so one must return to the rear exterior of the church to undertake the guided tour.

The **crypt** is suspected by most authorities of being much earlier in origin than the upper apsoidal structure. Although both are said to have been consecrated at the same time in 1057, the crypt probably dates from the tenth century prior to the depredations of Al Mansur. There is an extraordinary flavor of the Pre-Romanesque here, in my estimation not unrelated to what we will discover in Asturias a few days hence. The building stones of the foundations, barrel vaults, and supporting piers are large, less graceful than formidable, with some keystones of the arches being quite massive. Note that the center arches rest upon short, round pillars of various heights, compensated for by supporting capitals equally varied in size and design. The whole arrangement suggests builders with limited resources and skills making do with materials at hand, yet building to last for eternity.

Some of the capitals have distinctively secular carvings in the low relief characteristic of, but more primitive than, the usual Romanesque. Again we are reminded of Asturias, where similar work was executed a century earlier.

As we will discover later, the regions of León and Castile at first retained a much stronger Visigothic heritage, later modified by Islamic influences brought north by Christian migrations out of the Moslem south. Only later, with the popularization of the pilgrimage to Santiago and the influx of French immigrants, were influences from France grafted upon that local development further west from here. Meanwhile, in the mountains of Asturias, where Visigoths and Arabs never gained much of a foothold, old Roman styles and techniques were preserved in an isolated, homegrown culture that lay at the heart of the first stirrings of the Reconquista.

Thus here, in the company of those Vascon workmen who a thousand years ago set about recreating a fitting house of worship idealized by recollections of another age, we complete our visit to El Salvador de Leyre.

Javier

Coming down from Leyre, return to route N240 and turn left towards Juesca. After about a kilometer, reaching "downtown" Yesa, take the right turn to Javier, birthplace (1506) of St. Francis Xavier. The sixteenth century castle of the Xavier family, now a school for Jesuits, presides over the village. The castle, a couple of hundred meters off the highway on the left, looks fit for the role of a family fortress, and has been well restored. The same is true of the tiny parish church at the left end of the castle, where the saint was baptized. A convent is located adjacent to the church, along with facilities for visitors and a museum (open 9 to 12.45, 4 to 7 daily).

Morning and afternoon tours of the castle are available. Most interesting, other than the castle itself, are the murals of the Dance of Death recalling the bubonic plagues of the Middle Ages.

Sangüesa

The grand successes of the Reconquista in the eleventh century freed the Way of St. James from the threat of Moorish slave merchants and raiders serving the Arab king of Saragossa. One consequence was a tremendous increase in pilgrims choosing to travel the now safer Aragonese Road. To encourage that lucrative traffic, the king of Aragon constructed a new bridge at a favorable spot on the Rio Aragon. While it was some ways off the then existing pilgrim road, the safety and convenience of the bridge gained immediate pilgrim approval.

Just a stone's throw from the bridge he built and garrisoned a functional but palatial castle. It served not only to protect his kingdom against possible Muslim attacks, but also to defeat bands of brigands who preyed on pilgrims. The castle, being close to where the action was on the southern frontier of the kingdom, soon became the vacation resort to which the king repaired between campaigns against the Muslims. Naturally, the nobles of the court followed and built residences of their own nearby.

Until then the inhabitants of the area had lived on a low mount, Rocaforte, about five kilometers north of the present town. They had chosen Rocaforte as a more defensible site for repelling the constant attacks of the Muslims. To aid construction of his new bridge and castle, the king relocated the townsfolk down from Rocaforte. Later they provided services to his court as well as to pilgrims. The town of Sangüesa dates from that time, and subsequently grew like Topsy.

Town, bridge and castle remain to this day, all reasonably well preserved.

Some sources say the king who founded the place was Sancho Ramírez of Navarra and Aragon in the late eleventh century. Others say it was his successor, Alfonso I, the Battler, who ruled until the two kingdoms split again at his death in 1134. Both men were highly successful monarchs. Sancho, working with Alfonso VI of León and Castile, was responsible for rehabilitating the old Roman roads and making El Camino de Santiago a viable route through Aragon and Navarra. He further encouraged immigration of Franks and other Europeans to help repopulate a region left relatively wild and desolate by centuries of warfare and the Moorish slave trade.

Alfonso the Battler won his appellation by victories over the Moors at Saragossa in 1118 and at Valencia in 1125, dying of wounds after the Battle of Braga in 1134. For a time he also claimed Castile and León, having married Urraca, daughter of Ferdinand I and heir to her brother, Alfonso VI. That marriage was annulled by the Pope on the grounds of consanguinity, although the true reason was political. The powerful nobles of Castile and León refused to accept the Battler as their sovereign. They repulsed his attempts to gain by force what the marriage had promised to give as a dower. Thus Christian Spain had to wait another three hundred years for unification under Isabella and a later Ferdinand.

The pilgrim route via Javier descends into Sangüesa at the Plaza de los Fueros, which one encounters rather suddenly as one comes down a hill on the narrow road into the town. Take an immediate right as you reach the square and look for a place to park in the next couple of blocks, most probably on a side street to the right. There is parking in the Plaza de los Fueros, but don't count on finding a space in that busy square.

Walking back to the plaza, tree lined with a central plot of grass and shrubbery surrounded by parked cars, on the far side you see the **Convent** of San Francisco. This is an active monastery of the Franciscan fathers.

The entrance to this thirteenth century church is located underneath the tiny bell tower. The interior is extraordinarily plain, like its portal, and is most notable for its fourteenth century cloister which, with its slender-columned arcade and spare stone traceries, is splendidly attractive for all its simplicity.

Our walk through town is for the most part a stroll down the Rua Mayor, which departs the far side of the Plaza de los Fueros. Rua Mayor, Main Street, was built along the original pilgrim road that headed on a bee-line for the bridge that made the city important. Rua Mayor, the most important street of the small town, has possessed that status since its founding. As you walk, take time to observe and admire the ancient residences that line each side of what continues to be a busy shopping street. Mostly brick, with some stone, they boast of upper galleries with deep-carved wooden eaves. On portals and windows of some you see high relief Gothic carving, or later Plateresque fancies that were vogue during the various periods when the homes were built.

Notably, in the middle of the second block, on the left, are the palaces of the Sebastians and the París. These stately old former homes of Navarran nobility, who flocked here after the Navarran royal family set up a number of palatial residences, are not the principal attraction, however. The town is most noted for its magnificent churches, which tell of the historic importance of the place. As noted, it grew like Topsy. It boasted of six parishes and eleven hospices during its medieval heyday when it was a playground for princes and prayer-stop for pilgrims.

Largest of the churches is Santa María la Real, situated near the royal bridge. More revered by pilgrims and somewhat older is the Church of Santiago, near the center of town. Also important was the Iglesia de San Salvador, a few steps further off the Rua Mayor.

The very center of town is defined by the intersection with the Rua de Santiago. Turn left on that street and after a hundred meters, on the left, is the crenellated campanile of the church of that same name. The **Church of Santiago** is twelfth century Romanesque with later Gothic renovations. The crenellations on the bell tower were not added until 1365. The main church was begun in 1120 and completed about 150 years later. Above the studded wooden doors of the front portal, perched on a giant scallop shell, is St. James himself, with a painted pair of adoring pilgrims kneeling alongside. Only the statue is old (late thirteenth century) placed here in the tympanum of this early Gothic portal in this century.

Oldest part of the church is the three-apse east end, which you see is the by now familiar Romanesque. Unfortunately, on the interior it is largely hidden behind the undistinguished eighteenth century retable.

Returning to the Rua Mayor, turn left and continue west towards the river. After a few steps, on the right, is the arcaded and richly carved **Ayuntamiento**. The Town Hall dates from 1570, built as a renovation of the south wing of the former palace of the Prince of Viana (who in Navarra was the equivalent of the Prince of Wales in England).

Proceed through the arcade into the tree-lined courtyard

behind, upon which, at the far end, faces the north wing of the original **palace**. Built in the eleventh century by Alfonso the Battler, he later donated it to a commandery of the Knights of St. John, the Hospitallers, stationed here to give aid to pilgrims and protect the pilgrim way. It was largely renovated during the thirteenth and fourteenth centuries, first by the Hospitallers and later to serve the princes as a pleasure palace. The main structure contains distinctive pairs of Romanesque windows. It is flanked by strong, crenellated towers that betray the initial function of the palace as a fortress against the Moors as well as being a royal residence for the Battler.

A few steps further down Rua Mayor, at No. 12 and 14, are a pair of outstanding examples of palaces of the nobility who established homes in Sangüesa to be near the kings and princes of Navarra. First is the Guendulain palace, then that of the Duke of Granada. The latter fifteenth century residence is perhaps the most impressive of the two because of the extravagance of its late Gothic windows.

A few steps more, at Calle Alfonso el Battalador, make a short hundred meter digression to the left. On the west side of the street you find the Palacio de Vallesantoro, now the **Casa de Cultura**. Note the spectacular carving on the wooden eaves, incorporating monsters and serpents and whatever else the fantasy of the artist contrived. The facade is baroque, with coats of arms and spiral columns alongside the entrance.

Inside, the three-storey wooden grand staircase, with galleries opening onto all three floors, is no less spectacular. Note the ancient stone columns supporting the structure at the corners of each level, each set of four a different design. Take a moment to visit its charming courtyard. In the lobby you may also obtain a detailed map of the town, with its most notable features located and identified by number.

Further along, where the street angles off to the left, is the **Iglesia de San Salvador**, on the left. Again we have a thirteenth-century church, but this one boasts of a much superior piece of workmanship at its main portal. Featured sculptures are the Last Judgment and Resurrection of the Dead.

Inside is a fifteenth century retable by Jean de Berrueta, featuring Saints George and Damian. Its sixteenth century choir stalls were salvaged from the one-time ruin of the monastery at Leyre.

Now walk back to Rua Mayor, turn left, and proceed to the piece de resistance of any visit to the medieval town of Sangüesa: the church of **Santa María la Real**. A Cistercian-style structure begun in the early twelfth century, it is a classic representation of the first stirrings of a transitional phase between Romanesque and Gothic, containing features of both in its original construction and, of course, much more Gothic in its later additions and renovations. We found the style merely tacked on to the Romanesque church at Leyre. Here it is the work of the founders. Nonetheless, we will find the style exemplified at its peak expression at the convent church of las Huelgas in Burgos a few days hence.

The Cistercian style retains the plain-faced simplicity of the Romanesque, but notably adds the soaring nave and crossing made possible by the Gothic arch. This church was recently designated a National Monument in recognition of the architectural pioneering that went into its construction.

As you approach, you see its octagonal tower, added about the middle of the thirteenth century except for its crenellated upper tier and Gothic spire. These were raised in 1365. But the greatest treasure of all is the Gothic extravaganza of the **south portal**, regarded by some experts as the finest on the Way of St. James this side of the cathedral at Santiago de Compostela. Most of the work was done by the sculptor Fransoze Leodegarius.

The portal almost defies description. The deep-seated Gothic archway over the bronze-studded doors contains an intricately carved Last Judgment in the tympanum. The three interior arches over the portal rest on side columns, decorated with the peculiarly elongated figure of a saint except for the depiction (on the far right) of the hanged Judas. The others, from the left, are Mary Magdalene, the Virgin Mary, the mother of St. James, St. Paul, and St. Peter. Above the archway are two levels of tiny blind arches, featuring Christ the King with his royal falcon and griffins close at hand, and the remainder of the Twelve Apostles, plus the Four Evangelists bestowing their benedictions from individual niches.

Gothic Portal, Santa Maria la Real

In the triangular coving straddling the upper archway is a hodge-podge of artistic fancy: the figures of animals, real and mythical; people of various callings such as musicians and blacksmiths; while the Gothic arches themselves are intricately carved over every inch of their surface with more figures of saints, animals and heaven knows what else.

The poorly illuminated interior of the three-aisled church is almost anticlimactic after the exuberance of the entrance portal.

As seems to have been the pattern with medieval church builders, the Romanesque triple-apse was built first and is thus the oldest structure within the church. Note the nicely proportioned blind arches and the carved capitals, one of which depicts the flight into Egypt. But the detail of the central apse is difficult to observe because of the altar retable installed during the Renaissance (1554). Sculptures in the altar are by Jorge de Flandes. In a central niche is the fourteenth century Virgin of Rocamador.

The Gothic vaults above the crossing rest on squinches, typical of the Cistercian style during the transition from the heavy piers of the Romanesque to the column supports of the Gothic.

Finally, we walk along past Santa María to the raison de etre for all that we have seen here in Sangüesa: the **bridge**. You find its spans in excellent repair and still much used by the townsfolk.

Eunate

Depart Sangüesa, crossing the Aragon River and head north. In a few kilometers turn left, continuing north toward highway 240 and Monreal. That town took its name from a now-ruined castle. It has little to remind us of the pilgrim route except for an ancient **bridge**. To see it, turn left at the sign and wend your way down to the river. The twin-arched footbridge and its flagstone approaches are in excellent repair and still very much in use by local residents.

After leaving Monreal you find a local road to the left, NA5000. Proceed along that route for about ten kilometers, passing through hilly but fertile and productive farmland and crossing both A15 and N121. Soon, sitting all by itself in the middle of a grassy valley with vineyards and orchards climbing the low wooded hills nearby, we spot the distinctive octagonal form of the Church of **Santa María de Eunate**: Holy Mary of the Hundred Doorways, a Basque name probably derived from the archways in the arcade that surrounds the church, and which once probably supported a wooden roof between it and the main structure (open 10:30 to 1:30; 4 to 7; closed

Mondays).

Nothing is known about the origins and history of this remarkable structure. Experts in such things believe it dates from the early twelfth century, given its design. Here we find the plain face, squat sturdiness and round arches of the Romanesque yet with Gothic blind arches in its walls, which suggest the late twelfth century as the most probable time of origin. Most peculiar is the fact that the sides of the octagon, both in the church and surrounding arcade, are unequal, being elongated on the north side. A monkish construction error, or did it serve some arcane purpose?

Some sources attribute the church to the Knights Templar, perhaps because the octagonal design, similar to the Church of the Holy Sepulcher in Jerusalem, was often used by the Templars. Consensus believes it to have been a funerary chapel serving pilgrims. This opinion is based on the graves and scallop shells found within and near the arcaded enclosure around the church. The six-meter distance between arcade and church is believed to have been roofed, providing shelter for passing pilgrims unable to make it to Puente de la Reina for the night. The latter town is less than six kilometers farther on.

The arcade is supported on three sides by square pilasters, but on the north is a row of round double-columns with fancy capitals. The inner circuit of the arcade is paved with small river stones arranged in a herringbone pattern. The outside course, between the arcade and the surrounding wall and gate, is grass covered. On the church's far side the wall becomes a retaining barrier against the nearby field, its surface near the top courses of stone.

The angled sides of the church meet at embedded round columns with Corinthian-like capitals at the eaves. The quarried stone roof descends from the double-arched, flat two-sided belfry at its center, which has a Mozarabic flavor. Towards the south is a square tower, half engaged to one wall of the church, and topped by a small, octagonal roofed turret. Inside the tower is a stairwell leading to a door opening upon the main roof. Some think the stairs up the tower allowed a

71

lantern to be placed to guide pilgrims to its refuge after nightfall. East of the tower is the protruding semicircular apse with blind Romanesque arches in its five flat sides, and round pillars at each corner, repeating the design of the main church structure.

Santa Maria de Eunate

The main door, made of wood with iron slats, faces north. It sits within a Romanesque arch that rises from round columns with carved capitals at each side. A smaller door in a plain-arched entry is set into the west face.

The vaulted **interior** is severely plain and barnlike, with wooden benches facing the tiny altar. Behind it, elevated on a pedestal, is a multihued Madonna and Child.

The dome is eight-ribbed to match the exterior form, with a keystone atop. The ribs rest upon round columns engaged to the walls. Of the four Romanesque arches in the walls of the apse, two are blind, and two contain small windows. These few windows, and small apertures in each segment of the dome, contain thin slabs of alabaster that, translucent, permit soft light to filter through for interior illumination of the chapel.

The interior of the apse is most attractive. It holds a simple marble pedestal altar table set a step higher than the nave. The apse opens through a tall, double-layered Romanesque arch, bases of each arch seated on round, engaged pillars similar to those we saw outside at the corners of the church. The interior apse has rough ribbed vaulting above two levels of blind arches with side columns, the copy of what you viewed on the exterior. This is a peculiar place that leaves one with strange, unsettled feelings about it.

The church was closed when we first arrived, thus we proceeded on to Puente de la Reina, settled into our hotel, and returned to view the place after it reopened during late afternoon.

Obanos

From Eunate the road follows the pilgrim track for the few kilometers to Obanos, a village on a low hill just to the right of the highway and a kilometer short of Puente de la Reina. At an old hermitage in the hills above Obanos the Navarran and Aragonese Roads joined for the push west to Santiago de Compostela.

You need not visit Obanos. The village offers nothing remarkable or new to our explorations. The parish church contains a thirteenth century image of the Virgin salvaged from the one-time hermitage where the routes met, and the Ayuntamiento is nicely endowed.

Obanos is best known today for its outdoor theater where, every year in late August, the townspeople present a pageant in which hundreds of them participate. It is called *The Mystery of San Guillén and Santa Felicia*. The latter was a princess of Aquitaine who, on pilgrimage to Compostela, chose to abandon her royal past and live the life of a devout. San Guillén was her brother. Despairing of her choice, he sought to win her away from her new life. Enraged by her refusal, he murdered her. Filled with remorse for what he had done, he too made a penitential pilgrimage to Compostela, after which he spent his life in prayer at the nearby sanctuary of the Virgin of Arnotegui.

Proceeding on toward Puente de la Reina, a half kilometer short of the old walled town you come upon the junction with route N111, the main road west from Pamplona. Where the Navarran and Aragonese roads meet is a **statue** of a pilgrim, a piece of modern metallic art erected in 1965. It commemorates the union of the two pilgrimage trails represented by these modern highways. From here, the inscription says, the ways to Santiago are but on66e.

Your day is drawing to a close, so let me advise that the hotels you see straddling the highway junction near the pilgrim statue offer the most convenient and amenable halting places for the night. After you have taken your room, perhaps there is still time left for an evening stroll through the amazing little town of Puente de la Reina, the east portal of which lies but a half kilometer west along N111.

THE CITIES OF THE BRIDGES

Along the pilgrim's road a river, particularly one in flood, was a daunting obstacle for anyone traveling afoot. The chronicles tell of ferrymen who were little more than extortionists, and highwaymen whose favorite prey were pilgrims stalled at a river crossing.

At Sangüesa we learned how construction of a bridge drew pilgrims several kilometers off a more direct route when assured a safe and easy crossing. The commercial opportunities that developed when throngs of pilgrims converged at the crossing then led to development and economic sustenance of a prosperous town.

Today our journey leads us to a pair of historically prominent cities owing their existence to bridges along El Camino de Santiago. The first is Puente de la Reina, Queen's Bridge. Further along is Estella, a town known to pilgrims of centuries past as Estella la Bella because of the beauty of the place, both natural and as enhanced by the works of man.

Puente de la Reina

Puente de la Reina, bridging the Arga River, was created early in the eleventh century at the command of Elvira, the Doña Mayor (the First Lady), queen of Sancho the Great of Navarra. As at Sangüesa, a new town immediately sprang up at the east end of the bridge. Its population was mainly French, encouraged by the king to immigrate and settle along the pilgrims' route so as to serve the throngs of their countrymen drawn to the spot for safe passage across the often dangerous Arga.

While built at the order of the queen, the bridge was none the less part of a coordinated public works program sponsored by the kings of Navarra and Castile during the eleventh and twelfth centuries to ease the passage of pilgrims through their respective domains. Nearly a thousand years later Elvira's bridge still stands, majestically spanning the river and continuing in use by townspeople and pilgrims.

Arriving at Puente de la Reina, a half kilometer past the bronze pilgrim that stands where the Aragonese and Navarran roads meet, you may park your wheels in the open area beside a modern church to the left of the highway just before it curves sharply where it meets the central town. There you find yourself just outside the formerly walled perimeter of old Puente de la Reina. It is a town smaller than Sangüesa, and even more spectacularly medieval. Streets and structures seem frozen solidly in the ancient stone of centuries past.

Bear left as you walk from your car and enter the old town through a barrel-vaulted, tile-roofed **passageway.** It lies between the comparatively small, chapel-like Church of the Crucifix and, opposite on the left, an old pilgrim hospice. The latter was refurbished in the eighteenth century and is known as the Convento de los Reparadores. Both structures are situated just outside the one-time main gate of Puente de la Reina, so as to provide comfort to pilgrims arriving after the town gates were shut for the night.

Beyond the archway and church is Rua Mayor de los Romeros, the Main Road of the Pilgrims. That street, you will see, leads straight to the bridge at the far end of town.

Turn your attention first to the **Iglesia** del Crucifijo, the sturdy square tower of which rises immediately on your right. Step back a few paces along the street so you can view the polygonal lantern placed atop it during the Renaissance to house its bells.

The original church was built by the Knights Templar in the twelfth century after a king of Navarra, Garcias VI, gave the town to the knights in 1142. The gift served as a benefice in exchange for protection and care of pilgrims by the knightly order. Not incidentally, the knights also served as a de facto national guard ready to defend Navarra from encroachment by the kings of Castile or – less likely this far north by that time –

a Moslem raid.

Observe the symbol of the Templars posted over the front entrance of the squarish church that lies behind the sturdy Romanesque campanile. The church is rather peculiar in its overall design as the result of later modifications. The Templars built it with a single-nave in the Romanesque barrel-vaulted style. In the fourteenth century, after the Templars were disbanded, the more tractable Order of St. John took over ministering to the pilgrims. Under their management, the north wall was knocked out and a second, Gothic-style nave added. That later addition, known as the Chapel of the Crucifix, contains the famous cross from which the church takes its name.

The entranceway is generously carved with scallop shells and various grotesques and plant life typical of the early Romanesque tradition. Inside, the principal attraction is the **crucifix.** It is a life-sized wooden representation of Christ nailed to a Y-shaped cross (sometimes called St. Andrew's cross). The experts say it is of fourteenth century German origin, probably the gift of a pilgrim. The stark realism of the thing is a shock to many visitors if unprepared for what they are about to see. Other crucifixes merely suggest the sufferings of Christ. Here is His agony made tangible. It is the first of three such macabre yet fascinating works that we will encounter on our way to Santiago.

The **tomb** of the knight, Jean de Beaumont, who founded this fourteenth century chapel for display of this crucifix, is another fixture in the place. He lies beneath the pavement between the Chapel of the Crucifix and its predecessor.

We will see many reminders of the Templars preserved in stone along El Camino de Santiago in the days ahead. So seat yourself here in the presence of this strange, life-like effigy of the Redeemer and the tomb of His knightly defender of His Faith, and let us refresh your memories of those bellicose monks who built this place. They belonged to the Order of the Knights of the Temple of Solomon, better known as the Knights Templar.

77

The Order was formed in 1118 after the First Crusade. It was intended to defend the Holy Land in general, and the sacred places of Jerusalem in particular, from the counter-thrusts of the Saracens. The Templars were an immediate military success, attracting many young, landless knights to the defense of the Cross. They gained a reputation for being tough, competent fighters with no fear of the infidel or of death itself. They gave allegiance to God alone, represented by the commanders of their order.

Such renowned fighters quickly gained the attention and interest of the kings of Western Europe, including those of Spain. Like medieval monarchs in general, the Spanish kings were always finding excuses to attack their neighbors or their own wealthy subjects, using the grounds of treason or heresy as excuses for confiscating their lands and riches. What better mercenary fighters could they find than these? Thus Garcias VI of Navarra followed the lead of other European kings and gave the Templars rich properties and large tracts of land in exchange for military services to the Navarran crown.

By the fourteenth century the order had become so powerful it was virtually a law unto itself in all the kingdoms of Europe. One result was that the Templars assumed a level of arrogance and wealth that proved to be their undoing. Their downfall came when King Philippe of France started a disinformation campaign that his fellow monarchs happily conspired to assist and often expanded upon. The purpose was to break Templar power and confiscate their wealth.

The Templars were accused of the worst sort of moral and religious sins, from homosexuality to trafficking with the Devil. Their lands were seized, and their commanders tried and executed along with many of the rank and file, who otherwise were dispersed. The last grand master, Jacques de Molay, was executed in 1314. His name is prominent in modern Masonic lore, but the current Knights Templar lack true connection with the medieval order of the same name. In any event, you now find yourself in a church founded by those stalwarts at a time when they were considered favorites, not threats, by the royal houses of Europe.

Leaving the church, a few steps take you inside the thirteenth-century walls of the town. On the ancient buildings along the Rua Mayor you will see the sign of the Templars more than once, along with the carved coats of arms of a host of forgotten noble families. Several of those homes deserve appellation as mansions, spacious and imposing as they are. Then, about halfway through the town, we arrive at the beautiful Romanesque portal of the **Iglesia de Santiago.**

The church of Santiago is single-aisled, twelfth-century Romanesque, given a fifteenth century Gothic refurbishment that included spectacular ribbing designs in the ceiling vaults. The bell tower is eighteenth century, the work of Ventura Rodríguez. For me the most attractive element of the church is its **portal**, graciously carved, with a distinctive Moorish flavor to its basic Romanesque design.

This deep-set arched portal, its five column-supported arches converging above a studded double door, is at first glance standard Romanesque. It is so time worn that many of its details are now obscure. Difficult to make out or not, the work on this portal was a masterpiece of the French Romanesque as designed and executed by Mozarabic artisans who added distinctive touches of their own, such as the cusps with their carved decor in the archway directly above the door. Later today, if you choose to walk up to the thirteenth-century Church of San Román in the village of Cirauqui, you will find a Gothic portal with similar cusps and companion touches of the Mozarabic – or, more appropriately, Mudéjar, given the time of construction.

The principal object of a pilgrim's visit within this church is a fourteenth century gilded wooden **statue** of the Apostle in the garb of a pilgrim. St. James is barefoot, with walking staff and scallop shells on his hat. Find him on the left wall of the nave beneath a gilded canopy of obvious baroque origins. Gilt and the baroque are everywhere in this church. But there is a change of pace. On the opposite wall of the nave, carved simply but nicely of stone, is St. Bartholomew.

The altarpiece is more eighteenth-century gilded baroque, illustrating the life of St. James. Note the elegant carving of the crucified Christ. The polished wood **floor** is nothing other than tomb lids and their markings. This is a feature we have seen before and is common to many of the churches we visit during our journey to the shrine of St. James.

On the Rua Mayor again, continue west to the queen's **bridge.** You will be disappointed in this first view of a span that experts describe as the most beautiful Romanesque bridge in Spain, and perhaps anywhere, for its beauty comes of its graceful lines and proportions as seen from the side, rising on six slightly pointed arches from massive piers set firmly in the river bed. In contrast, now you see only the pavement of the bridge and its low side walls as they climb toward the center of the span. But we will gain opportunity for that superior view later when we depart the town.

Width of the bridge is five meters, copying the standard dimension of El Camino de Santiago as (and where) improved by the early kings and the monkish helpers and hermits who aided in the work. Mounted on the rail of the span in centuries gone by was a statue of the Virgin del Txori (Virgin of the Little Bird). It now stands in the church of San Pedro, the tower of which you spy above the rooftops on the right as you look back toward town from the high point of the bridge. It seems that birds, fresh from their bath in the river, often perched on the Virgin and sprinkled her with water as they fluttered their wings and preened their feathers. They appeared almost as if they were trying to clean the statue itself. To see such a bird "at work" was an omen of good fortune.

Returning through town to your automobile, walk along another street parallel to Rua Mayor. There is much else to see, including the previously mentioned **parish church** of San Pedro, which is thirteenth century but basically Romanesque; and the Iglesia de la Trinidad, which has an interesting Renaissance facade.

Back to your car, now follow highway N111 through town and cross the modern steel and concrete bridge over the Arga

River. On the other side, immediately exit the highway to park on the right. Get out to have the **view** of the Queen's Bridge that we promised.

Tis a nice view. The bridge is all that the experts say it is, humped above its broad central arch, mirrored in the quiet flow of the river, with the green foothills standing beyond and giving way to the snowy peaks of the Western Pyrenees in the distance. (Or were those merely billowing clouds posing to the eye as far off mountains?)

Cirauqui

On our way again, about five kilometers brings us to Mañeru, a village once the property of the Knights of St. John. Generally known as the Hospitallers, they were another product of the First Crusade, formed to aid sick and weary pilgrims in the Holy Land and on the pilgrimage routes. Soon they developed a military arm to provide physical protection against Saracens and bandits alike, but their primary mission was always to provide hospitals for sick and weary pilgrims.

Five kilometers further is Cirauqui, perched on the brow of a tall hill rising on your left. If you wish to visit the hilltop village, leave the highway at the first of the two Cirauqui exits. A scholar of architecture will certainly want to make the ascent into town to see the Mozarabic touches on the portal of its church of San Román, plus a second church, that of Santa Catalina.

The way up through the village is along a typical narrow medieval street through several archways, with armorial carvings on the faces of the buildings. None of that adds much to what you have already experienced in Puente de la Reina and Sangüesa, so most of us may be excused from the climb. Instead we attend to another historic treat that this tiny village offers traveler and pilgrim alike.

For that, leave the highway, turning left at the second exit; then, on the frontage road that parallels the highway, you immediately find an old stone water trough alongside the road. Park next to it and get out. (If you got off at the first exit to visit the town, later follow the frontage road along N111 around the foot of the hill below the village until you arrive at the water trough, which sits on your right near the crest of the next rise.)

A bright yellow arrow marking the pilgrim's trail is painted on the water trough, pointing the way west. Look back across the gully to the hill occupied by Cirauqui and let your eye follow the pilgrim track as it descends the hillside to meet the stream below. Spanning the stream and its gully is an old, very dilapidated **stone bridge**. Much of its superstructure is missing, and its right side has fallen away, but it is still passable for a pilgrim on foot. The bridge is Roman, and so is the remnant of road leading down to it from where you stand.

The Roman Road at Cirauqui

Walk down to the bridge to gain the experience of putting your feet down, one after the other, on an authentic **Roman road.** Five paces apart, edging the sides, are large flat stones with squared edges, separated by a pavement made of irregularly shaped chunks of rubble set down to make an even surface. A couple of thousand years ago a traveler could walk east from this spot, following a network of such highways all the way to Persia.

Here is one of the few places along our route where the old Roman road, with one of its many bridges (of which few remain) and original paving stones, is easily accessible to us. Beyond the bridge your eye can follow the road as it climbs to Cirauqui and disappears with a left turn around the hilltop.

According to Aymery Picaud's guide for pilgrims, this stream crossing was very dangerous for pilgrims traveling on horseback or with mules. He warned that the stream was poisonous and certain local folk would hang about the bridge, urging pilgrims to water their animals here. The animals would die almost immediately, after which the locals skinned them and made off with the hides.

While interesting, Picaud's medieval tale takes nothing away from our modern encounter with this Roman road and bridge. From now on, when someone mentions the engineering feats Romans accomplished with their road building, or you read about them in some history book or magazine article, you know the subject first hand. You can also understand why the Spanish in the days of the pilgrimage and later called the Roman roads the Calzada (a paved highway), for that they were.

You also might wonder what a Roman road is doing here. When you are in your car and again heading west on N111, which more or less follows the route of this Roman road, we will answer that question.

Now, on your way again, here is a brief introduction to Rome and its roads in Spain.

Although Carthage was defeated and driven out of Hispania in 206 BC by Roman arms, the power of the indigenous Spanish tribes remained unbroken. More than that, their age-old sentiments for independence were indefatigable. The consequence was virtually constant warfare as Roman legions sought to extend the dominion of the Republic, often with disastrous results for the legions. More than once the Romans were on the verge of being thrown off the peninsula.

Just as the American Plains Indians (admired by their opponents as the best light cavalry in the world) were overwhelmed by the sheer numbers and superior arms and organization of Blue Coats, Rome eventually brought the resources of an empire, and the discipline of its legions, to bear upon the disparate armies and citadels of the Spanish tribes. Even with that power, however, it was a task that took more than two hundred years to complete. Not until 69 BC could a Roman army, led by Julius Caesar, drive up the Atlantic coast of what is now Portugal. It forged its way as far as present-day La Coruña on what was little more than a plundering expedition. Afterwards the territory was again abandoned to the natives. (In recognition of the success of that expedition Caesar won his consulship.)

According to some authorities, an odd fact of history is that the need to maintain a large military force in Spain for so extended a period had the effect of creating Rome's first professional "standing army." That permanent organization of legions later was expanded to compass the entire empire and is given credit for being the instrument by which Rome eventually extended its borders from the Atlantic to Persia. That it also turned the empire into a military dictatorship (once the legions granted allegiance to their commanders rather than to the Senate and city of Rome) was but another consequence of the centuries-long struggle for the pacification of the Iberian tribes.

Thus while Spain was the first mainland conquest of the Romans outside of Italy, it was not until the reign of Augustus that Cantabria, Asturias and Galicia were finally pacified – though never Romanized. That "final victory" was the result of the so-called Cantabrian War. The road you walked upon near Cirauqui was probably built in preparation for that war. It permitted quick deployment of the Roman legions and facilitated their resupply and reinforcement.

The Cantabrian War was provoked by tribal raids against Roman towns, but the intent of the campaign was to bring under Roman control the rich gold and silver mines of Asturias west of the then non-existent Roman town of Asturica Augusta, now the city of Astorga. For in the first centuries BC and AD, Asturias was the principal source of gold and silver for the entire empire. Augustus no doubt concluded that it is better for an emperor to own such riches than to trade for them.

Thus in 26 BC Caesar Augustus personally trod this road as he led seven legions against Cantabria, Asturias and Galicia, invading and defeating each in turn before the end of 25 BC. Succeeding revolts, however, prevented complete pacification until nearly fifteen years later. At that time the most powerful hill tribes were forcibly moved down into the flatlands where the proximity of a legion permanently based at León assured their docility. These fierce tribes grudgingly accepted the dominion of Rome, but not its civilized demeanor.

After the Cantabrian War, the Roman army in Spain was reduced from seven legions to three. The others were transferred to the Rhine-Danube borders. Two more were sent to Germany early in the first century AD. So where once as many as ten legions had been required to win and maintain tranquility in Hispania, now only one remained. It was the famed Seventh Legion at León. It stayed until the final days of the empire, keeping the peace among the hill people of Northern Spain.

The last Spanish legion, the VII Gemina (twin), was formed in 70 AD by Vespasian, largely from Spanish recruits. In fact, by the fourth century AD the legion was comprised almost entirely of Galicians from the same mountainous region that they kept pacified. The requirement of Roman citizenship for enlistment indicates that many recruits were of Italian stock descended from retired legionnaires granted land near the borders they defended.

The grant of land, in recompense for service, became common practice at all fringes of the empire. It assured Rome of generation after generation of loyal troops ready to defend the frontiers against the barbarians. Indeed, abandonment of that tradition led to crushing military defeats at places as far apart in time and geography as along the Rhine in Germany and at Manzikert in far off Anatolia. Those defeats stripped the military veneer from Roman power, exposing the internal political rot that led to dissolution of the empire.

Speaking of defeats, driving west, five kilometers after Cirauqui we pass Lorca, site of one of the many losing battles the Christians of the Reconquista suffered at the hands of their Moslem adversaries. In 920, Sancho I of Navarra was soundly defeated here.

The town of Lorca had a pilgrim hospice and church, but most of us will pass it by. The same goes for the village of Villatuerta, which has vestiges of the San Román hermitage and a hospice of the Knights Hospitallers.

Estella is something else, and there we will stop both to visit and perhaps to spend the night if your itinerary so suggests.

Estella

Modern Estella is a city of about thirteen thousand people. Its name comes from a meteor shower, falling stars, if you will, that in 1085 alerted a group of shepherds to the hiding place of the statue of Our Lady of le Puy (in French, the Hill). While the Latin tongue of the clerics would have named the place Stella, the name meets halfway with the Castilian Estrella.

Originally a Roman town (named Gabala or Gebalda) along the road to León and Astorga, it deteriorated during the Muslim period into a small village that the Basques called Lizarra. The village subsequently gained increased stature less from discovery of the statue of Our Lady than from erection of a bridge across the Ega River. That attracted the pilgrim trade.

Of even greater importance for municipal development was the fact that the twelfth century kings of Navarra set up their court here in Estella, the better to defend their kingdom against the expansionism of the kings of León and Castile. That particular defensive ploy eventually failed. Castile absorbed the place along with the lands around. But Navarran strategy won success for a while, and the grand palaces, churches and fortresses of the king and his retinue gained the town the appellation, Estella la Bella.

On the near side of the river was the native Navarran settlement; on the far side was the French quarter where pilgrims found shelter among their own, and where we will discover much of what is see-worthy in the town.

Approaching Estella, you come upon it suddenly, practically hidden as it is in a narrow, steep-sided valley. The main road virtually bypasses the old town via a modern bridge and a tunnel through the mountain, Montejurra, that lies on the far side of the river. That mountain was the site of one of the battles of the Carlist Wars of the nineteenth century, when Estella was the headquarters of the revolutionary forces.

A number of such battles were fought in this vicinity, for Estella remained the center of the Carlist movement in both wars (1833-40; 1870-76). In the second Carlist War the town became not only the headquarters for Don Carlos María, pretender to the Spanish throne, but also was home base for his military arm, the red-capped Requetés.

Such freewheeling independence was not something of a modern quirk of character for the Basque townspeople. Local tradition has it that although the Arabs occupied the region for about two hundred years, never once did they enter the Christian Estella – even though the Muslims occupied all the hills around the town. Later, when Ferdinand and Isabella expelled the Jews from the rest of Spain, Estella gave them sanctuary.

Just before the highway crosses the river and enters the tunnel, pull off the road and park in the open area on the left near a small modern steel footbridge that spans the Ega. Across the river you see a distinctive old building, a church, now standing alone but once hemmed in by houses of tradesmen along a busy street. This is the **Iglesia del Santo Sepulcro**, a funerary chapel that ministered to the local French population and transient pilgrims. We decided to cross the footbridge and visit this church before pursuing the traditional route into town on the near side of the river.

This time-stained, twelfth-century Romanesque single-aisled church has a semicircular apse and a thirteenth-century Gothic facade. It looks its age and much at home in its dilapidated surroundings at the foot of the mount that rises behind. It stands across from a grassy park above the river. It has been closed and inactive for at least a century. No matter, its facade and portal, a Gothic piece dating from 1328, is a treasure to behold. In ages past, pilgrims said the **portal** could only be similar to the entrance into Heaven itself, splendid as it was.

Iglesia del Santo Sepulcro

The peak of the tympanum depicts the sufferings of Christ on the cross; below is the Last Supper, above which are the three Marys at the Holy Sepulcher. Above the portal to each side of the peak of the Gothic arch a tall frieze runs the length of the facade, containing niches occupied by images of the Apostles. Note that the lintel above the door is supported at both ends by the bare hands of a pair of bearded saints. Greeting you from pedestals at ground level beside the portal are, to the right, some no-doubt sainted Bishop of the pilgrim days, while a pilgrim-garbed Santiago stands on the left. Around to the back we found an archaeological team excavating near the foundations of the church and in the devastated space near the foot of the mount that towers behind.

Near the hillcrest far above the church is the vast **monastery** of Santo Domingo. That former monastic church and school was built through the generosity of King Theobaud II of the French dynasty that ruled Navarra after the thirteenth century. It was designed in the style of Cistercian early Gothic. Abandoned in the past century, the place now serves as a home for the elderly. We chose not to include it on our walk since it would add little to our experience.

Recrossing the footbridge to your automobile, leave your car where it is, cross the highway, and walk the couple of hundred meters into old Estella. Your way parallels the river and leads through a long plaza jammed with parked cars. At its west end, turn left to cross the Ega on an old-style stone **bridge**. This places you on the original pilgrim path. The bridge, however, is a modern replacement (1971) modeled after the ancient span, destroyed during the Carlist Wars a century earlier.

On the far side of the bridge, turn right on the street paralleling the river. This is **Calle de la Rua**, the old pilgrim route through town. It is a narrow, cobblestoned street, lined with centuries-old two, three, and four-storey homes of stone and stuccoed brick, all abutted wall to wall. Follow this street to where it ends at the Plaza San Martín.

About fifty meters along the Rua, on the right, is a sixteenth-century structure that was the palace of the governor at that time. Just before you reach the square, standing on the right at number 6, is the Palacio de Fray Diego, now the **Casa de Cultura.** This Renaissance mansion sports fascinating window frames decorated with assorted monstrosities in the Plateresque style. Opposite, but further on at the edge of the Plaza de San Martín, is the sixteenth-century Ayuntamiento, now the Palacio Justicia, and offering us an eighteenth-century Plateresque facade. It is located on the one-time site of the church of San Martín, which catered to pilgrims during the early centuries of the Camino.

In the center of the pleasant little plaza is an attractive eighteenth-century **fountain**, la Fuente de los Chorros (the fountain of the spouts), with four caricature face masks spouting water. Atop is a globe sporting a seated lion atop, clutching a plaque displaying the royal arms of Navarra. Rising across the way, behind a row of trees, is the **Palace** of the Navarran Kings. Today it is an art museum featuring paintings by Gustavo de Maeztu (1887-1947). It is open from 11 to 1, and 5 to 7; closed Mondays.

The palace was built in the twelfth century by Sancho the Wise. It is regarded as the most important example of secular Romanesque architecture in all of Europe. Its original interior is almost entirely lost to the construction of the art gallery, as you will see if you elect to view Maeztu's work. Finest face of the place is to your left, where it fronts on Calle de San Nicholas.

At street level is an arcade of four Romanesque arches rising from stout pillars. The arcade is now closed off by iron grilles. Above that are four broad windows, quartered by round pillars, each supporting a leg of tiny Romanesque arches above fancy carved capitals. At each end of the facade are engaged columns, one stacked atop the other, also with carved capitals.

Your attention is directed to the bottommost of these capitals on the end away from Plaza San Martín. Look closely and you will see the time-worn figures of two knights jousting on horseback. The rider on the right with the oval shield is **Roland,** whose fate we recalled at Roncesvalles. On the left, shown breaking his lance on Roland's shield, is the giant,

Ferragut, the Saracen lord of the town of Nájera, situated a few kilometers west of Logroño. Roland fought the giant, reputed to have had the strength of forty men, and slew him in single combat. The event added even more luster to Roland's already legendary fame. The capital bears the signature of its creator, one Martín of Logroño.

Next to the palace, on the left, is the local tourist information office where you may obtain a map of the town to aid in later explorations on the other side of the river.

Now turn and face away from the facade of the king's palace. Ahead of you, on the right side of the plaza, is a long, broad staircase leading to the twelfth century **church** of San Pedro de la Rua, located on a level high above the square. The green curtain of a wooded hillside forms a kind of backdrop beyond.

When the church of San Pedro is closed, the information office will arrange a guided tour of the church and its cloister. Guiding us through the church on our recent visit was a very agreeable and intelligent young lady who obviously loved her work and was fascinated by the history of her land and people. She conducted the tour in Spanish (for we were the only English speakers in the group of about ten travelers), but she was kind enough to answer our questions in English when her Spanish escaped our comprehension.

Dominating your view as you climb the stairs is its tall, square campanile, rising from a boxy, fortress-like structure that literally broods over the town below. This is the oldest church in Estella, although it was given a Gothic face-lift in the fourteenth century. The **main portal**, which opens into the north side of the three-aisled nave, is immediately at the head of the stairs. You will recognize the cusps in the portal's Gothic archway, expressing the Mudéjar influence upon its builders, and similar in concept and design to those portals we saw at Puente de la Reina and Cirauqui.

The carvings on the archivolts and column capitals are entirely lacking in religious symbols or human figures. Instead you see geometric and arboreal designs, plus a couple of griffins. The tone of all that is essentially Romanesque and expresses pagan Roman and Muslim influences rather than Christian, yet it has the style of early Gothic. Above the entry is a Gothic **window** that contains the only original fourteenth-century stained glass that survives in this church. Everything else was blown out in 1572 when the Spanish crown in the person of Philip II, fearing the always restive Basques of Estella, blew up the fortress of Zalatambor that stood atop the cliff just behind the church and its cloister.

Inside, we find the nave divided by two rows of arches above an assortment of massive piers. To the left of the altar observe the unusual column carved to display three intertwined snakes. The choir apse has Romanesque stalls, and three tiny semicircular chapels spaced around the rear wall.

The crucifix in the capella mayor is fourteenth-century Gothic. Among the sculptures are a Romanesque Madonna in the right apse, plus St. Peter and St. Andrew, each of late Renaissance origin. The Madonna on the left is known as the Virgin of Bethlehem.

The chapel to the left behind the grille is the **Chapel of St. Andrew**. It once housed a famous relic, the Reliquary of St. Andrew, said to contain a shoulder blade of the saint. Thieves made off with it several years ago and it has never been recovered. How it came to be in Estella in the first place is perhaps a neat commentary on the story of pilgrimage as such.

Everyone came. Kings and peasants, cardinals and the lowliest of monks. And they came from everywhere in Christendom. Many never made it home. Some died, overcome by illnesses or the rigors of the trail. Others were overcome by something else: the emotions rooted in a deeply religious experience, after which they found places in hermitages and monasteries along the way where they could fulfill an impulse to serve God by providing assistance to their brother pilgrims.

The particular story that interests us here pertains to a Greek bishop from Patras. It appears that he not only traveled incognito, but did so under a vow of silence as further expiation for whatever sinfulness drove him upon his pilgrimage. Whatever his motives, he never made it to Santiago. He died here in 1270, unknown and untended by the usual cortege that medieval bishops were wont to have. Perhaps some plague was suspected as the cause of his death, for he and all that was his were quickly interred in the common cemetery set aside for poor and nameless pilgrim dead here in Estella.

That night a church attendant noted a strange glow coming from the bishop's grave. After due consideration of the dangers involved, the authorities decided to exhume the body and investigate. They discovered papers revealing not only the identity of the victim, but also that he was carrying a sacred relic, the shoulder blade of St. Andrew. Inquiries directed toward both Greece and Rome verified the authenticity of the find. To honor St. Andrew, the Navarran King Carlos II commissioned a golden reliquary to contain the relic. Thus pilgrims thereafter were able to reflect upon the life of the saint as they passed this way on their sacred journey. As for the bishop, he was reinterred with much greater respect in the cloister of this church, which we now will visit.

The door exiting to the **cloister**, executed in Romanesque style, lies directly across the nave from the portal where you entered the church. You will be disappointed to learn that only the north and west galleries of the cloister remain intact. The others were destroyed when chunks of the fortress came tumbling down the mount when it was blasted apart.

The galleries are supported by paired columns (with exceptions to be noted) topped by carved capitals illustrating Biblical scenes and natural motifs. In the north gallery are portrayed the life of Christ and the Saints Peter, Andrew and Lawrence. On the west, the capitals depict animals and various plants, subjects more typical of Muslim artistry, and suggesting (as did the entry portal) the importation of Mudéjar talent from the south of Spain for the building of this place.

Near the northwest corner of the west gallery, you find several of the most peculiar **columns** you have ever seen, with strangely angled shafts. Oddest of all is a quadruple which one commentator described as "having its legs crossed." In the south side of the cloister is the tomb of the Bishop of Patras, a plain, geometric stone sarcophagus, its lid peaked at the center along its longitudinal dimension.

In the tiny shrine in the northeast corner you find beneath the pair of Gothic arches the tiny **sarcophagus** of a child. It contains the remains of the nine-month old prince whose death in the care of a negligent babysitter brought an end to the centuries-old Basque dynasty that had ruled Navarra since the expulsion of the Moors and Franks.

Now, descending towards the river via the Plaza San Martín, make your way across the modern bridge over the Ega River. On the far side, walk a block further and turn right. After about fifty meters, on the left, you find a broad **staircase**. It takes you high up on the rocky shoulder of the hill above the lower town to the fortress-like church of San Miguel Arcangel.

Going up the stairs you follow in the footsteps of millions of pilgrims who have climbed these steps since the Middle Ages. Arriving at the church, which in its twelfth century form was Romanesque, we circle around to the right to seek out the porch on the north side that shelters the portal beneath. On the way we pass a small separate structure, the **chapel** of St. George, in which a wooden statue portrays the saint, mounted on his charger, sword waving above his head, trampling an unlucky dragon underfoot.

The north **portal** that we seek, which experts rave about, is a survival from the original twelfth century church that otherwise was later made over into a less interesting early Gothic.

Authorities agree that the portal is an outstanding masterwork of the Romanesque period. For that it was lately given the extra protection of a steel and glass porch roof.

Again we find the typical pattern of five receding arches, each smaller than the other as they regress toward the aperture of the doorway, each archivolt carved in intricate detail over every inch of its surface, each supported at both ends by a round column. Here the columns have excellent capitals on which are carved scenes from the life of Jesus, depicted chronologically from left to right, from the Annunciation to the Crucifixion with a couple of secular scenes from the hunt thrown in at the right end to please the hunters among the medieval congregation, caballeros and freemen alike.

In the **tympanum,** Christ reigns, royal hawks and griffins at His side. Beside the archway stand the Evangelists and fathers of the church. An inscription once informed viewers that the image of Christ as shown "is neither God nor man, but represents God and man." The assertion was no doubt a medieval reminder to the faithful that adoration is reserved for Divinity and not for mere chunks of stone, no matter how beautiful and moving.

In the **covings** all sorts of figures are clustered about. In the center are guardian angels, and to the sides are prophets and scenes from the gospels, plus martyrs and saints. On the walls beside the portal are, on the left, the descent into Limbo, with St. Michael weighing the souls (shown as children) and a dragon slaying. On the right is the Resurrection, with a pair of angels and the trio of Marys as they learn of the empty sepulcher.

The church interior is of less interest. Massive piers support the Gothic ribbed ceiling, all the typically stout design of transitional Gothic. It contains a fourteenth-century **altarpiece** of painted stucco adorned with scenes depicting the burial of the Count of Eguía and Muruzabal. In a side chapel is a statue of St. Crispin, attributed to the seventeenth-century sculptor Juan de Imberto. Most notable is the statue of the Virgin, known as Nuestra Señora de la O.

From San Miguel you may make your way on foot north up the hill to the Basilica de Nuestra Señora del Puy, Our Lady of the Hill. We decided that it was a warm day, too warm for the hike to the top, so we went back to our car and drove up. The way up by car goes past the broad Plaza de San Miguel, so we walked back down on the streets we would follow going up to the Basilica, thereby familiarizing ourselves with the way, which is generally well marked but requires a couple of intuitive guesses as to turns on the way up. The map you obtained at the tourist office will be most helpful here.

As mentioned upon arrival at Estella, tradition would have us believe that the statue of the Virgin was discovered on 25 May, 1085, by shepherds guided by falling stars. Art authorities believe the statue is the work of a French artist of that eleventh century. Traditionalists insist it is a Visigothic work of much earlier vintage. In any event, the legend holds that the statue was found here on the side of the hill where you now find the basilica. The latter is a modern structure dating from 1951. It is star-shaped with lots of modernistic stained glass and concrete that, inside, is faced by stucco and courses of brick arranged in varied designs.

You find the famous **statue**, silver plated and bejeweled, beneath a finely fashioned canopy above the tabernacle of the high altar. It is a spectacle worth the trip up the hill to see.

Outside, enjoy the finest view that you will have of the Estella la Bella so long beloved by pilgrims. Including this panoramic view, we now have seen the best the town has to offer. Yet there is much more if you have time.

A student of history or architecture must also see the church of San Juan Bautista on the Plaza de los Fueros (Romanesque with a spectacular Renaissance high altar); and, on that same plaza at No. 13, the house where the pretender, Carlos María, lived from 1872 to 1876 during that second chapter of the Carlist Wars.

Irache

After Estella we visit the Monastery of Irache, occupied by the Benedictines at least as early as the ninth century and reputed to be the oldest of the pilgrim hospices on the Navarran section of El Camino de Santiago. To reach it drive west on N111 (A 12) through the tunnel and out of town. On the far side of the nearby village of Ayegui is the one-time monastery we seek. Look for the turn off on your left, with the usual yellow sign announcing its location. The complex of buildings is easily visible a few hundred meters from the highway. (Open 10 to 1:15, 4 to 7 Wednesday to Sunday.) Sunday Mass is at 11.

Irache has a peculiar history. It is believed to have been founded in the Visigothic era and was one of the early Benedictine chapters. Its hospice for pilgrims – the very first such establishment founded in Navarra on El Camino de Santiago – was built in 1050 by Garcia de Nájera during the peak of Nájera's golden age.

The Cistercians took control of the place during the early Renaissance, and in 1522 established a monastic school that became a university in 1615. The Napoleonic Wars and the repressions brought on by the restored Spanish monarchy spelled the end of the already weakened monastery. The university was moved to Sahagún in 1824, and not long afterward the monastery here at Irache was abandoned. Restoration began in the nineteenth century and was more or less complete by 1942, although work continues. It is now a national monument, with an Ethnological Museum in development, and buildings apart from the church are being revamped into a parador for wealthy pilgrims.

The architecture of the place is as varied as its history. The twelfth-century Romanesque church of Nuestra Señora de Irache was much modified in the Cistercian style, with an extremely deep-set Gothic archway leading to a Romanesque-transitional main portal sandwiched between a tall, square Herrerian bell tower and a much larger three-storied building that once housed the university. It takes a bit of sorting out to put it all in architectural perspective.

The **university** building, also of Herrerian style, dates from the seventeenth century. All three floors have been restored to serve as a Parador.

The plain stone face of the church in the seventeenth century was set off by the Herrerian **bell tower** (1609) with its fancy balustrade and ice cream scoop dome with a cupola and cross, with decorative roof cornices. Then, in the eighteenth century the church was further assaulted by addition of a baroque crown topping a new facade extending out from the original structure. As a result, the twelfth-century **main portal** is now deeply set back beneath the Gothic archway of the facade. Featured high up in the facade and crown are the Virgin Mary and St. Veremundo, abbot of the monastery during its most glorious period near the end of the eleventh century.

Gain entrance by means of the main door of the "university wing," through which you pass into the **"new" cloister**. Begun in the mid-sixteenth century the cloister was not completed until a century and a half later. Compared to what we have seen elsewhere during our explorations, these late Renaissance galleries are rather a disappointment, no matter that they are regarded as excellent examples of the style and the times.

The intricate Gothic vaulting and arches of the cloister lift from ponderous piers adorned with Neo-Classical columns and capitals. Carvings on the capitals deal with myths, both pagan and religious, with several religious scenes.

Now for the church, which is much more interesting.

Enter through a rather remarkable **doorway,** dated 1847, with both Plateresque and classical touches on the archway and its supports. After such exotic fare, the plain Cistercian simplicity of the interior is almost shocking. Yet a moment later we are struck by the beauty of it all. It is the beauty of proportion and harmonious agreement of parts with whole, a character we will have occasion in the days ahead to remark upon in several other churches of similar design. Those Cistercians knew how to build a church to be a proper monument to their Faith in God.

The main structure of this Church is regarded by the scholars as Cistercian transitional Gothic, three-aisled, with a nice dome (redone in the Renaissance) above the crossing, located at the fore of three semi-circular Romanesque apses. The dome rests on **squinches** shaped as giant scallop shells above the supporting pillars. The central apse, according to experts in such things, suggests the influence of builders from Cluny. Its arches rest on columns with strikingly decorated capitals. Note the blind arcading in the walls, and the massive piers supporting the archways, which we recognize now as a sort of trademark of the early transitional Gothic.

Also note the triumphal **arch** leading to the main chapel, its capitals showing, on the left, battling troops and, on the right, the Adoration of the Magi. The main chapel is beautifully illuminated by the gentle flow of sunshine through thin alabaster sheets in the windows. Presiding is Nuestra Señora de Irache, with her Christ Child. They sit atop a triple pillar, decked out in silver plate with raiment decorated in gold. The statue is said to date from the twelfth or early thirteenth century.

In the **sacristy**, we discover it fully restored in modern dress but for its remarkable vaulted ceiling on which the pendatives have painted carvings of the saints and fathers of the church.

Adjacent to the church is the **"Plateresque Cloister,"** named for the style in which it was executed by Martin de Oyarzabal and Juan de Aguirre in the sixteenth century, followed by a long list of others who completed the work over succeeding decades.

From the courtyard, with its central fountain, the galleries have an unexpectedly plain face, considering that it is dubbed "Plateresque." You see a low stone railing supporting square pilasters and unpretentious Gothic arches. The decor is within the galleries, where capitals of the pilasters, the corbels supporting the interior arches, and the keystones of the arches, are delicately carved. The capitals are carved to depict scenes from the life of St. Benedict, the childhood of Christ, and the Passion. The keystones bear the images of Christ, the Virgin, and various saints, monks and prophets. The corbels are pagan, their figures drawn from Greek mythology and monstrosities of medieval fantasy.

And here in this architecturally butchered old monastery boasting of a church with such an admirable interior, we conclude our travels for today. Next door, however, is the famous winery, Bodegas de Irache, which may suggest some wine tasting.

99

THE WAY TO LOGROÑO

After Pamplona the next large city along El Camino de Santiago is Logroño, with a population of about 120,000. Our plan today is to explore the pilgrims' Way to Logroño, see the city during late afternoon, then push on another thirty kilometers to Nájera. There we will find lodging and spend the morrow plus a second night.

Since arrival in Nájera will be rather late, and as Nájera is a small town with only a single full service hotel, the San Fernando, call ahead from Estella to assure confirmed accommodations. If you encounter a problem, there are a couple of other hotels, plus comfortable hostals within a block or two of the San Fernando.

Logroño and Saint James

Logroño is located on the border between the provinces of Navarra and La Rioja. In times long ago, Logroño was a border town between Castile and Navarra, many times fought over by Christians and Moslems alike. Throughout most of the early Reconquista the kings of Navarra staked out this territory until faced by El Cid, military chieftain for the kings of Castile. El Cid won it for Castile in 1076. Later, while soldiering in the pay of the Arab king of Saragossa, El Cid laid waste to Logroño in partial payment for rather shoddy treatment by the Castillian monarch. Later still, with the indomitable El Cid retired to his grave, the Navarrans took back the town and held it for another couple of hundred years.

Tied closely to Logroño is a legend that stems from the dawn of the Reconquista. It sprang from miraculous events a few kilometers south of the city near a one-time castle (now a ruin) known as Clavijo. The legend tells of the swashbuckling adventures of Santiago Matamoros, St. James the Moorslayer. It deals not with some medieval personage who won the sacred status of sainthood by feats of military prowess. It is rather the definitive chapter within a lengthy catalog of miraculous events and escapades featuring none other than St. James the Apostle. It is one of many fantastic tales handed down from grandfathers to grandsons as a cultural memory of events that may or may not have roots in actual history.

First, the Biblical facts. St. James the Apostle was the eldest son of Zeberde and Salome, sister of Mary, mother of Jesus. James was present at the Crucifixion and, about fifteen years later, was beheaded at the order of King Herod Agrippa. He was first among the Apostles to be martyred.

Now the story as it took shape in Spain.

When the Apostles heeded the command of Jesus and went out to teach all nations about the New Kingdom preached by Christ, legend says that James traveled to Spain. He landed on the Atlantic coast at the Roman town of Iria Flavia, now known as Padrón. This part of the legend is consistent with maritime fact. Before the time of Christ, Phoenicians and others for a thousand years sailed their ships through the Pillars of Hercules and up the Atlantic side of the Iberian Peninsula to reach he mines of Northwest Spain. Iria was thus a long-time Phoenician and Roman port of call to load shipments from the mines, and a logical place for a passenger from the East to disembark.

James announced the Gospel in Spain with little success for about seven years. He preached across the peninsula from west to east, probably moving from town to city along the same Roman road we now follow, but in the opposite direction. By the time he reached the city of Caesar Augusta (Saragossa) his apparent failure as an evangelist left him deeply depressed. His enthusiasm was restored, however, when visited by an apparition of the Virgin Mary (who, by all other accounts, was then still alive and well in Asia Minor near Ephesus).

The Mother of Jesus presented James with a small image of herself, set upon a pillar of jasper. Now called the Virgin del Pilar, James housed it in a small chapel and it remains to this day in the Saragossa cathedral as the most revered relic of the

Spanish early Christian Church.

James organized his few converts and created a bishopric in Caesar Augusta, then a relatively new city. It had been established by Augustus as his headquarters while conducting the multi-year campaigns of the Cantabrian War.

Before returning to Palestine, James promised his tiny colony of Christian converts that he would return, and expected to land at Iria as before. Unfortunately, he was martyred in Palestine and buried in Caesaria. But that proved not enough to break his promise. His disciples reclaimed his body, found uncorrupted and with its head mysteriously reattached, and carried it secretly to Jaffa to find transport to Spain. In the port there appeared a stone boat manned by a band of knights. They took charge of the Apostle's corpse, after which the boat, a sort of barge with neither rudder nor sails, magically made in seven days what at the time was a months-long voyage to Iria.

The funeral barge was met at the shore by members of the tiny Christian community. After considerable difficulties with local authorities (who were won over by mysterious events that foiled their attempts to prevent the corpse from being put ashore), St. James was reinterred in a Roman Compost Terra (cemetery) at what is now Santiago de Compostela. Thereafter, as the centuries rolled, the burial place was lost and forgotten. Still, the tradition of the return of St. James is said to have remained alive in the cultural recollections of the people thereabouts, the tales grandfathers tell to grandsons.

Enter a lonely hermit. One night about the year 815 the hermit saw a bright, star-like illumination over a vacant field that once had been a Celtic and later a Roman burial ground. Other strange lights flickered like fireflies around a clump of bushes. He hurried to report the peculiar phenomena to the local bishop, who immediately investigated. The earth was moved away from the spot. A tomb was uncovered, revealing a sarcophagus containing a still-uncorrupted body.

But whose? A subsequent vision informed the bishop that the body was that of St. James which, as the bishop was aware, local tradition always said was buried in those parts.

Meanwhile, a host of miracles took place as local folks began paying homage to the saint at his newfound sepulcher.

The kings of Asturias by then had extended the Reconquest into Galicia, where the Islamic tide of conquest had never achieved more than tenuous success. So in recognition of the discovery, Alfonso II commissioned construction of a small church over the tomb, the site of which became known as Santiago de Compostela. "Compostela" is believed to be derived either from the Roman Compost Terra, or from Campus Stellae, which means starry field. Or maybe it is a combination of both.

A few decades later came the Battle of Clavijo. It took place about the year 850 (some sources are precise, saying the date was May 28, 844) not far from Logroño. While Moorish sources are silent on the event, the chronicles of the Reconquista literally trumpet how St. James appeared upon the battlefield and snatched victory from the proverbial jaws of defeat.

The story goes that the Christians had been bound for years to supply an annual tribute, including one hundred comely virgins, to the Caliph in Córdoba. When the Asturians decided enough was enough and withheld payment, the Caliph sent a punitive expedition to teach the Christians proper manners for a vassal state. The Asturians mustered their meager force and rode out to meet the challenge.

The outnumbered Christians, led by King Ramiro I, were overrun and on the verge of being massacred by the forces of Abd al-Rahman II. Then St. James took a hand in the affair. The saint, mounted on a great white horse and brandishing a sparkling sword, suddenly appeared on the field and won his sobriquet of Santiago Matamoros – St. James the Moorkiller.

Santiago is reputed to have slain virtually the entire army of six thousand Moors that day as he turned sure defeat into victory. Nor was that the last of his military escapades. At least thirty nine times more during the following centuries the battle cry of "Santiago!" brought the saint and his sword to the aid of the Reconquista at crucial moments when only a miracle could save the day.

Little wonder then that Santiago de Compostela is the most sacred site in Spain and St. James is revered as the spiritual father of the Spanish nation. In gratitude for his life as well as his victory, King Ramiro dubbed St. James as patron saint of Spain immediately after the battle, and ordered that thenceforth every church in Spain must give annual tribute to the shrine of Santiago at Compostela, a practice that continued until 1812 and the disorders brought by the Napoleonic Wars.

Among the legendary miracles worked by the saint was one that led to the scallop shell (some versions refer to it as a cockleshell) becoming the badge of the pilgrim. The story goes that a bridegroom, riding along the Atlantic shore on the way to his wedding was swept, along with his horse, into the sea by a gigantic wave. His bride-to-be appealed to Santiago and, voila, the bridegroom, still astride his horse and festooned with scallop shells drawn from his watery grave, was raised up, alive, from the surf.

The bones of St. James did not rest quietly in his shrine forever. In 1589, when Sir Francis Drake threatened the Spanish coast with a large fleet and army, the priests of Santiago removed his sacred relics to a hiding place away from the threat of the English freebooter. Unfortunately, when the time came to recover the relics and return them to their resting place in Santiago de Compostela, they were nowhere to be found. That loss, coupled with the decree of the French King that his subjects no longer could journey to Santiago (he thought the wealth of France was being drained into Spain by the expense of pilgrimage and donations to the Spanish shrines), reduced the flow of the faithful to a trickle. The glory days of the pilgrimage trail thus ended and Northern Spain was left to its own economic devices. While the wealthier monasteries survived, and the town and city churches made do with what they had, the scores of hermitages and tiny hospitals and pilgrim shelters along the Way were for the largest part abandoned for lack of need and income.

The pilgrimage business remained mostly a thing of the past

until, in 1879, the relics were rediscovered and authenticated by a panel of archaeologists and medical doctors. After that the Way of St. James again became crowded with pilgrims and the occurrence of miracles obligingly resumed. So now we travelers encounter – or perchance become – modern pilgrims taking the shortcut to Heaven known as El Camino de Santiago.

Today our travels along that shortcut lead west from Estella on the road to Logroño. As it was yesterday, the route is N111. Our first stop will be in the old Roman town of Urancia, now called Los Arcos, about twenty kilometers west of Estella.

Los Arcos

In a countryside of low, rolling hills with fertile valleys in between, route N111 evades the small town of Los Arcos; but the modern highway was not the route of the pilgrims. To find it, take the Los Arcos exit and drive the kilometer to town center. There turn right and drive a block to the **Plaza Mayor** (which isn't all that grand) dominated by the tall, Baroque campanile of the Church of the Assumption (Iglesia Parroquial de la Asunción). To one side of the square is the seventeenth-century Puerta de Castilla that spans the route by which the pilgrims left the town during centuries past.

Tiny as Los Arcos is, the town once had a decade or so of larger pretensions when it harbored the court of Charles III, The Noble, of Navarra. It may be thought that the grandness of its parish church derives from that, but the time frames do not match. Charles reigned from 1387 to 1425. This church seems to have originated after his death dating from a period when Navarra was politically unsettled by problems of royal succession. Navarra, you see, was unfortunate in that Charles outlived his sons. Though he willed the kingdom to his daughter Blanche, the male chauvinists of the day took issue with his choice and plunged the state into a generation of rebellion and counter-rebellion before the matter was settled by the good old royal trick of a poison potion administered by a wicked stepmother.

In any event, Los Arcos was always a prominent stop along the pilgrimage trail. It gained a French district by order of King Sancho IV in 1175, followed by development of the usual hospices and shrines. Few traces remain of all that, but this **parish church**, details of which span at least three centuries, is worth a visit to see, if nothing else, its choir stalls.

The church is probably late fifteenth century with a Plateresque main portal where Mary reigns from above, with Peter to her right and St. Michael opposite, and a spray of those ubiquitous scallop shells overhead. The bell tower with its fancy belfry is sixteenth century, a fact which leads us to expect the busyness of the interior decor. There, in what is unfortunately a poorly illuminated interior, you discover the gilded extravagance of the baroque high altar, which is seventeenth century with a fifteenth-century retable displaying a fourteenth-century Madonna, the latter probably of French origin. Best feature of the interior, as promised, are the **choir stalls,** which are as elegant as any to be found on this junket, and deserve close study and the caressing touch of your fingers upon the time-polished wood. Outside there is a tiny but attractive Gothic cloister of fifteenth century origin.

Torres del Rio

The "River Towers" is a small town looking down upon the tree-lined banks of the Linares River. It is located about ten kilometers beyond Los Arcos just off N111 by a hundred meters or so. There is but one real attraction here, the Church of the Holy Sepulcher. It has an unusual feature the scholars of architecture make much ado about.

The church is thought to have been founded by the Templars, if only because of its octagonal form and name, similar to that of their temple in Jerusalem. But that is a mere guess. It served pilgrims both as a refuge and as a funerary church, as at Eunate and Roncesvalles. A light was said to have been placed in the turret atop the structure in order to guide pilgrims to safety when darkness caught them still on the road. Again, this is similar to what was said about Eunate – which was also thought by some to also have been a Templar church, had a similar polygonal form and probably dates from the same period.

The construction is twelfth-century Romanesque, in three storeys, the corner angles filled by columns as at Eunate, and with typical round-arched windows in the uppermost of the three levels. Above it all is a dome with a lantern, supported by cross-ribbed **vaulting** such as you probably have never seen before. And that is what attracts the attention of the architects.

Best view of the vaulting is from dead center of the building, looking up, no matter how tough that is on your neck. From that centered perspective you best see why this style of ceiling construction is known as star vaulting. It is a technique borrowed from Moorish architects of the south, and later adopted by many architects throughout Western Europe if only because that open center between the cross ribs allows support for a lantern or cupola above. That the eight-pointed star the eye picks out of the vaulting is very pleasing aesthetically was a further factor favoring transmission of the technique north from here into Europe by pilgrim architects and itinerant French builders who worked along El Camino de Santiago.

As at Eunate, this church has a small apse protruding from one side, plus a turret, with stairs leading to its top where a lantern was hung at night as a guide for late-arriving pilgrims.

Viana

Another ten kilometers closer to Logroño is Viana, founded in 1219 by Sancho the Strong as a fortified town to protect against raids from Castile, the old border of which is now just a few kilometers ahead. In the early Reconquista, the kings of Navarra controlled this countryside almost to Burgos – except during the eleventh century era of El Cid when, as mentioned earlier, the Castilians pushed their eastern frontier all the way to Logroño.

Probably a Roman town originally, Viana was called Cuevas before Sancho built and garrisoned his fortress. Later, Charles III of Navarra made the town the seat of Navarra's crown prince, a practice that thenceforth continued. Recall that we visited the prince's pleasure palace at Sangüesa. Peculiarly enough, after a Navarran dynasty gained the throne of France, the Dauphin traditionally was also given the title, "Prince of Viana," no matter that by then Viana was firmly and permanently in Castilian hands.

The **walls and gates** of Viana are still quite prominent, particularly on the west side of town, but not much remains of the hospices and shrines of the pilgrims. The same can be said for the palace of the Prince of Viana. But there is something else worth a stop within its walls. It is the **church of Santa María**, a massive and interesting structure for all its being a mere parish church in a small town. Just wait until you cast your eyes on its portal! We can only conclude that the church is a living vestige of the town's glory days when it was the capital of a principality.

The tall, square tower of the church is easy to spot as you approach Viana. Exit the highway and make your way through the narrow, cobblestone streets with old houses emblazoned with noble coats of arms.

A church was located on the site from very early times. It was leveled to make room for the original version of this church in the fourteenth century. But the fifteenth and sixteenth centuries saw an almost complete rebuilding and expansion of the structure, and still more was added in the seventeenth.

What you see as you approach across the Plaza de los Fueros is a stout, tall tower with large and deeply recessed blind arches in its sides below a square belfry topped by a cupola. It rises above a fantastically sculptured portal, and is appended to one corner of a lofty Gothic church with sturdy buttresses.

The **portal** is a most amazing piece of work. It was constructed during the Renaissance in Neo-Classical style by Juan de Goyaz, who worked on it for almost twenty years (1549-67). A sculptor rather than an architect, he created the portal as a sort of triumphal arch. If nothing else, it was the triumph of his life. Its detail is beyond description. You can study it for an hour and not touch on everything. Needless to say, it focuses on religious themes such as the mysteries of the Rosary, but does include a few grotesques here and there for comic relief.

Most notable is the tableau of the **Crucifixion**, the centerpiece within the bay-shaped interior of the portal. While the domed ceiling is ornately carved in square medallions, below it, on the semicircular face of a starkly plain wall surface, are the crucified Christ at the center, the two thieves hanging from their crosses at the sides, and the Marys standing to each side beneath. A Roman soldier aims his spear at the side of Christ. Below that is a panorama of the descent from the cross and much more.

Inside, you find a plain, well-proportioned Gothic design featuring a rather spectacular **triforium** with elegant stone traceries in the windows. The high altar is backed by a seventeenth-century gilded retable in well-done but typically confused Plateresque.

The Chapel of San Juan Bautista was an addition of the eighteenth century, and is noted for the **paintings** in its dome, executed by Luis Paret y Alcázar in 1787.

As you no doubt may have learned by now, my sketchy remarks on the highlights of such edifices as this are intended simply to introduce the character of the place. Often I will tell you to sit and observe the place in quiet contemplation, perhaps while I tell more of its background. But if, as here, I have little more to say about details, there is still the presence of the place surrounding you. If it has its emotional impact upon your psyche, do not just walk away from such a place when I finish. Stroll quietly among the columns and piers investigating nooks and crannies, sit and contemplate (as the religious folk recommend) the works of the saint celebrated here, or simply the evidence of spiritual commitment to God and His works that the place embodies.

No, you need not be religiously inclined yourself to grasp the feelings cast into these stones, for your discoveries on these travels through Northern Spain deal with men's dreams and foibles, inspirations and practical applications of their lives as expressions of varied relationships with deity, and not with God as such.

Hopefully you will be able to gain entry to the treasury, housed in the Sacristy, which contains an excellent collection of old religious objects.

A hundred meters west down the street from Santa Maria is the burned out hulk of the thirteenth century church of San Pedro. Its **portal** is an addition from a later period, probably the Renaissance given its Neo-Classical temper. It is definitely worth a moment's contemplation, featuring Peter enthroned above the whole.

Logroño

Again it is about ten kilometers to our next stop, the old Roman town of Julia Briga. The place, of course, is now Logroño, situated on the banks of the Ebro River and dominating the broad, fertile valley with its seemingly limitless vineyards, orchards, vegetable farms and grain fields. It is capital of the modern province of La Rioja, home of Spain's finest red wines and once the primary bone of contention between the kings of León and Castile and the kings of Navarra. It became Castilian for good under Alfonso VI in 1076.

In Logroño we find a modern city of more than a hundred thousand people. They are as heavily involved in industry as in agriculture. So our experience of this city will be quite different from that of the past several days when we explored old pilgrimage towns that retain much of the character of that former time. Yet Logroño still has its old town, one which – as we ought to expect by now – grew up at the end of a bridge. This one crossed the Ebro River, so nearby the remains of that bridge we find much of what we wish to see in Logroño.

N111 crosses the Ebro on a modern steel bridge, the Puente de Piedra. Off to the right you see an eighteenth century construction, the Puente de Hierro, that took the place of the eleventh century pilgrim bridge thrown across the river by the bridge-building saints of the Calzada, Dominic and John. Further upstream you may catch a glimpse of the single arch remaining of the twelve-arched span constructed by those saints.

Park your car along the street by the far end of the bridge so we can get out and explore. Walking from the bridge, make an immediate right turn into the Calle de la **Rua Vieja.** That narrow, cobblestoned street, parallel to the river, was the main thoroughfare of medieval Logroño. Not long ago it had become somewhat of the local skid row, but recent revitalization of the district has made a pleasant difference.

About a three-minute stroll brings us to the first landmark of principal interest. This is, on your left, the **Iglesia** de Santa Maria de Palacio, a twelfth-century Romanesque church that once was part of a royal palace used by Alfonso VII of Castile. He gave palace and church to the Templars in 1130. Only the church still stands, although much modified in the fourteenth, sixteenth and eighteenth centuries, so that it retains few features of its Romanesque beginnings. The entrance is around on the far side, a block left on Calle Palacio.

The tall (45 meters), pyramid-shaped Gothic spire that rises upon the church above a lantern tower, is a creation of the fourteenth century. Beside it is a squat, fat belfry that stands above the portal, which is a sixteenth-century work of Jean de Riba. Inside, the **altarpiece** is by the sculptor Arnao de Bruselas and the painters Francisco Hernández and Pedro Ruiz. It dates from 1561.

In the Chapel of Nuestra Señora de la Antigua, located on the left side, is a thirteenth-century image of the Lady, displayed on a gaudy baroque retable. The tomb with the recumbent statue of its occupant is that of Juan de Vergara. Back in the main church, a small Romanesque door that was part of the original twelfth century structure opens out into a small and mostly ruined fifteenth-century cloister.

Outside the church, continue along the Calle Palacio a couple of short blocks. Cross Calle Marqués de San Nicolás, making a one-block jog to the left, and proceed along Calle San Bartolomé, where you quickly spot the tall and square Moorish brick tower of the church of San Bartolomé, again on the left side of the street.

This is the **oldest church** in Logroño. It features Romanesque twelfth-century apses set before a transitional Gothic nave that proportionally is shorter than we are used to seeing. An extremely well done, life-sized **Crucifixion**, is suspended above the altar from the single rib vaulting the sanctuary. As for the facade, it is early fourteenth century, and has one of the finest Gothic portals that we will find during our explorations. The coving sculptures feature scenes from the life of St. Bartholomew.

Exit the church going left and through the plaza, leaving it to your right. After a block you will spot the **cathedral** with its twin towers on the left. Known as Santa María de la Redonda, the cathedral faces away from you onto the Plaza del Mercado.

The inappropriate name for the cathedral comes from the original, round Templar church that first occupied the site. That structure was demolished and replaced by the original version of the present church in the fifteenth century.

The baroque **facade** and twin towers, built in 1742, are perhaps the most striking features of the church. The portal, constructed as a large niche covered by elaborate sculptures, almost clashes with the plain faces of the lower portions of the towers, no matter the fancy baroque details in their upper sections. The portal and towers were designed by Martín de Beratúa.

Entering the church, we discover a Gothic vaulted nave with the usual somber cast, but more high-flying than anything yet seen on our travels since we left Pamplona. The two side aisles have the unconventional feature of being as tall as the central nave, while the massive columns seem never to end. The **high altar** is the first Churrigueresque work that we have encountered, its retable rising all the way to the ribbed ceiling. Churrigueresque, as you see here, is an especially ornate variation of the baroque.

The apses are polygonal, with an ambulatory featuring a gaunt-ribbed, ghastly Crucifixion with Peter and John looking on. The sixteenth-century choir stalls were the work of Arnao de Bruselas. The rejas, or **grille**, is thought by some to be exceptionally finely done. The dome was decorated by José Bexés in the eighteenth century.

Most interesting of the many chapels is that of Nuestra Señora de la Paz. It is located at the very rear of the nave, where that Lady presides in solitary glory. It boasts of an excellent **retable**, Plateresque, dating from 1541. To the side is the tomb of its founder, Diego Ponce de León.

Now we return to the Calle de la Rua Vieja, using Calle Mercaderes to make the transit in the direction of the river. At the Rua Vieja we turn left, cross the busy Calle Sagasta (look right to view the Puente de Hierro) and, walk another block into a small square across which you see the **pilgrim church** of Santiago. High above its portal is a sort of diorama of the old Moorslayer himself, war pennant flying, as he gallops into history at Clavijo. Brandishing his sword, we see him riding his charger roughshod over a battlefield littered with severed heads of unfortunate Moors. It and the portal below are the work of Juan de Raón, completed in 1662.

The present church was designed in the sixteenth century by Juan de Corella. It is single-aisled Gothic with six columns. The high gilded altar retable dates from 1649.

Check for its hours and, if convenient, on the Plaza de San Augustín you may visit the seventeenth-century Palacio del Espartero, now the La Rioja Provincial Museum. While not outstanding, it has some nice pieces.

With that we have completed our planned tour of Logroño.

To return to your car, use the modern thoroughfare hacked through the old town, the Calle Marqués de San Nicolás that you crossed on your way to the church of St. Bartholomew. You will find some of the city's finer restaurants and shops along this street. Where it jogs to the right, save a few steps and turn left towards the Rua Vieja, where, after a right turn you are about a hundred meters from the Puente de Piedra and your wheels.

To exit Logroño, follow the signs through the center of town pointing towards Burgos, which places you on route N120 for Nájera.

The Way to Nájera

Beyond Logroño and its valley we begin the transition into rougher country that constituted a formidable barrier between the lush valleys of the upper Ebro basin and the Meseta, the comparatively arid, treeless and sparsely populated high plateau of central Spain. The latter is an oven in the peak of Summer and a refrigerator in the depths of Winter. No matter, it is Old Castile, where in the Middle Ages landless Spanish and foreign knights carved out fiefdoms from territories held for centuries by Moorish kings.

During the thirty kilometer drive to Nájera there is nothing much to be missed as you hurry westward through the wine country. There are bodegas by the dozen and vineyards by the kilometer in all directions. Navarrete is the only significant town along the way. Just west of it is the site of a famous battle, where Pedro the Cruel (Peter I) won back the throne of Castile in 1367 with the assistance of Edward, England's Black Prince.

Pedro earned his sobriquet the old fashioned way: By torture and murder. His first victim upon taking the throne was Leonora de Guzman, his father's long-time mistress. With that he avenged his mother's shame. But his mother was no favorite in the eyes of the young king. He made her watch while he slaughtered many of her closest friends and servants. Other victims were several of his illegitimate brothers, his first wife, and a pages-long list of aristocrats; but he missed murdering another of his father's bastard sons, Henry, Count of Trastámara, who fled to France.

Henry returned with a legion of mercenaries, captured Burgos and claimed the throne of Castile as Henry II. Pedro fled to England and, promising all of Biscay plus tons of riches to the English, won the Black Prince's assistance in gaining a hard-won victory over Henry in the Battle of Navarrete.

Pedro did not savor his victory over the Trastámera family for very long. He welshed on his deal with the Black Prince, then had a field-day executing just about everyone who had accepted Henry and made the mistake of not heading for the hills when Pedro returned to power. Those who escaped joined Henry in a new attack that overwhelmed Peter two years later, March 13, 1369. After that battle, when the defeated Peter was brought into Henry's presence, Peter attempted to kill his brother with a hidden dagger. That bit of treachery was his last. He died a moment later under the blades of Henry's aides. Some say that Henry himself struck the finishing blow.

Another half dozen kilometers further along is the village of Ventosa, site of another Roland legend. To the left as you drive are a pair of low mounts, the second of which is known as the Poyo de Roldán, Roland's Hill. Legend has it that Roland tossed a huge rock down off that hill and struck the giant Ferragut in the head, incapacitating the Moorish lord such that his Christian slaves were able to escape.

In any event, in the late eighth century this was a land ruled by the Moors and Ferragut no doubt was a real Moorish chieftain. A giant or not, if he was to survive in the rough and tumble of affairs here on the frontier, he had to be physically powerful as a leader of fighting men, and politically Draconian dealing with friend and foe alike. That made the man both hated and feared by the Christian slaves who worked the rich lands Ferragut held here in La Rioja. For that his name lived on in local lore for centuries later. He became the local bogey man, so to speak.

As you approach Nájera from Logroño, leave N120, bearing left towards town center. The oldest part of town is situated on the far side of the Najerilla River backed up by reddish sandstone cliffs that locked the original town between those rock walls and the west bank of the river. In the twelfth century the stream was spanned by a seven-arched bridge erected by that inveterate bridge-building monk, San Juan de Ortega, of whom we shall learn more in a day or so. His bridge, and the adjacent hermitage where he sheltered pilgrims, were wiped out in the past century to make way for a more modern bridge, which you find next to the hotel San Fernando.

Arriving at Nájera you discover a small town of about six thousand people. Small as it is, your selected lodgings are easy to find. The San Fernando, as we mentioned earlier, is not the only hotel in town but has comfortable quarters and its own spacious parking lot, which by now you recognize to be a rarity among in-city hotels.

NÁJERA
THE HEART OF THE RECONQUISTA

If the Reconquista's middle years had a spiritual heart, you find it a few kilometers south of Nájera at the Monastery of San Millán de la Cogolla. If those same middle years possessed a dynastic heart, it pulsed in Nájera itself, visible at Nájera's pantheon of the kings of Navarra and Castile. There we find the earthly remains of the monarchs who placed a Christian lock on Old Castile and paved the way for the drive south into the heart of the Caliphate at Córdoba.

That Nájera's pantheon should memorialize monarchs of both Navarra and Castile-León does not surprise a student of Spanish history. La Rioja was a rich plum that changed Christian hands more than once after it had been torn away from the Muslims. In the eleventh century, Nájera was the royal seat of Navarra until El Cid and Alfonso VI incorporated La Rioja into the Kingdom of Castile. After that the town became no less favored by the kings of Castile.

Some say Nájera is an Arabic name (Naxera), one that describes the town factually as the "place between the rocks." While there are other opinions, I like that one best. Yet the town is far older than the Arab conquest and even predates Rome's Cantabrian War.

Nájera was recaptured from the Arabs in 923 by a joint campaign of Christian forces led by Ordoñio II of León and Sancho I of Navarra. The ancient landmarks we find in the town today were the creation of still another Navarran king, Sancho III, the Great; his son, Garcia, and their immediate descendants.

In the early eleventh century Sancho the Great made Nájera his western headquarters and held court here more often than not. It was a matter of regal priorities and military necessity. At that time La Rioja was Navarran nearly to Burgos, and that was where the action was. Arabs still raided these parts at the turn of the millennium, while the kings of Asturias and León pushed eastward from their forward positions around Burgos where the counts of Castile achieved autonomy as the tenth century drew to a close.

The first opportunity for Spanish unity came under Sancho the Great during the early years of the eleventh century. He expanded his Navarran kingdom to include Aragon and Castile as well. He ruled from Barcelona to Zamora, and seemed on the verge of uniting all of Christian Spain. Then, two years after Sancho died in 1035, his son Ferdinand inherited (through his wife Sancha) the Kingdom of Asturias and León when king Bermudo III died without a male heir. Unfortunately, the opportunity for total unity of the Christian states was already lost. At his death, Sancho had divided his kingdoms – Navarra, Aragon and Castile – among his sons. Ferdinand was given Castile. Combined with his wife's inheritance of León and Asturias, Ferdinand was the most powerful of the Christian kings.

Ferdinand established his throne at Burgos, dominating the table lands of Old Castile and the mountainous territories leading to the Atlantic, north and west. His armies became the first Christian force powerful enough to sortie south past Toledo to Seville. He also expanded his holdings in Castile at the expense of the Muslims and placed many of the Moorish "Taifa" kings under his "protection," awarded in return for substantial tribute, of course. Meanwhile Ferdinand took healthy chunks of La Rioja away from his brother Garcia, king of Navarra.

Garcia reigned in Nájera until his death at the hands of one of his own men at the Battle of Atapuerca in 1054. His son, Sancho IV, the Noble, became the last of the Navarran kings to use Nájera as the seat of his court.

Sancho IV, at a church synod he convened here in Nájera, took the first steps to substitute Latin Roman Catholic liturgy for the Mozarabic rites that then dominated the Church in western Navarra, plus the Kingdom of León and Castile including Galicia. After his death, the seat of Navarran royal power moved east again when Sancho Ramírez reunited the kingdoms of Navarra and Aragon in 1076, and Alfonso VI took Nájera and upper Rioja into his kingdom of Castile.

Nájeran prominence in regal and church affairs did not end with the takeover of the city by the Castilians. King Alfonso VII, known as the Emperor, installed Prince Sancho (later Sancho III of Castile) in Nájera as guardian of his eastern frontier. Here Sancho married Doña Blanca of Navarra. Their son, later King Alfonso VIII of Las Navas de Tolosa fame, was born here in 1155. Later, Alfonso's son, Ferdinand III, the Saint, was here proclaimed king, although his coronation was mounted months later in Valladolid. The streets, hotel and other features of Nájera today, which are named after the saint-king, are reminders of Ferdinand's many connections to this city throughout his life.

Such is the historical background of the place. Back near the roots of that history, the Monastery of Santa María la Real was founded in Nájera by the Navarran king Garcia in 1052. It was erected to memorialize and protect a cave in which the future king, then a young prince, discovered a sacred image of the Virgin Mary. He constructed the monastic building with its back set against the tall, purple-red sandstone cliffs that gave the town its name.

Originally Garcia pledged the church and its monastery to the shelter of pilgrims. For that he had to relocate the pilgrim track a few kilometers northward to bring the pilgrimage trade to the door of his new monastery. Soon afterwards he further dedicated the monastery as a mausoleum for the kings of Navarra. Later still, after La Rioja was surrendered to the kings of León and Castile, the new sovereigns continued to use the monastery as a royal pantheon For that it became the most important landmark on our list of things to see in Nájera.

No less see-worthy is the monastery of San Millán de Cogolla. It too was built with its back set against a rock wall, in this instance located on the side of a low mount a short distance south and west of Nájera. It also contained a cave, one that had especially sacred connections to San Millán himself, a hermit of lowly origins who came to possess saintly powers. This second monastery is different in every manner imaginable, including spiritual tone. While Santa María was given the flourishes due a pantheon of kings, San Millán never lost the rustic simplicity of its humble origins, no matter the extravagant constructions of its later occupants.

There are two monastic complexes at San Millán. They are called Suso and Yuso, upper and lower. The upper is oldest, built upon the hermit's cave in rustic surroundings. Fragments of it date from the Visigothic period. More of it dates from the era of the Muslim conquest, before the early Christian kings of Navarra recaptured these lands from the Moors. It opens to visitors at 10 am, a half hour earlier than the lower complex of buildings, which were a grandiose product of the Renaissance, quite out of character of the saint they honored.

The monks conduct guided tours only at the lower establishment, which remains an active monastery. So plan to be present first at the Suso Monastery a bit before 10 am, then tour the Yuso Monastery afterwards, completing that tour by the closing time of 2 pm. There is then enough time left in the afternoon for the drive back to Nájera for resumption our explorations at the Monastery of Santa María la Real. Since the latter has visiting times similar to those at San Millán, we will take advantage of its late afternoon hours between 4 and 7:30 pm.

Go west out of Nájera on route N120. At the village of Azofra, about six kilometers beyond Nájera, turn left onto a side road that after twelve kilometers brings you to the Monastery.

Cañas

On the way to or from the monastery of San Millán visit the Cistercian convent of Santa Maria in the village of Cañas. Our route winds through the village, birthplace of Santo Domingo de Silos, first a monk at San Millán de Cogolla, then founder of the famous and still very active monastery of Silos near Burgos. In fact, in 1994 a recording of their Gregorian chants became a huge best seller in Spain, outdistancing even the most popular rock and pop recordings. One newspaper headlined: "It's a miracle – Gregorian chant tops Spain's pop chart."

In Cañas, at the Cistercian convent, be sure to see its comparatively tiny Gothic chapel that boasts of exquisite **stained glass** and a museum of religious art. Situated next to the highway on your left (while going out), you can't miss it.

The convent, founded in 1170, contains tomb sculpture regarded by experts as among the finest of the medieval period: The thirteenth century **tomb** of Doña Urraca López de Haro (1170-1262), once abbess of the place, was a member of the aristocratic Haro family that dominated Nájera and its environs for several hundred years. We will see more of the Haros later today at Santa María de la Real, where several are buried in the company of the kings they served.

You meet the former abbess portrayed recumbent as a devout lady holding a shepherd's crook and flanked by a pair of ministering angels. At her feet, in prayer, are doll-like figures of novices. On the sides of the work are carved scenes from her life: on one side we see her as a novice, kneeling in prayer; as the abbess with her prayer book; and being greeted in heaven by St. Peter. Opposite we are shown her burial, attended by three bishops; a group of mourners; and her funeral procession of nuns. It is a stirring piece of work.

The nuns of the present convent are noted for the quality of their **ceramic ware**, which you may purchase in their novelty shop during your visit.

Beyond Cañas comes the village of Berceo, where Gonzalo de Berceo, the first poet to compose in the Castilian dialect (which became the language of all Spain during the next several centuries) was born late in the twelfth century. He wrote while a monk at the monastery of San Millán. The poetic work was titled *Miracles of Our Lady.* Gonzalo explained that he worked in Castilian vernacular for no reason other than he found Latin too difficult to master. All one-time students of that classical tongue may sympathize with him for that

In vernacular prose he also documented the lives of several local saints. Among those was an account of the life of San Millán called the *Vida de San Millán de la Cogolla.*

At Berceo you are coursing through the heart of the Cárdenas Valley in the foothills of the Sierra de la Demanda. Here the open fields and farms have almost entirely given way to hills and woodlands. The village is small and decrepit, half abandoned. You pass through on its narrow main street, after which the road divides, the right branch heading for the monastery.

San Millán de Cogolla

The founding of San Millán de Cogolla takes us back to the leading edge of the Visigothic era. It was one of the first monasteries founded in all of Europe, and later a primary repository of learning during the cultural debacle of the Dark Ages. Its time-scarred walls contain a treasury of legend as well as religious and architectural artifacts spanning the centuries from the Visigoths to the Renaissance.

The legends deal with miracles wrought by a solitary hermit, San Millán, beside whose cave a band of loving disciples founded a monastery within his century-long lifetime. He died on November 12, 574, and was interred in the cave where he had spent most of his life.

The monastery flourished throughout the Visigothic period, and was scarcely affected by the Muslim conquest until a vindictive Arab chieftain, raiding northward near the turn of the millennium, looted and vandalized the place. But as we shall see when we visit the monastery, Sancho the Great and his son Garcia renovated and expanded it in truly royal fashion. Fortunately, they left the earlier constructions nicely restored but essentially undisturbed. For that we thank them. They allowed us to see one of the most important surviving cultural landmarks of our entire sojourn in Northern Spain.

As for the earthly remains of San Millán, Sancho had them dug up and placed in more distinguished quarters: a green alabaster sarcophagus that is one of the outstanding artistic features found on our visit to the upper monastery.

The physical destruction of Arab raids had no negative effect on the influential spiritual status the monastery had attained within the Spanish psyche during the centuries of the Visigothic and Arabic presence. Reverence for San Millán and his works, generation after generation, made this the holiest place in Spain for centuries. The Moors could ravage the place, but not its spirit.

The monks of San Millán for hundreds of years maintained one of the few places of advanced learning in the West during the Dark Ages. Later, those monkish scholars became avid students of Eastern wisdom imported to Spain by the Arabs. Indeed, it was through these monks at San Millán that the Arabic system of numbers, and the concept of zero (which some say these monks invented), were introduced into the Western mind and displaced the cumbersome methods of mathematics based on Roman numerals.

You will be disappointed to learn that much of this great old monastery is very much abandoned, though not exactly derelict. Its noted library, relics and artistic wonders once were saved by removal to Madrid. Now many of them have been returned with the repopulating of the lower monastery. Among those priceless items was an interlinear translation of the Latin Bible in Castilian, the earliest surviving example of the birthing language of Spain in written form. Perhaps it was from the likes of that Bible that Gonzalo took his Latin lessons. Gonzalo thus was not the first to write in the Castilian dialect. The earliest known writings of that sort were produced by a monk named Munio, who lived at the monastery of San Millán perhaps a century earlier.

San Millán de la Cogolla (St. Millán of the Hood, a name which we assume implies a trait of the hermit to keep his features buried beneath a monkish cowl) is located well off the pilgrim track, but the fame of the place caused hordes of pilgrims to make the detour. If for nothing else they went to gawk at a place where a bona fide miracle worker had lived. Perhaps they also hoped for a miracle of their own as they dallied for a while in meditation and prayer over the sacred relics of the shepherd saint.

Many stories are told of San Millán. They agree that he was a plain, untutored, simple shepherd who as a young man appears to have had a remarkable spiritual awakening, after which he retired to a hillside cave to pray and meditate on first and last things. In a culture that bred respect for holy men, San Millán had a streak of no-nonsense common sense that led the local villagers to seek him out for advice on matters both religious and mundane. Some stories suggest he may have had the power of precognition and the healing touch, too. It is said he could restore sight to the blind and cleanse the leper. Soon people from roundabout came in groups to listen to him preach, later to be joined by others from afar as word of his works spread. To serve them he is reputed to have worked a miracle with wine similar to that performed by Christ.

San Millán was born in the year 473 and died in 574, a lifetime that spanned the fall of Rome and the coming of the Vandals and Goths. The many who came to hear him soon decided to build a shelter near the cave so that others could worship with and learn from him. The first church was built by his cave in 537. By mid-century it had become a Benedictine monastery, one of the earliest chapters of that pioneering monastic order. It celebrated a living saint who drew crowds of pilgrims from great distances even then.

No sooner had San Millán died than even greater multitudes of pilgrims began to journey to his tomb. This happened centuries before the vogue of pilgrimage to Santiago de Compostela. Why? Pilgrims respond to miracles as proof of divine powers, so there obviously were miracles aplenty.

After the coming of the Moors, the saint is reputed to have taken a page from Santiago's book and aided the Reconquista with a bit of Moor slaying of his own. Or so the legends tell us.

The Benedictines stayed until the nineteenth century (1835), surviving Moorish raids, anti-clerical attacks by money-hungry monarchs, and even the depredations of Napoleon's troops who looted the place before they withdrew from Spain during the Napoleonic Wars. But the combination of the First Carlist War and the long decline of the pilgrimages before the rediscovery of the relics of Santiago, was more than could be endured. The place was abandoned to the elements and only recently reoccupied by a congregation of Benedictine monks, who have attempted to restore and preserve what centuries of monkish endeavor had created.

The lower, Yuso, monastery comes into view first as you approach, its octagonal lantern and columned cupola rising above the landscape. But at the next intersection bear right so as to pass by the massive hulk of Yuso and continue up the steep grade for another kilometer or so by road to the older, smaller, but for me more magnificent, Suso Monastery. It is in the high end of the valley, near the crest of a low mount and smack up against the outcropping of rock that contained the hermit's cave.

As you climb the switchbacks towards Suso, you get only an occasional view of its square bell tower and red-tiled roofs framed against the backdrop of the wooded hillside. Where the road dead ends, park on the side to the left. Best to leave the small open area on the right clear for occasional tour buses, which, believe it or not, manage to come up here along the same narrow access road you used.

The Suso monastery is less than fifty meters further from where you park. As you approach on foot, you can tell from the variations in wall construction that this is an agglomeration of building styles derived from a double handful of centuries. The **main church** was built with Mozarabic flourishes during the ninth and early tenth (929) centuries, incorporating Visigothic beginnings, particularly in the chapels carved out of the live rock of the hillside. On these travels along the Highway to Heaven we encounter the Mozarabic in such distinct purity of form in only two places: here at San Millán, and later near León at San Miguel de Escalada. So now it becomes time to

125

answer the question: Mozarabic? What's that?

The Mozarabs were Christian migrants from Southern Spain. They came in a flood from the ninth to eleventh centuries as the Christian kingdoms gained footholds in the flatlands below their mountain lairs, and vindictive persecutions of Christians began in the Moorish lands to the south. Yet after centuries living under Moorish rule, the Mozarabs were fully inculcated into Arabic ways of life. Christian, their Bible was written in Arabic for they spoke no other language. By the same token, the educated Christian churchmen were well versed in Arab arts, science and knowledge, as well as in the mathematical forms that these monks introduced to their brethren elsewhere in Europe.

The artisans among them brought Moorish architectural traditions and techniques along with their tools and skills. Notable among those architectural variations was the horseshoe arch, which the Arabs themselves had adopted from the Visigoths. The Mozarabs melded it with Asturian pre-Romanesque barrel vaulting, and applied decorative touches that – as we have already seen in some of the early Romanesque – betray their Moorish inspiration.

Approaching the church we climb through a sloping court-yard leading to an arcaded **porch** on the near, downhill, side. It obviously was recently restored. Best feature of the porch is the view from its arcade, looking down over Yuso and across the valley beyond.

Note the sarcophagi lined up along the porch. Several of them formerly reposed out in the courtyard burial ground you just walked through. They include the tombs of three queens of Navarra, attracted here by the religious prestige of the place. Among the tombs on this porch is that of Gonzalo, the poet who toiled here with his pen, whose hand was a power in turning Castilian into one of the world's finest literary languages.

Enter the church from the porch, passing through a horseshoe-arched side door. Inside the church, we discover a double-aisled structure in which a row of **horseshoe arches** separate the aisles and support a heavy superstructure lightened by round-arched niches. Above that rest the rafters of the roof. (Outside, you may have noted the carving on the rafter ends. The finesse of their artistic decor is another sign of the Mozarabs who built the place.) The horseshoe arches rest on slender round pillars with plain, thick capitals that blend into the horseshoe.

To your right another pair of taller horseshoe archways open into the Mozarabic equivalent of an apse. These arches rest on heavy piers, as does the rearmost of the horseshoe arches along the nave to your left. Note that the archways that extend beyond that pier are Romanesque, also resting on round columns. Their **capitals** are quite different, although they also are simple in concept, of a plain-faced design reminiscent of those we saw in the crypt at Leyre, which dated from about the same time. Here again is the pre-Romanesque tied closely to the Visigothic.

What you observe in this physical change of archway design is, then, evidence of the tenth century extension of the ninth century church structure. The change reflects the greater influence of Spanish Romanesque, a design style just then being reborn in Spain and spread by monks and itinerant artisans on the move between monasteries. The influence of French Romanesque was still a generation or two in the future.

The far wall of the nave is built immediately against the rock face of the mount. Near the forward end are passages into small **chapels** set into caves, in part man made, hewn into the live rock of the hillside during the lifetime of the saint himself. In the cave chapel opposite the entrance door you find the recumbent image of San Millán atop a twelfth century **sarcophagus** (empty; his remains were moved to the Yuso Monastery in 1053). It was carved from a block of green alabaster, with ministering monks depicted around its sides. One bearded fellow is shown seated, head thrown back in despair at the death of his teacher, holding the saint's relics in a chest on his lap. The sarcophagus is believed to stand in the cave where the saint lived out his hundred years and one.

Back in the main church, forward of the nave, on the left, is a small chapel containing an **osuary** with the bones of monks and pilgrims who died here. The apse behind has a peculiar cube-like form, and its corbel vaulting and carving is unmistakably Mozarabic. Note the vestiges of painted stucco around the horseshoe arch on the right.

Now take a moment to savor the feel and the look of this place. There is nothing like it anywhere else in the world. Whether you have a religious leaning or not, this monument of stone – honoring a very special spiritual presence – is worth a pause for quiet contemplation. No miracles are promised, but you will walk away feeling better for it.

On the drive back down to the Yuso Monastery enjoy the panoramic **view** of the valley and, of course, sightings of the lower monastery. The church is on the near side of the comparatively massive complex. The octagonal tower stands above the apse end. The round Romanesque window over the blind arch on this end stands above the main entrance.

The original Yuso monastery was built in 1053 by King Garcia of Navarra. It was needed to accommodate the expanded monkish populace of this sacred "national treasure" as the result of the religious fervor stemming from the Millennium (anticipated world's end, and all that). It also memorialized the success of the kings of León and Navarra in fending off the last powerful attacks by the Moors, which led to a subsequent increase in the flow of pilgrims along the suddenly much safer Camino de Santiago.

When El Cid ravaged La Rioja in the latter part of that century he appears to have left this place undisturbed. Further growth and grandiose monkish aspirations soon ruled that Yuso should be demolished and completely rebuilt during the sixteenth to eighteenth centuries. So what you find now is basically a Neo-Classical complex of structures with Baroque accretions tacked on.

Park in the paved area beside the monastery and walk to where you can look down into the large, sunken courtyard surrounded on three sides by monastic buildings. The church is seen rising beyond the wing to the left. Descending the stairs into the courtyard, the visitor's entrance is located in that wing on the left. You may pass through directly to another courtyard that leads to the church, or first you may be conducted on a tour of the monastery's **museum.**

The tour takes you via a lower gallery of the cloister into the sacristy, then to the upper galleries of the cloister to the Salon of the Kings, adjacent to which is the library. As the monk (or perhaps a lay person; recently for us it was a young lady) conducts your tour in Spanish, let me fill you in on details you may not be able to catch.

The double-door **portal** into the cloister at the start of the tour is Plateresque, featuring pairs of "twisted" or "cable" columns (we will see the granddaddys of this architectural style in Asturias). Decor of the sixteenth century **cloister** is rather spare compared to what we have seen elsewhere, and is notable only for the quality of its vaulting. Its architect was an Italian, Andrés Rody. Its upper galleries contain a couple of dozen not remarkable paintings, many by the eighteenth century artist José Bexés. The earliest were done in the seventeenth century by an otherwise unknown artist named Spinosa. Portrayed are scenes from the life of San Millán. A turn around the galleries to study the story they tell is suggested.

The **Salon de los Reyes** (Hall of the Kings) contains paintings by a noted clerical painter, Juan de Ricci. Portrayed are Fernán González, who may be thought of as the founder of Castile; the Navarran kings Garcia and Sancho the Great, who were mentioned earlier as patrons behind the founding of this Yuso monastery; and the Castilian King Alfonso VII.

Most interesting for book people is the **library** with its collection of rare illuminated manuscripts, hymn books and parchments, plus some very early printed books. There you also find the ivory-paneled, time-darkened wood **reliquaries** of San Millán and his principal disciple, San Felices. The reliquaries were remade in 1944 from the broken parts of their predecessor pieces. The originals, jewel studded and set in gold, were destroyed in 1809 by French troops who stole the gems and precious metals when they plundered the place while retreating in the face of Wellington's Peninsular Campaign.

The ivory panels on the chest of San Millán were carved during the eleventh century between 1067 and 1081. Those of San Felices date from a few decades later. They are regarded as representative of the finest Romanesque sculpture extant. Many of the originals were removed to (and some still remain at) various museums before these you see were reassembled here. Most of the panels depict scenes from the life of San Millán; some deal with the life of his disciple, others portray the Last Supper.

The looting and vandalizing of Spain's national treasures by Napoleon's army will be mentioned again and again as we explore the Way of St. James. That these ancient churches and monasteries were despoiled is but a reflection of the anti-clerical aspect of the French Revolution, which continued as a feature of the Empire created by Napoleon. Yet the French did not escape with their loot, and many paid for it with their lives.

The French had more than Napoleon's penchant for empire driving them into Spain. In 1793, after King Louis lost his head, the Spanish king declared war on the French revolutionaries. Spain was defeated, and it took little urging in 1808 for Napoleon to cross the Pyrenees to vanquish an incompetent Spanish king who was hated by his own people. What Napoleon did not count on was that the Spanish people hated the French more than they hated their king. They rose against Napoleon and soon were aided by British troops, who defeated Napoleon and restored Ferdinand VII to the throne – followed by another twenty years of his regal stupidities.

As Wellington made his final drive north in 1813, the French recalled all their far flung contingents in Spain and concentrated them near Vitoria, some fifty kilometers north of here. Napoleon's brother Joseph, king of Spain by the Emperor's command, led the French in one final attempt to stop Wellington. The French defeat was worse than a rout. It was a complete disaster. Left behind were not only all their big guns, but also the army's baggage which, as one historian remarked, contained "…an amount of spoil never before won in modern times by an army. The accumulated plunder of five years in Spain was wrenched from the French in one fell swoop. Dollars and Napoleons strewed the ground."

Unfortunately, the work of vandals can never be fully restored.

Brighter by contrast with everything else is the seventeenth century **sacristy**, white with gilded Baroque stuccoes. Honored position is given to Nuestra Señora de los Angeles.

The sacristy presents a strange contrast with your first impression of the **church interior**. The rear of the nave when we visited revealed itself as a cavernous gray hulk of a place, lending a feeling a gloom and maybe even of desolation, stripped as compared to its original incarnation before it was abandoned a century ago. It has a central nave and two aisles. Its architect was Tomás Rodi.

Forward of a tall grille is a structure having an entirely different character, nicely restored and cared for, with pastel blue dominating the apse and walls around the sanctuary. The festively gilded high altar contains eight paintings by the artistic cleric, Father Ricci.

The **portal** leading into the church is Neo-Classical and relatively plain as such things go, with the saint solemnly greeting you from above the door. The inscription reads "1642." Looking to the portal leading from the courtyard in front of the church to where you originally entered the monastic buildings, you see above it a Baroque piece featuring **San Millán** on a charger, assuming his legendary role as a Moorslayer, the field strewn with fallen Muslims. The architect was Pablo de Basave, with sculptures by Diego de Lizarra. The pair of Renaissance dandies standing on tall pedestals beside the saint add an incongruously secular flavor to the piece.

As we end our visit here, perhaps you share my preference for the older monastic site up the hill where San Millán lived and provided everything else here with a reason for being.

131

Santa María la Real

The Hotel San Fernando and its spacious parking lot are situated on the east bank of the Rio Najerilla. Next to the hotel is the busy Plaza San Fernando, where you may dine, sip coffee or, in the evening, enjoy something stronger. North of the parking lot, the town's main streets meet the Puente San Juan de Ortega, which conveys traffic across the river.

Given its name, one might suspect the bridge traces its ancestry to the ancient span built by San Juan, one of the pair of bridge-building saints about whom we will hear more on the morrow. But this is a later bridge, more or less a reconstruction that replaced the structure San Juan was commissioned to build over the Najerilla early in the twelfth century.

You may drive or walk across the bridge on your way to Santa María la Real and its Pantheon of the Kings, the most important landmark of the town. Best choice is to walk and gain a better feel for this oldest part of present-day Nájera.

On the west side of the river our route plunges directly into the narrow streets of the old town. After a block turn left on Calle Martires, which leads to **Plaza la Cruz**. On your left is the parish church from which the square takes its name. Continue beyond the square for another block, turn right, and a block later the street deadends at the **Plaza Santa María**, named for the monastic structure that rises on your left between the town and the cave-pocked cliffs.

In the precipice behind the monastery notice the dark openings of **caves** large and small. Some are accessible via stairs hewn into the rock, and their openings are guarded by iron handrails. They provided sanctuary to the populace in times of flood or Arab raids. In one of those caves Prince Garcia, in 1032 and then a youth of sixteen, discovered an ancient statue of the Virgin. Tradition grew that the figure was made by St. Luke of the Gospels. Whatever its origins, Garcia vowed to provide the Lady a proper home. When he became king in 1035 and established his capitol here in Nájera, he was as good as his word.

Such is one story of the origin of Santa María la Real. Another sets the date of the find in 1044 when the king was out falconing and his bird pursued its quarry into a cave. Following, Garcia discovered the falcon and its prey perched amicably beside the statue of the Virgin. In any event, he was moved by the experience to build a home for the Lady, and by 1054 the place was completed and thriving in the hands of industrious monks dedicated to the service of Christ and to pilgrims heading west to the tomb of His Apostle.

As related earlier, in 1076 Navarra and Nájera passed into the hands of Alfonso VI of Castile. He awarded the monastery to monks from Cluny in 1079. They managed the place for the next four hundred years or so. Under their auspices the monastery was rebuilt early in the fifteenth century in a rather plain-feathered Gothic style under the direction of architect Pedro Martínez de Santa Coloma. For that, the Romanesque monastery Garcia built is not what you see now.

Call this the **red church**. Its walls of dressed stone share the color of the cliff that rises behind. The face of the church reminds one of a fortress, with plain, tall, forbidding walls with round towers set into the corners. The only fancy decor is its Renaissance-built main portal, and four lonely little pinnacles, one crowning each corner of the otherwise plain-faced campanile.

Entrance to the complex is from a small courtyard through an ancillary building. The way takes you down a corridor that leads first to the **cloister**, which is deemed to be the finest architectural element of the complex. El Claustro de los Caballeros dates from the early sixteenth century (1528) and boasts of delicate stone traceries of the Plateresque style filling the exterior archways above tall, very thin, strangely fluted columns with blooming capitals. Note the variations in the design of the traceries, archway to archway, variations so compatible you must pay attention to notice.

Each arch support is a formidable pier, backed by a massive buttress. On each pier, facing into the galleries, is one of a pantheon of saints, Apostles and fathers of the church, most with their heads smashed off by French vandals, each otherwise perched comfortably on a pedestal above a slender engaged column. Starting at a point just above their heads, the ribs of the vaulting fan out in their graceful, arcing ascension to their juncture overhead.

A number of **tombs** are situated in gallery walls of the cloister. They belong to lesser nobility (from which the cloister gained it name), plus churchmen and wealthy merchants who made their fortunes here along El Camino de Santiago. At the northeast corner is a large chapel with monumental tombs of medieval churchmen. In the northwest corner of the west gallery, in the fanciest niche of all, is the tomb of Diego Lopez de Haro, the Good, who held high office in the court of Alfonso VIII. Its reliefs show women grieving and men ranting and tearing their hair while monks go about covering his coffin. Note the exquisite detail of the roses in the coffered ceiling.

A **Gothic doorway** leads into the church from the cloister. Inside you discover a three-aisled church with stellar vaulting above the nave and its aisles, and groin vaults at the transept. The interior stonework is a pale ocher and unusually plain, typical of an earlier Gothic style than you might expect to find here.

The high altar **retable** is seventeenth century Baroque. On its left about halfway up is featured a statue of King Garcia kneeling in prayer. The Madonna of the piece, Santa María la Real, sometimes known as the Virgin de la Terraza, is twelfth century and Romanesque and not the Lady the prince discovered. She was lost sometime and somehow during the centuries.

Now turn to observe the elegance of the late fifteenth century dual-level **choir stalls** high above the rear of the nave. The symbol of St. James is carved on the seat backs. These Gothic works in wood were made by local artists, Nicolás and Andrés de Nájera. Above the center seat is the figure of Garcia himself, depicted in wooden high relief in full armor, stoic in his very real role as defender of the Faith and its followers. He stands beneath a delicately carved canopy that blends into a similar series of carved canopies extending over all three sides of the upper level of choir stalls. These are stalls you will remember as among the finest to be seen upon our journey. Take time to experience the detailed quality of the work.

Beneath the choir, behind a grille at the rear of the church, guarded by a pair of armed footmen wearing the colors of Garcia and his queen, Estefanía of Barcelona, are the principal **royal tombs** and the entrance into the sacred cave where the statue of the Virgin was discovered. Finest tomb by far is the twelfth century tomb of Doña Blanca de Navarra, Queen of Sancho III of Castile and granddaughter of El Cid. She died in childbirth. Her child became king of Castile, Alfonso VIII, dubbed The Noble, and a warrior who proved to be a true chip off the old block of El Cid.

Alfonso was what his time required, a warrior king who defeated the feared Almohades at Las Navas de Tolosa in 1212. Once Alfonso had broken the back of Moorish power in Spain it was all downhill for the Moslem hosts until Ferdinand and Isabella united their kingdoms of Aragon and Castile by marriage in 1469 and expelled the last of the Moors in 1492 after a ten-year siege of Granada.

Doña Blanca's tomb is prominently displayed apart from the others and on the church-side of the grille, its sarcophagus and fancy lid situated beside the entry into the crypt. The surface of Doña Blanca's tomb is covered with intricately carved Romanesque reliefs that the experts describe with superlatives. Around her carved figure are the king, attendants and mourners. Elsewhere are carved Old and New Testament biblical scenes, principal of which depict Christ with his Apostles. No king has a finer memorial. Here lies a lady who obviously was as loved for herself as she was respected for her position, her lineage, and the heroism of her son.

Among nearby tombs in a chapel to the right rear of the church are those of the Haro family, the Dukes of Nájera, and others of lesser import on the noble scale of things.

Now for the **pantheon** of kings of Navarra and Castile.

With them are the tombs of their queens, all in a line, all showing the wear and tear of nearly a thousand years, including the disastrous effects of the eighteenth century. Then the French army pillaged the church and tombs. Later the place was abandoned in 1835 at the time of the first Carlist War. It was not reoccupied until 1895, when it was taken over by a colony of Franciscans, who tend it to this day.

At the entrance to the **crypt**, one to each side, are the polychrome figures of King Garcia and his queen, kneeling, facing into the cave – now a tiny chapel – where the statue of the Virgin is said to have been found. In the chapel, poised above its altar, is a Virgin; but it is a thirteenth century polychrome piece that hardly satisfies one's expectations. And that provides a rather unsatisfactory conclusion to what otherwise has been a fascinating experience.

Outside on the street, retrace your way a few steps to find another church, this one much smaller. It is the **parish church** of Santa Cruz, once the royal chapel associated with the monastery and a nearby royal palace. Originally it was a twelfth century structure, but most of what we see is of later origin. It comes to us from the sixteenth century and suffers much from Baroque modifications in the seventeenth. The dark green marble facing on the sanctuary walls, and the tall marble pillars in the side altarpieces, are more Italian in character and mood than they are Spanish. The scene is reminiscent of churches of the same period in Florence or Venice. Most attractive is the great dome, rising high above the crossing, and brightly illuminated by windows around its drum. So ends our exploration of this spiritual and dynastic heart of the Reconquista.

THE BRIDGE-BUILDING SAINTS

During the late years of the eighth century the Asturian kings drove south out of the Cantabrian mountains into the region of León. In the ninth century they forged east across the Meseta to the barrier presented by the Montes de Oca. At the same time Navarra pressed its borders westward up the fertile Ebro Valley and along its tributaries until it, too, ran up against the eastern flank of that same mountainous barricade. Caught in this pincers, the Moors retreated south – but not without a fight. Indeed, there were many. Nor did the loss of Nájera in 923 end their presence in the region.

El Camino de Santiago west from Nájera through the Montes de Oca in the tenth century thus was a stretch of road where both angels and pilgrims feared to tread. Politically it was a no-man's land between Castile, Navarra, and the Moorish kingdoms to the south. It was a wild and untamed piece of geography notorious as one of the most difficult segments of the entire pilgrim route. More, there was a scarcity of safe havens.

The old Roman towns long since had been depopulated by centuries of strife and raids by Muslim slave traders. Villages were poor and ill defended from the depredations of Christian and Moor alike. The few remaining towns were armed camps with tall defensive walls and citadels ruled by local warlords little better than robber barons. Nearby castles were manned by unruly, "independent" warrior knights. Banditry ruled large stretches of the road where the king's men were reluctant to venture even in force. Here the pilgrim more than ever took his life in his hands to dare proceed a step further on his sacred quest for salvation.

Sancho the Great of Navarra (970-1035), followed by his sons Ferdinand I of Castile and Garcia of Navarra, finally brought the bellicose lords of Castile and La Rioja under control. But the lot of the pilgrim improved only slightly. What we would call the infrastructure of roads and services in the borderland between Nájera and Burgos – Navarra and Castile – remained pathetically inadequate.

Problems have a way of producing problem solvers. In this instance it was a Benedictine monk. He earned canonization as Santo Domingo de la Calzada (St. Dominic of the Highway) and spent a lifetime building bridges, roads, and hospices serving pilgrims along the route through this dangerous no-man's land between Nájera and Burgos. Dominic also became known for miracles, an essential qualification for sainthood.

Dominic was born in 1019 in a village not far from here, up the road towards Burgos. Like San Millán he was an untutored shepherd lad with the feel of God in his bones. It seemed appropriate therefore for him to join the brothers at San Millán de Cogolla. They turned him away. They were a pretty sophisticated lot of scholars by then, full of grandiose ideas and devotional hubris. That was about the time they began construction of Yuso, having outgrown the simple faith and ways of their founder. So, given Dominic's humble origins, and given the laborious tasks upon which he spent most of his life, he may have been rejected as much because of a rough manner and burly appearance that did not suit the cultured image the monks of San Millán then projected of themselves. Certainly it could not have been for lack of brains, considering the accomplishments of Dominic's life.

After several years serving a bishop in Italy, Dominic returned to La Rioja and took up the meditative life of a hermit. He established his hermitage not far from where he lived his childhood. The place he selected was at a strategic location where El Camino de Santiago crossed the Rio Oja. Soon he became obsessed with the notion that something had to be done to ease the way for pilgrims. Thus, with his own hands, he built his first bridge. It crossed the Oja near a small village. Nearby he built a pilgrim hospice.

A town soon grew up beside his bridge. First the people called it Burgo de Santo Domingo. Now it is known as Santo Domingo de la Calzada, no doubt to distinguish him from the many other saints Dominic who worked miracles along the Way of St. James.

We visit Dominic's town today along the way of one of our longer transits on this shortcut to Heaven. Tonight's destination is Burgos, involving a journey of about 110 kilometers. Make an early start.

On the way we encounter another place also named for a sainted bridge builder. We speak now of St. Dominic's principal disciple, San Juan de Ortega (originally known as Juan de Quintaortuño), who built a number of bridges and a fair distance of roadway himself. The original pilgrim bridge we saw at Estella was his work, as was the span at Nájera.

Today, nearly a thousand years later, several of the many bridges built by Dominic and his disciples still stand along the Way of St. James. That first bridge, spanning the Oja on twenty four arches, though many times repaired and modified, is one of those still in use. One wonders where this poor peasant boy learned to build so well. Maybe that was one of his miracles.

Santo Domingo died in 1109 at age ninety. He and San Juan, their working lifetimes taken together, devoted more than a century to improving the pilgrim road in this remote western district of old Navarra. By the time San Juan died in 1162, their joint efforts had made this stretch of El Camino de Santiago as good or better than any other section of the Way between Roncesvalles and Santiago Compostela.

Santo Domingo de la Calzada

Approaching the town the highway aims like an arrow at the tall, pointy tower of the cathedral, which targets what we come to see.

The Rio Oja is at the far side of this busy modern town where we find today's business thoroughly mixed with vestiges of its medieval past. Among those vestiges are defensive walls and towers built by Pedro the Cruel. They remind us that this town is within the region where Pedro and Henry of

Trastámera fought it out for the throne of Spain. Not until Henry's son, Juan I, was crowned did the royal succession get sorted out and regal affairs return to normal. Strangely enough, Juan received his crown right here in Santo Domingo de la Calzada in 1379.

Park on or near the cathedral square. The **cathedral** is on the north side and a **parador** is on the west. Both structures were originally built under the direction of Santo Domingo himself. Amazing, isn't it, what the little shepherd boy become master builder was able to accomplish. But what limits are there when you can work miracles?

In 1098, Dominic erected his original pilgrim church on land donated by the Castilian King, Alfonso VI. The present cathedral still retains – in the apse, ambulatory and apsoidal chapels – much of the original Romanesque design that delighted its founder. In 1158, however, the powers of the time replaced the main structure with a large Gothic edifice deemed more suitable for containing the tomb of its beloved founder. Thus it became one of the first Gothic churches to be constructed in Spain. It gained the status of a cathedral in 1232, even before its construction was finally complete in 1235.

The separate **bell tower** was replaced in 1762 by the architect Martín de Beratúa, whose work we saw earlier on the cathedral towers in Logroño. As at Logroño, Martín's sixty-nine-meter-tall tower contrasts the plain sides of its rectangular lower structure with profuse ornamentation on the upper octagonal belfry and the tower spire that gradually narrows to its cross-bearing pinnacle. Martín at the same time redid the nearby **portal**. His entryway is eminently Baroque on Neo-Classical foundations, yet calm enough to meld with its Gothic environs much better than Baroque ordinarily does. The saint is portrayed garbed in a fine cloak while greeting you from the center niche above the portal. He is accompanied by Sts. Emeterio and Celedonio.

Entering from the square, you gain limited access to the south transept where, beneath a Gothic baldachin and protected by a grille, you discover Santo Domingo's elaborate **tomb**. His recumbent figure is a twelfth century work, regarded as one of the best examples of Spanish Romanesque that survives. The surrounding mausoleum is an alabaster work by Juan de Racines, completed in 1513. Some sources say the design was by a Frenchman, Felipe Bigarny, whose best work lies ahead of us in Burgos.

To explore the remainder of the church and its museum, walk back outside and around to the front of the cathedral and its portal, known as the **Christ door**, situated within a transitional Romanesque-Gothic porch.

Taking stock of the nave with its high stellar vaulting, you find the clean lines of early Gothic there and in the aisles. The high altar and choir are both early sixteenth century work. Reliefs on the gilded retable of the high altar are by Damián Forment, with paintings by Andres de Melgar. This Baroque work is thought to be Forment's masterpiece.

You thought you heard a rooster crow? No, your ears are not playing tricks. Walk forward for the view from the interior side of the saint's mausoleum, and there look to the west wall of the south transept. You see an arched door with a richly painted mural in the tympanum, surmounted by what can only be described as a fancy Plateresque **chicken coop**. There behind an ornate grille are housed a cock and a hen, very much alive, to remind us of a miracle worked by Santo Domingo in response to the tearful prayers of a despondent couple whose son was unjustly hanged. The mural above the door tells the story pictorially.

It seems that while a German couple and their teenage son were staying at a local inn, the son rejected the amorous advances of a chambermaid. As scorned women proverbially do, she worked a bit of hell's fury on the lad. She secreted a silver cup in his luggage and reported the alleged theft and the suspect to the authorities. Protesting his innocence to the end, he was led to the gallows and hung. Across the transept from the chicken coop, beneath the window, is a piece of wood salvaged from the gallows on which the boy died.

His parents prayed to Santo Domingo (some sources prefer

Santiago) for the soul of their son. Evidently the saint elected to provide greater relief than that sought. For when the parents returned to view the body, still hanging from the gallows, the boy spoke to them. Thereupon the delighted parents dashed off to the magistrate to have their son taken down and freed. Such a miracle was proof enough of his innocence.

The magistrate had just sat down to dinner when the couple arrived. A roasted cock and hen were spread on platters ready to carve. The magistrate laughed at their story and told them that if their son was alive, then so are these birds – whereupon the cock began to crow and the hen to cluck.

The son was cut down, alive, and the family happily continued on their pilgrimage to Santiago, where they now owed prayers of thanks for the special favor of not one, but two amazing miracles.

In the sacristy is an interesting collection of paintings. The fourteenth century cloister is not remarkable, being Gothic with a touch of Mudéjar. Its galleries are now enclosed and turned into a **museum** containing rather less than average fare. But do take a quick spin around the interior of the church for a look into the **chapels**. The fifteenth century retable in the second chapel on the north side has gained considerable approval from the experts, as has the chapel on the south side adjacent to the transept. In the Chapel of St. John the Baptist, at the right rear, are rather well done tombs of several notables, including Don Pedro Juárez de Figueroa (d 1418), and the fifteenth century founders, the Count and Countess of Ciriñuela.

The chapels lining the ambulatory are not remarkable except for the semicircular Romanesque chapel at the rear. This structure is believed to be a vestige of the **original church** built by the saint himself. It is regarded as being of the purest Romanesque.

The wood carving on the **choir seats** is unique in my experience, in that only female saints are honored on the bottom row, while male saints and Apostles are shown above – chauvinistically dominating the female of the species, as usual. The central throne contains the figure of Santo Domingo. Each figure is carved in Plateresque low relief, often in a scene taken from life. It was designed and worked by Andres de Nájera, with assistance from William of Holland. It dates from 1521.

Some authorities think much more highly of this church than I do, but my preferences stem simply from a private matter of taste rather than from thorough grounding in architecture and its related arts and sciences.

Back on the plaza we find an old chapel of Romanesque style. It is the chapel of Nuestra Señora de la Plaza. But the real treasure among everything else on this square, including the cathedral, is the old Hospital del Santo built by Santo Domingo. It is now a **parador** operated by the Spanish government. It was building at the same time as the original pilgrim church back in the eleventh century.

Dominic established his hospice by enlarging and renovating a run-down structure that once had been a residence (let's not call it a palace, as some do) used by the peripatetic kings of Navarra before Ferdinand I of Castile took this part of La Rioja for his own. Dominic received a grant of the place from Ferdinand's son, Alfonso VI, who generously subsidized Santo Domingo's work along the Calzada for encouragement of the pilgrimage trade. All religious motives aside, it was a money maker for the realm and one sorely needed to support the seemingly eternal wars against the Moors. It also encouraged immigration, no less sorely needed to repopulate the land after so many centuries of war and depredations of Arab slave merchants.

The hospice was remodeled in the sixteenth century, and again in the past century when it was converted into a forty-four room luxury hotel. None of that detracts from the Romanesque elegance of the original construction. You are welcomed inside to pause for refreshment and to enjoy the ambience of eleventh century stone vaulting with beamed ceilings above polished marble floors decorously occupied by assorted antique furnishings. The stone stairways leading off into the corridors to the private rooms, and the spacious public lounge with its heavy old furnishings, add to the quality of

143

one's experience of the place. Certainly the pilgrims of old never had it so good, but given the rigors of the pilgrim trail, they probably felt they did when they stumbled in here and found shelter and care from the ministering hands of St. Dominic himself.

Before leaving the vicinity of the cathedral, walk across the square from the parador to where a few more steps take you into another and larger plaza. There, on the north side, is the **Ayuntamiento** of the town. It is a Renaissance structure with long arcades in front, a loggia above, and a facade bearing the arms of Charles V. The latter was Charles I of Spain, who spent the greater part of his life campaigning more or less ineffectually around Europe as Charles V, Holy Roman Emperor. Europe at the time of the Reformation was not a place in which grandiose imperial plans might succeed easily or generally. He ended up chucking it all and retiring to monastic life south of here in Extremadura, where he lived out his life in peace.

Following the old pilgrim road through Santo Domingo's town you find, near the far end, the **convent church** of San Francisco. The refectory is in ruins and the church seldom open. The church is sixteenth century and is admired by architects as an excellent example of the Herrera style. It should be, as Juan de Herrera, originator of the style, was the builder. The date was 1569.

Herrera was chief architect to King Philip II, successor to Charles V. His designs expressed his rejection of the extravagance of the Plateresque style. He switched to a severely plain, even ascetic, style often called "desornamentado." While I find Plateresque aesthetically confusing, Herrera is a bore. The style would better serve a bank or stock exchange. There is great geometrical precision and impeccable proportion but it lacks that quality that I prefer in any church from the smallest chapel to the most grandiose cathedral – the sense of divinity that has an air of awesomeness about it. But this place is a page of cultural history, so get out and have a good look if you find it open.

Inside, the most notable piece is the alabaster **tomb** of the founder of the church, Bernardo de Fresneda. Architects have another opinion. They are fascinated by the strangely flattened but pointed arch in the choir.

On the way out of town, park near the tiny shrine beside the road at the river bank and get out for a view of Santo Domingo's **bridge**. Its superstructure has been refined by modern improvements that allow it to be used even now to serve the main highway west to Belorado.

Belorado

Across the Oja and driving west again on N120, another twenty-five kilometers brings us to Belorado, the only good-sized town on the way to San Juan de Ortega. Pause in Belorado for lunch, or perhaps picnic beside the highway after your visit.

The modern road to Belorado bypasses most of the old towns of El Camino de Santiago. If you wish to take the time and have more than a casual interest, practically all of them offer something worthwhile to the eye. One of these villages, Viloria, was the birthplace of Santo Domingo de la Calzada. Its parish church still uses the baptismal font at which the saint was baptized nearly a thousand years ago.

Belorado dates from Roman times. To get there, turn right off the highway, following the road into town as far as the first spacious plaza, which you find on your right. It provides ample parking. Walk beyond that plaza for fifty meters through a narrow alley between buildings into the **Plaza Mayor**. It is arcaded on all sides, and extremely attractive. At its center is a circle of trees around a spacious bandstand. On one side of the plaza is the church of San Pedro, which deserves a look-see. With its square campanile, round windows and arched doorway it is pure Romanesque. The sightseer's gem in this town, however, is the sixteenth century **pilgrim church** of Santa María. The problem is that it is difficult to find and get to.

We found it by driving back out of the square where we parked, turning left at the red light by the gas station and driving for about a half kilometer. From there it is possible to look back across town and see Santa María where it is backed up against the cliff of a hill across town. You also can spot a one-lane, mostly dirt road heading in the direction of the church from the road you are on. Follow it to the cream colored, stuccoed church.

Abutting it to the right is a still-active pilgrim hostel operated by the church. Off to the left of the church is a very modern monastic house built against the cliff and in part occupying ancient **cave dwellings** within the face of the cliff. Note the metal stove pipe exiting one of the cave openings, and the modern windows enclosing others.

The star-vaulted interior of the church is its most interesting feature. The vaults rise from large round columns, with a pretty dome lifting above the crossing. The stone altarpiece in the chapel in the right apse contains two images of Santiago: below as a pilgrim; above as El Matamoros. On the main altar is a twelfth century seated virgin, and the Holy Family is shown on a side altar. This is a church my wife enjoyed immensely for reasons of her own private tastes in decor and mood.

A few kilometers beyond Belorado the highway passes through Villafranca Montes de Oca, an old Visigothic town originally named Auca. It gained its newer name when repopulated by French immigrants lured here by the kings of Navarra. The mountains of the same name are off to the right and dead ahead as you drive west. Once wild and densely forested, this part of the pilgrim track was regarded as the most dangerous. It was infested with wolves of both the four-legged and two-legged variety. The going was difficult also because the way climbs steadily to the pass called the Puerto de Pedreja. It rises to nearly 1200 meters and Winter comes early here.

San Juan de Ortega

After another dozen kilometers look for a side road to the right that leads through the village of Santovenia de Oca to San Juan de Ortega. Our destination is more than five kilometers off the main road, but right on the old track that pilgrims still walk.

There isn't much to be found in San Juan de Ortega these days besides the church that the saint built with his own hands. But don't think you are going to find just a rough pile of stones being passed off as a church. Like Santo Domingo, his mentor, Juan the bridge builder knew how to work with stone as both artist and engineer. The results he achieved make for an outstanding piece of business.

Juan was born about 1080 in the village of Quintaortuño, near Vivar, the birthplace of El Cid and not far from Burgos. The time of Juan's childhood was during the period of El Cid's greatest victories – including the conquest of Valencia.

Besides building so many bridges and sections of roadway, Juan also managed to make a pilgrimage to Jerusalem. During his return he experienced a shipwreck that nearly cost him his life. He attributed his rescue to St. Nicholas, patron saint of sailors. For that Juan vowed over the relics of St. Nicholas at Bari, Italy, that he would build a pilgrim church and a monastery on the Way of St. James if only he could be granted a safe journey home. The church we see was fulfillment of his pledge, and he refused to find an easy way to do it. Instead, Juan chose this wild area of pilgrim peril in the Montes de Oca as the site of his holy endeavors.

Juan named the place Ortega (Ortegas: Nettles). First he erected a chapel to serve pilgrims during construction of the main church. That latter church was finished in 1142 and dedicated as promised to Saint Nicholas. Juan meanwhile staffed the associated monastery and pilgrim hospice with Augustinians whom he himself recruited.

Upon his death in 1162, Juan was interred in a simple stone sarcophagus placed inside the chapel he himself had built.

147

Would that his works had been left alone thereafter. Not a chance. Three hundred years later, early in Isabella's reign, the powers that were decided that what Dominic had done for his pilgrims was no longer good enough for the saint himself. A stupendous Plateresque mausoleum was constructed within the old chapel to shelter a new and more prestigious sarcophagus. It was supplied by devout admirers of the saint's power with miracles, which continued throughout the centuries after his death.

By all accounts, a particular specialty of Juan as a miracle worker was the cure of infertility in women.

Queen Isabella, who was certain she had been miraculously so favored by San Juan, subsequently decided that such a beautiful mausoleum and its powerful saint deserved a resting place more elegant than the run-down edifice that Juan's little chapel had by then become. Thus Isabella ordered Juan's chapel torn down and replaced by something more appropriate to her regal taste. But that was not the end of her interventions.

Another donation by Isabella led to extensive rebuilding of Juan's own church, so that now little but the apse remains of his original structure.

Presently, we find that only the church and the later chapel built at the order of the Queen remain whole, accompanied by the semi-ruin of the monastery, plus a few houses, some deserted, in what remains as a small clearing in the wilderness. The monastery was abandoned in 1835, another casualty of the Carlist Wars. Yet now it lives again, long-served by a lone priest ministering mainly to pilgrims.

In its own way you will discover Juan's church to be as nice a place of devotion as you will find anywhere on this junket along El Camino de Santiago. No doubt the fact that it is now a national monument accounts for how well the church is maintained. But there is more than that contributing to the appeal of the place. More even than the helpful demeanor of the priest who kept the church active – and a delightful, friendly place he made of it. He offered food and shelter to pilgrims making their way along the track, putting them up in a renovated section of the former monks' dormitory off the cloister.

After his death church authorities have turned those responsibilities over to others who are thought by some to be less amiable servants of El Camino. Hopefully you will find better.

In its remote setting this is a place that takes you back half a millennium to the pilgrim trail as it used to be. Approach the church along a dusty street, with the Neo-Classical facade of Isabella's **chapel** on your left. The priest's quarters lie in the monastic complex intervening between the chapel and the church, the facade of which stands facing you.

A broad, deep-set round archway, protected by a fancy iron grille, leads into the chapel that Isabella built. The neatly maintained interior is divided by still another grille, protecting the chapel with its tall retable beyond it on the right. The grille bears the arms of the Catholic monarchs, Ferdinand and Isabella. But the saint's mausoleum rests here no longer. In 1966 the main church was refurbished still again and the saint's elegant sarcophagus was moved into the church and put down at the crossing near the apse built by Juan himself.

Outside again, as you approach the **church** someone familiar with California mission construction immediately is struck by the similarity between the New World churches and this one. The flat, slab-sided belfry with its three bells, each in its own aperture and stacked one on top of two, is Mission style at its best. The cultural connection between Spain and California comes to life right here. Observe the simplicity of the church facade, plain-faced stone, its portal opening beneath a Gothic arch with a round Romanesque window above and an end gable with an unobtrusive medallion beneath the peak of the roof. Very simple. Very ordinary. Then step inside and forget about the rustic simplicity of California Mission style.

The nave and side aisles are pure Gothic: sedate, meditative. High-flying ribs radiate upward from massive piers and solid round pillars; decorous capitals merge beautifully with the whole rather than demanding attention. Attention rather is

149

focused on the fabulous Plateresque **mausoleum** of San Juan, located behind a grille at the crossing.

This is Plateresque at its best. It is a work large enough to be significant, small enough to be coherent. Thus it escapes the confusion so often rampant in the Plateresque. Beautifully proportioned, it is said to be the work of one of the great masters of the form, Gil de Siloé, a Flemish master who served the court of Queen Isabella. Within is the sarcophagus, the saint shown recumbent, with scenes from his life carved around its sides. The Baroque statue of the saint, at the center exterior of the mausoleum, with other figures at the corners, are rather commonplace church art. But they are only minuscule distractions from the Plateresque majesty of the whole.

We have noted bits and pieces of Plateresque art in stone and iron grilles at a number of locations previously, and there is much more to be encountered later – some every bit as fine as what you see here, including more by Gil de Siloé that the experts award even higher marks. So for the uninitiated, perhaps it is time to tell about this singularly Spanish style of artistry while your eyes relate to the stone traceries and filigrees that are among it defining features.

As you plainly see, Plateresque is a flamboyant style. It was developed in the late fifteenth and early sixteenth centuries from Italian and Mudéjar influences, with a Baroque richness laid atop Gothic fundamental structures. Emphasis is on pure decor often having little relationship to those underlying structures.

The term Plateresque is derived from "platero," a silversmith, because of the similarity the filigree-type decor and carvings have to the work of Mudéjar workers in precious metals. The style was developed in Segovia by Lorenzo Vázquez. In Northern Spain it is generally found only here in Castile, except for isolated minor creations such as we have encountered, and as in the retable-like facade we will see on the main portal of the Hostal de los Reyes Católicos in Santiago.

The structure of the **crossing** where the sarcophagus of San

Juan lies in such elegant surroundings is the work of the saint himself. It and the apse behind are all that remain of the church he built. They have a nice design touch about them. Note the receding archways of the central apse, giving the impression of much more depth than there is.

The Apse of the Church Built by San Juan Ortega

Above, on a Romanesque capital supporting the crossing, is a sculpture of the **Annunciation**, known as the Miracle of Light. Planned for or not, twice a year at the equinox, March 21 and September 22, at exactly 5 pm (solar time), a ray of sunlight focuses on the midsection of the Virgin.

A door from the north side of the crossing (usually locked) leads out to the shambles of the late seventeenth century cloisters, once no doubt very fine. To one side is a semi-restored wing of the monastery, now used as a dormitory for pilgrims.

Inside the church, take time for another viewing of the

saint's tomb, then descend into the **crypt** for a pleasant surprise. The saint no longer reposes in his fancy mausoleum upstairs. He is down here, once again finding his eternal rest in the simple sarcophagus that claimed his body a thousand years ago. The plain, rough limestone of his sarcophagus is placed with pleasing contrast on a large dais of polished granite.

Finally, before you leave, walk around outside to the rear of the church for a view of Juan's **apse**. The central apse is semicircular, with superimposed Romanesque blind arches. The shorter side apses nest as quarter circles where the central apse and crossing meet. Juan the bridge and road builder turned out to be quite an architect. These attractive walls have turned back the ravages of time for nearly a thousand years and have the look of being good for a thousand more.

From San Juan de Ortega the pilgrim track continues on to Burgos through a series of small villages, across at least one of Juan's bridges, and the Sierra de Atapuerca. Only parts of the way are passable by car, even using a four-wheel drive vehicle. Thus we return to N120, there turning right toward Burgos, now about twenty-five kilometers distant.

Passing through the low hills and villages approaching Burgos on N120 you begin to catch first sight of the Meseta, the vast plateau of Central Spain. Low rolling country at first, between Burgos and Leon it becomes a flat plain about a kilometer in altitude, with an occasional upthrust of rock on which sits the inevitable castle.

Arrival in central Burgos via N120 is on Calle Vitoria, a broad one-way boulevard that leads into the heart of the city. In the final half-kilometer of that street, and on side streets left and right, are many hotels of all classes. In-city parking for once is not impossible, and any one of these establishments is convenient for our in-city walking tours tomorrow. Besides our excursions on shoeleather, we will also use our wheels to see the Cartuja de Miraflores to the southeast, and Las Huelgas and the Hospital del Rey to the west.

BURGOS
THE SHIELD OF CASTILE

While Nájera was the spiritual and political heartland of Christian Spain during the middle years of the Reconquista, Burgos was where the action was. It became a strategic anchor for the Reconquista virtually from the time the Asturian kings burst out of the Cantabrian Cordillera to dig a Christian foothold into the Meseta for the first time in more than a hundred years. At first it was the staunch shield against which Muslim kings futilely launched thrust after thrust in defense of the Caliphate. Later it became the royal seat from which the kings of León and Castile expanded their domains further south against Islam and forged eastward at the expense of their Christian brothers in Navarra.

The Arabs and their Moorish minions didn't give up these lands without many fights, large and small. Unfortunately for the Caliph, Alfonso III of Asturias and León developed a winning strategy. During his nearly fifty years on the throne, he devised tactics that first expelled the Moors from the vicinity of the mountains and then pushed them far south across the Meseta. For that achievement Alfonso earned the title, "The Great."

Alfonso's plan was simple enough. Starting from the vicinity of León, he leap-frogged east and south with formidable lines of castles that he and his successors pushed relentlessly forward until they met the natural barriers of the Montes de Oca on the east and the Rio Duero to the south. These geographical limits defined the land that came to be known as Old Castile, the egg out of which modern Spain was hatched. That proliferation of castles gave the region its name.

In those early days, the knights Alfonso recruited to garrison the castles of Castile had to be anything but foppish and fainthearted gentlemen. Bearing the brunt of Moorish raids was daily fare. Rallying for major campaigns was a yearly event.

Both sides annually assembled their armies and sortied onto the Meseta to carve large chunks out of the territories of their adversaries. It was a way of life that offered adventure and the medieval version of upward mobility for landless knights in search of fiefs, titles, and well-dowered maids to wife.

One such recruit was a German freebooter by the name of Belchides, who wed the daughter of an Asturian Count, Diego Porcelos. In 884, at the urging of and financed by his father-in-law, Belchides carved out a piece of Moorish territory for himself, commanding a castle Porcelos built on a hill overlooking the Arlanzón River within sight of the Montes de Oca. He called the place his Burg, German for city or town. The Castilian suffix quickly made it Burgos.

As the furthermost bastion of the Asturian Reconquista, Belchides' fortress stood on the front line for centuries. First task was to fend off the Moors. Later Burgos led the fights against the kings of Navarra for rights to the Montes de Oca and the rich land of La Rioja. The accumulated lore of sieges and battles at Burgos led its people to refer to their city with pride as "The Shield of Castile" or "The Head of Castile."

Less than a century after its founding, Burgos became the political center of Old Castile. Its count, a feisty and formidable fighter named Fernan Gonzales, in 950 declared Castile independent of the king at León. We have already told how Fernando I (1037-65), Prince of Navarra and through his mother a descendant of Fernan Gonzales, inherited Castile. As a true prince, he promoted himself to king rather than accept demotion to the status of a mere count. Then, through marriage to the princess of León, Ferdinand combined Castile, León, Asturias and Galicia into the Christian powerhouse that eventually united all of Spain.

Fernando made Burgos his capital, the better to be near the scene of the continuing action against the Moors in Saragossa, Toledo and elsewhere in the south. So it remained for five hundred years, no matter that at various later moments Burgos shared the royal court with Valladolid and Toledo after the principal action of the Reconquista moved south into

Andalusia. The capital was not permanently established elsewhere, however, until the reign of Philip IV in 1621, who moved his court to Madrid.

What we discover in Burgos, then, is a modern city proudly displaying all the accouterments that come of a royal court that lavished its wealth on the place for half a millennium. We gain our first taste of it at the Cartuja de Miraflores. In the streets and churches of Burgos we also find the monuments – and the names – of the warriors and monarchs who preserved the reputation of Burgos as the Shield of Castile. Among them was the incomparable Rodrigo de Vivar, El Cid Campeador, who lived and fought here nearly a thousand years ago. And there are names of modern fighters, too, who no less shaped the face of modern Spain.

First was General Mola, who on July 23, 1936, after José Calvo Sotelo was assassinated by the Republicans, turned the army against the government. He established the Junta de Defensa Nacional here in Burgos, making it the de facto capital of the Nationalist insurgency. A few months later, on October 1, Francisco Franco – whose roots are found in this northwest region – was installed here as head of state for the new regime, which headquartered in Burgos throughout the civil war.

The selection of Burgos as the Nationalist capital was no accident. Its historic reputation as the Shield of Castile, and thus of all Spain, had not been forgotten.

Yet one name perennially overshadows those of all the monarchs and military despots who wielded power here. The man was Rodrigo de Vivar, El Cid Campeador, by turns military chieftain of kings, mercenary with sword for hire, and champion of his age. His deeds are legend. He had the blood of kings and his heirs were kings, but he never sought the throne. He was more powerful than most of the monarchs of his time, and at moments of his life was richer too. Why not a king, then? Because of an oath given to a jealous and suspicious sovereign to whom Rodrigo pledged fealty here in Burgos. Rodrigo was first of all a man of his word.

Burgos for a thousand years has been the city of El Cid.

Much of his legend was made here and in the nearby territories. His is a legend larger than life, yet the legend does insufficient justice to the real man. It romanticized the deeds of a hard-headed realist, a buccaneering man of his times whose greatest moral virtue was his word. When he gave it one could bank on it, even a murderous ingrate and thief who became his king. But Rodrigo was no gentleman. He was in full measure a man of his time: rough and ready, yet religious enough that in 1064, as a young man in his early twenties he, too, made the pilgrimage to Santiago.

A book could be written about the legend that grew up about El Cid, and many have. Early among them was a twelfth century epic, the *Poema de Mio Cid,* probably more often called *El Cantar de Mio Cid.* It occupies the same position in the Spanish mind that *The Song of Roland* has among the French, but more so. Roland has receded into mere literature. The legendary deeds of El Cid still retain vitality in Spanish consciousness. Nevertheless, the real man is far more interesting than the legend. The best recent work about him, in terms of scholarship and readability combined, is *The Quest for El Cid,* by Richard Fletcher (Knopf, 1990).

Rodrigo possessed natural gifts of horsemanship and mastery of arms, talents supported by uncommon physical strength and endurance. Add to that a steely courage well-tempered by common sense. In single combat Rodrigo thus became a formidable warrior and a dreaded adversary. Moreover, his habit was to be stubbornly loyal to whomever he pledged his word or sword. That combination first made Rodrigo the personal champion and trusted companion of King Sancho.

More than that, Rodrigo possessed an instinctive military sense, coupled with decisiveness and daring. With the experience of a few campaigns he became the greatest battlefield general of his age. Add to that a charisma that made men ready to fight to the death under his banner, no matter what the odds. Put such a mix together and you understand the basis for the legend of El Cid, a leader renowned for winning battles that were deemed unwinnable, and who defeated powerful enemies who should have overwhelmed El Cid just as they previously had destroyed everyone else who dared challenge their might.

Rodrigo achieved all that before he was thirty years of age.

The man's Christian name was Rodrigo Diaz de Vivar, Roderick Diaz of the town of Vivar, about ten kilometers north of Burgos. His father was a distinguished soldier who campaigned under Fernando I. His given name is of Gothic derivation, suggesting family connections with the old Gothic nobility that led the surge down from the mountains of Asturias two hundred years earlier. That his uncle was king of Navarra further assures the historian that his family had not come lately to nobility.

Rodrigo was well educated for the time, literate even in Latin, though never overly facile in that classical tongue. Later he became fluent in Arabic, and in his elder years enjoyed the company of Arab scholars, much as did his Sicilian contemporary and fellow freebooter, Roger de Hauteville. But his true calling was at arms. His was a natural talent demonstrated from the moment he began training at the age of twelve, which was the usual time for such things.

At age fourteen, befriended by the young Prince Sancho, Rodrigo was brought into the court of Fernando I. Dubbed a knight by Sancho's own hand, Rodrigo was nineteen when he embarked upon his first campaign under the command of Sancho himself. At age twenty two, in 1065 when Sancho became king of Castile, Rodrigo was made Armiger, the chief of Sancho's army and his personal champion at arms.

Sancho's reign lasted but seven years, during which time his Armiger became famous as El Campeador, a term taken from the Latin: campi doctor, literally meaning "teacher of the military arts," which in fact was one of the functions of the Armiger. But the title meant more than that. It recognized his exploits both in single combat and as a leader of troops in the field. In the eyes of his contemporaries he became "the man who wrote the book" on armed combat and war.

The sobriquet, "El Cid," came later. It comes from the Arabic, Es Sayd, which translates as My Lord, or Master. It was a title bestowed on Rodrigo by a coalition of five Arab kings that he defeated in battle, after which he graciously granted them life and freedom – and won their everlasting personal loyalty. From then on he was known as El Cid Campeador, The Lord and Master of Military Arts.

Sancho's brother and successor, Alfonso VI, distrusted and hated El Cid initially because the latter was the favorite of Sancho, whom most authorities believe Alfonso murdered. Alfonso's hatred was exacerbated when Rodrigo, chief of the army, proved himself so powerful that he was able to force Alfonso to swear publicly that he had no part in the death of Sancho. For that Alfonso bore a life-long grudge. Soon the king trumped up reasons to confiscate Rodrigo's lands and wealth and banish him from the kingdom with little more than his horse and the clothes on his back. Having sworn his loyalty, Rodrigo could not bring himself to rebel against the injustice of his sovereign, no matter that the army would have followed him to a man. So began El Cid's career as a soldier of fortune.

The popular legend would make Rodrigo a crusader who turned the tide against the Moslem invaders of Christian Spain. In fact, fate thrust El Cid into the world as a mercenary soldier for hire, selling his sword to the highest bidder, of which there were many among the covey of Christian and Moslem kinglets of the time.

The Caliphate at Córdoba by then had broken down. Moslem Spain had disintegrated into a quarrelsome nest of minor kingdoms that fought amongst themselves as often as against the Christian states of the north. Pledging his sword to the Moslem king of Saragossa, El Cid fought his own uncle, the king of Navarra, and won handily. Not long afterwards, still serving the Moslem king of Saragossa, he won an impossible victory at Almenar over the Count of Barcelona. The battle and its spoils made him both rich and famous. Later still, when the king of Catalonia came south with a much larger army than that fielded by El Cid, the Campeador wiped out the Catalans, captured the king and his train, looted the camp, and ransomed them off.

Such escapades soon gained Rodrigo a personal following of landless knights – both Christian and Moslem- out for adventure and booty. It was an army for hire that he led in the service of Moslem and Christian potentates alike – and finally to take territory in his own name. The place he took was Valencia and the region thereabouts, a Moslem stronghold that theretofore had fended off everything the Christian kings of Castile and Aragon could throw against it.

His greatest military achievements were against the Almoravides, a powerful African Moslem force that in the eleventh century set out to conquer all of Spain, Moslem and Christian alike. Alfonso VI met the Almoravides and his army was destroyed. No one, Christian or Moslem, was able to stop them. Only the unfinished conquest of the Moorish kingdoms of the south saved the Christians from the same fate as the old Gothic kingdom three hundred years earlier.

El Cid saw the troubles caused by the Almoravides among the Moorish states as an opportunity for conquests of his own. In 1094 El Cid took his army south and captured Valencia, an Almoravide city. The main Almoravide army, fresh from conquest of Bajadoz, then moved against Valencia to besiege it. El Cid chose to lead his forces out of his fortress and take on the much larger Moslem army outside the city walls. He destroyed the besiegers virtually to the last man, the first time an Almoravide army had met defeat by anyone, much less having the misfortune of being wiped out.

In 1097, an even larger Almoravide force came over from Africa and moved north against El Cid to avenge the loss. El Cid, although supported by troops led by the king of Aragon, was so greatly outnumbered he decided it would be better to escape and fight another day. But the Almoravides sprang a trap and forced their intended victim to fight. Again El Cid led his troops to an impossible victory. With it, the Almoravide threat to the Christian kingdoms was broken forever, although the Africans remained a power in the south for several decades to come.

Rodrigo had three children. His son, Diego, was killed battling the Moors near Toledo, where the Almoravides decimated the army of Alfonso VI. His daughter Christina married an Aragonese prince, and through her his grandson, García, became king of Navarra in 1134 when Navarra and Aragon split. Another of Christina's children, Blanca, became queen of Sancho III of Castile. Their son, Alfonso VIII, thus a great-grandson of El Cid, was the victor at the decisive battle of Las Navas de Tolosa in 1212. Rodrigo's other daughter, Maria, was wed to Ramon Berenguer III, Count of Barcelona, who was of the ruling house of Catalonia.

El Cid died in Valencia in 1099, probably of complications from old wounds. His wife carried his body back to Castile for burial at the ninth century Benedictine monastery of San Pedro de Cardeña, located about twenty kilometers south of here. Tradition has it that his warhorse, Babieca; his sword, Tizon; and later his wife, Jiminia, were all interred there with him. Their remains were stolen by French soldiers in the nineteenth century, and not returned to Spain until 1921. Rodrigo and Jiminia then were laid to rest, as we shall see, beneath the cathedral floor in Burgos.

La Cartuja de Miraflores

When "walking through" the pages of this book to check the details before calling it complete, my wife and I arrived early enough in Burgos that, after checking into our hotel, we visited the Cartuja de Miraflores that very afternoon. Don't miss seeing the place. It is ranked with the Burgos cathedral and the Convent of Las Huelgas Reales as one of the trio of "must" places to see during any visit to Burgos. Hours are daily 10:15 to 3 and 4 to 6.

To get there, from Calle Vitoria turn left a block to the Rio Arlanzón, and left again along the river for a kilometer before taking the bridge across it. On the other side, immediately bear right down the ramp leading off the bridge so as to take a left beneath the bridge and drive along a pleasant avenue through a parkland to the Cartuja. After a couple of kilometers you will see, in a wooded, park-like setting on a low hill, La Cartuja de Santa María de Miraflores (The Carthusian Order of Holy Mary of the Place for Viewing the Flowers).

These lands were once the hunting preserve of Enrique III and his son, Juan II, who constructed a small palace on the site 1441. Damaged by fire in 1452, it was donated by Juan to the Carthusians. Juan then ordered construction of a church at the monastery which would serve as a funerary chapel for himself (d 1454) and his queen, Isabel of Portugal, parents of Her Catholic Majesty, Queen Isabella. The church was designed in the Gothic style and construction begun by Juan de Colonia (John of Cologne), who was also architect in charge of work on Burgos cathedral. After the architect's death, the work was finished in 1499 by Juan's son, Simón.

The high altar and royal tomb, plus another tomb for Isabella's brother Alfonso, were the handiwork of Gil de Siloé, commissioned by Queen Isabella. We met Siloé's artistry earlier at San Juan de Ortega. There his style was Plateresque. Here we find something the experts say is Gothic, and thus somewhat different but no less elegant and flamboyant. Perhaps, but for me what they here call Gothic is still very much submerged in a froth of Plateresque.

The monastery is still very much active, so movement here is restricted to the church and its immediate environs. Approach is from the west, to discover a Gothic portal leading into what otherwise appears to be a rather plain-featured church, so different from the flamboyant Gothic the architect gained fame for on the Burgos cathedral. In the tympanum of this portal is a rather ordinary Pieta. Emblazoned to the left are the royal arms of Castile, while to the right of the portal is the personal insignia of King Juan II. High above, near the top of the facade of the church, an angel holds the royal arms of Ferdinand and Isabella.

Inside you find a single-aisle design with typical Gothic

vaulting above. Forward of the nave are a pair of choirs. The first, the Choir of the Brothers, contains stalls in a Renaissance style by Simón de Bueras, completed in 1558. Beyond is the Choir of the Fathers, with Plateresque stalls worked in dark walnut by Martin Sánchez of Valladolid in 1489.

All that is indubitably very fine work, but given your experience during recent days these choirs come to stand as more or less standard fare. But now we move forward a few steps and reach the chancel. What we discover here is very definitely not more of the same.

The chancel, elevated slightly above the floor of the nave, sits in a polygonal structure slightly broader than the nave. Above is a tall ribbed ceiling and (when the sun is right) a blazing display of Flemish stained glass. First to gain your attention is the centerpiece, the retable of the main altar, completed in 1499. It is intricately carved of wood, gilded and painted in many colors by the master, Siloé, assisted by Diego de la Cruz. The scenes on the retable are formed in a pattern of medallions, the principal and largest at the center devoted to the Crucifixion. You can also find the Last Supper and, not unexpectedly here along El Camino de Santiago, the figure of St. James (at lower right) in pilgrim garb. At the Last Supper, note Judas at the right end, clutching his bag of silver beneath the table. The gold laid on the work is said to have come from the first hoard brought back from the New World by Columbus when he came to Burgos to report to Ferdinand and Isabella on the achievements of his second voyage.

Before the altar, enclosed by a low grilled railing, is the tomb of Juan and his queen. On the north wall in a niche is the tomb of their son, Alfonso. Both tombs are the masterful work of Siloé, and considered to be among the world's finest funerary monuments. In this instance his work is indeed described best as Gothic sculpture at its acme.

The regal tomb is shaped as an eight-pointed star. It is worked in exquisite detail in white marble of local origin, believed to be from a quarry near Santovenia, the village we passed through on the way to San Juan de Ortega. The reclining figures of the king and queen (she holding an open book) are surrounded by biblical personalities, some of which have been vandalized – a product of the Napoleonic Wars when French troops spitefully looted and abused the monuments of a land they were being driven out of by Wellington and his Spanish allies.

Vandalism notwithstanding, the work of Siloé here is regarded as perhaps the greatest piece of Spanish Gothic sculpture ever worked. It is resplendent with cherubs, scrolls, canopies, armorial crests and lots more, the intricate and precise detail of which defies description. Yet despite the bits of gaudy nonsense involved in the display, there is nothing here that suggests the romantic and superficial fantasies of the Baroque. There is a realism, a naturalness carved into the essence of the figures of the royal pair and everything else that evokes the archetypes lodged in the soul of Spain at the moment of its greatest power and grandeur.

The monument of Alfonso, whose early death gave the throne to Isabella, is no less highly regarded. It was worked in alabaster by Siloé, and depicts Alfonso, kneeling at a low table, along with a panorama of animals and carved scenes. It is said that the man wearing pince-nez at the lower left of the sculpture is none other than a self-portrait of the artist himself. The adjacent retable of the Annunciation is a work by Pedro Berruguete dating from the same period as everything else here: the latter decade of the fifteenth century.

Earlier today at San Juan's mausoleum we mentioned Siloé's connection with his royal patron, Isabella, whose munificence made possible the magnificence of what you discover here – and who is no less responsible for much of what you will see on the morrow in Burgos. Here at Miraflores, of course, her generosity is not unexpected. What she did here was simply to memorialize her parents, for whom she had deep respect, and her brother, whose untimely death became her ticket to historical immortality as the female half of Los Reyes Católicos.

Of the pair, Isabella was no doubt greatest both in mind and charismatic personality. Ferdinand was cunning but un-enterprising, too quick to give up the struggle when the going got tough. Isabella made a conscious effort to be on the scene to give him backbone when necessary. Indeed, in the final campaigns against the Moorish kingdom of Granada, when Ferdinand was ready to chuck it all and go home – and the morale of the army suffered from their knowledge of his weakness of spirit – Isabella dramatically appeared on the scene astride a prancing war horse, decked out in her own suit of armor. With lance and battle pennant flying she paraded among the troops. The sight of the royal Amazon in her shiny metal garb provoked the army to new efforts and shamed Ferdinand to once again take up the fight and move on to claim the victory that Isabella knew was at hand.

A mere glance at Spanish history convinces one that Isabella was author of the Spanish state not only as the government of a nation, but as a monarchical institution recognized by aristocrat and peasant alike as the legitimate center of authority from Gibraltar to the Pyrenees. She was, quite literally, the mother of Modern Spain, dragging Ferdinand and everyone else along with the inevitability of her iron will. While the kings of the early Reconquista had made Spain possible, Isabella realized the fullness of that possibility and brought the Reconquista to fruition.

Where Ferdinand was self-centered and greedy, Isabella saw her first duty as monarch to tend to the prosperity of her kingdom. Key to that achievement was the benevolence of God, which she sought out through a life-long campaign to propagate her Catholic faith. She thus originated the policies that ultimately gave Moor and Jew alike the choice of baptism or exile, and led to four centuries of the infamous Inquisition. Cruel, arbitrary and evil by our standards, the product was a Spain which otherwise might have torn apart into a dozen pieces. Multiculturalism was and is a prescription for disaster, as modern Europe is just discovering the hard way.

Ferdinand would have closed his fist and denied Columbus the financial backing to discover the way west to the New

World; Isabella had the imagination to accept Columbus' vision, and her beloved Spain was rewarded when the reality turned out to be entirely different and much richer than their wildest dreams. Out of Isabella's entrepreneurial gamble developed the wealth that, combined with the spirit evolved from the centuries-long Reconquista, made Spain the first world power in the West since the fall of Rome.

Later on, the power and wealth of Spain were squandered by Charles V and those who followed – much as has happened to America in recent decades under Lyndon Johnson and his successors – weakening the state until Napoleon disposed of the Spanish monarchy and placed his brother, Joseph, on the throne. The monarchy never afterwards recovered its vitality or the link with the people that Isabella forged. That situation bred the Carlist Wars of the nineteenth century, and the dictatorships of the twentieth century, before Juan Carlos amazed the skeptics and established a strong, constitutional monarchy that even the Republicans and Socialists respected

The same greatness of vision that allowed Isabella to create modern Spain also gave full rein to Siloé here at Miraflores. And we will view more of his work and her influence upon the arts of her era as we explore the extraordinary wonders of Burgos.

Before you make your way out of this monastic church, visit the Chapel of San Bruno, situated next to the Choir of the Fathers. There you find in the stark white plastered plainness of the chapel a strangely lifelike painted wooden statue of the saint by the Portuguese sculptor Manuel Perrerira. As the monks say of it, "Why doesn't this monk speak?" Obviously because he observes the order's rule of silence.

Finally, next to the Choir of the Brothers, is the tiny Chapel of Nuestra Señora de Miraflores, containing seventeenth century frescos dealing with the life of the Virgin. Next to it is the Chapel of the Reliquaries which, as the name implies, contains relics of a company of saints shelved in the retable.

Perhaps by now the crowd around the royal tombs has thinned. If so, before making our way back to Burgos, have one more leisurely look at the work of Gil de Siloé. It is the experience of a lifetime as far as the art of the Spanish Renaissance is concerned. Surely you will find more of Gil's work in Burgos on the morrow, but here, in my estimation, is his masterpiece.

The Pilgrim Route through Burgos

We begin our explorations of the Shield of Castile by following the pilgrim route through Burgos to the cathedral. That route takes a modern pilgrim along Calle de Vitoria, familiar to us as the route of our own arrival. On the near side of the canal-like tributary of the Arlanzón, turn right on Calle de San Lesmes. Across the way after thirty meters or so you spot a fragment of the old **city walls** next to which the tributary served as a natural moat. Hemmed in by modern buildings, what you see are the remnants of a round tower and a bit of the adjacent wall.

After a hundred meters you come to a plaza where, to the right, stands the Marceliano Santa María **Museum.** This is an art museum devoted to the work of a local impressionist painter (1866-1952) for whom the museum is named. It was installed in the renovated Benedictine Monastery of San Juan Evangelista, which dates from the fifteenth and sixteenth centuries. Arriving there we have come upon the road trod by the pilgrims of old, who gained shelter at this monastery located just outside the old walls of the city.

In the center of the square stands a bronze equestrian **statue** of Alfonso III. The statue was erected in 1984 in commemoration of the founding of Burgos a thousand years earlier. For it was during the reign of Alfonso that Diego Porcelos engineered the founding of the city with the strong arm and sword of his German son-in-law.

Across the plaza is the Church of San Juan Lesmes, patron saint of Burgos and one-time prior of this monastery. Juan Lesmes was a Frenchman invited to Castile by Alfonso VI to help the Castilian Church replace the prevailing Mozarabic liturgy with that of the Latin Church. This came after Cardinal Rainerius (who became Pope Paschal II) in 1190 held a Church council in León that read the riot act to the Spanish Church, enforcing an edict by Pope Gregory VII, the great reformer of the Latin Church, to fall into line with the Latin liturgy or else. After succeeding in that task, Juan stayed to care for pilgrims. Recall that in Nájera we learned that similar liturgical reforms were being instituted by the Navarran king at about the same time, no doubt for the same reasons.

The original **church** on the site, built in 1074, was Romanesque, replaced by a Gothic edifice in the fourteenth century, then remodeled more than once in later times. The church of today is rather ordinary fare, nicely vaulted inside, with a good Gothic main portal and a retable that is worth a moment to view. Inside is the tomb of the saint, his figure carved recumbent upon it.

Across the stream west of the church was the San Juan Gate of the medieval city. The pilgrim route continues across the lion-guarded **bridge**, through the one-time gate and beyond along Calle de San Juan. After the street jogs a couple of hundred meters farther along, occasionally visible in the distance above the roof tops is the hill topped by the ruins of the fortress that for centuries was the Cabeza de Castile. We will visit it on another day.

After a couple hundred meters, at Calle de Santander, one of the city's leading shopping thoroughfares, depart the pilgrim track for a brief detour. Go left down Calle de Santander for about a hundred meters. On your left you will find the **Casa del Cordon**, named for the peculiar carving of a Franciscan monk's waist cord on the facade around the main portal. To see the portal, on the far end of the building, turn left and walk toward the next plaza about twenty meters. In the tympanum formed by the inverted "V" shaped by the cord carved above the door are a dazzling sunburst and the armorial shields of the original owner of the palatial residence. That owner was the fifteenth century Constable (army chief), Don Pedro Fernández de Velasco, conqueror of Granada.

While house guests of Don Pedro in this residence, Ferdinand and Isabella on April 23, 1497, received Columbus and his gold after his second voyage to the New World. Years later Ferdinand, a tired old man and again in residence here, listened to Ponce de León tell of the fabled Fountain of Youth – and hopefully sent Ponce off to find it. Now the building is a bank, since only money is forever young.

Backtrack up Calle de Santander to Calle San Juan, turn left and resume the pilgrim track. Note that the street name has changed to Calle de los Avellanos at the jog to the left, still proceeding west. Another hundred meters brings you to the Calle San Gil. There turn right up the hill for another short detour. After about thirty meters, around the corner on the right, is the **church of San Gil**.

San Gil dates from the fourteenth century, but has been remodeled often times since. This is a church that appears hardly extraordinary, but go in anyhow. There you discover the sixteenth-century Chapel of the Nativity, the masterwork of Felipe Bigarny. Most extraordinary is its star vaulting and retable. Virtually anywhere but at Burgos this chapel would be a sight excelling all such sights for a hundred kilometers in all directions. But this is Burgos where the treasures of Miraflores and the cathedral eclipse the beauties of San Gil and everything else between Logroño and León.

In the Capilla Mayor, the wooden retable is Baroque behind an altar by Diego de Siloé and a fifteenth-century gilded pulpit. An unusual painting of Christ hangs in the Capilla de Santo Cristo.

Outside the church, look up to your right before descending to the street again. Far above, atop the hill, is the castle that formed the boss of the Shield of Castile. Should you wish later to climb to the **fortress** Porcelos and Belchides built on the hill above their town, this way offers access to the easiest route. After a block, bear left up Calle Corazas which leads into the park surrounding the ruined castle. As you might expect, it was a place well known to El Cid. Among other things, he was married there, attended by the king himself.

The final edition of the castle was created by an extensive remodeling in the thirteenth century. It was made uninhabitable by fire in the eighteenth century (1736), then blown up by the retreating French in 1813. We don't plan to walk up there now, but the way is not difficult. The view from the broken ramparts is excellent.

The castle can also be visited by automobile along the same route. Alternatively, leave Plaza de la Catedral going west on Calle Nuño Rasura and wend your way up the hillside to gain access to the road that climbs past the site of El Cid's own villa, then through the park on the far side of the fortress ruins.

Now, descending from San Gil, you find that Calle Avellanos now becomes Calle de Fernan Gonzáles, along which you resume the pilgrim path. The massive hulk of the cathedral is now dead ahead but nearby buildings make it still out of sight at a distance of about three hundred meters. The street soon slopes down to where you stand alongside the towering mass of the great **cathedral** on your left.

For the while, simply let your eyes feast on the place as we walk, taking in the larger views of things. For before exploring the cathedral, we have another memorable church to visit. It is the church of San Nicolás, on your right immediately after you are past the cathedral. Over its main portal you will be greeted by a seated San Nicolás created by Juan de Colonia, artist and architect, patriarch of three generations of the Colonia family who worked both on this church and the cathedral across the way.

The construction of San Nicolás was financed by a wealthy merchant family in the fifteenth century. Its best feature is its massive **altarpiece**, or retable, donated by a member of that family. It was carved in alabaster in 1505 by Francisco de Colonia from a design by his father, Simón. In contrast to most retables seen during our journey, here we discover only a touch of color, gilt, added sparsely and only where emphasis appears appropriate. Its magnificence extends wall to wall, floor to ceiling. Center of it all is the Virgin encircled by a flight of angels. Most of the remainder is devoted to scenes from the life of San Nicolás. Someone counted all the carved figures in those scenes. The number is said to be 465, which is a startling amount no matter that the piece is renowned for its quality rather than the sheer quantity of its representations. Again we find Gothic Plateresque at its best, a clear rival to the brilliance of Siloé's artistry at the Cartuja de Miraflores. All of it was the work of three generations of the Colonia family.

Leaving the church, walk across the street to the railing. There look down into the **Plaza** de la Catedral. From this lofty perch you get what I consider the best view of the cathedral of Burgos, seen in all its Gothic splendor. This sight will be remembered vividly for the rest of your life. There is nothing like it anywhere else in the world. It is a structure in which the Gothic of Germany and France was given a fantastic Spanish Mudéjar flavor found both in the extravagant detail and in the grand plan of the thing.

As you stand overlooking the plaza in front of this massive edifice, built of an especially tough white limestone, let me tell you something of its history, which explains its singular character.

Burgos was not a cathedral city until Alfonso VI ordered the bishopric moved from Oca and built a cathedral on the site in 1075. A hundred and fifty years later that original structure was torn down to make way for something more appropriate for the Cabeza de Castile. In 1221, Fernando III celebrated his wedding by laying the cornerstone of the present cathedral – but it was centuries before it took the form you see today.

Some say an unknown French architect designed and supervised local artisans in the thirteenth century construction, which included the central nave, aisles and principal entrances. Others attribute the design to a master builder named Enrique, who designed the León cathedral. After studying both, you may agree with me that the same hand definitely was not at work in both places.

The development and adornment of chapels, cloister and the like occupied the fourteenth century, and major construction

170

did not resume until the fifteenth century. Then the front spires and the Constable's Chapel at the far rear of the edifice were erected. The gigantic lantern above the transept dates from the sixteenth century, and that made the whole into what you see today – the third largest cathedral in Spain (after Toledo and Seville) and one that the experts place among the dozen or so finest and most distinctively wrought cathedrals in all the world.

Our plan is to examine the exterior now, then return at opening time tomorrow. That strategy allows a leisurely examination of the interior during the best light of day, so as to gain the full effect of the place.

The **west facade** fronting the square contains the main Puerta Real, also called the Puerta de Santa María, with two other entrances to the sides. The facade was reworked to the present dreary configuration at its lower level in the eighteenth century. Its fantastic hundred-meter tall openwork spires, the rose window and balustrade capping the stone tracery between them, are the work of John of Cologne (Juan de Colonia) in the fifteenth century. In the gallery above the rose window are eight kings of Castile. The lower frieze depicts the Biblical kings. The two minor doors have bas reliefs that are the work of Juan Poves in 1653.

The detail of it all is indescribable, and we attempt it only in the most general terms. For those with more than a casual interest in the place, purchase of a well-illustrated cathedral guidebook is recommended. One thing such a book is sure to mention is that the open-work spires and other decor of the structure give it a strong resemblance to the cathedral in Cologne, Germany, where John grew up and learned the art of the master builder. Why did he move to Spain? That was where the money was.

Now turn your attention to the magnificent **lantern** that rises above the crossing. Octagonal, each angle is filled by a column so profusely decorated that its internal structure is lost in the froth of ornamentation. Between the columns are paired windows fringed with stone traceries, with balconies at each level and wedding-cake spires above. The original lantern tower was built by three generations of the family of John of Cologne, including himself, his son Simón, and grandson Francisco. Jean de Vallejo rebuilt the lantern after a structural failure in the mid-sixteenth century, without disturbing the style of it all.

Now retrace your steps along the northern exterior of the cathedral. First we pass along the Capilla Santa Tecla, its external face rather plain-feathered compared to the main structure. Beyond, abutting the north transept, is the exterior of the Capilla Santa Ana, after which one arrives at the north portal of the main cathedral, the **Puerta de la Coronería**. This is the door the pilgrims once entered as they paused at the cathedral for devotions in a chapel dedicated to St. James. But don't expect to find that chapel when we explore the interior of the cathedral. Santiago's chapel was dismantled and the space taken over by the newer Chapel of Santa Tecla .

This beautiful portal, the Puerta de la Coronería, is a thirteenth century work. The tympanum features Christ in Judgment, with the blessed and the damned sorted out below. Note the detail of the carvings of the Apostles on the stone doorposts, even to the flowing fabric of their garments. These are considered to be masterpieces of the time. On the right post is Santiago himself, Bible clutched to his breast by his left hand, and a sword (broken) grasped by his right. Inside the portal (which ordinarily is not open), descending to the main level of the cathedral almost eight meters below, is a double staircase by Diego de Siloé, the famous Golden Stair (1525) with gilded bannisters and carved reliefs. We will see it when we study the interior.

To the left of the Puerta de la Coronería, in an alcove down a stairway, is the **Puerta de la Pellejería**. That doorway, located on the cathedral's main floor level, is an early sixteenth century Plateresque fantasy of detail by Francisco de Colonia. Its reliefs depict the martyrdoms of John the Baptist and John the Evangelist, the latter steaming in a pot of boiling oil.

After passing the tall exterior of the transept you now can

observe the rear of the cathedral. There the Capilla Mayor abuts the transept while the **Constable's Chapel** is crowned by still another set of glorious openwork spires that shoot skyward from its octagonal tower. Note how the heights of the spires, from the tallest at the fore of the cathedral, to these above the Constable's Chapel, step down in perfect proportion.

The Constable's Chapel is the architectural design of Simón de Colonia. While impressive enough from the exterior, tomorrow you will learn why many experts consider the chapel's interior design and decor to be the greatest feat of artistry in architecture that comes to us from the Spanish Renaissance. It is that work which made Bigarny's Chapel of the Nativity at San Gil pale by comparison.

Now continue around the cathedral and descend along its east end to Calle Paloma, where you turn right along the exterior of the cloister. Where the cloister's wall ends at a strange, round tower with a fat and fancy Gothic spire, you have arrived at the broad expanse of the Plaza del Rey San Fernando. On your right, several stages of a broad stairway lead up to the most beautiful portal of the cathedral.

This is **El Sarmental Portal**. The tympanum is carved with the figures of the Four Evangelists, each busy writing at his desk, while Christ teaches and other Apostles look on. This is the door pilgrims enter today when they pause to pray on their way to Santiago de Compostela. Above the portal is a nice rose window with more stone tracery above, featuring a baker's-dozen angels, topped by a balustrade with Gothic spires to each side. Pause a moment to appreciate the elegance of it all. We will see it again, closer up, tomorrow.

Now walk around to the west front of the cathedral, standing close to look up and get a dizzying impression of the immensity of the place. Also examine whatever exterior detail grabs your attention. Take whatever time you wish, viewing the details of the facade and towers from near and far and several perspectives. Each sight of the place seems entirely novel to the eye.

El Sarmental, the Pilgrims' Portal

Now depart the Plaza de la Catedral via the narrow street at the west side of the square. In a few steps beyond a hundred meters you approach another church, much smaller than those you have visited so far today. It stands to your right. Walk to its far end, where there is a tiny plaza, a place full of history. We came here for that, and not to see this commonplace old church.

This is the **church of Santa Agueda**. In the year 1072, Rodrigo de Vivar, Armiger of the murdered King Sancho, forced the new king, Alfonso VI, to place his hand on a silver lock and swear not once, but three times, that he had no part in the murder of his brother, King Sancho. Around where you stand were gathered the lords and ladies of Castile, plus the commonfolk. Their eyes bulged wide with amazement as an angry king reluctantly obeyed the demands of Rodrigo, who only then would kneel and swear fealty to the new king. And no matter how ill-treated he was by Alfonso in later years, Rodrigo never broke that oath even though it was within his power to have driven Alfonso from the throne virtually at any time.

Now return to the cathedral square, cross it and continue east, making a jog to the right to reach the Plaza de Jose Antonio. Here you are but a stone's throw from the Calle de Vitoria and your hotel where we began our explorations.

El Cid and the Arco de Santa María

We continued our walk through the history of Burgos late on an afternoon after a tardy lunch. Walk with us toward the river and the Plaza de Miguel Primo de Rivera, dedicated to the dictator who ruled Spain from 1923 to 1930. A year later, Alfonso XIII fled the country, the Republic was established, and its radical excesses brought on civil war and the establishment of Franco's regime here in Burgos.

Highlight the square, however, is not the statue of a dictator, but the famed equestrian statue of El Cid. It is a modern work (1955) by Juan Cristobal, with the crusty Campeador in full armor astride his warhorse, Babieca. He is brandishing Tizon, his mighty sword, in the direction of the Moorish enemy to the south in al-Andalus.

There is nothing pretty about the image Juan Cristobal created, but it is memorable in the extreme. This fierce and confident warrior, full beard flying in the breeze, conveys the character of a personality something other than the man portrayed by the clean-cut Charlton Heston who played El Cid on the screen. Heston came across as someone we might admire as capable and courageous. A gentleman.

Cristobal's artistry personifies the fiery charisma of the legend, the ask-no-quarter give-no-quarter freebooter ready and able to ride roughshod over whatever enemy dared stand in his way. Whether your imagination approves of the image or not, the spirit and character of the real man probably were captured quite accurately in the figure represented here.

Now exit the square toward the river, which you pass over on the **San Pablo Bridge.** Mounted on the bridge are eight stone figures depicting the principal characters in the life of El Cid. The sculpture is modern, of the past century. Personages include his wife, Jiminia; his son, Diego; and the Moorish king of Saragossa. They and the others are identified on plaques beneath the respective statues.

Beyond the bridge continue straight ahead about two hundred meters to Calle Miranda. Turn right on that street; then, after another hundred meters, you arrive at the **Burgos Museum**, otherwise known as the Casa de Miranda (1545). It opens at 5 pm for two hours. Buy a museum guide for information on the extensive detail of the place.

Casa de Miranda is a refurbished Renaissance palace containing a fine collection of Roman and Visigothic antiquities. Adjacent is the Casa de Angulo, a building of similar origins, containing items from the Reconquista and later, including some beautiful work by Gil de Siloé. One such piece is the tomb of Juan de Padilla, who died in the assault on Granada (1492), which ended the almost eight hundred year Arab presence in Spain.

From the museum continue west on Calle Miranda about a hundred meters to the Plaza de Vega. There turn right toward the river, which you cross on the **Puente de Santa María**. Ahead of you on the far side is a stupendous pile of masonry called the Arco de Santa María. Rising behind it in the distance are the Gothic spires of the cathedral, and behind that the hill where the counts of Castile built and defended the fortress that became the Cabeza de Castilla (The Head of Castile).

The **Arco de Santa María** is the front door to all that. It sits on the site of the medieval main gate of the city, the same gate through which El Cid rode off to banishment and the creation of a legend. The gate you see is a fourteenth century functional structure turned into a sixteenth century show-off piece with crenelated battlements and round towers above and to each side.

Adorning the facade are niches filled with statues of the city's historic greats. In the first tier are the two judges (Nuño Rasura and Lain Calvo) who established a civil government in the early city, and (in the center niche) the founder, Diego Porcelos, father-in-law of the German soldier of fortune who defended the castle and named the city. Above are Fernan Gonzáles, who turned the city into his own autonomous county seat; Carlos V, the erstwhile Holy Roman Emperor who reigned at the time the facade was built; and El Cid. The winged warrior on the face of the blind arch above them is the militant archangel St. Michael while, within a canopied niche atop the whole, reigns Santa María with her Christ Child cradled in her lap.

After a close-up study of the famous portal, turn back toward the river and walk east along the **Paseo del Espolon.** By this time the way should be thronged with the people of Burgos out on their evening promenade. Join them. Stroll the three hundred meters or so back to the Plaza de Miguel Primo de Rivera. Enjoy the feel of a Spanish evening among the paseantes of Burgos. Then work your way back along the Espolon to some sidewalk cafe that struck your fancy. Enjoy a bit of refreshment, or perhaps an aperitif in anticipation of the dinner you plan for tonight.

Burgos Cathedral: The Interior

This second day in Burgos is devoted to the interior of the cathedral (open 9:30 to 1; 4 to 7) and, later, to whatever your fancy may be for the remainder of the day. Be on your way early and spend an hour or so window-shopping, for we will pass along some of the city's more elegant shopping streets.

Later today you may return for purchase of an irresistible something seen in one of the shops.

We again commence our explorations by heading up Calle de Vitoria to the Plaza de Miguel Primo de Rivera. Stay to the right and exit the northwest corner of the square. A block further on is the smaller Plaza de Santo Domingo, across which is the foot of Calle Santander where you walked yesterday. As promised, here is your opportunity to have a look into the shops along it.

Don't spend all your time on Calle Santander. There are other nearby streets that deserve a look. A few steps further west is Calle Moneda on the right, and another square on the left. This is the Plaza de José Antonio, sometimes called the **Plaza Mayor**. It is exactly that – the largest square in the city. It is ringed with two and three storey buildings with arcaded walks at street level. Off the arcades are all sorts of shops, cafes, and what have you, making it one of the busiest spots in the city. On its south side is the Ayuntamiento (Casa Consistorial), a seventeenth century edifice by Ventura Rodríguez, the same architect who made such a mess of the cathedral's lower facade.

Depart the square at the west end, up a street that takes you through an underpass to Calle Paloma. Turn left and soon you are in familiar territory alongside the cathedral cloister. You know the way from there to **El Sarmental**, which always deserves another look. There is no hurry. Take time.

Entering the cathedral you find yourself in the south transept, probably awestricken by your first impression of the place. At your left is the entrance to the Chapel of the Visitation. To the right a fascinating wooden **doorway** leads to the cloister (but is not the visitor's entrance, as you will learn later). These doors, with splendidly carved panels, are worth more than a moment's study before exploring the bowels of the cathedral.

Portrayed on these panels is the Entry into Jerusalem and Jonah emerging from the whale's mouth. Also see Peter and Santiago seated in the lower panels. The portal surrounding the

178

doorway contains archivolts and side posts carved only with florals, making the tragic scene within the tympanum all the more effective. There we have a polychrome representation of the Descent from the Cross.

Our plan is to tour the place in a clockwise direction, which leads us to the nearby Chapel of the Visitation first and to the cloister last. There is no way we can describe the details of this fabulous place in a way that would satisfy a church buff or someone expecting to delve into the most arcane elements of religious art and its history. For such a level of interest, a host of guidebooks devoted to this cathedral are available in the souvenir shop beside the cloister entrance nearby. Hopefully you will find one that is a true guide and not merely a general, helter-skelter presentation of a bucketful of fascinating facts and pictures. If you find only the latter, let these pages be your guide, and use the other as a supplement filling in the details where we leave off. For this book is intended for the casual traveler more interested in history than in artistic detail, no matter that at times the beauty of things demand that we rise to a greater measure of such detail.

In the Chapel of the **Visitation**, designed by Juan de Colonia, the most remarkable piece is the tomb of Alonso de Cartagena by Gil de Siloé, whose work we encountered first at San Juan de Ortega and again at the Cartuja. After you have seen what he has worked here in this gigantic cathedral, you must stand in astonishment at the inventive mind of this master of the sculptor's art. How could he have accomplished so much in a single lifetime? Only because Queen Isabella gave his imagination free rein and backed it with the wealth of a united Spain fed by the virgin riches of the Americas.

Now proceed toward the crossing. You cannot keep your eyes away from the interior of the **lantern** that towers fifty-four meters above your head. The polychrome fan-like adornments that rise above the piers to support the octagonal tower with its double windows and star-ribbed ceiling are a combination able to take your breath away – and not just because you are bending your neck far back to take it all in.

The eight-pointed star with pendant bosses in the center of the dome, with its stone traceries through which light filters down, surrounded by the geometry of the ribbing above the side windows, is an engineering marvel that rests heavily on design innovations borrowed from Arab architects to the south. Don't expect ever to see its like again. Not on this scale, anyhow.

Give your neck a respite and look left down the nave. It is about half the length of a football field. Total length of the church is eighty-four meters. High above are Gothic windows full of stained glass. The vaulting is Gothic with Plateresque decor, the work of Felipe de Borgoña (aka Bigarny) and Juan de Vallejo. In the center of the nave, shielded by a lofty grille topped by a Crucifixion and the grieving Marys, are opposing banks of choir stalls, 103 in all, carved in walnut by Felipe Bigarny in the early sixteenth century. Depicted are Biblical scenes and not a little mythological nonsense. The man obviously had a sense of humor tolerated even by the Inquisition.

At the center of the choir, carved of wood and covered with enameled copper, is the **tomb** of the Bishop, Maurice, who was charged with getting the building of this cathedral off the ground back in the thirteenth century. Just a glance around tells you there is no doubt that he not only made it happen, he made it first rate to boot.

Now walk back along the south aisle of the nave where the first side chapel is the Chapel of the **Presentation**. Here the principal work is the tomb of Gonzáles Diez, Bishop of Lerma, carved by Felipe Bigarny as sort of an encore to his choir stalls. Another tomb by Bigarny is that of Diego de Bilbao, whose place of eternal repose is adjacent to the pier to your right. The unusually sedate retable, executed in Neo-Classical style, is by Sebastiano del Piombo.

Near the far southwest corner of the nave, which you now approach, turn left down a broad passage. Beyond a pair of glass doors it becomes the Capilla del Santíssimo Cristo. It contains a **Crucifixion** that may be shocking for those not warned in advance, simply because of the stark realism of the crucified figure of the Cristo de Burgos. The illusion before you is the crucified Christ in the flesh, an effect that even the master illusionists of Hollywood would be hard put to improve upon. More, it has stood here for hundreds of years in apparent incorruptibility, which is somewhat of a miracle in itself. Some report that at Easter time it both sweats and bleeds from the wounds caused by the crown of thorns.

Pilgrims have left records telling of it since the thirteenth century, and it may be older. Some of its disturbing effect is soothed by its background. It stands tastefully framed against a deep purple backdrop and carved, natural wood retable.

Church lore attributes the work to St. Nicodemus, said to have modeled it from memory of the living Christ immediately after the Crucifixion. It was said to have appeared floating in the sea off Spain, from whence it was rescued. The life-like figure has real human hair and fingernails, and once was said to have human skin also. Lately it has been determined that the skin belonged to a buffalo. No matter, it is too real and intimately personal and we were relieved to get back into the precise orderliness and expanse of the main structure.

Crossing the nave near the west portals of the cathedral, high up at the very top of the far wall near the rear of the north aisle, is another bizarre feature known as the **Papamoscas**, the Flycatcher Clock. This sixteenth century timepiece marks the hours by opening the mouth of the comic gentleman who sounds the bell as the hour is struck. For it does keep proper time.

The rose window in the west wall is large, ornate and pleasing enough in design, but the stained glass lacks something of the quality you will find, for example, at León. The problem is that all the original glass in this building was blown out by concussion when the Napoleon's troops blew up the castle on the hill behind the cathedral.

Here at the rear of the nave by the main doorway, turn for a view forward. High up, the triforium galleries are blind, but with charming stone traceries providing decoration. Note the male and female heads decorating the upper arches.

Walk forward on the north aisle of the nave. Immediately to the left is the newest of the chapels, the Capilla de **Santa Tecla**, a design executed between 1731 and 1736 by José de Churriguera. While not one of the better efforts of the Churrigueresque style of the Spanish Baroque made popular by the Churriguera family, it is one of the few pure examples of the style encountered on our travels with St. James. The blue and red stucco decor of the retable and stuccoed dome and ceilings is a bit unsettling after the quiet grays and browns of the main edifice. This chapel originally was the Capilla de Santiago that for pilgrims was a mandatory place to visit. The saint is still remembered here in the presence of the equestrian statue of Santiago high above the altar.

Just this side of the transept is **St. Anne's Chapel**, built by Simón de Colonia in 1488. There the main attraction is the retable made by Gil de Siloé and Diego de la Cruz. Heavily gilded, you find St. Anne meeting Joachim, the Virgin and her Christ child, and much more. The prominent tomb is that of a Bishop named Acuña. And here as elsewhere in this cathedral, the sculptural adornment of the place seems unending, as if there was no will to ever stop adding detail upon detail, Apostles piled on prophets, angels to the side of saints, or whatever.

Again at the transept, look left to its north wall. There, mounting to the Coronería Portal, is Diego de Siloé's fantastic **Golden Staircase** that we mentioned as we toured the exterior. The flowing marble work with its statuary and reliefs, presided over by a pair of crouched griffins, was done by Diego himself. The gilded ironwork was by a Frenchman named Hilaire. The portal itself is hidden behind a protective wooden doorway.

Forward of the north end of the transept is the tiny Chapel of San Nicolás, the oldest chapel in the cathedral, but for all that little tended.

Now we are back at the crossing. Take your eyes off the attraction of the lantern for a moment and glance down at the pavement beneath. Inlaid in the floor are the reddish **funerary tablets** of El Cid and Jiminia, who found repose here when their bones were returned from France a century after being stolen from their resting place at San Pedro de Cardeña during the Peninsular War. And also look south to the rose window above El Sarmental. I think you will admire it much more than the one seen at the west end of the nave.

Look forward from the crossing into the **Capella Mayor**, with its sixteenth century retable. It is a bit different from most we have seen, in that its Gothic high relief is contrasted with Neo-Classical background structures. It is the work of a team of brothers, Rodrigo and Martín de la Haya. The cathedral, dedicated to the Virgin Mary, naturally features the Madonna as the centerpiece of the retable, surrounded by scenes from her life. The tombs at the altar foot belong to members of the royal family of Alfonso X.

Walking into the ambulatory, note that the rear wall of the retable is decorated with what is called a **trasaltar**, on which are carved scenes of the Passion, the Ascent to Calvary, the Crucifixion, Descent from the Cross, and the Ascencion, all by Felipe Bigarny. Seated below are the church fathers and twelve Apostles, the latter dolefully contemplating the awful things happening above them.

Directly across from Bigarny's triumph of artistry is the entrance to the **Capella del Condestable,** the richness of which makes Bigarny's work suddenly seem something less than first rate. The facade above and around the doorway is but an indication of the fabulous wealth of sculptures within. It is Gothic sculpture infused with Spanish Plateresque on an architectural design that hearkens back to the age of the Romanesque. As within the chapel itself, the tremendous detail of artistry on this portal defies description.

The Constable's Chapel is just that. It was commissioned in 1482 by Hernández de Velasco, victor at Granada, Constable of Castile. You perhaps remember that we visited his once palatial Casa del Cordón on Calle Santander. Here you find him with his wife, recumbent in their home for eternity amidst the grandest single expression of monumental sculpture in all of Spain, Miraflores possibly excepted.

Juan de Colonia created the basic design but his son Simón was responsible for actually building the structure that contains such a wealth of artistry. Look to Juan's imagination for the origin of the star vaulting and lantern, octagonal cupola and stone tracery. The decor hung upon those vaults, walls and altarpiece was a cooperative effort of the greatest artists of the era, including Simón himself. The armorial work is by Diego de Siloé. The Gothic archways and balustrades are by his father, Gil.

Beside the tombs, which were carved by Felipe Bigarny from Atapuerca marble, is a stele of Granada marble for inscribing the names of their descendants. The tombs have the usual recumbent forms of their occupants, he with his sword, she with her pet dog asleep at her feet. For me, the realism and modernity of this display of Renaissance sculpture were astounding, no matter the conventions of tomb art that have been maintained.

The **retable** and side altar are the work of Felipe Bigarny and Diego de Siloé. The entrance grille was the work of Cristobal Sandino in 1523. Lost among such sheer magnificence are the fairly common touches of the polychrome inlays in the floor surrounding the tombs, and the alternating dark and light stone blocks in the five steps up to the raised altar.

Relevant to our travels with St. James, you will find him here perched on a corbel at the lower right beside the retable. He is garbed as a pilgrim, walking staff in left hand, holy book held at his side in his right hand, and with scallop shell badge pinned on the center of his hat.

On the southeast side is the door to the tiny **sacristy** tucked into a corner of the chapel. The door is pure Plateresque. In the sacristy is Leonardo da Vinci's painting of Mary Magdalene. (Some say it is more likely a work of a pupil of Leonardo's by the name of Gian Petrino.)

Now make your way back to the south transept and the entrance to the cloister. Admittance is through an anteroom just outside the main **sacristy**, the star feature of which is Diego de

Siloé's Christ at the Column. Most impressive to me was its elaborately stuccoed ceiling, dome and cupola. The wood paneled chests for storage of vestments are rather standard fare for such things.

You find the groin-vaulted **cloister** literally cluttered with a museum's bounty of tombs and religious art by a whole host of sculptors worked in wood, terracotta and stone. Each blind arch offers a niche containing its resident saint, depicted life size, standing above a sarcophagus upon which reposes an equally life sized effigy of its occupant. Also included is a group comprised of the founders of the present cathedral, Ferdinand III and his queen, Beatrix of Swabia. On the far (east) side are three additional chapels. Approaching from the north gallery you find the chapels of St. James and St. Catherine, then the sacristy, with the chapterhouse at the extreme corner.

The Capilla de Santiago is now a museum full of **altar plate** (Museo de la Plata), tapestries and religious goods drawn from all the centuries of the cathedral's existence. The showstopper here is a silver processional carriage carrying a gigantic mobile tabernacle, the whole of which must contain a ton of silver, all splendidly fashioned into a phantasmagoria of figures and forms. Even the wheel spokes and rims are sheathed in silver. I have never seen anything like it. Its origin was in Madrid, 1901.

St. Catherine's is very different in character and contents. It contains manuscripts and documents including the marriage contract of El Cid and Jiminia. The **carved cupboards** have various scenes, among them depictions of Moorish kings paying homage to the king of Castile (found at the base of the ribbing on the left wall). Others show lion hunts and the feasting that afterwards celebrated the success of the hunt.

In the Chapterhouse (Sala Capitular) are tapestries of the fifteenth and sixteenth centuries. Woven in Brussels, they show inspirational religious scenes. Note the diptych by Van Eyck. Best of all, however, is the wooden **ceiling**, intricately fashioned in the Mudéjar style with ivory inlay work.

In the starkly bare sacristy adjacent to the Sala Capitular is a battered old **chest**, once the property of El Cid, that hangs on the wall. According to lore, he pawned the chest with some Jewish "bankers," telling them it was full of gold and other riches – but he forbade them to open it to judge the worth of the thing. Although it is said the bankers knew the chest was filled with sand and rock, they banked on El Cid's word and lent him the money to finance his capture of Valencia. El Cid later recouped his pawn with the wealth of the conquered city. One version of the story goes on to say that when the chest eventually was opened the sand and rock were discovered to have miraculously turned to gold.

Back in the cloister, resume your circuit of the galleries, paying attention to the detail of it all according to your personal tendencies.

The tour of the cathedral is now finished, but take time for a second look – and perhaps a first look at details you missed first time around. Do not stint on time spent in this place. It is one of a kind and quite possibly you may never return here again.

Finally, I recommend that you spend the remainder of the day enjoying the hospitality of Burgos in whatever fashion you wish. On a past trip we walked back along the shopping streets, found a pleasant cafe for a light lunch, then climbed past San Gil to hike up to the ruined fortress. Coming down, we took the west access road past the weed-infested barrenness of El Cid's estate, and thus returned once more to Cathedral Square and a view of its fantastic towers.

Another option and a must see for the history buff is the Museum of Human Evolution. Its prize displays came from the archeological site at Atapuerca, some 20 kilometers east of Burgos. Several sites have been excavated in the Atapuerca mountains revealing fossils and tools that tell of a culture of hominids that flourished in this vicinity 800,000 years ago. They are said to be the oldest human-like beings discovered so far in Europe. Those who would like to visit the archeological site can make arrangements at the museum. Reach the museum from the intersection of Calle Vitoria and Calle Santander.

Head south over the bridge across the river to the intersection with Paseo Sierra de Atapuerca. There you see the museum as the very modern building to the left on the Paseo.

In the morning, departing Burgos for our transit of the Meseta, we will visit Las Huelgas and the Hospital del Rey.

THE MESETA

West of Burgos is the Meseta.

The Meseta is what the name implies: A tableland, gently rolling at first, then flat from horizon to horizon. In Summer, it becomes a golden sea of wheat ripening in the hot, stifling breezes of the season. Further west it turns largely into sheep country. It is rich agricultural land, the meaty bone of good earth that Muslim and Christian kings fought to hold for the five hundred years between the Arab conquest in 711 and the decisive Christian victory at Las Navas de Tolosa in 1212. In the while, anywhere the least pimple of a hill thrust up from the plain, someone raised a castle on it. This was the heartland of Old Castile.

The combatants perhaps didn't know it then, but the game was winner take all. To take and hold this core territory of the Iberian Peninsula was to gain all of Spain – eventually. The eventuality arrived in 1492 when Granada fell to the armies of Los Reyes Católicos, Ferdinand and Isabella, led by their Constable, Pedro Hernández de Velasco, whose home and tomb we visited in Burgos.

For a pilgrim afoot the way west from Burgos to León is even now regarded as a long, monotonous passage across unrelenting flatness, hot as a griddle in Summer, cold as an ice-floe in Winter.

Much of our route to León lies off the pilgrim track taken by the hiking fraternity. Modern roads – or any roads at all – don't go that way all the way any longer. Yet we will be able to visit the pilgrims' principal stopping places along the Way as we transit the Meseta.

Before venturing out into the Meseta, however, we must visit a pair of landmark institutions on the pilgrims' route as they depart the city of Burgos. One is the Hospital del Rey, once a large establishment on the outskirts of the city. Its development dates from the twelfth through sixteenth centuries, and was devoted to the care of pilgrims. It lies immediately on the pilgrim way. The other, closer to central Burgos and a short distance off the main track, is the convent of Las Huelgas Reales.

The Hospital del Rey, established in 1195 by Alfonso VIII, was rather conventional pilgrim fare historically and architecturally. Las Huelgas is justifiably famous in both respects.

Las Huelgas Reales

Still an active Cistercian convent, Las Huelgas Reales was originally a Summer palace for the kings of Castile. From that it took its name, which means the royal resting, retreat or recreation place. In short, it was a royal pleasure palace, an escape from the less amiable confines of the grim-walled castle above the city.

In 1180, King Alfonso VIII, at the urging of his wife, Eleanor (daughter of Henry II of England and sister of Richard the Lionhearted), donated it to the Cistercians as a convent for daughters of royal and aristocratic families. While some such ladies truly had the call to the religious vocation, for many the nunnery was merely a way for their families to remove them from the opportunity of marriage. That strategy saved the dowers and claims upon titles and land that their families chose not to allow. Today the nuns are of more pedestrian origin and dedicated to an especially rigorous Rule of St. Benedict compared to other Cistercian convents.

Under the terms of the arrangement with the sisters, Las Huelgas continued for centuries to be used by the royal family as a place of retreat from the affairs of the world. In 1199 it also became the royal pantheon that eventually contained the tombs of no less than fifty kings, queens, and other members of the regal line. Additionally it served as a hostel for aristocratic or regal pilgrims en route to Santiago.

In one of its chapels, King Ferdinand III, the Saint, was

knighted in 1219, commencing a tradition that continued for centuries. Alfonso XI was crowned there in 1331. Pedro the Cruel was born and spent his early years in the place, although I doubt that his early association with the nuns can be blamed for his malevolent disposition. More recently, General Franco found shelter in Las Huelgas during the Civil War while he organized his government.

To find Las Huelgas proceed west along the south bank of the Arlanzón on N620 for about a kilometer past the Puente Santa María. Where a pair of streets converge from the left to meet the highway, take the converging street on the right. A sign at the intersection points to Las Huelgas.

Our way is along a street lined by neatly appointed upper-middle-class residences that reminds one of Pasadena, California, and the streets near the Rose Bowl. After a half kilometer that street dead ends at a tree-shaded avenue that runs along in front of Las Huelgas, which you see rising behind an iron picket fence and a spacious courtyard. Closed Monday, it is open from 10:30 to 1:15, and 4 to 5:15 pm, except Sunday, 11 to 1:15. The interior is accessible only on a guided tour. Unfortunately for many of us foreign travelers, the guide's commentary in Spanish is delivered too swiftly for the unaccustomed ear. Take heart, for we will prepare you for the tour.

As you face the monastic buildings from the street, entrance to the church is through a portico off to your left. To your right at the far end of the courtyard you see a Gothic-arched gateway set in a rubble wall with crenellations atop. It opens upon another large courtyard. Pass through the archway and, on your right at that point, you will see the entrance to the ticket office for the tour. With ticket in hand, walk back through the gateway and make your way to the church entrance where, inside in the transept, the tour will organize and begin.

While approaching the church, note the peculiar juxtaposition of Romanesque and Gothic arches in the entrance **portico**. This speaks volumes on the architectural character of the place. While you wait for the tour to form, be seated on one of the benches along the wall of the transept and let me tell you more about Las Huelgas.

The church, built between 1180 and 1230, was designed specifically to serve as the pantheon for the royalty of Castile. It is regarded as one of the purest examples of the Cistercian style of architecture, which marked the transition between Romanesque and Gothic and utilizes building designs adapted from both styles.

The nave has three aisles. The center aisle, containing the nuns' choir behind the screen separating that choir from the Capella Mayor and the public spaces of the transept, was intended for the tombs of kings and queens. The left aisle was reserved for princesses, the right for princes. And so it was done. On the tour you see the files of royal tombs lining the aisles – but with exceptions. Some princesses are entombed among the princes, probably as the result of later sortings out of things.

Most of the tombs were looted by French troops in 1809, but since only gems and the like were stolen, much of historical value remained. The Caudillo, Francisco Franco, in the 1940s ordered the tombs opened and their contents (other than the bodies) removed and prepared for display. The consequence produced the only museum extant that is able to show original garments and fabrics worn by royalty down through the centuries. It is known as the Museo de Ricas Telas, which was established by Franco's order. The garments, as we shall see, are displayed in humidity-controlled and air conditioned cabinets to assure preservation.

From your seat in the transept, look forward into the apse and Capella Mayor. The **high altar** is Baroque, gilded and rather standard stuff for such things. Rather startling is the unusual array of organ pipes above the choir stalls on the right. Also note the peculiar pulpit of gilded ironwork located at the face of the nuns' choir screen. It pivots so that the preacher may address either the nuns' or the public's side of the screen. A fresco on the front of the screen depicts the royal donors, Alfonso and his queen, kneeling in devotion.

191

The tour takes us first into the **nuns' choir**. In the center of the nave, forward of the rows of choir stalls, Alfonso and Eleanor lie in twin sarcophagi resting upon reclining lions. The tapestries alongside are of sixteenth century origin. The place has a somber, peaceful mood, resulting mainly from the dark wooden files of choir stalls, which as such are rather ordinary. Meager illumination from outside comes through round Romanesque windows set between Gothic arches.

Note that the tombs in the side aisles are labeled as to their occupants, and observe the rough-cut wood planks that comprise the flooring. My point is simply that the layout and decor of the place fundamentally remains as it was first constructed and has been dutifully and nicely maintained throughout the centuries.

A Mudéjar **wooden door** with intricate carvings displaying obvious Arabic motifs leads from the nuns' choir into the Claustro Mayor. Built originally in the thirteenth century, this cloister reveals its Mudéjar origins despite many renovations, particularly during the fifteenth century. Even those changes were accomplished with Islamic flavors, reflecting the work of Moorish artisans who remained behind as Christians after the expulsion of the Muslims from Spain.

Note that while the vaulting is Gothic, sections of it after restoration have been left unfinished to reveal the delicacies of the Mudéjar workmanship in some of the ribbing that later renovations had obscured. As you first enter the cloister, also note another spectacular Mudéjar carved wooden door beneath a ribbed ceiling of similar style. As you circle the **cloister**, note particularly the peacocks and stars in the original ceiling work, left exposed instead of covered by the smooth stucco surface of the restoration. These are motifs that only a Moorish influence might have inspired.

In a small shrine off the cloister you will find a strange polychrome **wooden statue** of St. James. The arm, outstretched and holding a sword, is articulated. Formerly this statue was located in the nearby Chapel of St. James (not shown on the tour). For centuries the princes of the royal house came to that

192

chapel and knelt in vigil before this statue when they came of age for knighthood. The arm of the saint was lowered to place the sword upon them so that they were said to be knighted in the Order of St. James by the "hand" of the warrior saint himself.

The Order of St. James, as we described in more detail elsewhere, was founded in the tenth century specifically to help bring some semblance of law to El Camino de Santiago. Thus while the foundations established by the order often provided material and medical assistance to pilgrims, its principal role was patrolling the pilgrimage route and ferreting out bands of brigands and thieves. Think of them as a medieval highway patrol.

Off the west side of the cloister is the aforementioned **Museo de Ricas Telas,** where the tomb-wear of royalty is displayed. And a fine display it is; one that you should not merely walk through. Seamstresses among you will make sure you dally there an appropriate while. It is spectacular.

Adjacent is the **chapter house**, a large, tall room, with graceful Gothic arches. In it you find more museum displays and something else of history. It contains a rich display of tapestries, paintings of royalty and abbesses, and such like fare. Featured is a fancy embroidered tent flap, a trophy torn from the tent of the Arab king that Alfonso VIII and Sancho the Strong defeated at the Battle of Las Navas de Tolosa.

Here you stand in the presence of modern history, too. In this room the short-statured Francisco Franco in 1936 stood on the wooden dais at the fore and assembled his government for the first time in a ceremony wherein all swore allegiance to the new Falangist regime. Later, on 2 December 1937, Franco here presided over the initial meeting of the new Nationalist Congress.

A liberal spirit may rue those days, but for Spain it was a time of choice between the stern discipline of Franco or the murderous anarchy of the Republicans. We might not regard that as much of a choice, but that is another story. Enough to remark that Spain chose and in the end emerged as a politically and economically prospering member of the modern family of democratic nations. More, it came to fruition under a king who restored an emotional underpinning to the political unity of Spain such as the nation had not enjoyed since the era of Los Reyes Católicos.

Next door to the museum is the entrance to a much smaller, Romanesque cloister, the **Claustrillos**, or little cloister. It is much superior in mood, with a sort of coziness beneath gently sloping beamed ceilings and Romanesque archways supported by double columns with elegantly carved capitals. In the interior courtyard the landscaping is a geometrical design comprised of low, square-trimmed hedges and rose gardens. If one were a nun, there could be no better place than this for a prayer walk.

The convent rooms off this cloister are believed to be vestiges of the original palace of the kings. Thus it is not unexpected that beneath the changes wrought by the years, the modern workmen discovered touches of the original Mozarabic artisans who built the place at the order of the early kings of Castile, as well as the Mudéjar of later renovations.

Off this cloister, and not accessible to the tour, one finds the diminutive **Chapel of Santiago** de la Asunción. It may be seen by special permission. It is approached through a neatly kept garden to the side of which is a flagstoned path flanked by tall hedges and ivied walls which focus upon the chapel entry. This is marked by a horseshoe arch straddling the round columns that serve as doorposts. Nothing grand here, we think as we approach the tiny door into the equally tiny chapel made of brick. Look again. This is pure Mozarabic, reminiscent of doors and walls and roofs that one expects to find only in the Arab south, as at the Alhambra.

Inside take particular note of the artesonado ceiling, so called for its wood-panel (artesón) decor. Most important here historically was the peculiar wood statue of St. James, formerly enthroned at the fore and before whom the royal princes once stood their vigils in preparation for knighthood.

The Hospital del Rey

From Las Huelgas return to N620 and turn left to continue on the Way west. After a couple of kilometers, just this side of a railway overpass, about fifty meters off the highway on the left, is the Hospital del Rey. Its remnants are nicely restored and preserved within the bounds of a campus of the University of Burgos.

The Hospital del Rey was founded in 1195 by Alfonso VIII, abandoned in 1835 during the Carlist War, largely turned to ruin by fire in 1837, and later used as a military barracks during the Civil War. The entrance gate (Puerta de Romeros) is sixteenth-century Plateresque, featuring the scallop shell of the pilgrim with Santiago seated beneath. The gate opens onto a courtyard where, on the left, is the hospital church, dedicated to San Amaro. He was a Frenchman named Amer who, on his way back from his trek to Santiago de Compostela, decided to spend the rest of his life here in service to his fellow pilgrims.

Originally a Gothic structure, the church has been too often remodeled to retain much of its original form. The bell tower and the interior are Baroque. On its Renaissance portico you find Santiago Matamoros rather less gloriously represented than you have seen him elsewhere on our explorations. The porch below Santiago guides us to a much more significant relic of the early days of pilgrimage. Attend closely to the exquisitely carved, high-relief panels of the wooden doors. This is a hand-me-down from the original Gothic church, and illustrates the culture of the pilgrimage as it was those centuries ago. The view of these doors left an impression of the El Camino experience that particularly stands out amongst all others encountered on the Way of Saint James.

One scene on the right-hand door depicts a pilgrim family, much the worse for road wear, presenting themselves before prosperous, well-garbed church folk. Note the gaunt-ribbed mother breast-feeding her infant as they walk along. Here you see a bit of artistic realism suggesting much of what a pilgrim endured as he trod the Way to Santiago. The experience was no walk in the park, as the saying goes. For a poor pilgrim it was practically unendurable but for the promise of Salvation at the end.

The left-hand door panel displays an armored St. Michael, and St. James in pilgrim garb with staff in hand bestowing his blessing upon a kneeling pilgrim.

Unfortunately the church is seldom open, which leaves us little more of note to observe here at the Hospital del Rey, other than the fine new buildings of the university itself, surrounding a grassy quadrangle situated beyond the church. Note the ruined, isolated grouping of massive piers and an arched portal, all that remain of the old hospital itself.

Castrojeriz

From the Hospital del Rey, continue west on route N620 for another kilometer or so to the junction with N120. Here the highway follows the pilgrim way along the old Roman road to León. It leads through Villabilla (now more like a built-up suburb of Burgos) to the village of Tardajos. There El Camino de Santiago bears left to Rabe, beyond which the Way becomes a dirt path unsuited even for four-wheel-drive vehicles. So we must depart the Way and stay on N120 driving in the direction of León.

About twenty five kilometers west of Burgos you see the ruins of the fifteenth-century castle of Olmillos. Another five kilometers further, at the village of Villasandino, take the road left (BU404) which takes us to our first stop beyond Burgos.

Our destination lies at the foot of an unusually prominent pimple on the plain of the Meseta. It has the inevitable castle crowning its crest. The place is called Castrojeriz, a one-time Arab stronghold where the annual tribute of a hundred Christian virgins is said to have been transacted until Santiago Matamoros put a stop to such things by the ninth-century Battle of Clavijo. The distance is now fifteen kilometers to Castrojeriz along the poorest stretch of highway that we encountered along the Way. Hopefully it has been rebuilt before you drive along it.

The walls and towers of the ruined castle soon appear on the crest of a steep hill peeking over the shoulder of a low rise on your left. The town lies at the eastern foot of the castle mount.

The town of Castrojeriz is much older than its castle. It was Celtic (named Jeriz) and Roman (Castrojeriz) before it was Gothic and Arabic. The first Christian castle built here was raised by a Gothic count of Asturias in 760 during the reign of King Fruela I. It was one of the first bold thrusts made by the Christians as they abandoned the safety of their mountains. Modified in the ninth century, it became the seat of the Council of Castile, where pioneers of the Reconquista assembled to plot strategies against Moorish and Christian adversaries alike. It was rebuilt for the last time in the sixteenth century.

At the peak of the pilgrim trade the town of Castrojeriz possessed no fewer than seven hospices and teemed with activity. Today it is a backwater few tourists bother with, and far off the mainstream of today's Spanish economy. Because of that, once you get off the highway and into the town, you are as close to being in a rural medieval Spanish town as anywhere along our route of exploration. But first, drive east, skirting the town, heading toward Hontanas.

You are now on the original pilgrim route again, for the moment heading away from its destination. After about three kilometers turn around and park by the ruin of the fourteenth-century monastery and **hospital** of San Antón. You can't miss it. The road passes through the tall, stout arches straddling the one-time front porch of the church, arches that rise at least fifteen meters above the pavement. The desolated Gothic hulk of the monastery of San Antón is impressive as a gigantic ruin, probably the best display of unrestored ruination to be encountered along the Way. It is just plain, unreconstructed dilapidation – arches supporting nothing but sky, gap-toothed stone tracery within beautiful Gothic windows along the nave, rose windows at the end of the transepts gaping through tumbled-down walls, a farmhouse crouched for shelter against one outside wall, while the now roofless interior of the church serves as a storage yard for the miscellany of materials and implements that make a go of farming. One wonders at the melancholy thoughts of those who found their vocation here, when the day came to abandon this once so beautiful place, leaving it to fall to the ruin it has become.

The **main portal** lies between the pair of arches spanning the highway. It is cemented up, the flat, plain face of the closure detracting from the effect of the grand dimensions of that portal and partially dismantled facade. The details of its fancy carved archivolts are timeworn to the point that only general features are recognizable. Still they display a whole galaxy of saints.

The monastery was built in the fourteenth century by French monks. The quality of the stone work is as good as you have seen on this trip. It was a tall, graceful structure. Everything was built of dressed stone, with windows and portals finely tooled. It was dedicated to St. Anthony of Egypt, who in the fourth century invented the idea of the monkish life, long before St. Benedict decided to found the first order of European monks, the order that took their founder's name.

Pilgrim lore says this was a place of many miracles. San Antón's specialty was cure of digestive disorders. That I could use at times. But the monks had medical prowess of their own. The chronicles say the monks of San Antón even possessed a cure for the illness known as St. Anthony's fire, a curse similar to leprosy.

While we drove out here principally to see the ruin of San Antón, we also have the opportunity to share a pilgrim's distant view of the mount sporting the castle from which the town of Castrojeriz takes its name. While the land still swells and rolls hereabouts, the mount with its towered fortress rises sharply a full nine hundred meters off the plain – a natural watch tower from which to spot the dust of approaching Moorish raiders a dozen kilometers off.

Driving back into town, the first monument to be encountered is spotted from a considerable distance. It is a church which stands out particularly because of its tall campanile rising high quite literally out of nowhere on a deserted countryside. This is the Church of Nuestra Señora del Manzano (Our Lady of the Apple Tree). Here again you meet the transitional architecture of the Cistercians in this late twelfth century structure, no matter the Renaissance adaptations such as its massive bell tower with correspondingly large cupola atop. The portals are Gothic, with their receding arches showing less carving than we might expect, and a very large rose window above the main portal. A peculiar feature is that the thick low wall forming the courtyard around the front of the church has a built-in bench all along its limestone inner face.

The Church of Our Lady of the Apple Tree

The entire structure has a fortress-like mood about it, with its window slits and, around to the rear, the octagonal addition surrounded by a tall wall with a square bastion-like protrusion set like a tower to protect its gate. No doubt the architecture suited the nature of the time when it was built.

Inside is a medieval polychrome **stone statue** of the Virgin – one with a long history of miracles – from which the church was given its name. With it is a nice collection of religious objects from centuries past, including a St. Jerome by the seventeenth century artist Carduccio, and much more.

Compared to the mobbed experience of our visits to the cathedral and elsewhere in Burgos, the quiet dignity of this place is a welcome change. Among those more permanently resting here is a queen, Léonor of Aragon. I have no idea why we find her here in this out of the way location.

Now drive along from the church, following the yellow hand-painted arrows of the pilgrims' route that twists through town. In the center of Castrojeriz is the church of Santo Domingo on the right and, farther along, another dedicated to San Juan on the left.

Santo Domingo, a sixteenth-century parish church, has alongside it a museum containing antiquities removed from the ruins of other churches and monastic foundations that once flourished in this vicinity. Most valuable of its displays are Flemish tapestries reminiscent of works of Reubens.

The Gothic transitional church of San Juan is less interesting, but boasts of a Gothic retable in a side chapel that is worth seeing. The retable in the main church is standard Baroque, notable only for the painting of St. John that is its centerpiece. The church once was part of a large hospital for pilgrims.

Frómista

At the main highway crossroad at Castrojeriz, take the road west toward Melgar. This is a secondary road, a kind we will see much of between here and Compostela. But don't be concerned. As you by now have discovered, roads in Spain are generally as good as those in England or the United States, and those along El Camino de Santiago are especially well constructed and maintained, whether superhighways or country roads.

Soon you reach a left turn onto the road that leads to

Frómista. The road jumps along El Camino de Santiago from village to village between Castrillo Matajudios (the little castle of the Jew slayer) and Boadilla del Camino. Midway between the latter places we cross the Rio Pisuerga, once the frontier between the old kingdoms of Castile and León. Presently it is the border between the provinces of Burgos and Palencia.

Spanning the river, and still used by the modern highway, is the eleven-arched Romanesque bridge built at the turn into the twelfth century by Alfonso VI of León, who reunited the kingdoms in 1073 by murdering his brother, Sancho II of Castile. Near the bridge was the twelfth century hospital of St. John, of which few vestiges remain.

On the near side of the river is the village of Itero del Castillo. The castle on the hill belonged to the Dukes of Frias. A ruined hermitage lies at the foot of the hill. On the other side of the river is Itero de La Vega, with the still viable hermitage of La Piedad and an old church, San Pedro, with a thirteenth century porch. Both villages are slightly off to the right of the modern road. A student of the Camino will pause to visit them. We pass them by.

After about another ten kilometers we come to Boadilla del Camino, a larger village. Its fifteenth century church of Santa María is undistinguished architecturally, but contains an elegant collection of paintings and statuary, plus a strikingly carved Romanesque baptismal font, a Plateresque high altar and some nice altarpieces.

In the town you also pass a strange pylon carved of stone on a five-step pedestal. Some call it a cross. This fifteenth century piece is famous among connoisseurs of such things. It is a Gothic sculptured column revealing distinct Plateresque influences most evident in the intricacies of the crown-like carving at its top. Note the scallop shells integrated into the piece. Why this? Why here? It is nothing more than a fancy trail marker celebrating El Camino de Santiago.

Now it is only a half dozen kilometers to Frómista, one of the minor jewels along the Pilgrim way. A Roman town originally named Frumentum (wheat), it was destroyed in the tenth century during one of the many battles of the Reconquista. This region between Castrojeriz and León was a centuries-long battleground where the forces mustered by Moslem and Christian kings decided the issue of sovereignty that led to the founding of the Christian kingdom of León. Battle followed battle, campaign piled on top of campaign. It was a deadly way of life, generation after generation, the kind we see today only in Africa, the Middle East and the Balkans.

Entering Frómista you find yourself on the main pilgrimage street, the Calle de los Franceses. Just a short distance past the main intersection turn right to approach the rather small and quaint "Plaza Mayor." Two places of interest face each other across the square. One is the old pilgrim hospital of **Los Palmeros**, sitting behind a sixteenth-century arcade. Today it contains one of the better restaurants you will find during our explorations. In that restaurant is a fine artesonado ceiling, and you will enjoy traditional food served amidst the appropriateness of the fine old furnishings. It also has public telephones, which we used to check up on our son, who manned the family fortress in the wilds of Oregon during our absence.

Standing in front of Los Palmeros in the plaza is the statue of Pedros Gonzalez Telmo, a native of the town, born in 1190, and its most famous son. A Dominican father, San Telmo was confessor to Fernando III, the Saint. More significantly, for many years he devoted his vocation to seamen working the ports of Galicia and, for whatever obscure reason, his name became associated with the strange electrical phenomenon known to mariners as San Telmo's fire.

Now walk across to **San Pedro** on the other side of the square. The church is fifteenth century, but is an "early" Gothic design, no matter its late date of construction. Inside are, most notably, several paintings by Ribera and Meng, plus a rather standard Pieta and other items of religious art. While the church is of no great architectural repute, structurally it is as nicely proportioned and finished as any parish church to be seen along the Way in the smaller towns and cities.

From the main square follow the signs a couple of blocks to the pride of Frómista. This is the church of **San Martín,** dedicated to a French saint and situated at the lower end of a nicely landscaped modern plaza. This small but architecturally significant church is now a museum piece and justly so.

The Church of San Martin de Fromista

San Martín de Frómista is especially delightful to see beneath a late afternoon sun when it takes on a golden-brown hue that allows the stern Romanesque features of the structure to take on a measure of emotional warmth. Otherwise there is a cold, fortress-like mood to the place: formidable round towers at each corner of its fore, the sturdy octagonal lantern over the crossing, and a facade and front portal made painfully plain compared to what we have seen elsewhere on our journey. Then the side windows, high up from street level, lend a first impression of archers' embrasures rather than the double windows of pure Romanesque style that they are. Note the horizontal checkerboard courses incorporating squares of lighter stone along the sides of the church. More of that white stone is found in the walls of the triple apse.

What we have here is an eleventh-century structure that

some authorities believe contains recycled stone that originated in some ancient Roman basilica. This idea developed because of the secular – indeed, pagan and obscene – character of many of the carvings, some so objectionable that they were removed during the late nineteenth-century restoration of the church.

Note that the stone blocks are relatively roughhewn. The **modillions** beneath the cornices, and the protruding bands along the exterior sides of the walls of the church, including towers and lantern, are all exquisitely carved. For me they suggest more a Mozarabic than a French influence. The modillions are particularly fascinating, most of them fashioned into the heads of animals, all different: a monkey here, then pigs, goats, sheep and cattle galore, plus an infant crawling up near the peak of the facade. That's enough to make a mother wince.

The original building with its beautifully proportioned, if plain, interior dates from 1066. The church was associated with a long-disappeared Benedictine monastery that in later times came under the domination of Cluny and gained protection from the Templars. It and the accompanying monastery and pilgrim hospice were erected by a French architect (undoubtedly assisted by Mozarabic artisans, as we suggest) under the sponsorship of Doña Mayor of Navarra, then the widow of Sancho the Great, who had died in 1035. Her intent was to provide material and spiritual shelter for pilgrims along this remote stretch of the Camino.

The church of San Martín thus is one of the earliest examples of the French Romanesque in Spain and is regarded as a classic example of the style. Many authorities believe it became the model for Romanesque design in Spanish churches all along El Camino de Santiago. The checkerboard exterior courses we mentioned became somewhat of the trademark for the style these builders helped create.

Inside we discover a barrel-vaulted nave and two aisles, while ahead of the transept stand conventional Romanesque triple apses, domed rather than barrel vaulted. A dome rises in the lantern above the crossing. The engaged columns on the four pillars at the forward end of the nave have capitals containing excellent Romanesque carvings that are primitive in style but elegant in concept and execution. Similar scenes grace the capitals of the tall columns supporting the ceiling ribs, and also the shorter pillars beneath the side arches dividing the central nave from the side aisles. One series of carvings depicts the experiences of marriage – including quarrel and reconciliation.

As mentioned, some of the carved capitals have been replaced. They are recognized by the "R" marked unobtrusively upon them, eleven in all. You will recognize them easily by the lesser quality of their workmanship. In the sanctuary find a rosewood statue of Santiago, along with a life-size, primitive crucifixion. Santiago bears a pilgrim's staff and wears the scallop shell badge.

Villalcazar de Sirga

From Frómista to Carrion de Los Condes, where we plan to spend the night, the distance is about twenty kilometers. The Way passes through several villages, each with its own parish church and each can boast of a fine old house or two. But we drive about fifteen kilometers before making our next stop, which comes at the church of **Santa María la Blanca** in Villalcazar de Sirga. Sirga is another word for "highway." Alcazar is Arabic for fortress or citadel.

Just as the "highway" isn't all that "high" in these parts any more, neither is the village. It would seem incorrect to call the place a town. But in its day it was a thriving mini-metropolis, and the massive church of Santa María la Blanca is proof enough of the fact. Nothing else in the village competes with its gigantic hulk, which stands high above everything and makes it plainly visible from afar as you approach.

Santa María was originally a Templar church with an attached convent and hospital for pilgrims. Its dedication is to a miracle-working statue of the Virgin still housed within its walls. For that, King Alfonso X (r 1252-84), the scholarly troubadour king, dubbed The Wise, wrote many of his more than four hundred Cantigas about this famous Lady of stone. His poetry sang of no less than fourteen miracles attributed to her intercession.

Alfonso had more connections with this particular church than that, however. It is also the place where his brother, Felipe, is entombed after he was murdered in 1271 by none other than Alfonso. The end of Felipe was as strange as his life.

Felipe had a calling to the Church. Being a prince of the royal blood, the fifth son of San Fernando, Felipe easily rose to the position of Archbishop of Seville. Before that he had studied in Paris with such prestigious theologians as St. Thomas Aquinas and St. Bonaventure. In 1258, however, when Alfonso (who suddenly became infatuated with an Arab princess) literally left his prospective bride standing at the altar, Felipe did penance for the family's shame by repudiating his vows and marrying the girl himself. No matter, she died not long afterwards of a broken heart.

Felipe evidently developed a taste for the wedded state. Soon he married again to Léonor de Castro, whose tomb lies next to his in this church.

The church had its foundations laid in the twelfth century and was finished early in the thirteenth. As you draw up to it, you see a building that, but for the Gothic arch above the tall, cavernous porch-like **vestibule**, appears to be pure Romanesque. And so it is. The final structure is transitional between the two styles, but not Cistercian, strictly speaking. Inside you will discover a tall, narrow interior with high Gothic arches resting on sturdy Romanesque walls with minimal exterior buttressing.

A broad staircase leads up from the street through marble-faced bastions on either side, while the church, with its grand **rose window** facing the road, is devoid of apertures anywhere near ground level. There is no doubt that the Templars built this place as much for a fortress as a house of God. Higher up are a few Romanesque windows.

Approaching the entrance you find it decorated with sculptures portraying scenes from both Biblical and Spanish history. A pair of friezes are above, with Christ in His Majesty presiding over the top row, and His Mother, with the infant Jesus, centered within the lower frieze. A thousand years of weather has robbed much of the sharpness from the finer details.

Inside you are on the south aisle of the three-aisled church where the towering vaults betray its transitional Gothic origins. Turn right into the south transept, which contains the **chapel of St. James.** In it are the elegantly sculpted tombs of Felipe and Léonor, their effigies recumbent in regal finery beneath the soft glow from the rose window.

Felipe reposes within the furthermost sarcophagus; Léonor lies near the iron grille that closes off the chapel. The reliefs on Felipe's tomb depict his funeral, and the same is true of his lady's. His tomb sculptures are by far the more elegant, however. And could it be that Léonor is gagged? What truth was she bound not to tell for all eternity? Note the use of color, now much faded, to highlight and vivify the sculptural details.

Beside the royal pair, at the far end of the chapel, is the tomb of a Templar knight accompanied for all time by his hawk and a sleeping lion. He was the Master of the Temple who directed construction of the place. The retable at the altar is typically Renaissance and worth but a short glance.

The Virgin Mother is thrice portrayed in this church. The polychrome figure sheltered by a canopy and seated on a pedestal facing into the chapel of St. James, badly abused by time and with the headless Christ Child on her lap, is believed to be the miracle maker. For you possessing the Faith, you need but ask and your prayer shall be answered one way or another.

Carrión de los Condes

The drive to Carrión is about seven more kilometers. We find it to be a bustling modern town no matter that it is chock full of monuments to the pilgrims of long ago. And it is a town of many legends.

A strong tradition links Carrión de los Condes with the annual tribute of the hundred virgins paid to the Moorish kings to stock their harems back in the eighth and ninth centuries. Perhaps both Carrión and Castrojeriz at various times were appointed sites for the transaction.

We recall that the Battle of Clavijo was said to have ended the tribute. Another legend told in Carrión speaks of an occasion when, while the transaction was taking place, a herd of wild bulls charged upon the scene, attacking the Moors but leaving the levy of young girls untouched. The Moors took that as an evil omen and put an end to the practice. I suspect there is truth to both legends, and that what happened was that the levy of virgins was a general practice of the various Muslim kinglets of the time, exacted wherever they possessed the power to coerce their Christian neighbors.

In any event, Carrión is a very old town sitting above the Rio Carrión on a low bluff, which in these flat lands made the place at least somewhat naturally defensible. For that advantage the town was an old Moorish strongpoint which later became an early outpost of the newly founded kingdom of León. It was taken from the Moors by Alonso Carreño about the turn into the ninth century. The place took its name from him, with Carrión being a corruption of his name.

The counts (Condes) entrusted with defense of the place became very important chieftains because Carrión figured centrally in guarding the fledgling Christian kingdom from incessant Moorish attacks.

At the time of El Cid, two sons of the Conde de Carrión are said to have gone off to Valencia to pay suit to the daughters of the great warrior. The story is probably fictitious in part or whole, but it is told in *El Cantar del Mio Cid.*

It was well known at the time that to whomever El Cid granted his daughters' hands in marriage, El Cid was prepared to grant fabulously rich dowries drawn from the wealth he had captured at Valencia. The young Condes were found acceptable, the deal was struck and the marriages took place. Then the lads headed for home with the ladies and their riches. Along the way the boys paused in a remote region, stripped and beat the girls and turned them loose, naked and bleeding on the road. The scoundrels thus returned home with what they truly wanted – the wealth of El Cid. They dared the insult and theft because with the pressure of the Almoravides, the distance from Valencia, and the strength of their own fortress, they were sure they had nothing to fear from the legendary warrior.

El Cid in fact was unable to chuck his responsibilities and gain vengeance by his own hand. Not a matter of fiction: In his employ was the deadliest band of cutthroats west of the Two Sicilies. The legend refers to them as "knights." Whatever they were, they made sure the young wastrel counts did not live to enjoy their ill-gotten wealth or brag that they had bested the powerful Cid. As for the girls, as told earlier, they subsequently went on to make fine marriages among the royal families of the Christian kingdoms to the east.

Carrión de los Condes is situated on the near side of the Carrión River. The first landmark as we approach is the tall **convent church** of Santa Clara situated starkly alone, high up on a hill to the left. The convent is thirteenth century and contains a well thought of Pieta by Gregorio Fernandez. Only the church still stands, an old barn of a place not in the best of repair. But do see it. Walk around to its far side and you find scraps of the convent that once abutted the church.

From the convent, proceed straight on into the center of the city where, on the narrow Calle Santa María, on the right, you find the church of **Santa María del Camino,** sometimes called "de la Victoria," in celebration of a victory near here by Bermudo I (d 1037) over the Arabs. A scrap of the old city wall is on your right as you approach.

The church is twelfth-century Romanesque with a spacious

porch which provided shelter for pilgrims. The porch is of most interest here. It was profusely decorated with carvings above the main portal. Some are reputed to depict the legend of the bulls saving the virgins; other sources say the figures are horsemen victorious in Bermudo's battle. Other scenes are of the Nativity. The porch has a modern wood-coffered ceiling.

Inside the church are a number of unremarkable seventeenth-century tombs and a Plateresque altarpiece. The central nave was later redone in early Gothic. The Romanesque cloister is worth a peek, but not great study.

Across the street from Santa María is a hotel and restaurant. The dining is excellent and the rooms in its new addition next to the restaurant compare favorably with three-star hotels but at a much better price.

From the hotel that evening we walked a couple of hundred meters west on Calle Santa María to the Plaza Mayor. Just off it on the right is the mid-twelfth-century **church of Santiago** – or what remains of it after most of the place was burned down during the Peninsular War. You find its facade crowded cheek by jowl with adjoining buildings, with a tall, square Romanesque bell tower above. The main portal is Romanesque, its carved archivolts containing twenty two figures of ordinary folks involved in daily activities, from cobblers and cooks to knights and musicians. The archway rises from round columns, capitals of which portray the salvation and damnation of the soul. The whole is regarded by some experts as among the highest quality Romanesque sculpture to be found on our travels this side of Santiago.

A second portal on the right, showing Gothic tendencies, is obviously of a later date. But what led to this ruin being selected as a national monument is the frieze that runs across the top of the facade. Centrally located above the main portal is Christ in His Majesty, the All Powerful, flanked by an angel and a hawk. In the row of niches to each side are the twelve Apostles. Although some of the figures have been badly vandalized, the work is regarded by the experts as outstanding for the time and style.

Still time for a stroll before dinner? Walk down from the plaza to the park by the Rio Carrión. It is a favorite of the townspeople for an evening promenade or a Sunday outing with a barbecue.

THE MOUNTAINS
WHERE THE RECONQUISTA WAS BORN

From Carrión de los Condes we plan a grand digression. It carries us far off our path along the now-familiar French Road. We will climb high across the spectacular Picos de Europa and down their northern flank to the sacred cave at Covadonga, birthplace of the Reconquista. The detour begins at the city of Sahagún. For travelers with a short fused schedule, this means that after exploring Sahagún you have a decision to make.

El Camino de Santiago leads directly from Sahagún to León, then some seventy kilometers away. Our planned detour takes us off the Camino for at least three days of explorations among the mountains of Asturias. If your schedule cannot afford those three days, head directly for León, detouring briefly at Mansilla de las Mulas to visit San Miguel de Escalada and Gradefes, places which in a later chapter we visit by means of a short backtrack from León.

With that advisory: Leaving Carrión de los Condes on N120, immediately across the river you find the monastery of **San Zoilo**, noted for its Plateresque cloister. One must stop to see it. Also found in the monastery are the tombs of the two young counts who are said to have made the fatal mistake of crossing El Cid and dishonoring his daughters. Their parents (founders of the monastery), half-dozen siblings and other relatives of the count are also entombed here.

San Zoilo was an early Benedictine foundation dating from the eleventh century, though virtually nothing of that founding edifice remains after the place was rebuilt during the sixteenth and seventeenth centuries. For a long period during modern times it was a seminary. Later it was abandoned and left in charge of caretakers until another drastic remodeling in the 1990s. Then, lo and behold, the main portal of the original Romanesque church was discovered beneath the accretions of the earlier renovations. While not as fancy as some we have seen, it has interesting archivolts which rest alternately on round columns and square pilasters engaged with the walls. The columns are believed to be of ancient Roman origin. Indeed, the columns and their carved bases and capitals are probably the nicest touches of the whole.

As for the **cloister**, it was the design of Juan de Badajoz, begun in 1537 but not finished until 1604, long after his death. The Gothic-arched galleries are studded with carved hanging bosses, while the ceiling between the ribbings is sculpted with scribed plaques and assorted frills and froth. The corbels beneath the ribs are decorated with skulls and bones, reminding us of our mortality amidst the eternal beauty of stone. Believe it or not, you will consider the galleries of Juan's cloister here to be rather plain if not second rate once you see the galleries he decorated, using many of the same design techniques, in the cathedral of León. Nonetheless, the experts are of an opinion that challenges mine.

The distance from Carrión to Sahagún is about forty kilometers, all on N120. We pass through or skirt a number of towns and villages, all of old Camino vintage. Until we reach Sahagún there are none with particularly see-worthy monuments recalling those centuries of pilgrimage or anything else.

At the town of San Nicolás del Real Camino we reach another border. This time we depart the province of Palencia and enter León. We are now plunging into the heart of the old kingdom of León, wrested from Muslim hands while the Caliph was still at the very peak of his powers. Not that the matter was settled with a single onslaught. León and the territory around it changed hands several times before the Christian hosts prevailed.

Sahagún

We remain in a land of legend. Sahagún marks the westernmost locale where the heroic feats of Charlemagne and his knights were made into legend. Indeed, Charlemagne is said by some accounts to have founded the town, naming it Cemala.

On the flatlands beside the nearby Cea River, according to the legendary history of the time, the Frankish king met an overpowering hostile force led by a Moorish giant. Miraculously, the Christian warriors prevailed. After the victory, the lances of the Frankish knights slain in the battle were driven into the soil along the riverbank to mark their graves. Again miraculously, the shafts took root, sprouted leaves and kept regrowing even when cut down. Now the grove of poplar trees near the medieval bridge crossing the Rio Cea, legend tells us, are descended from the lances of Charlemagne's valorous knights who died here a thousand years ago.

Beyond the river is the plain on which the battle was fought, and beyond that is more of the same. Flatlands. On this same plain a thousand years later another cavalry battle was fought, this time between a French contingent and a British force supporting the Spanish defense of Madrid against Napoleon during the early phase of the Peninsular War.

The British were led by Sir John Moore. He defeated a much larger French army on 21 December, 1808. A few days later, the tables were turned. A French column of more than fifty thousand men turned away from its Portuguese objective and marched north to cut off Moore and destroy him. Thus, from his base camp here at Sahagún, Moore's battalions began their historic retreat west along El Camino de Santiago to seek safety aboard the English fleet at La Coruña.

The retreat was a horrible disaster.

Traveling in mid-Winter without supplies, harassed by the French vanguard, it was an ordeal not unlike the retreat of the U. S. Marines from the Yalu – but worse. Moore himself died of wounds suffered at La Coruña, leading the rear guard while his surviving troops embarked. Some of the same troops later fought under Wellington and won revenge when they drove the French out of Spain.

In between the battles of Charlemagne and Sir John were centuries of warfare between Christians and Muslims for control of León and the land roundabout. Once León fell into Christian hands a great migration began. The Christians of the south, who had endured confiscatory Muslim taxes (of fifty percent of income, leveled as an economic incentive to convert to Islam) since the Arab-Moorish invasion in 711, suddenly found their persecution increased proportional to the military successes of their Christian brothers to the north. In response to those increasing tribulations the southerners, known as Mozarabs, during the late ninth and tenth centuries pulled up stakes by the thousands and trudged north to find new lives outside the orbit of Islam.

Most spoke only Arabic. They brought their Arabic Bible with them, along with their Arabic liturgy of the Mass and other Sacraments. The artisans among them also brought the manual skills and design know-how learned from Moorish master builders with whom they had apprenticed and served for nearly two hundred years.

Sahagún was one of the first places born of that migration. About AD 900 a monastery was established here by a colony of the so-called "black friars" who had fled Córdoba. They dedicated the place to San Facundo, a Roman martyr, and the name, Sahagún, is said to be a corruption of that name.

The monastery was always a shelter for pilgrims on the route to Santiago de Compostela. It grew steadily in importance no matter that it was twice destroyed by Moorish raiders. The final reconstruction took place in the eleventh century at the time of Alfonso VI, who induced Hugh of Cluny to send a company of Benedictine monks to San Facundo in 1079 as part of his move to reform the Mozarabic tendencies of the Spanish church. Alfonso at the same time obtained the companion migration of a town full of French tradesmen and others who settled around the religious community of monks.

The monastery, one of the grandest between Roncesvalles and Santiago, soon gained repute as "the Cluny of Spain" because of royal favor and the cultural and religious influence it wielded throughout the young Christian kingdoms. The monastery and the town that grew up around it also became as wealthy as they were influential. Some sources say that in the twelfth century Sahagún was the richest municipality along the entire Camino de Santiago, bar none.

All that is ancient history in more ways than one. The town is now a quiet backwater, much run down and disheveled. The monastery is but a memory except for bits salvaged for display in local museums. Its grand church of San Benito is a gigantic ruin. It was plundered by the French in the Peninsular war, and two decades later burned and turned to complete ruin during the First Carlist War. Yet the mark of its influence remains. In Sahagún you will discover, more unadulterated than anywhere else, the fruits of early medieval technology brought here from the Muslim south.

Another peculiar feature of the Mozarabic influence at Sahagún is that the skills of the refugee artisans were applied to brick rather than stone, which locally is not found in a quantity or quality suitable for extensive use in building. Perhaps you may have been fortunate enough to gain permission to see the distinctively Mozarabic brickwork in the chapel of Santiago at Las Huelgas, but that was a mere appetizer compared to what is preserved in Sahagún. Here its applications are of monumental proportions.

Sahagún is located on the flat between two rivers, the Valderaduey on the east and the Cea to the west. After crossing the Valderaduey, turn left off the main highway to follow the route into town and the Plaza Mayor. Exit the plaza on the far side and drive a couple of hundred meters further to park in the spacious Plaza San Benito near the prominent ruin of the church of the same name.

The church of **San Benito**, part of one of the most immense monastic establishments ever built along the Way of St. James, is mostly a ruin. Only its eastern section with its tall campanile survived the nineteenth century wars well enough to justify restoration as a modern clock tower. The main structure's cavernous Romanesque arches of red brick have been left standing open to the weather for nearly two centuries now. There is a stolid nobility about the place. It deserves a poem.

Near where you parked, on the end of the ruin opposite from the campanile, is the **Arco de San Benito**, spanning the street passing through its broad round archway. This portal, dating from 1662, rather remarkably is virtually whole and appears incongruous with its medieval environs. Nearby, occupying a rehabilitated rear section of the ruin, are the offices of the Guardia Civil, with parking for their vehicles located in the former interior of the church.

A few steps further, alongside the main ruin and saved from further deterioration by a protective roof, is the chapel of **San Mancio,** one of the earliest Gothic constructions in Spain and also with arches of brick. It contained the tombs of the benefactor of the monastery, Alfonso VI, and his Moorish-born queen, Zaida. Relics from all of this are now incorporated into a modern monastic building occupied by nuns of the Benedictine order, and operated as a museum open to the public. See it.

Walking back past San Benito toward the Plaza Mayor, you immediately encounter another church constructed of brickwork. It is dedicated to **San Tirso**. While not as grand as San Benito obviously once was, San Tirso is beautifully restored and maintained.

Why this church, virtually in the shadow of San Benito? San Tirso was begun in the late eleventh century as a parish church to serve the town that sprang up around the Benedictine monastery.

San Tirso achieves in brick many of the same architectural devices that marked Castilian stone structures of the time. Most remarkable is the tall tower above the crossing. Rectangular rather than perfectly square, with three levels of arcades piled one upon the other, the **tower** is a superb feat of architectural engineering. San Tirso is now a national monument intended to preserve this outstanding relic of the Mozarabic migration.

The San Tirso Church Tower

The entrance is to the side beneath and midway along the covered arcade that runs the length of the church. Ahead of the crossing is a pleasant chancel surrounded by three half-circle apses with **blind arcading** of the Romanesque-Mozarabic style. Note that the arches leading into the apses from the nave are all distinctively of the keyhole variety, though slightly less pronounced as such compared to those we will see at San Miguel de Escalada, or that we viewed at San Millán de Cogolla. The central apse is much taller than the pair alongside.

Now walk back to the **Plaza Mayor** and turn left past the Ayuntamiento, on the left. Continuing north from the Plaza Mayor you soon see another church. This one is dedicated to **San Lorenzo**. It is a twelfth and early thirteenth century edifice that, like San Tirso, is regarded as one of the best surviving

Romanesque-Mozarabic style brick edifices. Its tower is not as tall as that of San Tirso, and while it is similar in concept, it is much more artistic in design, distinctly revealing much stronger influences of the French Romanesque. For by then the Cluniac reforms and the immigration of Franks had been firmly established all along El Camino de Santiago.

The columns supporting the broader and thus airier arches in the lower and middle storeys of the tower lend a lighter, more graceful look. You see in the blind arches of the central and side apses a similarity in design to San Tirso, but with what I perceived to be a more Byzantine flavor in the style, a nuance mediated by Arabic sources.

In the large vestibule at the rear of the church were stored and displayed a half dozen of the lavishly decorated **"posos"** that groups of men carry on their shoulders during the Holy Week procession.

Inside the church note that, as at San Tirso, some of its blind arches are of horseshoe design. It is three-aisled and triple-apsed, with a transept and dome, all from the original construction. Interior decor is mostly sixteenth century stucco laid over the brickwork, with a Baroque altar containing a sculpture of the patron saint by Jean d'Angers. Note that the timbers supporting the roofs above the side aisles are pole construction, slender tree trunks hewn flat on two sides.

Finally, on the southern outskirts of Sahagún is the **Sanctuario** de la Peregrina, once associated with a vanished Franciscan monastery and pilgrim's hospice. The name came from a statue of the Virgin in pilgrim garb, now seen at the Benedictine nun's museum. The sanctuary church was completed in 1257. Recently restored (completed in 2011) as a national monument, it serves as a cultural and educational center. It gained distinction as a monument because here we find the unusual application of Mozarabic touches to a Gothic design done in brick. You will find nothing else like it along the Way. In effect it has a Visigothic influence peeking through Arabic stylistic designs worked on a French Gothic concept. Talk about multiculturalism.

The entrance consists of a Gothic **triple arch** with a horseshoe effect, something unique to be sure. The remnants of Moorish stucco work in the lofty vaults of the sacristy are especially noteworthy. Nearby excavations tell of the vanished monastery.

The Picos de Europa

From Sahagún drive north on C611. A hundred kilometers away are the mountains where Christians found sanctuary from the Arab conquerors and slave merchants. The tallest peaks are the spectacular Picos de Europa, the snow-capped backbone of the Cantabrian Cordillera. Today we negotiate the high passes through those peaks and gain shelter tonight on their northern flank not far from where the Reconquista was born.

Our destination is Cangas de Onís, some 150 kilometers distant. It was the first capital of the Asturian kings who traced their lineage directly to Roderick, last king of the Visigoths, who was slain during the initial and only pitched battle of the Arab conquest. The victory of the Arabs was so devastating that no force remained that was fit to stand against them.

One of the mysteries of history is why rich and powerful regimes such as that of the Visigoths can so often collapse in a single day, as it were. We observed it most recently in the disintegration of the Soviet empire. But there was no mystery about what happened to the Visigoths on the battlefield at Xeres, not far from Cadiz. It is a tale of treachery and intrigue, not unlike that now threatening Europe and America.

The Arabs were secretly invited into Spain by Julian, the spiteful son of a former king of the Goths. Julian felt he, not Roderick, should have been elevated to the throne. Thus while Julian and his supporters joined Roderick in the battle against the Arab invaders, their real intent was to have the Arabs get rid of Roderick. After three days of battle, however, the Goths were on the verge of winning and Roderick looked secure on his throne. That was too much for Julian to endure, so he pulled his troops out of the line during a critical stage of the fight and the Arab-led army of Moors slaughtered Roderick and the cream of Gothic knighthood, virtually to the last man. Most of those who managed to escape were hunted down and slain during the following three days.

Julian, too weak to face the Saracens on his own and understanding too late that they meant to take Spain for themselves, not for him, surrendered himself to the mercies of the Moors. The Saracens then marched north through Spain, methodically taking individual cities and towns by force or by terms, and within a year they controlled the entire peninsula. Only a handful of Gothic knights escaped to the safety of the northern mountains and there stayed free of Arab chains.

Later the Arabs marched four hundred of the leading Gothic nobility, male and female, and thirty thousand others, also of both sexes and all in chains, overland across North Africa from the Strait of Gibraltar to Cairo and Damascus to celebrate the triumph. After that exhibition, the surviving captives disappeared from history into slavery. The widow of Roderick was taken to wife by the Moorish commander. Julian disappeared, and his daughter was given to a noble Arab to add to his flock of wives.

Such was the story of the conquest, told in the proverbial nutshell. The crucial element – the seed that bore fruit in the Reconquista – was the escape of the tiny band of Christian knights who fled into the mountain fastnesses that we now are approaching.

After Cistierna the highway (N621) begins its climb into the Cantabrian Cordillera. Call these the rocky gray mountains, their sharp, precipitous peaks silhouetted on all sides as you drive.

At Riaño take N625 north about ten kilometers and you find you have now climbed into the high mountains. Continue on highway N625 for passage through the Puerto del Pontón at 1296 meters. It lies near the heart of the spectacular Picos de Europa and is the lowest of the three main passes that penetrate these mountains.

The Picos de Europa contain the tallest peaks of the Cantabrian Cordillera. Their weathered gray sawtooth summits and buttresses lift high above the green beginnings of life down below. Much of the year the rugged gray masses of stone are softened by snow, deposited by Winter storms that swirl among the crags. Here are the Summertime sources of the rivers you crossed down on the Meseta. The Torre Cerredo tops out at 2648 meters, and you gain a wonderful view of it from the Mirador de Piedrafitas (at 1450 meters). That viewpoint lies at the end of an access road that departs the highway just prior to reaching the Puerto del Pontón.

At a viewpoint on the pass itself there is an equally fabulous view of the Sajambre Valley, off to the right. Note that the farms in the narrow valley straddling the road are devoted to dairy and beef cattle. The short growing season at this altitude limits crop selection to grass and hay.

About twelve kilometers beyond the pass is the village of Oseja de Sajambre. A kilometer or so beyond it, on the right, a side road leads off about two kilometers to another mirador with a fine view. The sheer rock peak to the southwest is the Niaja.

Much of this huge and precipitous territory is a national park. To the east is a large game preserve, the last refuge of a local species of brown bear and the wolves that once preyed upon pilgrims down on the Meseta below. Yes, and the last wild horse herds in Europe. This is country that, a hundred meters off the road, is as wild and untamed as when the Christians fled here in the eighth century for refuge from the Arabs. Yet there are walking trails into the backcountry, and the dizzying cliffs that you see in all directions are favorite haunts of those devoted to the sport of rock climbing.

Continuing north on N625 you suddenly find yourself descending into the Desfiladero de los Beyos, a seven-kilometer long slash through the limestone mounts cut by the Rio Sella. The road follows the tortuous twists and turns of the river through the deep, narrow gorge. In places the rock walls seem to rise a kilometer above on both sides.

About ten kilometers after you exit the defile, the road to Priescas departs to the west through a similarly spectacular gorge cut through the rock massif by the Rio Ponga.

Past the intersection with the Priescas road we continue northward another ten kilometers to Cangas de Onís, first capital of the Christian kings of the Reconquista. It is situated beside the Rio Sella, which now flows through a wide, fertile valley.

If you did not dally too long over lunch and got an early start this morning, there is plenty of time remaining for a visit to Covadonga. As you pass through Cangas de Onís, however, take the precaution of verifying your hotel arrangements for tonight. As you will soon discover, this is a popular destination for Spanish visitors in all seasons. Our choice was a hotel on the highway east of town on the way to Covadonga. There is a Parador near town which we will visit at the end of our time in Cangas de Onis, so it might be convenient to stay there.

Covadonga

Take route AS114 east from Cangas de Onís for about four kilometers. Watch for the road to the right, AS262, that follows the Rio Deva to Covadonga. As you drive, let me brief you on the history of Asturias, and Covadonga in particular, at the birthing of the Reconquista.

With all organized resistance smashed, the Arabs drove all the way to the Cantabrian coast in their first surge of conquest, occupying all of the peninsula by 714. In 713 a governor was installed at Gijon on the Bay of Biscay, north of what is now Oviedo. At first the Arab governor attempted to follow up the conquest with pacification of the region. He met resistance from the handful of Gothic knights led by Pelayo (Pelagius), who some sources say was a one-time ne'r-do-well son of Roderick, the last Gothic king. Others said he was the son of a highly-placed member of the Visigothic king's court.

Pelayo's force lacked the strength of numbers to offer

pitched battle, but made life miserable for the Moors by ambushes and other harassments. In 718 Pelayo had the gall to have himself elected (after the Gothic tradition of choosing a monarch) to the throne of his father, no matter that the royal seat was now little more than an outcropping of rock, safe in the protection of the mountains.

Finally, the Arab governor, assisted by a punitive force sent from Córdoba by the Caliph in 722, mounted an attack on Pelayo's mountain lair, located at a place now known as Covadonga. "Covadonga" is a linguistic corruption of Cueva Dominica, Sacred Cave, where the final action of the subsequent battle took place.

When the Arabs approached to launch the attack, Pelayo and his tiny troop of about three hundred knights took up blocking positions in the **gorge** of the Rio Deva, which we drive through on the way to Covadonga. In these narrow confines Pelayo calculated that he could better defend against a force that outnumbered his own by more than ten to one. He knew it would be a fight in which no quarter would be asked or given.

The legends say more than six thousand Moors moved up the gorge against him, but that seems an unlikely number. In any event, the Christian knights were forced to retreat, falling back to the fortress-like lair they had established, centered on a large cave high in the side of a cliff, now the **Sacred Cave** of Victory.

We follow the route of their retreat as we exit the gorge and approach their last-chance redoubt through a small but verdant valley. It is what American mountain men called a park, rimmed by tall cliffs amidst the towering shoulders of the Picos de Europa. In the middle of the valley is a low, flat-topped limestone ridge containing the cave where Pelayo and survivors of his three hundred knights rallied for their last stand. Tradition has it that Pelayo and his men, prior to the final battle, prayed to an image of the Holy Mother that a hermit had hidden in the cave, and were rewarded by Her intercession in the battle.

At the fork in the road, near a concatenation of cafes, souvenir stands and the like, find a place to park. From there it is a brief climb to the cave, high up in the cliff face on the left. Visible atop a lofty pinnacle to the right is an attractive pink-stone basilican-style church with twin towers.

Where you find the road guarded by a pair of heroic-sized sleeping lions, take the long, red marble staircase up to Pelayo's cave. A small beige colored chapel is tucked back beneath the rock overhang of the cliff above. You may find a line of visitors already formed at the head of the stairs in the tunnel that leads off to the right through the heart of the mount. It was cut through the solid rock to provide a shortcut to the cave from the church you viewed from below, and from the monastic quarters nearby.

It is a rare day and hour when it is possible to come here to Pelayo's cave, find only a handful of visitors, and be able to study the chapel and its environs at leisure. Generally, for the sake of others crowding behind, you may pause a moment at this shrine commemorating the birth of Spain, then move on to exit between the guide ropes that separate the lines coming and going. It would be best to brave the line twice, attending to the shrine on this visit; later returning to view the ambience of it all.

Less than a cave, this is more a gigantic recess bowled into the cliff by a parent of the Deva a million years ago. It was to this place, the legend says, that Pelayo and his men retreated to make their final stand – and won the day. It was a miracle, they knew, attributing their victory to the intercession of the Virgin Mary, to whom they had said their last prayers, pleading either for earthly help or eternal salvation. Trapped with their backs literally against the rock walls of their hideout, Pelayo's men rallied to kill the Arab leader and decimate the attacking force, an event recalled in Spanish history as the first victory of the Reconquista.

Now this place is called the **Santa Cueva** and the chapel is dedicated to Nuestra Señora de las Battallas – Our Lady of the Battles. Her day of honor is September 8. You would do well not to be here then, when Covadonga is thronged to overflowing with Spaniards from all corners of the globe, drawn here to celebrate the beginning of their freedom from foreign bondage, and to honor the Lady and the warrior who made it happen.

Covadonga, The Sacred Cave

One wonders why the Moors allowed the victory to stand, powerful as they were at the time. The answer may be that their defeat at Covadonga was regarded for what it was – a miserable little flea bite on the backside of a wolf that was setting out to gobble up the rest of Europe. Then, after the stinging defeats his armies suffered in France, the Caliph probably lacked the will and the resources to invade these mountains again to set things aright for Islam. Soon the passes were defended by an organized and battle-toughened force of Asturs rather than just the rag-tag band of survivors from King Roderick's army of defeated Gothic knights.

In the cave's chapel, mounted above an enameled **altar** of modern vintage, is the much venerated statue of the Virgin, La Santina. It is of twelfth century origin with a masterful eighteenth century facelift. Behind the altar is an enameled copper panel depicting the kings of Asturias. Nearby, in a cave opening in the adjacent rock wall, is the resting place of the first king, Pelayo, and Alfonso I, who married Pelayo's sister Ermesinda, and through her came to the throne. With them are Ermesinda and Gaudiosa, daughter of Pelayo and queen of King Favila. The legend that Favila was unfortunate enough to have been torn to pieces and eaten by a bear, may explain his absence from this pantheon celebrating Asturian royal beginnings.

Now make your way through the tunnel to the broad **Plaza** de la Basilica, with a bronze Pelayo poised beneath his cross of victory. Perched high on this rock shoulder above the lower valley we find the basilica on the far side, the Hotel Pelayo to the right, souvenir shops and the like to the left, the museum to the far end of that building, and monastic and other Church buildings off behind. The square hums with activity in the service of pilgrims come to give reverence to this historic and sacred place.

The **church** was started in the nineteenth century and finished in 1901. It replaced a tenth century structure destroyed by fire. Modern though it is, it is predominantly neo-Romanesque with Gothic vaulting above the crossing and a mixed bag of styles in the twin towers. The entire structure is made of the pink marble of which we have seen so much hereabouts. Part of the cloister, and a pair of tombs therein, are vestiges of the tenth century construction.

The most interesting feature of this religious establishment is its **treasury**, which sits in a separate building across the plaza. It contains votive offerings to Nuestra Señora de las

Battallas deposited here in centuries past. One outstanding piece (kept in a steel safe opened during viewing hours) is a crown on which are mounted more than a thousand diamonds, and twice as many rubies.

Interesting also are a number of imaginative portraits of the early kings. Among them is Pelayo himself, who died in 737. He is depicted in war helmet and beard, wielding his cross of victory. Others shown are Bermudo I (d 795), Fruela II (d 924) and Ordoñio II (d 925), the latter pair reigning over the divided kingdom of Asturias after the death of Alfonso III, the Great.

So now you have seen it all at Covadonga. As you come out onto the plaza, however, take one last stroll between the monument to Pelayo and the parapet across the plaza in front of the church. The views are stupendous and worth a moment of contemplation. Only a few feet from where modern men have left their mark is the green wall of forest and the gray bastions of the mountains. They are not all that different now from what they were thirteen hundred years ago when Pelayo and his desperate followers retreated into the valley below, parrying the thrusts of a horde of Muslim attackers, falling back to the narrow confines of the rock walls near their sanctuary. There they stood and fought, gaining the same advantage that the Spartans did at Thermopylae: A few stout fighters in a restricted space could hold against tremendous odds, at least for a while. The difference was that here the Arab commander rushed to the front rank to rally his troops for the final victory and died in the attempt. His followers, shocked by their loss, fled the field and Pelayo's tiny legion achieved the first major victory of the Reconquista.

ASTURIAS

Events in France figured prominently in allowing the Christian resurgence in Asturias to gain momentum. From 719 onward, the main Arab thrust was directed into France. Asturias, by then isolated from the remainder of Christendom and too weak to pose a meaningful challenge on the Arab flank, was practically ignored while the Caliph stalked bigger game. France thus was the scene of the decisive campaigns that decided the outcome of the Arab conquest of Europe.

Nevertheless, Asturias remained a player in the game of conquest. After Pelayo's phenomenal success at Covadonga, his tiny force quickly multiplied in strength and grew in daring. Recruits streamed into the hills to fight under his banner. Soon the Arabs were virtual prisoners in Gijon. Worse, because of catastrophic reverses in France, further assistance from Córdoba suddenly was beyond the capability of the Caliphate.

After having occupied Gijon for only a decade, and virtually cut off from the rest of Spain by Pelayo's raiders and ambushes, the Arabs were forced to pack up and retreat south to León. The mountains of Asturias were thus reluctantly but surely abandoned to Pelayo's Christian knights. But for that fateful decision by the Caliph not to contest the mountain passes with Pelayo's growing band of fighters, the Iberian Peninsula even today would probably be an extension of Moslem North Africa.

It was, then, no mere coincidence that the Arab retreat to León coincided with the first major defeat the Saracen armies suffered in Europe. That setback came in 721 in France, at Toulouse, involving losses that required the Caliph to draw heavily on his military assets in Northern Spain in order to maintain pressure upon the Franks. The defeat of the Caliph's army at Toulouse proved to be only a temporary reversal. Reinforced from Spain and Africa, Moslem forces soon seemed unstoppable once again. By 730 the Caliph controlled

France all the way to Lyons and the Loire. Christian armies, one after another, were wiped out, the men killed or sent into slavery building mosques in Córdoba and elsewhere in Spain and Africa. The Caliph's dream of subjecting all of Europe to the Moslem yoke was on the verge of coming true.

The Arab scheme of conquest was smashed near Poitiers on October 25, 732. An alliance led by Charles Martel, chief of the Franks (and grandfather of Charlemagne), destroyed both the Arab army and its leader. The disorganized remnants of the Arab invasion forces then were swiftly driven back beyond the Pyrenees, and never again recouped the strength to challenge the Franks on their home field. A generation was required for the Arabs to revitalize and fill out the squadrons depleted by the stupendous disasters they suffered on French battlefields. As it happened, that was all the time the Asturians needed to make their mountains virtually impregnable to anything other than what George Patton liked to call "reconnaissance in force."

Pelayo reigned from 718 until his death in 737. He established his capital at Cangas de Onís and married off his daughter to the Duke of Cantabria, who succeeded Pelayo and called himself King Favila of Asturias. Pelayo's sister married another noble Asturian knight of his court. As fate would have it, she and her husband, Alfonso, turned out to be the progenitors of the kings of the Reconquista.

The daughter of Pelayo apparently was without issue, perhaps because of the early and untimely death of her husband. As we learned at Covadonga, Favila is said to have been killed and eaten by one of the bears that still roam these mountains.

Alfonso I was dubbed the Catholic. As a boy he had turned toward the church and become something of a scholar, joining the brothers at a monastery we will visit several days hence. The coming of the Moors changed all that. Alfonso's monastic refuge was destroyed by the conquerors and he fled north into the mountains where he took up arms and joined the resistance. The keen mind of the scholar thus became one of the best military brains of the early Reconquista.

During Alfonso's reign, which lasted until 757, he secured full control of Asturias, then expanded his domains east to Santander and west into Galicia beyond the present city of Santiago de Compostela.

Alfonso II (r 791-842), known as the Chaste, transferred the Asturian capital to Oviedo while extending his dominion over all of Galicia. He held the throne when the tomb of St. James was discovered in 814.

Alfonso II was followed by Ramiro I, famed as victor at the Battle of Clavijo, and Ordoñio I (d 866) both of whom set about reconquering the fringes of the Meseta. Ordoñio recovered León and made it the capital of his enlarged Kingdom of Asturias and León. That set the stage for Alfonso III, the Great, who fought off repeated attacks by the Moors – although they recaptured León for a time – and solidified the Christian hold on the northern reaches of the Meseta.

Cangas de Onís

Covadonga was the birthplace of the Reconquista. Cangas de Onís was where it was nurtured, capitol of the young monarchy until 774. In recognition of that beginning and the crucial role of the Astur tribes in defeating the Arabs, the eldest son of the Spanish king and queen has always been given the title, Prince of Asturias. But the city itself long ago lost practically all physical evidence of the heritage stemming from Pelayo and his stalwarts. Surely there is the Capilla de la Santa Cruz, originally erected to house Pelayo's Cross of Victory. We will take a look at the modern version of that tiny edifice.

In the vicinity, with no connection to the history of the Reconquista, there is a particular site one ought to see while hereabouts. East of town less than three kilometers, north of the highway about a kilometer, is the famous Cueva del Buxu (boo-coo), where cave drawings of animals and geometric figures have been discovered dating from the old stone age. The drawings are tiny and generally difficult to make out after so many millennia (estimated age is about 25,000 years), so they are spectacular only in terms of their value as artifacts telling of the so called Magdalenian culture, which thrived here on the north coast of Spain.

In deference to the fragility of the cave and its treasures, only a couple of dozen people are admitted to the cave in any one day (closed Mondays). In groups of four or five persons, the first tour of the low ceilinged, narrow passages starts at 10 am. On the recent day when we explored the cave, my wife and I were the thirteenth and fourteenth persons to arrive, although we got there more than a half hour early. We were so early only because we had spent the night at a hotel near to the turn off to the cave, not really thinking there would be so many people wanting to join us in poking about in a hole in the ground. Besides, it was past the peak of the tourist season. Yet we were joined by a young German couple with a pair of teenage girls, a pair of French university students, and Spanish people of all ages and backgrounds from pre-teens to retirees, blue-collar folks to professors.

Best advice is to be at the cave even earlier than we got there. At least a dozen more than the allotted twenty five were turned away, as the rule is strictly observed by the guide. We were fortunate to share our tour, which lasted about a half hour, with a student of archaeology and his wife, who spoke some English. Thus with our less than technical proficiency in Spanish, the commentary of the guide was clarified by our companions. Nonetheless, even someone with little capability in the language and not fortunate enough to have a knowledgeable translator, will find the tour fascinating. Pictures, after all, speak for themselves.

The road up from the main highway finds a rather unobtrusive sign on the left indicating the walkway up to the cave. Park along the road wherever you can find a shoulder wide enough. From there hike up a little-used farmer's tractor path that girdles the steep mountainside for about a kilometer between a mix of forest and precipitous pasture on either side.

The brief path to the cave, where it turns off through the woods to the right towards the face of a cliff, is well marked. From there climb the crude stairway and steep incline about a hundred meters up to the mouth of the cave. You find it obstructed by a locked wooden door set back into the cliff about ten meters. Remember, first come, first served, with the limit set at twenty five.

Visiting the cave means that you will get a late start on the road, but that is no real hardship, as we are not traveling far today. Our destination is Oviedo, the long-time capital of Asturias, just a little more than seventy kilometers west of here on a good highway all the way.

Capilla de la Santa Cruz

Returning to Cangas de Onis from Covadonga or Cueva Buxu on A114, exit onto the Avenida de Covadonga, which runs parallel. Continuing toward the center of Cangas de Onis, take a right on Avenida de Contranquil and after about 200 meters you encounter the Capilla de la Santa Cruz. It is a tiny structure of quarried stone with an entrance stairway nearly as broad as the building, with a flimsy appearing roof above it. Tradition has it that this was the first Christian church built after the Muslim invasion.

How faithfully the current structure, built in 1951 on the site of the original, mirrors that original is not known. The chapel was erected by King Favela I, successor to Pelayo, in 737, and consecrated as the royal church on October 27 of that year. Such a less than imposing structure speaks to the limited power and wealth of his birthing kingdom.

The site was originally a Celtic burial ground and shrine. In the fifth century, a Christian chapel had been built directly over the burial ground. Enclosed within the chapel foundations was a Celtic dolmen, a large, natural flat stone laid across other stones much like a table or an altar. These were used by the Celts as cemetery markers. Such a site for a Christian chapel was not unusual for, as we have seen in our explorations of both Sicily and Greece, Christian evangelists seemed universally ready to co-opt the sacred places and even the gods and spirits of their pagan converts.

For whatever reason, Favila had his chapel sited upon that earlier Christian structure above the 3000-year-old pagan dolmen, complete with a burial chamber decorated with rock drawings and paintings. After nearly a thousand years, the chapel was completely rebuilt in the seventeenth century. Come the Spanish Civil War, it was reduced to a pile of rubble in 1936, leading to the reconstruction in 1951. The dolmen was fully excavated during the 1951 rebuilding and now exists as a kind of crypt beneath the existing chapel. A port located in the chapel floor exposes the dolmen to view.

The chapel gained its name by becoming the sanctuary which kept and displayed the Cross of Victory carried by Pelayo at Covadonga. (We will see it at the Cathedral in Oviedo.) One local story has it that King Favila and his queen were buried there, no matter the companion legend that he was killed and eaten by a bear.

On the way west to Oviedo out of Cangas de Onís take a moment to view the old bridge over the Rio Sella. Its long graceful arch, soaring high above the river, is seen to your left as you cross the modern highway bridge. Find a place to park in the small plaza on the far side of the river. From there, walk the thirty meters or so between buildings to stroll up onto the cobblestone pavement of the old span.

What you find is a large, sturdy structure built to withstand the floods of a thousand years. And it has. Some say it is of Roman vintage, rebuilt in the thirteenth century. Others say it is simply Romanesque, built probably in the eleventh or twelfth century. Still other opinions would have it be a Gothic construction, perhaps of the sixth or seventh century. Whatever its origin, it is a beautiful, ivy-covered stone structure with a single hump-backed main span with two short arches beneath the approaches.

If your interest is technical, such as that of a civil engineer fascinated by ancient feats of engineering, walk across the bridge and, on the east side of the river, you will find a stairway down to the riverbank where a detailed inspection of the structure and its footings can be made.

Monastic Church of San Pedro

On your way again, you find that the highway snakes west along the Sella river towards Arriondas. After about two kilometers, across the river on the right is the village of Villanueva. At the far end of the village is the formerly abandoned monastery of San Pedro, with a church that far outshines the Capella de la Santa Cruz. Today the monastery is a hive of activity, having been converted into a top quality Parador. The monastic church, once just an empty barn of a place, now has a beautifully appointed interior and appears fully functional.

On our first visit, the place was deserted and locked up tight, so we drove back through the village, going past the site of the new bridge to a small general store near the old one-lane bridge that, until the current century and the Parador, was the only river crossing available to the community. We learned from an elderly gentleman resting beneath a tree that the lady at the counter in the store held the key. She entrusted it to our care without questions or second thoughts. Later, when we returned the key, we purchased the fixings for a picnic lunch to be enjoyed later along the road. The photograph of the church shown here was taken upon that occasion.

The original church of San Pedro was built at the order of Alfonso I. Local tradition has it that it was consecrated on 21 February 746, which was tenuously confirmed by the archeological evaluation of the site during the construction of the Parador. Considering that was but a decade after construction of the Capilla de la Santa Cruz, the size and character of the church was a significant indication of the progress of the young Christian kingdom.

The Monastic Church of San Pedro

The monastery was added in the twelfth century, operated by Benedictine monks. Renovations and remodelings during the seventeenth, eighteenth and twentieth centuries modified the church such that the only parts of the original church structure that remain are the apses and adjacent portal. In 1685 even the tower was redone. The design of the whole, however, is said to preserve that of Alfonso's and the Benedictine's remodel of the original. Fortunately, portal and apses contain the architectural gems that make a visit to this place so interesting. The Parador also has two rooms containing displays of items recovered during the archeological evaluation of the site during construction of the Parador.

The portal stands within a porch beneath the fat, square, and squat Romanesque bell tower. The portal's archway, sans lintel or tympanum, we found ornately carved around a paneled, time-darkened wooden door. It is a Pre-Romanesque entryway that deserves close study by experts and ordinary folks alike.

The sculptured decor is characteristically Roman, with triple arches rising from capitals carved with florals, as are the archivolts, except for the capitals on the left. Those at the far left of the portal depict Favila's strange demise. As we see, he kissed his queen, Gaudiosa, goodbye, and went off hunting with his falcon on his arm. Then he was waylaid, killed and eaten by a bear. No doubt the intent of Alfonso was to provide a sculptural obituary honoring his predecessor.

Continuing to the right, the next capital depicts a dragon being stilled by an angel, followed by a display of four hawks perched atop the inner doorpost column.

At this portal, and in the decorations we will examine in a few minutes while walking around the exterior of the apse, we experience our first encounter with Asturian art and architecture, which is a pre-Romanesque style imbued with traits drawn from Rome through the Visigoths and Byzantium, the great empire of the East.

Perhaps one of the most fascinating aspects of these cultural discoveries in Northwest Spain is the sophistication and audacity of the artisans and builders employed by the Christian kings of the early Reconquista. In the Christian west, except in Southern Italy and the provinces of Byzantium, architecture in the grand style was virtually a dead art until the Age of Charlemagne. Yet here in these isolated mountains of Northern Spain during the eighth century we find a rejuvenation of the arts, and their independent persistence while virtually cut off from Christian Europe for the best part of two hundred years.

Here we discover the work of builders who displayed a connection with the culture of ancient Rome filtered through Byzantium and the old Visigothic civilization of the south. Just as Pelayo and his companion knights escaped north to fight again, at least a few of the master builders, artisans and artists who served the Visigothic kings in Toledo or elsewhere found safety here in the mountainous north. And just as the Gothic knights found brides among the Asturian tribes and produced the phalanx of warriors who recaptured Spain, so did these builders create the foundation for a novel cultural expression

237

that came to be the artistic underpinnings for a new Christian civilization.

We discovered echoes of that influence, we recall, as far distant as Leyre on the borders of Aragon. There it was soon overwhelmed by the surging cultural presence of France in general and Cluny in particular. In the Pre-Romanesque crypt and apse of Leyre, built two hundred years after this church at Villanueva, we found traits suggestive of the builders who learned their trade here in the mountains of Asturias. I suspect that what they had in common was their Visigothic antecedents.

A century later, Asturian builders met the Mozarabs down on the Meseta, and we saw the melding of their arts and crafts at San Millán de Cogolla, and the coupling with French Romanesque as well as the Mudéjar at Sahagún. But here, and in Oviedo, we discover the pure Pre-Romanesque of the Asturian cultural revival.

Leaving the portal, circle around the exterior of the apse. Of note are the elegant carvings of the modillions, high up beneath the edge of the roof. They are all different, depicting both human and animal figures, while some are merely geometric in design. On the central apse the modillions are separated by carved panels. Most are geometric in design, but several display a few primitive human figures. The tall, narrow window in the central apse, with a low-relief floral frieze above the arch and cylindrical columns to the side, betrays a distinct Byzantine influence.

Inside the church, the domes of the central and side apses and the barrel-vaulted ceiling were frescoed. The frescoes are survivals of the seventeenth century rehabilitation of the place by the monks. The arches and their capitals, however, repeat a primitive pre-Romanesque style of sculptural decoration. Note at the central apse, on the right hand capital, we see a bear pouncing on Favila. Opposite, on the left hand capital, farmers are shown tending their oxen. Despite the rehabilitations of the place during the course of centuries and the lavish appointments of today, here you share the view of Alfonso I and the early kings of Asturias. Where you walk now, they walked and prayed more than a thousand years ago.

At the rear of the nave a door permitted egress down a stairway into a vestibule opening left into the tiny, two-storeyed cloister. Here we found a pure, plain Romanesque construction with strange, flattened arches in the upper galleries. Entry into the cloister was through a beautifully conceived triple-arched portal, decorated in the Roman style with floral capitals above the side columns. There was solitude and peace here no matter the artistic recollections of man-eating bears and kings who, generation after generation, fought the Moslem tide to a standstill. Some of that monastic flavor has been preserved to be seen as you explore the Parador.

Oviedo

We find Oviedo situated in a broad, fertile valley surrounded by mountains ranging toward ever taller peaks silhouetted in the distance.

Oviedo for more than a thousand years has been the capital of Asturias. Now the center of a coal and copper mining district and a city of about two hundred thousand people, Oviedo is very much a modern city in all respects. Yet it has neither forgotten nor lost respect for its origins – although it came close to that in the 1930s during a workers' revolt and later when the Republicans took the city during the Civil War. The fighting in both instances severely damaged much of Oviedo's fabulous heritage dating from the early days of the Reconquista. Like the Bolsheviks that they emulated, or the tzars of political correctness in our own time, the Spanish Republicans and local communists revealed little respect for a past they were determined to overthrow and hoped to obliterate.

Oviedo recovered from the destruction of the 1930s, just as it had when the Moors flattened the place in 789. We have already described how the theological scholar, Alfonso I,

239

turned warrior king and forcefully expanded the Asturian realm from the vicinity of Cangas de Onís to encompass Santander, Galicia and the edge of the Meseta even to the vicinity of León.

The towns and villages of the Meseta meanwhile were largely depopulated. The inhabitants fled to the mountains to escape enslavement or worse at the hands of the Moors. The Asturian kings welcomed the refugees with land and helped them form new villages and towns. This was the principal work of Fruela I, who consolidated the realm his uncle Pelayo and father Alfonso had created. One of the places where those refugees settled was in Oviedo and its valley. Oviedo was founded by Fruela in 761 alongside the Benedictine monastery of San Vicente on a hill known as Ovetum.

Alfonso II, the Chaste, was on the throne when the Moors destroyed Oviedo during a "reconnaissance in force" in 789. The destruction became an excuse for Alfonso to rebuild the town and make it over into his capital city, which it became in 792. He built sturdy walls to defend it so that never again could the Caliph work vengeance on the Christian city that, at the end of the eighth century, already was a spear pointed at the heart of the Meseta.

After Alfonso came Ramiro I of Clavijo fame, and then Ordoñio I, who moved onto the Meseta in force. He established his capital at León so as to be closer to the scene of military action. Alfonso III, the Great, then began the reconquest and repopulation of Old Castile before his death in 910.

We recite the names of these kings and note the broad scope of their accomplishments because the most important of the historic and cultural artifacts that we visit today in and around Oviedo are products of their era, which lasted about 150 years. It was a time of momentous achievements during which the kings of tiny Asturias fought toe to toe with the most powerful empire on Earth. It was a period of constant war and preparations for war, an era when even the saints had to be deeply involved in the fight. How else could the Christian kings have won, after all?

Santiago! After Ramiro's time that rallying cry brought the

famous Moorslayer to the side of desperate men overrun by Moors on the open vastness of the Meseta. Then too, since the time of Pelayo, fighters trapped with their backs against the wall of a ravine in the mountains had still another call. Santa María! She was not known as Our Lady of the Battles for nothing.

Somehow, whether through divine intervention or not, these Asturians won out. The old Gothic aristocracy that Pelayo represented merged with the Astur descendants of Celts in the mountains and Iberians from the plains. They created a Christian sanctuary in mountainous Asturias while intermingling their blood and consolidating several dialects with common Latin roots. These mergers of blood and fresh cultural beginnings produced the first truly "Spanish" kings: Ramiro, Ordoñio, and Alfonso the Great. Between them they created the political and cultural foundations upon which modern Spain was raised.

The highway leads directly into the heart of Oviedo and to Calle Jovellanos. On this street and nearby are hotels of many classes, all convenient to our initial explorations of the old city, which begin as soon as we get settled. However, our recent visit found the city streets so torn up for repairs and improvements that parking and normal driving through the streets was virtually impossible. One glance at the situation and we decided to stay at a hotel in the suburbs. Our selection is located a half-dozen kilometers north of Oviedo off the Autopista, A66. Exiting at the Lugones off ramp going east there are a couple of three-star hotels along the highway within the first kilometer. Then, to explore Oviedo, we drove back into town and found public parking without being concerned whether it was convenient to a desirable hotel or not.

Our explorations of old Oviedo commence at the northwest corner of the Plaza de Alfonso II near the eighteenth century Camposagrado Palace (now a courthouse) and the Heredia Palace, a sixteenth century construction now with offices of the regional government.

This square has been the center of affairs in Oviedo since

Alfonso II rebuilt the place after the Saracens leveled it in 789. Off to the right is the Plaza de Porlier where, facing you, is the public library, ensconced in the seventeenth century Palacio de Toreno. On the far left of the square is the cathedral, which indubitably is the eye-catcher here. Its Gothic tower and spire stand eighty-two meters tall. The gigantic pointed archways leading into its front porch, with the rose window above at center, immediately command attention.

Fruela I built the first church on the site in the eighth century, only to have it destroyed by the Moors along with the rest of the town. Alfonso II built anew, but only fragments of his work remain after later reconstructions. The present cathedral is a product of the period between 1328 and 1528 except for the tall west tower, completed in 1539.

But there is much more to this square than the cathedral. As we said, this broad plaza has been the center of activity in Oviedo since Alfonso II laid it out and rebuilt the city late in the eighth century after the Moors had done it in. On your left, looking east, is the Heredia Palace (sometimes called the Valdecarzana Palace, dating from the seventeenth century), with ironwork balconies and the royal arms on the facade at the center. It was a former royal visitation palace. Beyond that, in the far corner, is the Garden of the Reyes Caudillos (the Royal Leaders), memorializing the early kings of Asturias. Those kings were in fact leaders of the old style of warrior kings, who led their troops into battle and shared the rigors of campaigning in the field.

Across the street from where you stand is the Balesquida Chapel, founded in 1270 by Doña Balesquida Giraldez. At the altar is a life size image of Nuestra Señora de la Esperanza, garbed then in a matrimonial gown beneath a flowing green cape. From a distance Our Lady appears lifelike enough to be preparing to step down to walk among us.

On the street again, walk to the right, circling the square and gaining different perspectives of the cathedral as we go. A few steps beyond the chapel, at No. 11, is the Llanes House, while at the southwest corner of the square at No. 15, is the fifteenth century Casa de la Rua, the oldest house in Oviedo.

At the southeast corner the square is the Church of San Tirso, originally constructed between 812 and 816 by Alfonso II and restored practically from its foundations in the seventeenth century. Little of the original structure is be found therefore other than the round-arched triple east window, now blind. The capitals of the window's four columns have the same florals that we saw at San Pedro near Cangas de Onís. The cornice above it, known as an afiz, is a Moorish touch that is inexplicable, given the time and place. We pass by its seventeenth century interior, but someone who has a thing for churches may pause for a look. Nothing particularly interesting.

Now pass along the front of the cathedral, peering through the grilles into the porch. The west portal was built by Pierre Buyeres. The relief above the main doorway is the Transfiguration. The wooden main doors are ornately carved, featuring Christ (on the left) and St. Eulalia (patron saint of Asturias) poised to greet the faithful as they enter.

Continuing past the cathedral a few steps, we come to the walled garden of the Reyes Caudillos. Inside, occupying large niches along the east wall, are statues of the Asturian kings in various heroic poses. Rising at one corner is the square Torre de los Pelayos, with a Gothic gingerbread spire.

Now return to the cathedral entrance and go inside. First move to the rear of the nave to sit for a moment, looking forward to the sanctuary. For me, the retable that graces the center of this interior view of the cathedral has a stunning effect. In the vast milieu of Spanish church retables, this one is something else. It is carved of wood, gilded and painted, created by Giralte of Brussels and Jean de Balmaseda early in the sixteenth century. Rising above is a grand display of stained glass in tall windows between arching ribs that peak high above the sanctuary. The colors of the glass blend beautifully with those of the retable, which are predominantly blues and reds bracketed or framed by golden filigree.

You may have gathered by now that while I often find the

monumental detail of the gaudy altarpieces of Spain to be fascinating, or at least interesting, with few exceptions I balk at treating them as true works of art in an aesthetic sense. They are religious artistry, to be sure, and some elements of the pieces may be true works of art in their own right; but the entire extravaganza of religious scenes and symbols is ordinarily just too much to stomach without suffering a severe case of aesthetic indigestion.

The retable in this cathedral at Oviedo is, I repeat, something else. I am not sure why. In concept it is similar to many others. But here, if anywhere, is an example of the retable as a genuine work of art. Perhaps it is because of its ambience: The vaulting, stone tracery and stained glass in the triple windows rising in the apse above, the elegant but plain marble slab of the altar, the gentle curve of the altarpiece as it fits into the semicircular apse behind, the sense of it being framed by the tall, pale piers supporting the towering vaults where nave meets chancel. Then there is the ceiling, painted a striking blue with crushed lapis lazuli. The choir screen is low and unobtrusive so as to take nothing away from the glory of the altar and the retable that rises behind.

The splashes of color and their composition, with blues and reds against a broad background of filigree gold, I find very pleasing. As for the scenes depicted, they almost do not matter as far as detail is concerned as one takes in the whole effect of the thing. At top center is the tableau of the Crucifixion. Below that is the Annunciation. Finally, enthroned above the tabernacle and garbed in robes of imperial crimson, sits Christ in Judgment. To the sides are a couple of dozen scenes from the life of Christ, all so vividly portrayed that anyone conversant with the Good Book will find it brought to life, so to speak.

An interesting feature of the retable is that the donors, Juan de Condamo and his wife, are shown, he on the left, she on the right of the scene where Mary is lamenting over the body of her Son. The donor was the architect who designed the remodeling of the cathedral between 1458 and 1489.

In the nave the triforium has balustrades with stone traceries mounted above, and stained glass windows a level higher. Turn to the north aisle and the seventeenth century Capilla de Santa Eulalia. It is Baroque, featuring an eleventh century silver gilt casket containing the remains of the lady, who is the patron saint of Asturias. Her reliquary is deposited high up in a Baroque centerpiece.

Continuing forward to the north transept you find the Capilla del Rey Casto, Alfonso II, the Chaste. Outside its entry is a Baroque altar supporting a Madonna with a spectacular halo of golden rays and accompanied by ministering angels. It is the work of Jean de Villanueva Barbales, done in 1741.

The chapel of Alfonso stands on the site of the original church built by Fruela and structurally dates from the ninth century, although it was given a Baroque overhaul in the eighteenth century. It remains a little church of its own, with central and side aisles and even its own tower when seen from the exterior. It was intended to be the pantheon of the Asturian kings. Among the few tombs here is but one belonging to a king: Fruela I, whom you find in the left rearmost side chapel.

More notable are the sculptures around the inner face of the entry, at the sides featuring Sts. James, Peter, Paul and Andrew. In the covings are a dozen musicians, along with a company of saints studiously consulting scrolls of the Holy Word. To the left of the entry is Nuestra Señora de la Luz, a sixteenth century work.

From Alfonso's chapel, walk back towards the crossing and follow the ambulatory around to the south transept. In the ambulatory is a whole string of chapels, all named on plaques, none particularly exceptional.

Now for a visit to the Cámara Santa, which is the highlight of any tour of this cathedral. The room contains very special antiquities that any visitor to Oviedo must see. You may see it by yourself or see it on a guided tour, conducted in Spanish, so let me describe its main features for you.

From the forward side of the south transept climb the stone stairway to reach the Cámara Santa. It is a special treasury built by Alfonso II in the ninth century to safeguard the Holy Ark containing sacred relics preserved by the Visigothic Church prior to the eighth century. The Arca Santa was brought to the mountains from the Visigothic capital of Toledo at the time of the conquest to save the relics from desecration by the Moors.

The Cámara was heavily remodeled in the twelfth century, and again after 1934 when it was damaged in the workers' uprising that placed the city under siege. Yet the basic structure is still the one built at the order of Alfonso more than a thousand years ago.

First you enter a small, barrel-vaulted outer chapel, remodeled in the twelfth century. Inside, above the entryway, is a remarkable head of Christ literally emerging from the surface of the wall. Inside you discover a series of pilasters, each adorned with a pair of exquisite statues of the Apostles. These are much admired by the experts. Beyond is the smaller inner chapel that contains the hoard of the most holy objects that survive from the early Kingdom of Asturias and its Visigothic antecedents. Oldest is the famous cedarwood Arca Santa, covered with handsomely tooled silver plate, placed on a marble base and sealed within glass at the center of the chapel. It is about one and a half meters square and a meter tall. The ark was made, church lore tells us, by the Apostles. They used it to transport its sacred contents when they fled to Egypt from Jerusalem.

What does it contain? Thorns from Christ's crown of the crucifixion, one of the pieces of silver paid to Judas for his treachery, a bone of Moses, the heart of St. Bartholomew, a piece of the True Cross, a crumb of the bread fed the multitude after the miracle of the loaves and fishes, and more.

No less sacred is the jewel-studded Cruz de la Victoria, borne by Pelayo at the Battle of Covadonga. It was plainer stuff then. Alfonso III had it fancied up in 908 before placing it here in the cathedral to memorialize both the victory and the victor who founded the Asturian dynasty. You find it encased between a pair of angels above the ark.

Other honored items displayed here are the ninth century

cedarwood Cruz de los Angeles, a gift of Alfonso II, decorated with precious stones and gold filigree; a sixth century Byzantine diptych; a gold chest donated by Fruela II and much more on which to feast your eyes and let your imagination run. Several small silver caskets contain the relics of saints.

Exiting the Cámara Santa, climb another flight of stairs to the cathedral museum, which is as nice a display of historic church goods as you will see during our travels in Spain. The tremendous wealth of it defies detailed description.

The way out of the museum is a stairway leading down from the museum into the cloister, which encloses a paved courtyard that does nothing to lend attractiveness to the place. Originally constructed in the ninth century, the cloister was completely redone in the Gothic style in the fourteenth. The vaulting and stone tracery are not as fine as we have seen, but are presentable enough. The cloister contains several pilgrim tombstones and the more ornate tombs of church notables.

More interesting than the cloister as such, is the Capilla de Leodadia, located beneath the Cámara Santa. It contains ninth century tombs and a small altar, with a rather unusual stone fixture that probably was a tabernacle.

Off to the right from the chapel is the Sala Capitular, built in 1293. Its most notable item is a small marble frieze called the Retablo de las Lamentacions, depicting the removal of Christ from the cross.

The conclusion of the museum/cloister tour deposits you on Calle San Vicente behind the cathedral. From there, walk left through the archway to where Calle San Vicente ends at Calle Jovellanos. On your left is the Convent of San Pelayo.

The convent was originally a donation of Alfonso II early in the ninth century. It was rebuilt in the eighteenth century and restored after sustaining severe war damage in the 1930s. The convent is active and closed to the public except for its exposition hall (open 10-2 and 5-9 p.m., closed Sundays) which contains a fascinating display of old manuscripts, plus an assortment of archaeological finds, antique silver plate and paintings. Some of the manuscripts are well over a thousand years old and are composed in Gothic script. Among these treasures is the Pacto Monastico, the founding document for the San Vicente monastery, dated 781.

Turning back on Calle San Vicente toward the cathedral, the building next to the convent is the sixteenth century church of Santa María la Real de la Corte. Just past it is the Archaeological Museum, which if time allows you may visit now. (Somewhere along this part of your explorations you will run out of time and things will commence to close. If so, you are handy to your hotel near Calle Jovellanos, or to your parked car. That allows you to conclude your walk through Oviedo for now, and resume later this afternoon or tomorrow where you left off.)

The exterior of Santa María la Real has a Romanesque plain squareness about it, while its interior is done in Renaissance style, and contains the tombs of local notables. Nothing truly extraordinary here.

The museum (open 10-1:30; 4-6), on the right just past the archway, is a much more significant edifice. It is situated in the monastery of San Vicente, built by King Fruela I in 781. It survived the Moorish destruction of the city in 789 well enough to warrant reconstruction rather than replacement, and thus is the oldest building in the city. It has been remodeled and restored a half dozen times, but the original construction still lies at the heart of the thing. On the ground floor in rooms off the cloister is an outstanding collection of Asturian pre-Romanesque, Romanesque and Gothic art. On the floor above are items from Roman times and, on the top floor (in the enclosed galleries of the cloister), is a display of Stone Age artifacts (some from the Cueva Buxu), many of them more than 50,000 years old.

From San Vicente continue west along the calle of the same name. Beyond the cathedral is the sixteenth-century archbishop's palace, facing onto the Corrada del Obispo. There turn right and follow the twists and turns back towards Plaza Alfonso II. On your right as you walk is another face of the archbishop's palace, while on the left is the Velarde Palace, which now contains the Museum of Fine Arts of Asturias. Its entrance is around on the far side, on Calle de la Rua, which we will come to in a few minutes by walking round the block. Its collection spans from the Renaissance to the present day, featuring Asturian painters.

Having completed our explorations in the vicinity of the cathedral, we leave from the Museum of Fine Arts, going left along the Calle La Rua, the name of which reminds us that this also was a pilgrim way. English and Lowland Dutch often came by sea, landing in Gijon and walking south via Oviedo to León, where they joined pilgrims traveling the main route to Santiago.

Soon the Rua becomes the Calle Cimadevilla which passes through an arched passage beneath the Ayuntamiento into Plaza Mayor (Plaza de la Constitution). The Town Hall lends its street level arcade to the decor of the square. A cafe among the many arcades surrounding the plaza is recommended for lunch if the time is right, so that we may view the square and the people as we dine. The Town Hall with its clock tower dominates the square. On the west is the sixteenth century Jesuit church of San Isidoro. Oddly enough, a twelfth century portal from the original Romanesque church on that site has been reconstructed in the Campo de San Francisco, which is the main city park, a half kilometer from here along Calle de Fruela.

South, down Calle Magdalena past the Magdalena Chapel, a right turn after about a hundred meters to Plaza de Daioz y Velarde brings an art enthusiast to the San Felix Palace, an eighteenth century mansion turned into an art gallery. Among its treasures is El Greco's *Apostles*. The entire square is surrounded by well-kept Baroque mansions that suggest something of the life style of the rich and powerful a couple of centuries past.

The most popular promenade for Oviedans is in the Park de San Francisco, now about two hundred meters west along Calle Suárez de la Riva. A block beyond that is the Hotel de Reconquista, the city's leading hostelry situated in the former Old Hospital of the Principality.

Santullano

Sitting just a few meters west of Autopista A66 to Gijon (Hee-hon), easily visible as you drive into Oviedo from the north, is the church of San Julián de los Prados, more commonly known as Santullano. But it is as difficult to get to as it is easy to spot. The problem is that A66, where it meets the Ronda de Circunvalación (the circle of streets that compasses the center of the city), slices through and blocks the old city streets. That, coupled with the usual one-way thoroughfares characteristic of old cities, spells difficulties for the stranger.

Best solution arriving on A66 (or even coming from town center) is to bear west on the Ronda for half a kilometer until you reach Avenida de Pumarin. Follow it north through the Barrio de Pumarin for about a half kilometer to Calle Albéniz, and turn right. After about two hundred meters, where you meet Calle Teniente Alfonso Martinez, turn right and take the street that immediately runs obliquely off to the left. It opens a few meters further into the Plaza de Santullano. Find a place in the plaza for your car, (parking is rarely a problem here) and walk to the church, which faces you from a grassy park alongside A66 at the far left end of the plaza.

Compared to the cathedral and similar grandiose piles of stone that we have seen in recent days, Santullano doesn't look like much. But here is an instance where appearances are deceiving. This is as important a church, religiously and historically as well as architecturally, as will be seen during our explorations of Northern Spain. It was built by Alfonso II between 812 and 842, and thus is a companion piece to the

250

Cámara Santa at the cathedral.

Santullano is thought to mean "Saint of the Fields," probably recalling when this was once an agricultural area just outside the city walls. Tiny as this church may appear, it is the largest pre-Romanesque church in all of Spain, measuring twenty five by thirty meters. It boasts of a nave with exposed wood timbers supporting the roof, side aisles, and a broad transept. Small vestibules are at the south and west entrances, with a tiny room containing the sacristy added off the north end of the transept to balance the south vestibule. The three apses are barrel-vaulted with bricks, with the side chapels separated from the main sanctuary by blind-arched walls. The gray marble pillars astride the chancel have interesting floral carvings and rise to form an attractive archway between sanctuary and nave. Those gray pillars are Roman first century although their capitals are Asturian. Behind them, the pilasters on both sides facing the altar are also Roman, but much older, dating from before the time of Christ and the era of the Cantabrian wars.

Santullano

251

The central apse is peculiar, perhaps unique, in that it has two levels, with a hidden chamber above. The nave has clerestory windows and also windows in east and west ends. The stone traceries in those windows are pre-Romanesque, but perhaps of a slightly later date than the main structure. They feature repetitive patterns of a kind of lattice, and of the cross pattée, concaved, which is similar to St. George's or the Maltese crosses. Pilasters separate the central nave from the aisles.

The large crucifix in the sanctuary has no connection with the early beginnings of this church. It is artistically transitional, being Romanesque but for the crown, which is Gothic. It is believed to date from the twelfth century.

Most significant here are the murals decorating the interior walls. Though in poor condition after more than a thousand years, they are important because they betray the artistic connections of this remote corner of Spain, with similar works to be found in Ravenna, Rome and the eastern provinces of Byzantium.

The murals are believed to be copies of Roman originals, or at least inspired by such. Depicted are the classical buildings of a Roman city and other decor of a similar nature. Not a person is shown. Why? According to the parish priest, a scholarly sort who obviously loved to tell about his church, it is because the workmen and the founders of this church had been infected by an early medieval heresy known as Adoptionism.

Given that heretical influence, Santullano is the most singularly expressive edifice among all that we see as we travel toward Santiago. It is more than a landmark in architecture. It speaks artistically of the Roman Church under assault by an alien creed, no less than the Christian kings were then parrying thrust after thrust of Saracen swords.

Although the Muslim governors sustained their rule here in the northern mountains for little more than a decade, those few years coupled with their obviously superior material culture and subsequent highhanded treatment of the Asturians –

dealing with the weak Christian kingdom as a tributary state for more than a hundred years – prompted a long-standing sense of political and cultural inferiority among the Christians of Asturias. Little wonder, then, that Muslim secular power and wealth, based on the fanatical allegiance of Arabs and Moors to the Islamic Creed, begat seeds of doubt among the Christian faithful.

Meanwhile, cross-cultural dealings between Christian and Muslim included long theological dialogues between the mullahs and the priests, dialogues with effects that filtered down to the common folk of Asturias. The result, worse than doubt, was a general questioning of the Christian faith. That sharing of religious ideas thus led eventually to the birth of heresy.

Islam regards Christ as an important prophet and holy man, but not God incarnate. In the milieu described, most Asturians, from Bishops down to the lowliest peasants, were persuaded to believe that Jesus was not the Son of God, but a prophet who taught the Christian Way of Salvation. In effect, Jesus was demoted to the level of Mohammed and therewith this isolated Christian community had "adopted" a new concept of Christ from the Muslims.

The heresy of Adoptionism included the Islamic rule that a holy place should not display images of man as it honors the One God, whether named Jehovah or Allah. At the time when the church was built during the reign of Alfonso II, heretical beliefs thus made the Asturian Church exclude even representations of Christ in Heaven or on Earth. The murals they painted instead are secular portrayals that recall the art and architecture of Rome. That may seem odd, but it is evidence that even at that time the glory of Rome remained a powerful cultural memory. It spoke of an empire remembered for its cultural extravagance and economic good times, a kind of "heaven" that existed before the "hell" suffered after the coming of the Vandals, Goths and Moors.

Thus we find ourselves here in the artistic milieu of Ravenna, Rome and Constantinople, which Asturians last

253

contacted during Gothic times through the pervasive influences of Byzantium. For in the sixth century resurgence of Byzantine power, their reconquest of the former empire in the west reached even to the shores of Spain. Later, Byzantium maintained many cultural and economic contacts with the Visigothic regime. All that, for Asturians as they faced the Muslim horde, was but a happy memory couched within a culture worn to tatters, where alien devils triumphed and the good were martyred or sold into slavery. Thus we see Roman murals spread across the walls in the church of Santullano, built at the acme of the heresy, which flourished at a time while the Asturian Church was effectively isolated from the Latin Church of Europe and Rome.

Santullano consequently was built without representation of liturgical symbol or the human form. True, we do find the pattée cross in the latticework of the windows, but these are suspected to date from several decades later. That places their origins in King Ramiro's time, when Asturias began flexing its muscles on the Meseta. Meeting the Muslims on their home ground with a measure of success thus commenced to restore confidence in the power of Christianity and themselves, undermining the heresy.

Concurrent with the decline of Adoptionism and the resurgence of Christian power was the discovery of the body of St. James at Compostela. Perhaps the latter played a large part in that resurgence, particularly given the legend of Santiago Matamoros at Clavijo.

Monte Naranco

Ramiro I, victor at Clavijo (r 842-850), succeeded Alfonso II at just about the time when the church of Santullano was completed. One suspects that, with an experienced cadre of builders and artisans at hand and their work complete, he looked about for something else for them to do.

West of town is Monte Naranco. The obvious thing to do

254

was to put the builders to work on creation of a Summer palace high up where the breezes are pleasant and the views are royal on the shoulder of the mount. Fortunately, something of what they constructed remains for us to see today: the church of Santa María de Naranco, once part of the palace and thus not originally a church; and San Miguel de Lillo, which is believed to have been the chapel used by the royal court.

The way to Monte Naranco is northwest across the Viaducto Ingeniero Marquina, which spans the railroad complex next to the train station. On the far side a right turn followed quickly by a left up the hill on Calle Naranco de Buines puts you on the way to Monte Naranco. The road takes many twists and turns through the steep countryside for about two kilometers as it winds its way up the mount. First you come to the church of Santa María, a few steps down the mountainside off the road. A half kilometer further is San Miguel, dedicated to St. Michael the Archangel.

The interior of the buildings may be seen only on guided tours, again in Spanish only. Guided tours are available between 9:30 and 1, and 3 to 7 pm., visiting both sites. The exteriors may be seen at any time. Tour tickets are sold at a small office in the cellar of Santa María. Parking is easier near San Miguel, from which it is an easy walk back down the road.

What many regard as the piece de resistance of the Asturian artistic heritage is the church of Santa María del Naranco. Originally it was not a church at all, but part of Ramiro's palace – his audience salon to be precise. It was converted into a church in the tenth century, later abandoned, dismantled, rebuilt and is now a national monument. Best strategy here is to walk all around it first to get an impression of the place.

At ground level is a crypt-like barrel-vaulted basement containing three rooms, with Romanesque window openings at each end beneath the porch loggias. The east room contains a deep cistern, with steps going down into it. It is said to have been the royal bath, and had provisions to be heated. A small door exits this chamber to the outside.

The end porches are similar, one to the other, with tall,

arched openings to each side, and at the ends triple-arches rest upon columned supports with Corinthian-like capitals. Above the arches are carved medallions and simulated engaged pilasters rising to the eaves astraddle the tiny upper triple window. Taken together, the end porches comprise half the length of the structure. Buttresses lay against the side walls.

There is a Byzantine flavor to the blend of browns and golden yellows of the stone on which we find these architectural touches, more of which we will see inside. The column capitals also betray a Roman-Byzantine heritage, with carved florals reminiscent of San Pedro in Cangas de Onís.

Santa Maria del Narranco

Along the north side a double stairway is set against the building, each set of steps leading up to a small covered porch and the entrance to the main hall, or nave. A structure of matching size on the south exists only as lower foundation walls. Note that dressed and sized stone is used only at the corners of the building and to frame doors and windows. The bulk of the structure is built of rough-cut stone of assorted dimensions selected for fit rather than to achieve matching courses. The effect of proportion, decor and tonalities of stone, for all its primitiveness and the ravages of time, is exceptionally pleasing aesthetically. It has a delicacy and mood that leaves us in admiration of the unknown architect who devised it in service to his king.

The interior only enhances that response. The main chamber is barrel vaulted with engaged "twisted" columns (some call them cable, or rope style, since the twisting spiral ribs of the columns look something like the surface of a heavy cable or rope) supporting blind Romanesque arches all around. Above the junctures of the arches are round medallions and simulated carved pilasters like those we noted on the exterior. The medallions are decorated in low relief with long-tailed dragons, while the capitals display the figures of lions and wolves, with all of the representations essentially repetitive. In the capitals are small human figures, so primitive in style that they are little better than sketches done by children.

Amongst all this secular decor you find the Christian symbol only beside the niches above the exits to the porches. In each instance you see a pair of pattée crosses which are much like the better known Maltese Cross of centuries later.

From the east porch is a wonderful view of Oviedo and, on a clear day, the Picos de Europa. On this porch is a marble-slab-topped altar with rather crude linear reliefs carved on its lower sides. More twisted columns are paired on all sides of the pilasters and piers surrounding the porch. The west porch is similar, sans altar. Note the slots cut into the columns, obviously for insetting a railing the porches now lack.

Now walk with the tour group up to San Miguel de Lillo (aka Liño), where the same ticket gains you a tour inside the place, probably with the same guide. It sits in a mountainside nook among a grove of trees beside a hairpin turn in the road. In that parklike setting we find the surviving portion of the church.

At one time San Miguel was the royal chapel associated with Ramiro's palace, and thus dates from the middle of the ninth century. The structure was badly damaged by an earthquake in the thirteenth century, after which its forward end was demolished and a new apse built into the foreshortened edifice. The result is a cube-like building, about a third of the length of the original structure. Its height thus is much out of proportion to its length.

What you see of the original basilican-style church, then, is the three-aisled nave end. Note its almost fortress-like appearance, with narrow windows below. Above, however, are some of the most beautiful pre-Romanesque windows you will ever see. Their sculptures have lately been protected by glass panels.

At the church entrance to either side are bas reliefs of a primitive Byzantine style. Both are practically the same, and are thought by some authorities to be modeled after a Byzantine piece now at a museum in Leningrad. (I would guess that the Russian and Spanish carvings are both copies of a Byzantine original, now lost.) The scene at the top is believed to depict a Roman consul accompanied by his aides. Below is a scene involving combat with a lion, possibly a hunt, but probably an artistic recollection of Roman gladiatorial combat.

The pilasters along the south and north transepts have especially fine Byzantine-style low relief carving. We see a pair of mounted knights, swords raised high as if to strike. Note also the pair of men in long robes, hands raised and placing hats or crowns upon their heads. Some scraps of old wall murals can also be seen, though not comparable in quality or preservation to those we saw at Santullano.

A peculiarity of this edifice compared to other Asturian pre-Romanesque churches is that the central and side aisles are separated by columns instead of pillars.

Worthy of comment here is the fact that this church, built only a decade or so later than Santullano, now includes human figures in both sculpture and wall murals, but still is devoid of liturgical symbols. Note the stone traceries in the windows, which are simply geometrical. This church is virtually as secular in decor as Santa María, which after all was once part of a palace.

Best work is in the choir loft above the Romanesque arches at the sides of the loft. Again we find low-relief florals.

Viewing the windows from inside, note the peculiarly twisted, rather spiral-like "cable" carving decorating the column shafts. These "twisted" columns, we now see, were characteristic of Asturian architecture of the ninth century. So, in this very old setting, we complete our visit to the turf of the early kings of the Reconquista.

LEON

León is strategically situated at the confluence of the Bernesga and Torio Rivers in the northwest corner of the Meseta. First it was a Roman army camp guarding the road to the mines of Galicia and Asturias. A town grew up around that legion encampment and took its name from it. "Legion," as locally pronounced, quickly became "León."

From the first century AD the town was the centuries-long base for the famed Seventh Legion that kept the peace among the troublesome hill tribes in Northwest Spain. After the collapse of the Empire, the city fell to the Visigoths in 540. A couple of hundred years later most its people fled to the mountains to escape the Arab conquest. Death or enslavement was the fate accorded to those who stayed behind.

Moors repopulated the abandoned site in 717 and then, after the Muslim retreat from Gijon, the Caliph made León his forward strongpoint during the continuing wars pitting mighty Islam against the puny Christian kingdom of Asturias. Puny or not, the Christians under King Fruela seized León in 742, profiting from Moslem weakness after the calamity suffered by the Caliph's forces in France.

When Oviedo was flattened in 789, León held on, safe behind its formidable Roman walls.

A century passed before the armies of Islam recouped full measure of their former power, whereupon León was retaken by the Moors in 846.

The city fell once more to the Christians led by Alfonso the Great in 882, then was recaptured still again by Al Mansur in 988. That distinguished warrior died soon afterwards, and his successors held León for less than a decade before succumbing to the factional strife that tore the caliphate apart and allowed Alfonso V to win back the city for good.

None of that taking and retaking speaks of the countless sieges, raids and battles in the countryside roundabout. No part of Spain was more soaked in blood than here where Islam and Christianity fought it out for control of León for those three hundred years.

This brief recitation of events marking centuries of strife tells us that León, occupying its strategic site near the northern bounds of the Meseta, was the key to domination of Northwest Spain since Roman times. It also tells us that the outnumbered Christian armies, always able to fall back among the Cantabrian peaks to lick their wounds and raise up another generation of tough young mountain men, won a centuries-long war of attrition that sapped the wealth, resolve, and eventually the staying power of their foe. For without León to hold back the Christian tide, the whole of the northern Meseta – which history came to regard as Old Castile – lay exposed to Christian arms. It may have taken another four hundred years until Ferdinand and Isabella finished the Reconquest, but the most decisive roles in that struggle were played by those early kings and their squadrons of buccaneering knights who fanned out into the Meseta, each man determined to cut out and hold a chunk of Moorish territory for himself.

From Oviedo we follow the path of the Reconquesta south through the Cordillera Cantabrica on A66 and N630 to the edge of the Meseta and onward over the few kilometers further to León. Then, before exploring León, we head southeast, backtracking along El Camino de Santiago (via N601) to visit some of the earliest landmarks of the Christian resurgence onto the fringes of the Meseta.

Pola de Lena

About forty kilometers south of Oviedo, and five kilometers past Pola de Lena, is another ninth century Asturian church, Santa Christina de Lena. It dates from the reign of Ramiro I, who rode this way en route to the Battle of Clavijo. The location is well marked, sitting atop a hill just off A66 south of town. Unfortunately, there is no access to the site directly from

A66; therefore, exit A66 at Pola de Lena.

Pola de Lena is situated in a small valley couched in the northern face of the Cantabrian Cordillera. Follow the Santa Christina signs south through town and some five kilometers beyond to where a side road crosses over A66. From the bridge, look up to the hilltop above the rural railway station across the way. There you see the tiny, well-preserved **church** of Santa Christina de Lena. (Open 1 April to 31 October, 11-1, 4:30-6:30, closed Mondays.)

Turn right at the other end of the bridge and continue a couple of hundred meters to where the road ducks under a railway overpass. On the far side, park along the road. The path up to the church, marked by a relatively inconspicuous sign, is next to the house across the street. On our visit, the home was occupied by an accommodating lady who held a key to the church. She will oblige a visitor on off hours if she is at home. The path up the hill is steep, and may still be poorly graded and hazardous in wet weather.

Santa Christina de Lena, sitting all alone on the grassy crest of the tiny hilltop, was built in 845 in the Greek cross plan, modeled after the Visigothic style. There is a drabness about its exterior, and it is not as tall and stately as those you saw at Monte Naranco. Nor do you find exterior decor such as we found there. This appears to have been an ordinary country church and not a chapel serving kings. On the other hand, building techniques are similar, with profuse dependence upon blind arches, pilaster-like buttresses against the exterior walls, and scant utilization of evenly dressed courses of masonry. Indeed, some experts believe this church was designed and built at the order of King Ramiro I by the same architect and builders who did Monte Naranco.

The layout of the place is distinctive to itself, different from anything else we will see on our journey through Northern Spain. Entrance is through what is more properly called a **vestibule** rather than a porch, with stone benches lining each side. The interior is dark and gloomy, yet the sort of a place easily lit by an array of votive candles and a lamp or two. The single nave is barrel vaulted, and the Greek cross plan is completed by two tiny constructions, also barrel vaulted, astraddle the nave.

The **sanctuary**, six steps higher than the nave, is separated from the nave by a triple arch and a screen (iconostasis) decorated by geometric reliefs similar to the rather primitive sculptural reliefs we saw at Monte Naranco. Again we are viewing expressions of the heresy of Adoptionism, coupled with the Visigothic/Byzantine. influence in the Greek cross plan and iconostasis.

The pillars beneath the arches are smooth, of recycled Roman vintage, with floral capitals as at Santullano. The columns leading into the apse are the twisted, or cable, variety peculiar to Asturian architecture, with crudely carved medallions between the covings of the arches.

At the rear of the nave is a **choir** loft with a stone stairway leading up along the wall. The loft is illuminated by tiny windows that lend something of the demeanor of a fortress to this little church. Located as it is on a strategic hilltop not far from the then Moorish Meseta, one suspects that it indeed doubled as a fortified refuge against enemy raiding parties during those turbulent times.

Backtracking across the bridge over A66, turn left in the direction of Campomanes, where a decision is required. From there you can continue on N630 through the Puerto de Pajares (elevation 1380 meters) or take the more modern route A66, which tunnels through the highest mounts and connects with N120 about five kilometers west of León. The result is that A66 is much faster. But for a closer look at day-to-day life in the mountains of Asturias and the original route of the Reconquista, N630 should be your choice.

The road across the Pajares Pass is the old route followed by Muslim armies heading north to punish the Christian upstarts led by Pelayo and the later Asturian kings. Easy to see why anything but a sizable army could be ambushed and wiped out at any one of a hundred places along the way. Later this was the way south for Fruela I and Ramiro I, the former to capture

León, the latter to lose it again. The route is no longer primitive, but it remains a mountain road, full of twists and turns with steep ascents and descents. Use care. The day we crossed the Pajares four young people were killed in a plunge off the road when they tried to negotiate a curve at too high a speed.

Beyond the pass the countryside changes radically. The north face of the Cordillera, bathed in mountain mists and rain from the Atlantic, is heavily forested and green year around. Descending on the south, the forests fade and when Summer comes the mountainsides turn brown, blending into the sunburnt rolling hills and plains of the Meseta.

Arriving in León from the north on N630, turn right on Avenida Alvaro López Nuñez, then follow that main thoroughfare as it winds past a railway station to a right turn onto Avenida Suero de Quiñones and onward to the Antiguo Monasterio de San Marcos, now a well-known five-star Parador and not far from several other hotels of lesser repute and tariff.

Entering León from the west on N120 from A66 finds you on the Avenida de Quevedo. A right turn is required just before reaching the Bernesga River. This leads you past a railway station, where a left turn takes you across the Bernesga. There another left turn leads north along the river to the Parador of San Marcos or, as we stated, to some other hotel in that vicinity.

Check in at your selected hostelry, then we are off to make further explorations to the east.

Mansilla de las Mulas

After Sahagún the pilgrim track cuts across the back country on a direct line to Mansilla de las Mulas, nearly forty kilometers as the crow flies. Pilgrims afoot still go that way, but the highway takes a long detour southwest on N120 and then north on N601 to rejoin the Camino at the town of

Mansilla de las Mulas.

Backtracking from León, head east on N601 to reach Mansilla de las Mulas.

Mansilla de las Mulas is an old Roman town that was turned into a defensive outpost for the new Christian kingdom of León. It soon became a prominent stopping place on El Camino de Santiago. Most notable here are the remains of its twelfth-century defensive walls, some of which still stand in unusually fine condition, along with towers and gates on its eastern perimeter. While the town itself is picturesque, its contribution to our explorations of the culture and history of the region is minimal. A tumbled-down monastery nearby, however, is even more fascinating than the ruin we found at San Antón. The monastery, originally dedicated as Santo Noval, later became known as Santa María de Sandoval.

Approaching Mansilla from León on N601, a short distance before the bridge over the Rio Esla, a right turn leads to Mansilla Mayor (a small town, despite its name) and **Villaverde de Sandoval,** the tiny village of a handful of houses nearby the monastery we seek. The slab-sided see-through belfry of the monastic church, and the towering hulk of the thing itself, rise above the rich, flat farmland that extends for kilometers around. Park in the shade of one of the many trees in the grove beside the church and its walled courtyard.

The **monastery** was founded in 1177 by Count Ponce de Minerva, a political luminary who made his fortune as mayordomo for Alfonso VII. A colony of Bernardine monks from France were installed in the place, providing religious and social services until the Napoleonic and Carlist catastrophes of the nineteenth century. As it was with other places we have seen, abandonment and ruin was its fate thereafter.

The church is the best preserved part of the old establishment. It now serves the local parish, whose tiny congregation is rather lost in the broad and tall expanse of its interior. Form of the church is a Latin cross of transitional Gothic design with three naves. The apses, windows and walls are thus a conventional Romanesque, with Gothic vaults

265

superimposed. As at San Antón, we find an elegant construction using large, dressed stone blocks in measured courses. All in all this is a top-quality production of an architectural master and stone masons as originally built, no matter how nondescript it has become with time.

Observing the tall central and lower side **apses** from the exterior, note that they are constructed without blind arches to lighten the load, leading to an extreme thickness of the walls, which is clearly perceived in the casing depth of the Romanesque window in the central apse. The carved modillions have been worn to the point of oblivion by time and the elements.

Adjacent to the near side apse is a Romanesque **portal** of a strikingly singular design. Just as earlier on our travels we observed the cusps that were the trademark of Mozarabic builders, here the archway above the door contains a simple sawtooth pattern, one that I have seen elsewhere only on Cistercian transitional churches. But never were they quite like this.

With no tympanum, the portal has an open sawtooth arch above the doorway. The sawtooth design is repeated as a relief in the stone just beneath the semicircles of the plain-surfaced archivolts. To each side are three slender round columns, capitals of which are carved with geometric designs.

On the way back around from the apse end, observe the tiny graveyard beside the church. According to a posted notice, for a price, it is still possible to be interred there along with pilgrim folks from the time of the founders and since. One wonders whose bones would be disturbed to make room for a newcomer.

Pass by the main entrance to the church for now, but on a **side door** into the nave of the church, observe the sawtooth relief repeated, this time bordering the entrance from pavement to pavement around an otherwise plain-featured Gothic portal.

Now walk through the gate into the walled **courtyard** beyond the church. On the left of its dusty, barren expanse is a roofless, half fallen in second-story loggia of Romanesque

266

arches supported by round columns and Corinthian-like capitals. Even now there is an elegance about it. Windows gape emptily in the similarly roofless structure alongside.

Old monastery buildings across the courtyard on the right, you notice, are now barns used by a farmer, whose stylish modern house hugs the ruin of the monastic structure to the left. Residing in that home we found a stooped, gray-haired, elderly but vivacious lady who had the keys to the place. She made pin money showing travelers what there is to see of the monastic establishment and the church. She had more energy in her head and voice than in her legs. We knew her as Señora Mundo, for whom this church and its lore have been a large part of her life.

With cane in hand she removed the padlock from the wooden gate and guided us first into the ramshackle **cloister**. Originally Romanesque, it was given a Neo-Classical facelift in the seventeenth century, including addition of a chapterhouse. Strolling through the despoiled galleries that enclose the weed-choked and trash filled courtyard, there is a quality of sadness pervasive of the place. Note the *fleur de lis de Frances* in the capitals of the columns beside the doorway to the chapterhouse, indicating the long lasting influence of the French on this Bernardine foundation.

Back at the **main portal** of the church, we find it to be a relatively simple Gothic, with a Calvary in its tympanum. The capitals of the columns below the arches are carved to depict monks, heads lowered and hands clasped in prayer. The archivolts are covered with leafy foliage with an occasional infant birthing forth from the shrubbery of the topmost archivolt. My association was with the old story about babies being found beneath cabbage leaves.

Aside from the devout monks on this portal, it is significant how little religious form and few liturgical symbols are found in the decor of this church. We are still centuries removed from the profuse pandering of sinners to the saints and the Pantocrator found in the Romanesque of Navarra, or discovered everywhere in late Gothic and subsequent styles

(Herrera excepted).

The cavernous **interior** of this church reeks of age and decrepitude. The sanctuary and altar goods are so Spartan I was reminded of simple military outdoor services I attended in years past. The retable is seventeenth century, and not outstanding. Behind it, in the cove of the apse, is a much more interesting piece, a beat-up old retable of indeterminate age set up as a sort of trasaltar.

Then, expressing profuse gratitude to Señora Mundo, we departed her sovereign realm while she hobbled back to a seat on a bench against the wall of her home, there to discuss with her neighbors those strange Americans who took such a nit-picking interest in her church.

San Miguel de la Escalada

San Miguel de la Escalada is designated a national monument. It commemorates the Mozarabic migration of a millennium past, embodying one of the finest extant examples of Mozarabic architectural style. Some see it as second to none.

San Miguel is off the main highway, and also about ten kilometers off the pilgrim track. At the west side of the N601 bridge across the Rio Esla, take the road heading north. Follow it along the Esla River through several tiny villages. After about twelve kilometers it reaches the monastic church of San Miguel de Escalada. (Open 10-2 and 5-8, Wednesday to Saturday; Sundays 10-3.)

The first monastery on the site was dedicated to St. Michael and dated from Visigothic times. It was abandoned and destroyed with the coming of the Arabs in 711. In the late ninth century Alfonso the Great turned the site over to Mozarabic monks fleeing persecutions in Córdoba. Their finished church was consecrated by the Bishop of Astorga on November 20, 913, the same year the separate Kingdom of León was established by Ordoñio II. (After the death of Alfonso the Great, his three sons divided the kingdom. Garcia had Galicia;

268

Fruela II kept Asturias, while Ordoño governed León.)

Of the monastic buildings, only the nicely restored church survives, now a museum piece dedicated to its Mozarab founders. A caretaker and his family reside in the nearby home, and have been known to make the site accessible off hours.

In a pleasing pastoral setting, San Miguel de la Escalada is couched in a draw on the side of a low, broad hill overlooking the verdant, tree covered plain of the Esla valley. It is a basilican style church, with central nave and two aisles. The clerestory windows, seen from the outside, appear to be blocked with white stone, contrasting with the reddish brown and grays that predominate. When we go inside we will discover that the window coverings are thin sheets of alabaster that filter soft light into the interior.

San Miguel de la Escalada

On the south side is a pretty **porch** added in 1050. Its roof is supported by twelve arches that open onto a broad open area that once was the cloister. The horseshoe arches of the porch are supported on slender polished columns with Corinthian-like capitals carved with the distinctive acanthus flower. The porch gallery, at its east end, abuts a stout Romanesque tower, strongly buttressed at each corner. The tower is a thirteenth century addition, with a small single-aisled chapel inside.

Note the small double window at the end of the arcade and another above it in the tower. They also exhibit the horseshoe arch.

Inside, horseshoe **archways** lining the nave are supported by polished marble columns topped by an assortment of capitals, all displaying floral motifs of varied designs. Some are believed to have been salvaged from an earlier Visigothic church and even earlier Roman structures that graced the site. Above central nave and aisles is an open wood truss and vaulted ceiling supporting the roof. The artesonado decor of the central nave is of later origin, probably twelfth century, since it bears the armorial signs of León and Castile.

Dividing the nave from the triple apse are three grand horseshoe archways, while the apse interiors continue the horseshoe form. Separating the side aisles from the transept are **carved panels** of stone set up like a sort of balustrade. Note the carvings on the panels – birds, foliage and the like, so typical of early Islamic secular sculpture that the Mozarabic church copied, and so rare in later Christian church construction. Similar carvings are found in the frieze spanning the wall above the central apse and the triple arch at the fore of the nave. The experts see this as perhaps the most outstanding existing example of a merging of Mozarabic and pre-Romanesque Asturian artistic influences.

Off the beaten path as this place is, it is likely you will be all alone during your visit. Given the undisturbed silence at this remote location, there is ample opportunity for quiet contemplation of the lives of the refugee monks who built the place to glorify a God who promised them a new beginning and freedom from their yoke of persecution.

Gradefes

Depart San Miguel by continuing northward along the road, driving past the church and up over the hill behind. The road is extremely narrow, full of curves and occasional rough pavement. Traffic is practically nonexistent, and in three kilometers you meet a much better road where you turn right toward Gradefes, ten kilometers away.

If you have learned to admire the precise clean lines of Cistercian transitional architecture, you will love the convent church of Santa María la Real in Gradefes. Best of all, it has been beautifully maintained by the sisters such that for the first time you can get an idea of what a first-rate medieval convent church was meant to be for its inhabitants, without all the touristy and regal folderol we encounter at such places as Las Huelgas.

Find the church and convent on the far side of the village on the righthand side of a quiet street. There won't be a tourist in sight. We were met by no one as we entered the grounds, and wandered through the church by ourselves, no one in sight until, in the nun's choir, a happy faced young nun in toe-touching gray work habit and broad apron appeared with broom and duster and, after a pleasant smile in our direction, set to work.

Gradefes thus remains an active Cistercian institution founded in 1168. Construction of the place lasted well into the thirteenth century. The **apse** of the church is, as we by now expect, the oldest part of the structure, and is a fine Romanesque with an ambulatory. The remainder of the church is transitional Cistercian Gothic with thirteenth and fourteenth-century reconstructions.

The high capitals beneath the dome are perhaps the only really ornate feature of this sedately dignified church. No two of the **capitals** have the same detail. Mozarabic touches are found on everything except the seventeenth century gallery on the west side. The tomb sculptures are interesting but their eternal-rest occupants are of no historical import to anyone but

271

a Cistercian.

The **sanctuary** is truly magnificent in concept. It is exceptionally tall with Cistercian Gothic vaulting above Romanesque windows high over the altar, which is a plain slab of marble with the Madonna and Child seated upon a tall pedestal, backlit by the single window in the central apse. Surrounding the sanctuary are massive piers supporting the dome, with primitive Gothic arches between, rising from severely plain engaged round columns and capitals with a leaf at each corner – all but one, to the left above the altar – which has a moonface carved into its forward angle. On its opposite side, looking into the ambulatory, is a capital displaying a trio of monstrosities.

The **nun's choir** is separated from the forward nave by a low wall with a grille above. The ceiling of the choir is a flat white stucco with polychrome reliefs of fifteenth century origins applied to the original Romanesque barrel vault. The reliefs are florals leading to center medallions depicting the Virgin and major saints. The choir stalls are plainly carved, in keeping with the mood of the entire church. It is a place of God that is clean lined, elegant, plain of face but for the ceiling decor just described. It is a hallowed place communicating a mood that defines the nature of a church in some archetypal sense that tweaks at the heartstrings of our feelings about such things.

All in all, expect a very restful visit here with the sisters of Gradefes.

Driving back through the town of Gradefes, make the left turn to cross the Esla River, then turn right on N621 for the twenty-two kilometer drive back to Mansilla de las Mulas. If you do nothing else in Mansilla before you start back to León on N601, pause a moment to view the twelfth-century town walls. While we treat Mansilla as rather a wide spot in the road (which it is not), at the height of the pilgrimage it had four hospitals, two convents and seven churches.

León

In eleventh-century León, once the seemingly interminable battles at the city gates were finally over, the Christian kings constructed a monument to their victory, replete with a pantheon to commemorate the dynasty that did the job. That edifice survives as one of three great landmarks that keep alive the historic past of León and form cornerstones for our explorations within the city.

First and oldest is the church of San Isidoro, which houses the pantheon of those early kings of the Meseta. The second is the great Gothic cathedral, famed for its treasure of stained glass and dedicated to Santa María de la Regla, divine protectress of the by then distinctively Spanish regime. The third is the monastery of San Marcos. Once it was the best known and respected of all the great hospices that succored pilgrims on the road to Santiago.

Heed the need to get an early start to avoid untimely interruption at siesta time. Begin today's excursion at the east end of Suero de Quiñones, named for a famous knight whose romantic escapades on the pilgrim's Way will be related later during our journey. From the intersection of that street with Avenida del Padre Isla, walk east on Calle de Renueva. After two hundred meters, at the Avenida de Ramón y Cajal, our route meets the northwestern ramparts of the old city walls.

These walls were rebuilt by Alfonso V and his successors on Roman foundations remaining after the Arabs trashed the city when abandoning the place for the last time at the turn of the millennium. Given the security offered by these powerful walls, a stout round tower protruding every thirty meters or so, León and surrounding towns and monasteries (remember San Miguel de Escalada some twenty kilometers east of here) offered safe sanctuary for thousands of Mozarab refugees fleeing Moslem persecution in Toledo, Córdoba and elsewhere in the south. Indeed, Mozarabs soon became the majority among the inhabitants in this entire region as the northern Meseta was repopulated by refugees.

273

The melange of Asturians, Galicians, French and Mozarabs shared a common but by then remote Roman-Visigothic cultural heritage and little else other than Christianity. But even that religious basis for unity was fractured by distinct heretical tendencies including vestiges of the Adoptionism that once prevailed in Asturias and the vast differences inherent in the Arabic culture and language spoken by the Christian Mozarabs. Couple that with several Latin-influenced dialects of the northwest and the result was a Babel that cried out for the unifying power of the Roman church and the newborn tongue that became Castilian. Understanding that, we comprehend the importance of the invitation extended to French priests from Cluny by Alfonso VI to reeducate the Mozarab clergy into the Latin liturgy and sacramental rituals. His goal was to weld cultural diversity into unity that could translate into the political and military power needed to continue the struggle against the Moorish kingdoms to the south.

Local dialects and traditions aside, those two cultural factors – Roman Catholic Christianity and the language of Castile – have been ingrained into the collective unconscious of Spaniards ever since. Only in such terms may outsiders understand the compulsive Catholicism and proud Spanishness of a heritage born out of centuries of war and hardship. Here in León is where that sense of national unity germinated and took first root. It was a king of León, Ferdinand I, who first called himself "king of all the Spains."

Are such deepset psychological factors still operative in the Spanish psyche? Consider this: From Castrojeriz all the way here to León there are cities, towns and out of the way villages never mentioned here or in any other book on Northern Spain, that even today set aside a time each year to celebrate the end of a degrading national insult: the annual tribute of a hundred virgins to satiate the amorous fancies of the Moorish kings. In León it is called the Fiesta de las Cantaderas, celebrated each June in the cloister of the church of San Isidoro. Never mind that it all happened over a thousand years ago. The cultural recollections of the Moorish presence and the indignities and

274

suffering they inflicted on the Iberian people is not soon to be wiped clean from the slate of their collective memory. Not in Northern Spain to be sure, despite the surge of political correctness in Madrid seeking the rebirth of multiculturalism.

Now we stand beside the **walls** of León, which helped put a stop to all that. Archaeological investigations revealed that the history of these ramparts goes back to Roman Spain in pre-Christian times. Then the site is believed to have been the base for the Roman Sixth Legion, the Victrix, at the time of the Cantabrian War. Later it became the headquarters of the Seventh Legion, the Gemina, which we have mentioned before in its role as pacifier of the northwest from the first century AD onward.

The earliest permanent wall was about two meters thick and probably not very tall. The third century rampart with its many round towers, the much renovated remains of which you see, was more than five meters thick and still existed in its full circumference into the eighteenth century. Now less than half of it remains. It courses eastward from here for a half kilometer, then south for another half kilometer. It terminates at the church of San Isidoro at this end and the cathedral of León at the other.

The wall marks the borders of the original Roman camp that later became the powerful fortress. Camp and wall had the conventional Roman military plan of a gate on each side, with main streets quartering the camp north to south, east to west, from the respective gates. The east-west street is today's Calle de Generalísimo Franco, while Calle Cardiles follows part of the north-south road through the camp. The existing Puerta del Castillo is the old north gate of the fort, Porta Decumana. The cathedral is believed to stand on the site of the commander's quarters (Praetorium), next to the legion headquarters. Oddly enough, Ramiro I built himself a palace on the same site to serve as his own headquarters during his vain attempts to hold back the resurgent Moors in the mid-ninth century.

At this western section of the wall we turn right along Avenida de Ramón y Cajal where, on the left and abutting the old city wall is the sprawling complex of the royal collegiate church of **San Isidoro.** Follow around the end of the wall to reach the Plaza de San Isidoro and the south side of the church. Seen from the square, on the left is the stout, square bell tower, of distinctively Romanesque design. Some liken it to a watchtower overlooking the ancient ramparts. On the right is the south arm of the transept and in the center is the main portal of the church. To the left, near the tower, is the entrance to the pantheon and museum.

San Isidoro is the oldest of the three leading landmarks in the city. The first church on this site was built in the early ninth century, probably by Alfonso II, and dedicated to John the Baptist and San Pelayo of Córdoba, whose relics rest above the altar of the present cathedral. The earlier church was built on foundations of an old Roman temple devoted to Mercury. That church was destroyed by Al Mansur when he reestablished Moorish control of the northern Meseta late in the tenth century. After Alfonso V expelled the Moors from León a few years later, he rebuilt the church and gave it over to a monastic order. It remains a royal collegiate church to this day.

Ferdinand I began construction of an addition to the church in 1054. The addition was intended as a mausoleum for the kings of León. Soon he turned the project into a more ambitious plan for construction of the present church, which was far enough along to be consecrated in 1063.

Ferdinand's intent in rebuilding this church was to create a proper repository for the relics of Saint Isidore, which he brought to León from Seville. Isidore (560-636) was Bishop of Seville and the most important theologian in the history of the Visigothic Church.

Most interesting about the matter of the relics of St. Isidore was the continuing spiritual alliance felt by these Spanish kings with their then centuries-distant Visigothic heritage. For them there was apparently a need for a connection with both the church and the royal blood of their Visigothic predecessors, as if without it they somehow lacked legitimacy.

A fascinating footnote to this is that Isidore was known to

Ferdinand and his time as "el Doctor de las Españas," while Ferdinand was the first of the Spanish kings to call himself "el Rey de las Españas." The use of the plural form indicates the birth in Spanish consciousness of the notion of a united Spain, then still a half a millennium into the future. It probably could only have arisen out of the tremendous achievements and pan-Hispanic background enjoyed by Ferdinand.

Recall that Ferdinand I was the Navarran prince whose father united Navarra and Aragon, and then annexed Castile all the way to Zamora. When the old king died, Ferdinand's brother Ramiro became king of Aragon, while his brother Garcia ruled Navarra. Ferdinand inherited the leavings, a mere "county," Castile. As a bona fide prince, however, Ferdinand declared himself king of Castile, married Alfonso's daughter Sancha to unite Castile and León, then conquered Toledo and Seville and the lands known as New Castile. He topped that off by annexing large chunks of Navarra at the expense of his brother Garcia.

Those achievements made Ferdinand monarch over a land that included Galicia, Asturias, Santander and all the Meseta to Seville, and marked him as one of the great leaders of the Reconquista. But this first Ferdinand in the end could only dream of being el Rey de las Españas and achieving the national unity ultimately won by the fall of Granada in 1492 and annexation of Navarra in 1512.

Ferdinand I died while visiting this church just five days after Isidore's relics were installed here in 1065. His pantheon of the Spanish kings claimed his remains.

The pantheon, for which this church is best known, was completed in 1066 by Ferdinand's daughter, Urraca, long before the church itself was finished. Work on the church continued in fits and starts until Alfonso VII completed the job in the twelfth century under the direction of the architect Petro de Deo.

Our first objective is to visit the **Pantheon** (open 9-2; 3-8), which we reach through the entrance to the museum, and is accessible only by guided tour. The tour is conducted in

Spanish, so let me tell you some of the details of the tour, which takes you through not only the Pantheon, but also the treasury (tesoro), library and cloister.

The Pantheon is admired for its eleventh-century architecture and sculpture, and its twelfth-century wall murals. It presents one of the earliest and finest examples of Romanesque sculpture and architecture in Spain. The work of the artisans clearly shows their inheritance from Asturias and the Muslim south in the secular character of the decor on its capitals, no matter the pronounced Romanesque style adapted by the stonemasons. The murals, applied a century later, include many secular themes, but are largely religious.

The groin-vaulted ceiling is lower than you might expect to find in such a landmark, but fortunately so. It enables a closer view of its wonderfully preserved wall and ceiling frescoes. Some commentators have labeled the place as the Sistine Chapel of the Romanesque, but I find that rather too extravagant a comparison. Historic art treasures these may be, and they are indubitably outstanding for the period, but a near equivalent of the Sistine Chapel they are not.

These **frescoes** were applied in the years between 1157 and 1188 during the reign of Ferdinand II. Extensive as the work and its subjects are, we would no more attempt to describe it than we would Michelangelo's famous ceiling at the Vatican. Yet by now even the most liturgically naive of us may recognize the main characters of these religious representations. For sophisticated Bible scholars it can be a field day of recognition.

More than that, as mentioned above, there also are scenes drawn from the life of the times, showing people in their ordinary dress and activities, from grape harvesting to boxing matches. Or is it only a barroom brawl?

A small spiral stairway leads up to the **museum**, consisting of the library and treasury. The treasury is reputed to contain the most complete collection of precious objects of art and artifacts of Spain's Middle Ages. Most notable here is the raison d'etre for the entire establishment: The original silver reliquary of St. Isidore, donated by Ferdinand and Sancha, founders of the church. Another reliquary that formerly contained the remains of San Pelayo, and a relic of St. John the Baptist, are also present, recalling the dedication of the original church on this site.

Another select item is an agate chalice decorated with gold and precious gems, donated by Queen Urraca in 1063, perhaps in penance for the incestuous cravings of her youth. But there is so much more, including Muslim artifacts, medieval fabrics and a stone tablet bearing the seal of the Roman VIIth Legion, found in recent excavations around the church. Also notable are some medieval tapestries, some as old as the twelfth century.

The **library** takes you into another age, the Renaissance. The room was designed by Juan de Badajoz, showing his trademark ribbing and ornamental bosses here in glorious color: blues, golds and reds against white ribbing in a pale pink stucco ceiling. Its exhibits include bits of a Visigothic Bible, another dated about 960, and a fifteenth century breviary containing miniatures by Nicolás Francés. All these survived the burning of the library and looting of the pantheon by the French during the Peninsular War, when much else was lost forever.

Beyond the Pantheon is the **cloister**. It is sixteenth century in origin and typical of the Renaissance style in vaulting and general design, but not particularly noteworthy. Finally, take time to pay attention to the sarcophagi of the pantheon that make this place what it is. Oldest of its occupants is Alfonso V, followed by the founders, Ferdinand and Sancha. The assemblage includes eleven kings, twelve queens, and literally dozens of princes, princesses and others of the royal blood. You discover them lined up in the pantheon itself and also in the galleries and rooms off the cloister.

We now make our way outside to the square and move east to the eleventh century **Puerta del Perdon** (Door of Forgiveness), entrance (closed) to the south arm of the transept. The Crucifixion is featured in the tympanum, with the three

Marys at the Tomb, on the right. On the left is shown the Ascension of Christ. The artist is reputed to have been Estaban, creator of the world-famous portal of La Platería at Santiago de Compostela.

On the church exterior, the most architecturally ornate features are on its apse end. There you find it adorned with many late Gothic spires, while a fancy balustrade adorns the roof.

Now return to the **main portal** of the church. The entry is twelfth century and nobly decorated. To the sides of the tympanum are San Isidoro and San Pelayo. Both figures were salvaged from the decor of the early church and date from about 1060. Also from the original church are the friezes depicting various animals. The tympanum portrays Abraham sacrificing Isaac, with El Cordero (the Lamb of God) and a pair of ministering angels above. The equestrian statue of Santiago Matamoros atop the gable is eighteenth century, as are the balustrade and gargoyles to each side.

As for the **doors,** these are said to be the panels against which the armored fist of the Spirit of El Cid is supposed to have thundered the night before the Battle of Las Navas de Tolosa. His voice echoed across the square, calling on San Isidoro to rise to the aid of the Christian host and assure victory in the coming fray against the seemingly invincible Almohades. The Christians won, whether aided by the saint and the ghost of El Cid or not.

Inside this three-aisled, Latin-cross edifice we find an interesting combination of Romanesque with Mozarabic touches, early Gothic with Cistercian influences, and (in the choir) the gaudy flourishes of Renaissance Gothic. Somehow the melange fits together very nicely, for all it being a bit dark and gloomy.

The basic construction of the **nave** is Romanesque, severely plain with unusually tall barrel vaults and ribbing above Romanesque piers. The capella mayor is Gothic arched in an intricate pattern, while the side aisles are vaulted in a clam shell mode. Of the windows, more than half are Romanesque.

The finest touch is on the capitals, carved with secular motifs including knights, animals, floral wreaths and mythical monstrosities. The **choir**, inserted into the central apse by Juan de Badajoz in 1513, and the fairly standard retable behind the high altar dating from the same period, are late Gothic but not of the quality we have seen elsewhere.

Most spectacular for me are the gigantic **cusps** in the Romanesque arches leading from the central nave into the arms of the transept. These Mozarabic features are kingsized versions of similar arches we found above the portals of churches early in our explorations in Navarra near the borders of Castile. And note the secular character of the capitals upon which they rise, a sure clue to their Mozarab makers. More of that early Romanesque is found in the barrel vaults and walls of the transept, and also in the side apses, once you disregard the accretions laid on during the Renaissance.

In the north transept are two **chapels**. The first, forward of the north aisle, is that of San Martín, where daily Masses are said for local parishioners. The second is the Capella de los Quiñones, where we conclude our visit to this historic edifice.

From San Isidoro's plaza, walk south on Calle del Cid for about two hundred meters, making a left turn just as you approach the far end of the little park known as the **Jardin Romantico**. From there the distance to the cathedral is about four hundred meters. Follow the jigs and jogs of the narrow old city streets eastward to the Plaza de Regla. There, across the square, surrounded by an ironwork fence set into stone posts with sculptured figures, is León's **cathedral**.

Santa María de la Regla has the look of something one would find in the south of France. It is clean-lined, well-proportioned, no-nonsense early Gothic until it reaches the late Gothic gingerbread on its highest elevations, which are obviously of a later date than the rest of it.

The cathedral (open 8:30-1:30, 4-7) was begun in 1205 when Spanish Gothic was just beginning to shake loose from the Cistercian influence, and was completed a little more than a century later. The principal subsequent modification was the southernmost of the two west towers, which benefited from an open-work spire erected in the late fifteenth century by a Dutchman, Joosken van Utrecht. Around to the south, the facade of the transept was treated to more of the same at about the same time by the same architect. And note that I say "benefited," for while some authorities belabor the inappropriateness here of that later style of Gothic that we saw so much of in Burgos, my opinion is that Joosken's work added a certain interest to a piece that otherwise might be too balanced in its effect and tend to be boring as viewed from the exterior.

That is its character as seen from the outside. Inside is the most fantastic display of architectural use of Gothic structure and stained glass that the art has ever seen. That stained glass, coupled with the golden tone of the sandstone structure, led the place to be dubbed the Jewel of Leon.

As remarked earlier on these pages, one of the principal advantages of Gothic architecture is its ability to create massive and tall interior spaces with relatively light-weight supporting structures. That allows the builder to open up the walls with apertures for windows to an extent that the ponderous structures of Romanesque and transitional Gothic could never allow. Here at León cathedral that advantage is carried to the architectural extreme. The walls seem literally filled with stained glass that illuminates the interior space with an awe-inspiring display incorporating all the colors of the rainbow. But, as usual, before dashing inside to enjoy that symphony of color, first let us finish our examination of the exterior, details of which we discover are not a disappointment to the eye.

The structure is created of a yellow sandstone. After centuries of facing the climate of the Meseta, the stone – no matter the recent refacing of the bare-walled surfaces – shows weathering that has taken away the sharp edges of sculptural detail. Worse, some of the most accessible sculptures near the portals have suffered from vandalism: an arm broken off here, a nose missing there, part of a prophet's flowing robe torn away somewhere else. The structure has a Latin cross plan, with nave and two aisles, and is much smaller than the cathedral at Burgos. Here we have a structure less than a hundred meters long and forty wide. Its two towers are of slightly different heights, the right-hand spire being about four meters taller at approximately seventy meters.

The **facade** is dominated by a gigantic rose window above portals dating from the second half of the thirteenth century. The column at the center of the middle portal serves as the mount for Nuestra Señora la Blanca, crowned and with her Christ Child cradled in her left arm, accompanied by a retinue of saints to each side. St. James is among them, on her left above the damaged **column**, in part worn away from the touch of pilgrim hands. According to tradition, a pilgrim must rest his hands on this worn column supporting St. James. So if you have chosen to be pilgrim as well as a traveler, pay heed.

In the tympanum is Christ in Judgment above a frieze depicting the tortures of the damned. St. Michael presides on the left, weighing the souls before those found wanting of innocence and Grace are delivered to devilish torment. More of the same is carved into the three archivolts above.

The decor on the left portal (Puerta de Regla) celebrates the childhood of Jesus, while the righthand entrance (Puerta de San Francisco) displays the Dormition and Coronation of the Virgin, and an assemblage of the prophets.

The **south portal** into the transept is as impressive in design and detail as the west facade, no matter what it lacks in comparable height. We see a triple portal with towers (much smaller than in the west) alongside, and a huge rose window above. The sculptures astraddle the central portal are thought to be the best of the highly distinguished lot of thirteenth-century carvings that decorate the entrances of this cathedral. Again, as at Burgos, we discover the four evangelists hard at work at their writing desks while Jesus teaches from his throne above the center doorpost.

Walk further east for a view of the **rear** of the thing. This probably is the most beautiful apsidal structure of all the major churches in Spain. Note the fancy detail of the Plateresque wall of the sacristy, the delicacy of the flying buttresses and the beautiful proportions of the whole. This must have been a joy for its unknown architect to see it rise into reality out of the fantasies of his imagination.

Now step inside. First of all move forward to the crossing and pause for a moment to look around in all directions. Forget details of things for the moment. Just look, then proceed on an unhurried circuit of the interior, still viewing for impression alone. Take your time. Just look and seek no more than an impression: A grand and glowing panoply of **multi-colored glass** framed in stone. There are places where it seems that nothing but glass supports the roof and ceiling that soars sixty meters above your head at its tallest point. It must be held high by a crew of angels. Or so it would seem given its lack of material support.

Back at the crossing fill out your ethereal impression with a batch of mundane statistics. There are more than 1800 square meters of glass in these walls. There are 125 large stained-glass windows, some as tall as ten meters; three great rose windows, and 57 smaller apertures filled with stained glass. Each level of glass has its own **motif.** The lowest represents the natural flora of the region; above that are heraldic motifs of the kings and nobles of the land; highest of all are windows depicting the great figures of the cities of God and man: saints and prophets, martyrs and monarchs, Apostles and fathers of the church.

Because of occasional structural failures during past times, the glass dates from all the centuries from the thirteenth to the twentieth. The bulk of it is thirteenth century. Many authorities compare the display with that at Chartres. In the comparison, Chartres gains from sheer size, but loses in that its glass has a more limited spectrum of color and a less advantageous relationship to structure. Some opinion has it that the general artistry of the work here is not only as good as at Chartres, but makes better use of color, and not simply because the artists at León had more and different colors to work with.

Strangely enough, the León cathedral does not appear on

any authoritative list of the world's great churches. For that I disagree with the experts in such things. True, this place lacks the tremendous bulk of a Notre Dame or a Chartres, and its sandstone leaves something to be desired as a structural material with the strength and lasting qualities of limestone or granite. But the imaginative design fancies of the unknown architect who conceived of and built this place, and the results he achieved, place this cathedral virtually in an architectural category of its own. If Chartres deserves a place on the top-twenty list (and it always does), then León's Santa María de la Regla should stand there too. But that is merely one traveler's opinion.

As you probably have noticed by now, the church **nave** is peculiarly lacking in side chapels. The central nave conforms to the usual Spanish practice by having a choir rearward of the crossing, but here it is less obtrusive than usual. The stalls are fifteenth and sixteenth-century works by Juan de Malines and Diego Copin de Holanda. The Plateresque grilles to the sides of the capella mayor date from the choir designed by Flamen Jusquin in the fifteenth century, but were reworked in the eighteenth century.

The **trascoro** (the massive carved piece at the rear of the choir) of gilded alabaster was designed by Baltasar Gutiérrez in 1576. Some also see the hand of Juan de Badajoz in the work. Its rich display of carvings were the work of Esteban Jordán. Above the central arch is a crucifix by Bautista Vásquez.

The high altar is the tomb of Ordoñio I, who brought Christianity back to León. The **capilla mayor** also displays, above the tabernacle, the silver chest made by Enrique de Arfe in the sixteenth century, containing relics of the patron saint of León, San Froilán (Bishop of León, 900-905), behind which stands a massive triptych. Its paintings depict scenes from his life. The work takes the place of the conventional retable, filling the space behind the altar from pillar to pillar and floor to archways. It is a fifteenth-century work by Nicolás Francés. Note the fifteenth-century bishop's throne.

The apse contains an **ambulatory** with radiating chapels.

Against the trasaltar of the capilla mayor in the ambulatory is the tomb of King Ordoñio II (d 924), reposing in a niche below a Calvary. The royal insignia and Christ are flanked by a pair of Apostles and ministering angels. The chapels, starting from the right at the south transept, include the Capillas del Carmen, del Cristo, de San Antonio, del Salvador at the extreme rear, del Rosario, del Nacimiento, and de Santa Teresa at the north transept. Behind the Capilla de Santa Teresa in the north transept is the chapel of San Andrés, on the left, and behind that, the chapel of Santiago, now called the Capella Santísimo.

The thirteenth-century doorway to the chapel of San Andrés is particularly charming, while the chapel of Santiago is distinguished by the quality of its stained glass. St. James himself stands at the place of honor high above the altar, pilgrim staff in hand. The glass was made and set during the Renaissance and has a character quite different from that set in the earlier centuries. The chapel itself was designed by the father of Juan de Badajoz, whose work we have seen so often during our explorations. Featured above the altar is a Pieta by Roger van de Weyden.

The cloister is beyond beautifully carved wood **doors** at the end of the north transept. Seen from the exterior side, this is the Puerta del Dado (Dice), the oldest entrance to the church. Santa María stands on a pillar beneath the tympanum. The door is closed. To view it and the cloister, pass through the museum (open 9:30-13:15, 4-6:30), entrance to which is a few feet to the left of where you stand in the north transept.

From the anteroom of the museum another beautifully carved wooden door opens into the **cloister.** On the top left door panel is Santiago Matamoros trampling a passel of fallen Moors, sword swinging in deadly arcs.

No matter its reputation for being an elegant masterpiece of Jean Badajoz, the cloister, taken overall, is probably one of the least appealing of those we visit on our journey, other than those we found in complete ruin. This one is far from being a ruin. It was built during the thirteenth and fourteenth centuries, gradually fell into disrepair, and then was refurbished and remodeled by Juan Badajoz in the sixteenth century. His trademark pendative bosses are wildly profuse on the gallery ceilings, making a heavenly circus of the vaulting. His work in these galleries is much admired by the experts in such things, but somehow it does not rescue the character of the thing overall. So after earlier promising you his masterpiece, I now argue its disappointing character. But perhaps you agree with the experts and not with my Philistine taste.

The courtyard is completely paved, and has a disenchanting "parking lot" atmosphere. Perhaps this is what affected my overall opinion. The Gothic pinnacle with its twisted ribs, set out near the center of the courtyard, is a piece removed from the roof of the cathedral during one of its many alterations. Several more such pieces are assembled variously around the courtyard.

Notable within the galleries are poorly preserved **frescoes** applied by Nicolás Francés in the decade of the 1460s. Yet they conceptually are so broad in scope one is amazed at the work. Also notable are the Plateresque **stairs** leading into the chapter house, another work by Juan de Badajoz. The chapter house and stairs are located near the east end of the north gallery and are on the route of the museum tour.

The cathedral **museum** is located in rooms off the cloister. What you find is the usual collection of items drawn from church history, plus some truly remarkable treasures. These include a tenth century Visigoth Bible, a tenth century Mozarabic illuminated Bible, a painted stone statue of Ordoñio II, and an exquisite collection of Romanesque sculptures saved from the cathedral during its various modifications. Of interest to architects is a large stone block scribed with the plan for constructing the rose window in the cathedral. In other words, these things were not done freehand. Their plans were etched in stone.

After taking advantage of every moment necessary to satisfy your interest in the displays, when you leave the cathedral go across the street to the **Diocesan Museum**, housed in the Seminario Mayor. It contains three separate sections: a collection of paintings; a display of Roman antiquities; and an assortment of Mozarabic and Mudéjar artifacts. The gem of the place is a Mozarabic Bible, the oldest extant example of the Spanish Romance language. Among the paintings is Pedro Campana's *The Adoration of the Three Kings.*

Finally, walk west along Calle Generalísimo Franco where, incidentally, we are following the old Pilgrim track as it heads west through León to the old monastery of St. Mark. A couple of hundred meters west from the cathedral square is the Plaza de Botines that, on its further end, merges into the Plazuela de San Marcelo. On the near side, to your right, is the **Palacio** de los Guzmanes, a sixteenth-century palace now serving as the assembly for the Diputación Provincial. Its architect was Juan de Quiñones. With its corner towers and imposing facade it presents a nice face to the square. Its Plateresque patio is a further attraction.

To the right, forward of the Palacio, is the **Casa de Boitines**, a modern building dating from 1894. Once a private residence, it is now occupied by a bank. The building is particularly interesting because of its neo-Gothic design by the famous Catalan architect, Antoni Gaudi. Note St. George assaulting the dragon above the front door.

To the left of the square is the church of San Marcello (1588--1627), which houses the remains of the saint. Behind it on the left is the arcaded and elegant **Ayuntamiento,** designed in 1585 by Juan del Rivero. León's coat of arms adorns the facade. Inside there is a collection of paintings said to portray each of the kings of León, from its capture during the early Reconquista until today.

That brings us to the Plaza de Santo Domingo, where at least seven major thoroughfares intersect. Make your way around it (circling left is easiest) to reach the Avenida General Sanjurjo which heads northwest on a beeline towards the Antiguo Monasterio de San Marcos, about a kilometer distant.

In the parklike Plaza de San Marcos, facing upon the former monastery, there is an historic **cross** in the gardens opposite the hotel entrance. Nearly three meters tall, it once marked the pilgrim way. It dates from the fifteenth century and is called the *Alto del Portillo*. The Gothic carvings on it are mostly scenes from the Gospel. One scene depicts San Rafael in pilgrim dress.

San Marcos, built in 1168 alongside the San Marcos bridge over the Bernesga River, was the mother house of the Knights of the Military Order of Santiago of the Sword. Given the royal support of Ferdinand I, the Knights of St. James were for centuries protectors of pilgrims along El Camino de Santiago.

Ferdinand's queen, Doña Sancha, founded the hospital soon after the order was formed. Under her auspices it became one of the most important and active pilgrim hospitals along the entire Way, since León was an important junction where diverse pilgrim routes met. They came not only along El Camino de Francés that we have been following since Roncesvalles, but also from the south by way of Valladolid and from the north via Oviedo. San Marcos was the largest of seventeen hospitals and hospices in León.

When Ferdinand the Catholic, husband of Isabella, ruled Spain, the royal pair connived to make Ferdinand the Grand Master of the Order. The ploy was strictly political, a move designed to allow Ferdinand to peacefully disband the Knights of St. James. Why? Because by the sixteenth century the order of valorous knights had outlived its purpose of protecting pilgrims. Worse, it had become too powerful to be allowed to continue, as the organization posed a potential political threat to the throne. So under Ferdinand's stewardship the Knights of St. James disappeared into history, fortunately with more humaneness than the Templars had experienced two centuries earlier.

Not long before his death, Ferdinand decided to raze the old structure and build the present edifice as a properly prestigious monument to the centuries of good works accomplished by the Knights of St. James. His death interfered and it remained for Charles V to implement the plan. Building began in 1514 and continued well into the eighteenth century.

In 1837, the institution was closed, later used for a

veterinary school and then a military barracks. Today it is a posh five-star hotel and a museum.

The **main building** is two storeys tall and a hundred meters long, corniced end to corniced end. Having taken so long to build, it is a complex mixture of Gothic, Plateresque, Renaissance Neo-Classical, and even a bit of Baroque thrown in. Its facade, besides the usual carvings around windows and the like, contains medallions carved in high relief, all in a row at intervals along the lower face of the building. Depicted are famous people from Spanish history and the Scriptures. Since Charles V paid much of the tab, he is shown on his personal medallion, along with Augustus Caesar, Isabella the Catholic and many more. Such was the grand company in which the powerful but relatively ineffectual Charles fancied he belonged.

The experts say there is nothing else like it anywhere in Spain. The lower level of the facade was given a series of elaborately carved pilasters with Corinthian capitals. The upper storey has thin columns with sculptured swags hanging down. The main portal displays Baroque carvings of Santiago in scenes from his life and legend, from moorslaying to his prior demise. Astraddle the doorway are pairs of engaged Corinthian columns at the lower level, while above are sectioned columns that for all the world remind me of pairs of fancy candleholders. Above that is a typical Renaissance pediment with coats of arms, stone traceries within a round canopied look-through, and statues and pinnacles all around. It is all very Baroque or Plateresque, or Neo-Classical Renaissance, or whatever happens to dominate the feature your eye fastens upon at a glance. The **church** at the east end, completed in 1541, is dedicated to Santiago. It was designed in the Gothic style and is nothing to write home about. Symbolically it celebrates Santiago with the field of scallop shells decorating the broad archway that functions as a sort of front porch. In the chancel, note the profusion of scallop shells on the east wall.

The **Museo Archaeologico** (open 10-12, 4-6) is located in the old chapter house and the sacristy of this church. The entrance is forward to the left of the capella mayor. The outstanding piece in the Archaeological Museum is the Cristo de Carrizo, an eleventh century Romanesque crucifix with an ivory figure of Christ by an artist named Carrizo. The work is noted for the remarkable visage and eyes, life-like braided hair and beard. Another ancient crucifix is the Cruz de Penalba, which is tenth century Mozarabic.

Other items include ancient Punic funerary artifacts, evidences of the Seventh Legion and miscellaneous Roman antiquities

The **sacristy** itself is an elegant work by Juan de Badajoz, done in 1549. His trademark pendative bosses are here carved as masks. The ribs of the vaults are decorated with scallop shells, cherubim and garlands, while resting on corbels carved as heads. The effect of the intricacies of vaulting and associated carving is thought by some to be the man's architectural masterpiece. Meanwhile, the chapter house boasts of one of the finest Mudéjar artesonado ceilings and paneling to be found on our explorations of Northern Spain.

The two-level **cloister** was originally designed by Juan de Badajoz, but is the product of the sixteenth, seventeenth and eighteenth centuries. Its jewel is a relief of the Nativity by Jean de Juni. Decor includes more portrait medallions and Plateresque froth, but not so much that it would ruin the effect of a prayer walk.

The landscaped courtyard gives a pleasant air in front of sturdy buttresses that frame the broad archways of the lower level. There is an Arabic flavor to the daintier Ionic columns, balustrade and round-arched galleries of the upper level. On the upper level a door opens into the upper choir of the church. The **choir stalls** are admired by the experts. They were made in 1542 by Guillemus Doncel.

As for the modern Parador: It is furnished with antiques, the polished marble floors often display hand-woven rugs, and its three-foot thick walls are decorated with tapestries and old paintings, some a thousand years old. From the lobby a grand staircase winds upward to the rooms. Rooms in the tower have ceilings nearly seven meters high. Aside from television and other amenities that go with a modern luxury hotel, it offers a taste of the good life of centuries past.

THE WAY TO PONFERRADA

Today our destination is Ponferrada, another hundred and ten kilometers west along El Camino de Santiago. You may guess that it is a city which gained its name from an iron bridge. Not unusual perhaps, except that the bridge in question served the medieval town a full eight hundred years before modern engineers "invented" iron-work spans late in the eighteenth century.

On the way to Ponferrada we learn of many other odd things: A stone-throwing Virgin who worked miracles; a medieval knight who performed an iron-man routine deserving of the Guinness Book of Records (if such had existed in his day), and a beautiful storybook palace no one has ever had the courage to live in. Then, beyond Astorga, we traverse some of the loneliest stretches of territory the pilgrim faces on this shortcut to Heaven.

Our way today closely follows the original pilgrim path, which itself tracked the old Roman road that led to the mines in the mountainous region known as El Bierzo.

Leave León on route N120 for Astorga, driving past San Marcos and across the sixteenth century San Marcos bridge spanning the Bernesga.

La Virgen del Camino

The Santuario de la Virgen del Camino is our first stop west of León. Actually, the city's outskirts now envelop the small village that for centuries sustained itself serving the sanctuary and nearby farms.

The Virgin's sanctuary is easily identified by the tall, thin white pylon with a cross-bar near the top. It sits just off the right side of the highway, with a boxy modern church between it and the road.

The story goes that the Virgin appeared here in 1505. There was nothing much around the site then except for a simple hermitage and open pasturage for sheep. The Virgin, known for centuries hereabouts as Our Lady of the Road, greeted a lone shepherd with the request that he build a sanctuary in her name. Doubtful of his senses, the shepherd asked for a "sign." The Virgin picked up a small stone, then tossed it six hundred paces away, where it promptly turned into a huge rock. No longer doubting, the shepherd passed the word and a chapel was built as ordered. After that Her chapel became a place of many miracles. Even today there are pilgrimages to the place every year on September 15 and October 15.

Miraculous events worked by the Virgin were nothing new in these parts. Back during the early Reconquista a Christian from León, enslaved by the Moors, is said to have prayed every night to the Virgin of the Road for his freedom, asking that it be given on his birthday. His master, taking no chances, had the slave chained within a large chest and, for good measure, slept on its lid himself. During the night he woke to the sound of bells and hymn singing, with the chest nowhere in sight. Chest and prisoner miraculously had been carried north to Christian territory, where its grateful occupant offered the Lady his chains in way of thanks. They were all he possessed.

The **chapel** is a modern edifice built in 1961 when the rambling old buildings that originally graced the site were bulldozed flat to make way for change. The new sanctuary was designed by a Portuguese architect, a monk known as Fray Coello. Notable at first sight are thirteen tall bronze statues splayed across the facade of stained-glass and concrete, plus a set of stout bronze doors. These are the work of a Catalan sculptor, José María de Sibirachs. The gaunt-looking ultra-modern statues are said to represent the gathering of the Disciples at Pentecost. To me these caricatures of the Apostles give the appearance of starved men begging for alms or food to support their emaciated bodies. The Virgin seems miraculously poised in midair above the group at the center.

The **stained glass** in the facade is a product of shops in

294

Chartres, France, where the art form is still practiced in a style and excellence seldom found elsewhere today. The exterior structure near the base is dark brown, rough finished stone with smooth, light colored limestone above.

Inside is the much venerated statue of the Virgin of the Road, enthroned above the altar in a sixteenth century baroque retable quite out of place in these modern surroundings. Above it all is an energetic St. Michael smiting a phalanx of fallen angels with his sword, driving them back into Hell.

The **interior** is as boxy as the outside, with marble wall facing, ship-lap wood ceilings and polished wooden floors. Along the wooden wainscot are tiny illuminated name signs above hinged panels behind which are confessionals staffed by the fathers named. The altar and retable sit between rough-faced dark brown sandstone walls, and behind the retable is a small chapel featuring a remarkable and strangely macabre Crucifixion of bronze in the same style, by the same artist, as the Apostles hanging on the facade of the church. Also noteworthy in this place is the Pieta depicting the Virgin, in a white-lace stole, grief stricken as she holds the body of her Son. You share the pangs of her pain and sorrow, the work is so remarkable.

The sanctuary is a foundation of the Dominican Fathers, who are installed in a large group of buildings on the other side the highway. Walk across to visit their **Museum** of Natural Science, created from objects sent back from their far-flung missions. Included are pre-Colombian terracotta figures and implements, fossils, pottery and baskets made by Native Americans, mineral samples from around the world, and literally scores of stuffed animals and birds.

Hospital de Orbigo

From the Sanctuary, thirty-five kilometers on the road brings us to Hospital de Orbigo, a town named for a medieval care facility created beside the river Orbigo to aid pilgrims on the Way to Santiago de Compostela. To get there, we pass Villadangos del Paramo (Paramo: desert, which this region virtually was until modern irrigation turned it green with kilometer after kilometer of field corn and garden crops). This was the site of the decisive battle between Alfonso el Battalador of Aragon and the armies of León. Here the Leonese fought off the Battler's attempt to conquer León in the name of his queen, Urraca. As we related during our explorations of Navarra, Alfonso lost the battle, his queen and his dream of uniting the Christian kingdoms.

Centuries earlier, Alfonso III, the Great, of Asturias won a crucial battle against the Moors near here. That happened in the ninth century early in his campaign to evict the Moslems from the northern Meseta.

The main section of Hospital de Orbigo sits on the far side of the Rio Orbigo. It occupies the site of the original town at the west end of an historic bridge, the Puente del Paso Honroso, made famous by the deeds of Don Suero de Quiñones. Today the town is spread out in all directions and includes a small collection of homes on the near side of the river.

Since the modern highway skirts the southern extremities of town, Don Suero's bridge lies a kilometer north of where our route crosses the river. Reach the famous old bridge by exiting the highway at the turnoff just before the modern bridge. As you enter the congested locale, the left turn onto the old bridge is unmarked, so drive slowly and look left as you pass each narrow side street. The approach onto the bridge is easily visible, little more than a stone's throw from the intersection.

The structure you see is a much lengthened sixteenth-century rework said to be an honest remodel of Don Suero's bridge, which dated from Roman times and still exists as the four arches in the center section of the span. A couple of arches were blown up during the nineteenth century by the retreating English during the Peninsular War to delay the French advance. Neatly repaired, the existing bridge is more than two hundred meters long. It crosses the river and its low-lying banks on twenty arches, all modeled in the same style invented by the Romans a couple of millennia ago.

While the narrow, one-lane bridge is still used both for foot and vehicular traffic, be advised not to try to drive across it yourself. You may meet some farmer's tractor or truck coming the other way. That would present a problem it would be better to avoid within the limited confines found between the stone guardrails. Best advice is to stop and park by the near end of the bridge, both to appreciate the environs made legendary by Don Suero, and also to walk onto the bridge for a look at things from one of the pedestrian safepoints jutting out from the main span. At the middle of the bridge are a pair of memorial **pylons**. On them is inscribed the record of Don Suero's Quixotic iron-man performance.

Don Suero was a real-life knight from León. No doubt you recall traversing the street in León named in his memory. His was a prominent family whose name has been mentioned here more than once.

The occasion of Don Suero's historic escapade was during the Summer of 1434. By then the military supremacy of the mounted knight already had already been obsoleted by Swiss infantry tactics and gunpowder. But Don Suero, like the fictional Don Quixote, was a romantic who reveled in notions of chivalrous love and all the idealized nonsense that went with it. Besides, that's what knights were all about once their practical utility had waned.

Instead of jousting windmills in the company of a faithful Sancho, Don Suero and nine companions turned their lances against any and every knight who sought to cross this bridge across the Rio Orbigo. Why? Simply to demonstrate his love for a lady, Doña Léonor de Tovar, for whom he wore a kind of iron dog collar as a sign of his abject submission to her will. His companions no doubt went along for the sport of it, and to keep their friend from jousting more challengers than one knight ought handle in a day on the field of honor.

A jousting field was built and walled with wood in the best medieval fashion here on the east bank of the Orbigo in July

1434. A herald then was sent out each day for a month to announce the challenge to any knight who approached. Since 1434 was a Jubilee Year (St. James' Day fell on Sunday), travel along El Camino de Santiago was especially heavy. Gentle knights on pilgrimage were allowed to pass unchallenged and unharmed if they admitted that Don Suero's lady was the fairest lass of all. All others were challenged to defend their honor, including many would-be champions who hurried here seeking reputations instead of Santiago's indulgences.

Old sources tell us that no less than seven hundred and twenty seven knights accepted the challenge of personal combat. That involved more than twenty matches a day, and legend says Don Suero and his friends defeated them all. They faced knights from France, Italy, and Germany as well as those from Spain. Only one death resulted, but the scribe who recorded the affair listed more than three hundred broken lances and not a few sore heads and behinds. Dead was Claramont of Aragon, killed jousting Quiñones, albeit accidentally when his own lance broke and drove through the eye of his helmet.

Each night, the story continues, Quiñones and his friends held a merry banquet to fete their fallen adversaries before sending them on their way. As for his lady friend: She spurned his love in spite of his grand heroics at the bridge.

The month of combat ended, Don Suero led his companions as pilgrims to Santiago de Compostela. There he presented an offering of a golden bracelet to the saint. (Perhaps his lady had rejected the bracelet as a gift?) It may be seen in the reliquary chapel of the cathedral to this day. Also, even now on Holy Years, the current inhabitants of Hospital Orbigo commemorate the romantic episode.

Beyond the bridge the ancient Hospital de Orbigo was operated by the Knights of St. John. It is long gone, marked only by cross above a few scraps of ruined walls.

Astorga

Astorga is the gateway to the Meseta or to the mountains, depending on the direction you are heading. For that, Astorga in 14 BC became one of the most important citadels of the Roman occupation. Beyond it, west and north, rise the Montañas de León and the mining region of El Bierzo, situated in the western extreme of the Cordillera Cantabrica. The Way west across these mountains reaches the highest point on the entire Camino de Santiago, a point we will pass later today.

Astorga has always been a good-sized community since it was repopulated under Ordoñio I in the ninth century. At the height of the pilgrimage in the Middle Ages, it possessed twenty two hospitals, of which only one (adjacent to the cathedral) remains to be seen. Today the city boasts of a population of about 14,000.

The Romans called the place Asturica Augusta in honor of the Emperor Augustus. They used it as a staging point to the mines and to ship gold and silver out on the Via de La Plata, the Silver Road that led south to Salamanca and Zamora, and beyond into Andalusia. Later, El Camino de Santiago here met what became the pilgrim route along the old Via de la Plata.

Centrally involved with the mining traffic was a strange tribe of people known as the Maragatos. They were teamsters and muleteers who provided the means of commerce and transport in Northwest Spain since prehistory. Only in the last couple of generations have they been forced into other work by the coming of modern roads and alternate transport. The district west of Astorga is known to this day as Maragatería, the land of the Maragatos.

Astorga has long been "the capital" of the Maragatos. Stop at a bakery and try a mantecada, a distinctive type of roll that gourmands rave about but which for my taste was something of a disappointment. The local bread is no less well-spoken of, and in this instance I agree. Buy some, along with cheese, perhaps a few slices of ham, plus a bottle of local wine, and have a roadside picnic on your way west from Astorga.

The origin of the Maragatos was a mystery until recently. Formerly they were thought to be a tribe of Berbers converted to Christianity during the Reconquista. Lately an archaeological ethnologist, Dr. Julio Carro, demonstrated conclusively that this close-knit band of people are descendants of a Phoenician colony established in pre-Roman times when Phoenician ships and traders came here to deal for the output of the mines. He showed that local traditional costumes, now worn only on holidays, are modeled closely after Punic fashions discovered on figurines excavated from old Phoenician settlements. Some were discovered among remains of a Punic site near a village west of Astorga. Their name is believed to be a corruption of a Roman word for merchants.

Local legend also tells us that one of the heroes of the Battle of Clavijo was a native of these parts by the name of Pedro Mato. He is believed to have been a Maragato. When we arrive at the cathedral we will find him dissplayed, pennant in hand, atop the pinnacle at the apse end of that edifice. The town hall contains an ancient bit of fabric said to be from a pennant carried by the Christian forces who won the battle. Scientific tests proved it is the right age.

With Pedro Mato we again find an extraordinary cultural memory. It tells of a man and an event now twelve hundred years back in the dim reaches of history. Some historians doubt the battle ever happened, or at least maintain that it was never as much of a fight as legend would have us believe. Yet in the minds of these people the battle of those centuries past still lies just below the surface of everyday goings and comings and is as vividly important as if it happened only a few days before yesteryear.

Astorga still has substantial portions of its Roman walls, some six meters thick. The town needed such stout protection when this place was an outpost of the empire facing untamed hill folks in the era of the Cantabrian War. Pliny, the well-known commentator on Roman times and events, was Procurator of Near Spain (Citerior) during part of that time. He wrote of Astorga as a "magnificent city."

The walls failed against Al Mansur, the Scourge of God, who destroyed the place at the turn of the millennium when he rampaged north to Santiago de Compostela and flattened the holy city of the hated Christian infidels. But, as at León and Santiago, Astorga and its walls were rebuilt and the new city again became a safe haven for pilgrims.

For all its diminutive size, Astorga is a cathedral town. The cathedral is worth a passing glance only because of the remarkable conglomeration of styles juxtaposed in its construction. The real gem here is the bishop's palace, so grand that no bishop ever dared to live in it. Unlike the city or the cathedral, the palace is relatively new, begun in the late nineteenth century. Architect was Antonio Gaudi, displaying his distinctive Neo-Gothic style.

We saw some of Gaudi's work at La Casa de Boitines in León. That was the diddling of a child compared to what he did here in Astorga at the request of a friend who was the local bishop. Gaudi, never one for half measures, outdid the expectations of everyone and his design was approved.

Unfortunately, the bishop died with work in progress. Soon the locals found the courage to complain about the unbearable cost of the place. For such an unappreciative response to his creation, Gaudi threw up his hands and quit.

The work was eventually finished by others who followed Gaudi's design but worked more sensitively with regard to the people's purse and patience. The major work was thus completed by 1913, but the last stone was not set in place until 1961. Then, because of the continuing animosity of the townspeople over the extravagances built into the place, no bishop has since been bold enough to take up residence and enjoy what Gaudi's architectural fancies wrought. The palace was instead turned into a pilgrims' museum called *Museo de los Caminos.*

Cathedral and palace sit within the old **city walls** on the far side of town. With their round bastions at evenly spaced intervals, these ramparts are reminiscent of the walls at León. On our recent visit we parked below those walls on the

Avenida Murallas, from which, across the intervening open area, one gains an excellent view of the walls and the palace and cathedral standing above. But we didn't have to scale those walls like a rampaging Moor. A walkway and stairs lead up over the wall to the rear of the cathedral. Later we walked through the center of town to the Plaza de España, thereby gaining a closeup view of old-town Astorga.

If one chooses to drive into the old town to reach the cathedral, the route leads through the typically arcaded main square, the **Plaza de España.** Its seventeenth century Casa Consistorial (town hall) is extremely attractive, with twin towers and an unusual clock. The clock has two mechanical figures, dressed in the traditional costume of the Maragatos, that strike the hours.

Beneath the building to the left as you face the town hall is a dungeon-like cellar room, the ergastula, sixty meters long and ten meters wide. It dates from Roman times. Tradition has it that the place was a slave pen for unfortunates on the way to labor in the mines of El Bierzo.

Clustered together are the cathedral, the Diocesan Museum and the Bishop's Palace. The latter contains the Museum of the Way to Santiago de Compostela. The two museums have the same hours (10-2; 4-8). Take a quick but appreciative look at the cathedral first and then see the palace and the museums.

The **cathedral** is the product of three centuries of building guided by the hands of a series of architects, each with a different idea of what a cathedral ought to look like. It was begun in the fifteenth century by the famous architect, Juan Gil de Hontañón, whose son Rodrigo took command at about the turn into the sixteenth century. The job wasn't finished until just a few years short of the nineteenth century.

What we have here, then, is an edifice in which Gothic merges with Baroque and everything else that was popular in between the vogues of the two styles. Gil began construction on the Gothic apse, completed in 1471. The nave is Gothic trending toward Baroque. The west facade is pure Baroque, while the sacristy and south facade are Renaissance Neo-

Classical. So is the late eighteenth-century cloister, which is badly run down and worth little attention. The basic stone of the construction even changed with the times. Red marble and tan limestone are dominant, and contrast between the pair of towers, one red, one brown. And besides all that is a remnant of the old Romanesque structure that this structure superceded. You will find it as the Romanesque Chapel that houses a small statue of the Virgin.

Quite interesting is the seventeenth-century **west facade** with its extravagant decor, from the statuary around the portal to the complicated decorations of the structure towering above. It is Baroque with the distinct flavor of Plateresque. Above the door, carved in a pink limestone, is Christ shown sending his Apostles off to teach all nations. St. James is among them, kneeling, dressed in pilgrim garb. The low reliefs depict scenes from the career of Christ, including the Expulsion of the Moneylenders from the Temple and the Pardoning of the Adulterous Woman.

Some say the most notable feature of the interior is the Renaissance **retable** done in Neo-Classical style in 1562 by a trio of artistic Gaspars. It was carved by Gaspar Becerra, painted by Gaspar de Hoyos, and the reliefs done by Gaspar de Palencia. For me the finest feature is found in the Gothic choir stalls, also of sixteenth century origin, done by Juan de Colonia and Robert de Mémorancy. The latter artist also carved the pulpit.

The choir stalls are constructed on two levels, with a long overhead canopy, also richly carved, circling the upper level. The high **grille** at the fore of the choir is not regarded as artistically excellent, but is grand and aesthetically appropriate, which often cannot be said about some more highly regarded creations.

Note the stylistic differences in the supporting piers at the rear of the nave compared to those forward near the transept, and the stylistic shifts evident in the pendative bosses high up in the ceiling vaulting. All these are marks of the changing of architects and styles as the centuries passed.

In the left apse side chapel is a Madonna, much revered by the local flock. In the **trascoro**, note the delicacy of the marble inlay work on the altar face (including violins and horns) and around the silver-doored tabernacle. Also observe the florals and geometric figures in whites and grays against the tans and browns of the basic structure. Interesting all, and often a delight.

The Diocesan Museum is housed in a remnant of the old monastic Hospital of San Juan. The entry is to the left of the cathedral's main portal. Inside, the way steps down to the **cloister**. The latter is of Neo-Classical vintage and its galleries were a mess, hopefully corrected of late. Its courtyard was overgrown and offered a single attractive feature: a tall magnolia tree. St. Francis is supposed to have stayed here while on pilgrimage to Santiago de Compostela.

The **museum** is located on three levels accessed from the near gallery of the cloister. The treasury of the cathedral includes an especially valued item. It is a handsome gold and silver reliquary containing a sliver of the True Cross, donated in the ninth century by Alfonso III, the Great, to the then bishop of Astorga, San Genadio (899-919). The small chest is cruciform and jewel studded. As for the remainder of the museum, it is tastefully organized and neatly displayed, a welcome change from the confused hodgepodge one often finds in such museums.

Now to Gaudi's flamboyant **bishop's palace.** The whimsical Catalan architect gave it a tall and slender appearance no matter the fortress-like character of its towering gray granite walls. It stands poised behind a dressed stone and iron picket fence, looking like something cooked up in Disneyland, a fit companion to Snow White's castle of dreams. My favorite exterior view is from around to the right where you see the fanlike archway of the main entrance and towering facade. This I expect was the perspective from which Gaudi intended the place to be viewed.

The interior is not so spellbinding, but well worth the price of admission. Hopefully you will arrive when tour buses aren't disgorging a horde of tourists, as a visit therein is best enjoyed without such distraction.

While the museum is installed throughout the palace, the second floor is the most interesting and architecturally spectacular. It was given tall, Gothic arched ceilings with ribbing of three-lobed red glazed brick with various floral designs baked in. The second floor includes the throne room, audience room, a majestic dining room, and the bishop's private chapel.

The **museum** specializes in items related to the history of El Camino de Santiago and also includes a display of the traditional costumes of the Maragatos. These you find on plaster figures beside a wall cabinet in which is shown a collection of Maragato jewelry.

In the basement are the transplanted tombs of several local counts, and a collection of Roman antiquities discovered at sites nearby. On the third floor is a modern art gallery that is rather less than outstanding, but worth the visit if only to see more of Gaudi's imaginative artistry in stone.

There are seven other churches in this town. They date from the eleventh through the seventeenth centuries and a scholar of church architecture would find them interesting. We leave them to their parishioners since they add nothing new or particularly noteworthy to our itinerary. There are still fifty mountainous kilometers ahead of us on our way to Ponferrada.

To Ponferrada

West of Astorga you are coursing through the Montañas de León, mining country since ages past, and still a region of operating coal and iron mines. Along the Way the road climbs to an altitude of 1490 meters. Have your fuel tank topped off and your oil checked in Astorga. In the heat of Summer, carry a jug of water just in case of an overheated radiator while pulling up the steep grades.

A modern foundation established by the Franciscans stands

next to the road just outside Astorga as we exit the city on a local road, LE142, following a sign pointing the way to Santa Columba de Somoza. This secondary road serves a whole series of villages along the original path of El Camino de Santiago. The route is picturesque, at times quite lonely, and always a peaceful change from the main roads and their ever-present streams of heavy trucks and other vehicles. The road passes westward through the Maragatería and its Valle del Silencio.

Most of the villages along this segment of the Way once held pilgrim hospices. Such historic places are now reduced to sparse ruins or less. The quiet rusticity of these communities makes their busy past now seem quite improbable. Yet in their day they served the great and the small by the hundreds of thousands every year.

Ferdinand and Isabella came this way when they went on pilgrimage. So did King Louis VII of France, not once but twice. Among the notables were many medieval saints. Some were renowned for their good works on behalf of their fellow pilgrims. There were also "big name" saints. Saint Francis (founder of the Franciscans) and Saint Dominic (founder of the Dominicans) came this way and established monasteries at Compostela to serve their pilgrim brothers.

Your map may show Santa Colomba de Somoza and Foncebadón as substantial towns along the way. Don't believe it. Santa Colomba is viable enough as a village, but the Foncebadón we passed through was full of empty stone houses with gaping windows and thatched roofs in various stages of collapse and disrepair. Its populace consisted of a handful of shepherds and packs of unruly dogs. More recently several hearty souls have renovated a handful of the best preserved buildings and offered to serve the pilgrim trade.

Stop at Rabanal del Camino to see an eleventh century church of the **Templars**. It deserves at least a glance because of its peculiar construction. It has a towering sixteenth century facade rising through four stages to a gabled pinnacle far above the main structure of the church. Thus there is nothing behind the facade but a stairway up to a roofed landing at the second stage behind the twin apertures containing bells. Such a facade speaks of great but unfulfilled hopes. The squat Romanesque church, with an arcaded porch along its side, could never live up to such high hopes.

In or near Rabanal are remains of a hermitage and hospital, and fountains that a student of such things should stop and see. Altitude here is 1150 meters. There are a couple of active facilities for support of pilgrims.

Another half-dozen kilometers further is Foncebadón at 1430 meters. It is mostly a dilapidated shell of a town, as we indicated. A very old **tower** suggests the remains of a medieval hospice. Yet this remote place was once important enough that Ramiro II, king of León, here assembled an historic council of his nobles in the tenth century.

From Foncebadón we climb to the highest point along the entire route between Roncesvalles and Santiago de Compostela. The pass, at 1490 meters, is marked by the **Cruz de Ferro** (Cross of Iron) set in a large cairn of stones. The cairn was created by pilgrims who, as they pass, toss another stone on the pile. So add your contribution to the heap.

The iron cross is about a meter tall, on a ten-meter wooden staff. A stone's throw further off to the right is a small, modern hermitage, Ermita de Santiago, where a pilgrim afoot can find shelter from the storms that sweep across these mountains. Pause here by the cross for a while and enjoy the mountain views and peacefulness of the setting.

The mountains in these parts are rounded, gentle sloped, with newly planted pine forests. The taller and more rugged summits of El Bierzo loom in the distance through the haze.

El Acebo (Holly) is a livelier place than most along this stretch of the Way. "Picturesque" describes it very well. Its hospice has disappeared without a trace and its parish church, while very old, is not memorable. The town, however, is as pleasant as it is old.

From El Acebo, at 1150 meters, the decent toward Ponferrada now accelerates. Molinaseca is already down to 600 meters. There you find an old and neatly maintained Romanesque **bridge** on your left as you skirt the village. Some say it was a Roman bridge, now many times rebuilt.

This small town deserves a pause to walk along the picturesque old main street to see the house of Doña Urraca, Queen of Castile and León, who inherited the kingdom from her brother, Alfonso VI. We have alluded to the scandalous hint of an incestuous relationship between the two, and told of her annulled marriage to Alfonso el Battalador of Aragon and Navarra, who had his heart set more on capturing the kingdom than the queen. She married again to Raymond of Burgundy and, by him, had a son who put the realm back together by recapturing what El Battalador had taken. Her son was Alfonso VII, dubbed the Emperor.

Now it is not far down to Ponferrada, where you enter town across a medieval, Romanesque arched stone bridge.

Ponferrada

The sudden contrast of the modern city, Ponferrada, with the ancient villages just left behind in the empty vastness of the Montañas de León, has the effect of culture shock. With a population of fifty thousand, busy factories, and mountains of slag that tell of its centuries-old iron mining industry, at Ponferrada we suddenly fall once again under the thrall of contemporary civilization. The mines are now shut down but its past remains alive, even in its name. As mentioned at the outset of our journey along this segment of our highway to Heaven, the name, Ponferrada, was derived from an iron bridge across the River Sil.

The bridge was the brainstorm of a bishop of Ponferrada during the eleventh century (some sources place it early in the twelfth). The bishop's thought was to remove the river crossing from the list of hazards facing pilgrims. Meanwhile the project made use of the surfeit of iron that had difficulty finding more than a local market in those turbulent times. Such a structure at such a time could only have happened here, where mining and smelting of iron and (later) steel were king for more than two thousand years. History had to wait another seven hundred years before anyone else had the audacity and imagination to build iron into another bridge. That finally happened in 1779 in Coalbrookadale, a town in West Central England.

Ponferrada was a Roman town long before its famous bridge was built, going by the name of Interamnium Flavia. It flourished first with trade from the gold and silver mines that once pocked the mountains round about.

Arriving in Ponferrada, one of the most interesting things to see is located on the east side of town. It is a very old church, **Santo Tomás** de las Ollas, situated but a short walk from downtown Ponferrada. So after hotel checkin, walk (or drive) along the main street of town, going east a half kilometer to reach the side road left just past the hospital. Follow that street to the top of the hill where the church is on the left at the rear of a small plaza. The man in the house in front of the church had the entrance key when Santo Tomás happened to be closed.

Santo Tomás is said to be the oldest surviving church in the Bierzo district. It dates back to the early tenth century and the reign of Alfonso III. That places its origin in the earliest phase of the Mozarabic migration into the newly safe haven offered when the Reconquista forged south into El Bierzo. The migration, led and organized by St. Fructoso, was the first of many.

The church was associated for centuries with the monastery of San Pedro de Montes, which no longer exists. Now a millennium later, it remains active as a humble parish church.

The single aisle of the tiny church leads to an oval **apse** with blind, horseshoe arches and a Byzantine-style dome above. A total of nine horseshoe arches, including the great archway between nave and sanctuary, decorate the little church, revealing its distinctively Mozarabic character. The scraps of wall paintings at the fore of the nave are sixteenth century, while the main portal has origins in the twelfth century, although it has been lately restored. The Madonna is known as Nuestra Señora del Rosario. All in all, this is a very memorable experience.

In the other direction on Avenida de Astorga, a short walk leads through the old town and all that is noteworthy to see here. Passing the park on the right, bear left along Calle Ancha, a main shopping street, for a couple of hundred meters to the **Plaza** del Ayuntamiento. The town hall, nothing special compared to what we have seen elsewhere, faces you from across the square. It is Baroque, of seventeenth century origins.

Exit the square on the street to the right of the town hall, passing through a sixteenth century gate supporting a Baroque clock tower. Along this narrow passage, on the right, is the active convent of the Immaculate Conception (also sixteenth century). After a hundred meters or so you encounter the eastern bastions of the Templar's Castle, seen across the tiny Plaza de la Encina. Off to the left is the historic main church of the city, the **Santuario** de Nuestra Señora de la Encina. The church you see is of late sixteenth century origins, showing a mix of Gothic and Renaissance styling with Baroque afterthoughts.

The Lady from which the church takes it name is an image discovered by the Templars about AD1200 in a holm oak (encina) tree. She presides above the altar on a silver pedestal with a gold and red satin crown set against a blaze of radiant shafts of gold. Some authorities attribute the work to an unknown fifteenth century artist. In any event, the statue is held to have miraculous powers and is much venerated.

The nave is single-aisled Gothic. The nicest touch in the church is a seventeenth century **retable** by one of Gaspar Becerra's apprentices turned journeyman and artist. The altar front is a remarkable plate of tooled silver depicting religious themes from the Bible.

From the church and the plaza, walk down along the tall and forbidding walls of the castle to its entrance. The **Castillo** de la Orden Militar de los Templarios has afternoon hours from 4 to 7 (closed Tuesdays) as well as its morning opening. It was built in 1119 as the principal Templar headquarters in this mountainous section of the pilgrim route that they protected. Digs within and around the site suggest that it was erected on much older Roman foundations.

When the Templars were exterminated by the kings of Europe in the fourteenth century, the castle was taken over by the Spanish crown. Later, Alfonso XI awarded it to the Count of Lemos (a royal favorite).

Some of the castle has been excellently preserved. At first glance as one approaches, it seems as fit and ready as ever to repel attack, but once inside you see that most of it stands in ruins. The fortress is rectangular in form, although irregularly so, about 170 meters long by 90 meters wide. Scholars regard it as one of the finest remaining examples of Spanish military architecture dating from medieval times. Certainly it was remodeled and refurbished throughout the centuries, but the last major modifications were made in the thirteenth century.

The **main gate** is approached across a fortified bridge over a filled-in moat. The entrance is straddled by round, crenellated towers. Behind them rise an even taller inner keep with a pair of watch towers high above everything. Slots for a now vanished portcullis are found in the round-arched entrance passage that pierces the wall. Inside, the place seems less cramped, and the interiors remind us how relatively small of stature the people of the old times were. Climb to the top of the parapets to gaze across the battlements for a fighting monk's **view** of the surrounding mountains and the valley below where the iron bridge conducted pilgrims across the Rio Sil. Except for the slag heaps and the modern city roundabout, the watchman's view has a nice medieval effect. Closer by, across the street is the tiny sixteenth century church of San Andreas, and a block further down the hill is the fourteenth century pilgrims' Hospital de la Reina, which may be seen only from the exterior, although it appears in good repair. The hospital was a donation of Ferdinand and Isabella.

Thus, on these thousand year old battlements we conclude an eventful day of exploration.

EL BIERZO

Depart Ponferrada on highway N VI, driving northwest through the valley of El Bierzo. Historians say the Roman name for the region was Bergidum, the linguistic root that evolved into "Bierzo."

After about twenty kilometers we come to today's first stop, Villafranca del Bierzo.

Between Ponferrada and Villafranca is a parade of old towns and villages, many with origins far antecedent to events in Roman times when this region first entered our history books. Columbrianos has scanty evidence of a Roman fortified camp adjacent to the village. Near Cacabelos was another Roman castro that later became an Asturian fortress. Some of the tumbled-down ramparts and towers still stand.

Most notable of the religious foundations along this stage of the route is the Carracedo del Monasterio. Located in Cacabelos, its proper name is the Monasterio de Benedictinos de Santa María, founded by King Bermudo II sometime about the year 1000. The present church is eighteenth century, and not particularly appealing. The old cloister and much else about it are either ruined or vanished. We do not recommend a halt unless you are a dyed in the wool church buff.

Villafranca del Bierzo

This small city was another of the ancient communities occupied by Frenchmen lured into Northern Spain during the eleventh century by the kings of Castile and León. Standing tall ahead of us are the green-decked mountains of El Bierzo receding into the morning haze. They are humpbacked and breadloafed rather than rockfaced and topped by crags as in the Picos de Europa. Such relatively gentle slopes permit cleared farmland even on the crests of some mountains we pass.

Villafranca is as different from Ponferrada as farm from factory. It is a pretty town of nearly seven thousand inhabitants. It sits in a rural setting of small farms within a side pocket of a fertile valley surrounded by steep, low-lying hills. More distant on all sides are the tall mountains that contrast their wildness with Villafranca's peaceful pastoral setting. In the far distance to the north is Peña Rubia. Its peak reaches 2214 meters.

Near Villafranca we sense a further transition from León's Meseta into the mountains of Galicia. There is more involved in this than the mere difference between mountain and plain. It is a cultural thing. We enter a region, Galicia, occupied by a people possessing a language and heritage distinctly their own. Like the Basques of Navarra, they too are by nature restless and notoriously independent of mind. Their land, like that of the Vascons, also is greener, lending a natural lushness to their farms, a quality missing in the dry expanses of the Meseta. Even the houses differ both in basic color and construction. Now you find a grayness that comes from the local slate the builders use, and a style of overhanging balconies reminiscent of villages in France, but which retain a Galician traditional form. Perhaps it speaks of the millennial-past connection between the Gauls of France and Northwest Spain.

Gray stone does not necessarily mean that the town is less colorful. Villafranca has more than its share of centuries-old mansions built by old noble families, plus the sixteenth century fortress-palace of the Marquéses de Villafranca (still privately owned and inhabited).

After exiting N VI to reach Villafranca, watch for a right turn that leads up a winding street to the most prestigious historical landmark of the region. But don't expect something grandiose. What we seek is the relatively small and architecturally undistinguished **church of Santiago**. You discover it on the left a couple of hundred meters past the foreboding castle of the Marquéses, which stands on the right.

The church is a Romanesque, single-aisled, single-apsed structure dating from the twelfth century. Simple as is the construction of the tiny church, you may wonder why it is so notable.

The reputation of the church derives from both the decor and the function of its famous north portal. That doorway is known as the Puerta del Perdón, the **Door of Forgiveness**. Church tradition allowed that a pilgrim unable to proceed further because of failing health brought on by the rigors of the journey, could petition at this door for the same absolution he might receive in Santiago de Compostela. Why bestow it here? Because of the especially difficult terrain still ahead along the Way to Santiago, and because a worn-out pilgrim afoot already had demonstrated the strength of his faith simply by managing to make it this far.

Remember how far we have come and what we have seen. This is a far distance from Roncesvalles, nor ought one forget the earlier trek that brought the pilgrim from somewhere in France, Italy, Germany and beyond. This was not a journey to be attempted by the aged or infirm, but they came anyway. Many died before reaching Villafranca, creating the need for the funerary chapels, only some of which we visited, in which the main occupation of the fathers was to dispatch the spirits of perished pilgrims into the hands of the archangel for the weighing of their souls.

We saw the first of those chapels at Roncesvalles, and others at Eunate and Estella early on, where the obstacles along the Way of St. James were comparatively easy. Then came the bandit-infested Mountains of Oca, followed by the long, hot tedium of the Meseta. The chill of the Montañas de León and El Bierzo was welcome at first, but the steep grades soon became the last foot-crunching, lung-wrenching effort that an exhausted, ill-nourished body could take without breaking down.

In those days, under the conditions that prevailed, perhaps it was a miracle that any pilgrim made it this far. Worst of all, after Villafranca another range of high mountains still lies ahead. Then, in the end, after Compostela one still faced the long road home. For footsore pilgrims that must have been a daunting prospect if there ever was one. Perhaps that is one further reason why so many stayed on in Spain to serve other pilgrims instead of heading for home.

Here then, at the Puerta del Perdón, the mercy of God was dispensed to sick or worn out pilgrims by the Vicars of Christ on Earth. As the Lord admonished sinners of another age, so it was done here at Villafranca in His name: Go and sin no more, for your sins are forgiven you. Here was their shortcut to Heaven.

The Romanesque carvings surrounding the portal are time worn but still spectacular. Experts see them as the best between León and Santiago de Compostela. On the **keystone** of the archway sits a diminutive Christ in Judgment. The carved capitals above the round columns supporting the series of receding archivolts are regarded as the finest work. On the left are the Crucifixion, the Flight into Egypt and a covey of angels, among other things. On the right-side capitals are characteristic Romanesque florals and heraldic figures.

The exterior of the **apse**, semicircular with engaged columns and small Romanesque windows between the columns, is proportionally satisfying to the eye. Not the same may be said of the relatively dull interior walls. Note the scallop shells carved into the rather primitive baptismal font. A chapel to the right contains a Baroque retable with an unusual Pieta as its central figure. But all in all, save for its famous portal, the place is a disappointment to the eye and interesting only for its history.

On the way back down the hill toward the town, pause to view the fortress-like **castle** of the Marquéses. Large and rectangular with massive but stubby round towers with conical roofs at each corner, it was built in the sixteenth century. The wing to the left has been rehabilitated and remains livable. To the right we saw gaping windows and grass-covered parapets that testified to ruin in progress. A great place for a ghost story. We hope it is seeing better days.

Back down the hill from the castle, a right turn takes us to central Villafranca. A block above the Plaza Mayor (long and narrow, rather tiny due to the constrictions imposed by the surrounding hillside) is the church of **San Francisco**, once part of a convent of the same name. It was built by the Franciscans in the thirteenth century in the Romanesque style, now most evident in its main portal. The saint (which some stories say founded this establishment himself during his pilgrimage to Santiago) stands in a niche above the doorway, arches of which are carved with simple geometric designs. Arch supports are smooth-faced engaged pilasters. The vaulted nave was remodeled in the fifteenth century by Mudéjar artists who left their distinctive mark. Best touch is their artesonado ceiling.

West of Villafranca's Plaza Mayor a hundred meters or so is the Baroque church of **San Nicolás**, a seventeenth-century addition to the former monastery and Jesuit college that dominates the north side of the adjacent square. It was built by Gabriel de Robles upon his return after many years in the New World. Among its many sculptures is a Christ that he is believed to have brought from America.

Another hundred meters west, on the left of a small park, is the most important church in town, the **collegiate church** of Santa María of Cluny.

Monks from Cluny moved here in 1070 to build a monastery and church, after which they more or less ran things for a far distance around. The original monastic buildings are long gone and the church replaced by newer constructions. The present church is basically a Neo-Classical design from the sixteenth century, remodeled again in the eighteenth, and never quite finished after that. Rodrigo Gil de Hontañón, whose work we encountered in Astorga, created the original plan for the place. Oldest part of the present building is its square thirteenth-century tower with a much later, oddly-shaped cupola atop the belfry. The **apse end** presents the only attractive exterior face on this church.

The interior of its great dome, and soaring, Gothic-ribbed ceilings, are left in their natural stone, gray in the dome, a salt and pepper brown in the ceiling. There is a simple dignity to the church interior established not only by the dome and ceiling, but also by the unadorned fieldstone and mortar walls and the statuesque elegance of its gray round **columns**. The latter are at least three meters in diameter and more than twenty meters tall, smooth faced at the bottom and fluted at their higher elevations. The double-level choir stalls are attractive and appropriate to their setting, but artistically not outstanding.

While I can't say I admired this church, I felt remarkably comfortable in it.

Cebrero

Following N VI west from Villafranca the road climbs into the high mountains. Villafranca, couched in its pleasant valley at an altitude of 525 meters, gives way to Piedrafita, high in the Sierra de Ancares, where the Piedrafita Pass sits at 1110 meters.

During the ascent to the pass we enter Galicia and leave León. At the town of Piedrafita we also say goodbye to the main highway, turning south on LU634. For about three kilometers that road climbs still higher to Cebrero (spelled in Galician as Cebriero on some signs) at a lofty 1300 meters, the highest town or village on the entire Way.

We now are in a region the Moors never successfully penetrated except on raiding sorties. Like the mountains of Asturias, El Bierzo was a refuge for Christians fleeing the Meseta and its nearby foothills. El Bierzo served as a rampart behind which Alfonso I was able to win back Galicia and contest the Moors for León long before the eighth century was out.

Along our route is the usual assortment of villages, most of which have lost the marks of their history to the travails of time. There are also a few castles, mostly in ruins, perched on hills overlooking the valleys. Near the village of Trabadelo was a particularly notorious fortress owned by lords who preyed on pilgrims and held the rich for ransom. Alfonso VI put a stop to such piratical enterprises as part of his general pacification of El Camino de Santiago during the eleventh century.

The village of Cebrero once had a Benedictine monastery that operated a hospital for pilgrims. The monastery was abandoned with the decline of the pilgrimage traffic in the sixteenth century. Today a part of that old establishment has been attractively restored as a rustic hotel and pilgrim hostel serviced by inhabitants of the village and its surroundings. The principal object of attention here, however, is the town's tiny church, **Santa María la Real**, once associated with the former monastery.

The existing church structure has pre-Romanesque and, for that matter, even pre-Mozarab origins. Like everything else in these parts, it is constructed of rough chunks of gray slate. The church was rebuilt in the eleventh century on ninth century foundations. Its stubby, square **bell tower** is roofed in an arching corbel style that suggests the Byzantine, as in Apulia, but which we have heretofore learned stems from the influence of the Visigoths. The entrance is protected from the region's bad weather by a covered vestibule. Restored in the 1960s to its original form, Masses are still said here on weekends and holy days. The church has a plain, three-aisled nave with a rectangular apse and beamed ceiling. Interior walls are whitewashed except for the arches and columns. While none of that recommends the place as very special but for its antiquity, it gains that status by being the site of one of the most remarkable miracles ever recorded along the pilgrim way.

It is a Winter's-night tale. During Winter snow piles deep on the pilgrim track here in these mountains. Wind roars through the trees and drives the cold through the heaviest garments, penetrating to the bone. At such times, Pilgrims were held back in the lowlands and the mountain folk virtually hibernated during the worst of the season.

On such an occasion near the year 1200, most of the monks of the monastery retreated to the valley and a lone father was left to celebrate Holy Mass for the handful of locals who worshiped here in the church of Santa María la Real. The roads were seemingly impassable, yet no matter what the conditions, Juan Santin, a shepherd from a nearby village, fought his way

318

through the snow and cold each evening to hear Mass.

Santa Maria la Real, Cebrero

One particularly stormy day when the monk would have preferred to stay huddled by his fire, the shepherd appeared as usual, expecting to attend the daily service. The monk, grumbling and shivering beneath his vestments in the drafty, icy cold church, hurried through the Mass as fast as he could. As he came to the blessing of the bread and wine, the monk glanced over at the shepherd and wondered aloud at what sort of a fool would come out in such weather just for a bit of bread and a sip of wine.

The answer was a clap of thunder added to the howling of

the wind. Before the eyes of the monk and the shepherd, the everyday miracle of the Mass became observable fact to their eyes. The bread became flesh and the wine was blood that flowed to the rim of the chalice, while a voice rang out, "I too have come to hear the Mass, and I too am a shepherd."

Evidence of the miracle was carefully preserved and may be observed in the church to this day. It is held in a fancy **reliquary and flask** which, two hundred years later, replaced the original containers. The new reliquaries were a regal gift from the Catholic Monarchs, Ferdinand and Isabella, after they passed through here in 1486 on pilgrimage to Santiago de Compostela. The relics are displayed in a locked, glass-fronted case in the right apse.

An addendum to the story relates that Isabella wanted to take the relics away to the cities for display before great throngs of the faithful; but, when they were packed up and ready to leave, the mule refused to budge until the relics were removed from its load. Even the queen, well known as a woman of unrelenting will, and the one whom everyone knew wore the pants in the royal family, acquiesced to the sign of a Will more potent than her own.

Displayed above and behind the reliquaries are the **chalice and paten** that held the bread and wine of the Sacrament that day, both validated by experts as dating from the time in question. The chalice, known as the Holy Galician Grail, is regarded as an especially excellent piece of twelfth-century Romanesque goldsmithing. Also to be seen are a pair of **tombs** displaying carved human figures said by tradition to be those of the "monk of little faith" and the shepherd of the miracle. The Madonna, seen on the right aisle, is a Romanesque work of twelfth-century origin. It is known as Santa María la Real.

The **crucifix** above the main altar, life-sized, is a Romanesque work of about the thirteenth century. The cross is constructed of heavy beams rather than the spindly shafts one usually sees.

A few steps from the church is a locally sponsored Ethnographical Park. There, for the first time on our journey, we encounter the age-old stone and thatch-roof houses used by Celtic tribes that populated Galicia in pre-historic times. Known as **pallozas**, the round structures have stone exterior walls about five feet tall, with tiny doors and (or sometimes no) windows framed by sturdy granite lintels and doorposts. Atop the whole is set a conical thatched roof. Inside, a dividing wall supports the roof and separates human habitants from their farm animals. In two of the pallozas we found a small ethnological museum displaying the everyday items common to traditional Galician mountain living.

Communities of ancient pallozas are found scattered throughout Galicia, both as ruins and occasionally as serviceable structures still used for storage and farm use. Also to be seen on farms in the lower elevations along our route between here and Compostela is a structure called a horreo. We saw similar structures in the mountains of Asturias. The horreo is like a small barn or storage shed raised above ground on pillars of granite. Often they are decorated with crosses, giving the effect of being shrines or funeral monuments which, of course, they are not.

Route LU634 from Cebrero now heads west along the backbone of the mountains, navigating a series of passes higher than 1200 meters. We pass through Linares (flax fields), Hospital da Condesa, and many more small villages and towns. All are picturesque, with tiny churches of ancient demeanor but noteworthy only for a student of the times and its churches. San Juan de Padornelo had a hospital run by the Knights of St. John. Its chapel is now a mausoleum.

Soon we reach another pass. On the summit is a chapel dedicated to Mary Magdalene. A few kilometers onward is Fonfria (cold font, or spring), where its former hospice has vanished, and so has practically everything else but a few farmsteads. Now we are coming down from the higher elevations. The sometimes tortuous descent ends as the road curves gracefully through a series of narrow valleys containing an assortment of hamlets and small farms. Then we arrive at Tricastela, situated in another tiny valley. While this is a more vital community of some size, we pass it with only a glance. It had its pilgrim hospice, the Hospital de la Condesa, of which only scraps remain, while its once Romanesque parish church has been disfigured by an eighteenth century renovation, making it more of a pain than a pleasure to see.

In another narrow valley a dozen or so kilometers further, lies the village of Samos. There we find the Benedictine Abbey of St. Julian, and a pause is in order.

Samos

The monastery of St. Julian was founded in 655 during the reign of the Visigothic kings. Because of its protected location, after the Moors came the abbey performed much the same function as a cultural life-preserver here in Galicia as San Millán de Cogolla did in Castile and Leyre provided to Navarra.

The monastery of St. Julian was abandoned only briefly when leveled by the Moors during the first surge of conquest. The monks managed to preserve their library, quickly rebuilt their physical facilities, and resumed the religious, scholarly and educational activities for which they were well known, albeit for a while they could do so only with greatly diminished capacity. In any event, the religious community survived, eventually emerged as strong as before, and served as root stock for a local Spanish culture that developed during the early Middle Ages. None of that happened, of course, until Alfonso I gave the boot to the Arab overseers of Galicia, ending their short-lived control of the district.

Alfonso I, dubbed the Catholic, spent his youth here in Samos studying with the Benedictines during the decade prior to the coming of the Moors. That long association with the learned brothers of Samos made him the best educated of the Asturian and Leonese kings until the time of Ferdinand III, the Saint, almost half a millennium later.

But for the Moorish invasion, one suspects Alfonso might

have followed a religious vocation instead of becoming one of the great leaders of the early Reconquista. Rather than join the brothers in restoring the monastery, Alfonso's decision was to ally himself with Pelayo at Covadonga, taking up arms against the hated invaders who had destroyed his island of peace here in the valley at Samos.

While the monastery thus survived the adversities of the Moorish conquest and early Reconquista, it flourished most auspiciously during the tenth century after the migration of Mozarabic monks. Unfortunately, nothing much remains from that early period. Once the "disestablishment" of the church occurred in 1824, the place was abandoned, its priceless library dispersed as kindling material for the peasants, and the structures turned to complete ruin by fire in 1951. How interesting that zealots of all stripes, religious and otherwise – even today as we observe the politically correct dismantlement of our own cultural past – always have the "me-now" awarenesses and sensibilities of barbarians. But, as the saying has it and the monastery at Samos proves, that too shall pass, though not without grievous loss.

The monastic church of San Julián, neatly restored in recent decades, is an interesting structure found in a pleasing rural setting. It stands within a spacious complex of buildings on the left beside the main route as you pass through Samos. At the near end of the establishment, park beside the road to visit the oldest surviving construction, which is a Mozarabic arch in the tiny chapel of El Salvador. It lies a short distance away from the main complex. To find the **chapel**, from near where you parked, walk up a side street opposite the monastery for a distance of about a hundred meters. There, on the right, huddled beneath a thousand year old cypress tree that towers above it, you find the chapel.

What you see is no more favored in general appearance than many a well-tended old barn or cow shed you have seen along the route in recent days. Built of slate in the late ninth, or perhaps early tenth century, the gable-roofed chapel has a rectangular apse jutting out like a small shed. Inside, the nave offers but a single aisle. Entrance is through a Romanesque door on the near side, and only two small slits of windows pierce the walls on each side. It speaks loudly of the tough times faced by the colony of monks during the period of the early Reconquista.

Back down the hill to the main monastic complex, walk to your right along the highway to where a stairway leads down from the road into the courtyard around which the main monastic buildings are gathered. The restored **church of San Julián** was originally built in 1604. The Neo-Classical facade with its attractive double staircase and entry are the design of Juan Vázquez, a monk in residence here. They date from 1779, near the time when the high altar and sacristy were constructed.

The **interior** is barrel vaulted and plain of demeanor but for the polychrome saints decorating the squinches at the crossing. Even the high altar is less flamboyant than we are used to seeing on this trip. It is the design of a local sculptor by the name of Ferreiro.

The church has a pair of **cloisters**. One is a seventeenth-century design, styled classically, with prominent if not particularly attractive frescoes in the upper galleries depicting the life of St. Benedict. The statue centered in the courtyard is of a seventeenth century monk, Feijóo, who was the moving spirit behind construction of the church we have just seen. The other cloister is Renaissance Gothic, dating from 1582. In a corner stands a Romanesque **portal** surviving from the twelfth century establishment. The large fountain is known as the fountain of the Nereids.

Sarria

Our last night along the Way is spent in Sarria, the first good-sized town since Ponferrada. It is a bustling, modern community that for more than a thousand years has served as the market center for the farms and villages in the hills aroundabout.

Historically, the most important event that happened in Sarria occurred in 1230 when Alfonso IX died while on pilgrimage to Santiago de Compostela. While not noted on any list of first-rate historic places, the town has its share of picturesque holdovers from medieval times that are worth an evening walk to see. So, after you settle into your hotel, stretch your legs and build an appetite by a walk to the upper town where its distant past is more or less preserved. We say "walk," but there is a climb involved, passing up a couple of flights of stairs to reach the lower end of Calle Mayor where the pilgrims found their way through the old town that then huddled beneath the walls of a powerful fortress. All that remains of the fort today is a ruined tower and a few tumbled down walls. It was destroyed by the crown in 1467 for some now obscure reason.

From the near end of Calle Mayor it is about three hundred meters up the narrow thoroughfare to the modern church of **Santa Marina**, built on the foundations of a medieval edifice. From there, walking further uphill along Calle Mayor, you pass a former pilgrim hospice dedicated to San Antonio, now used by the local law court and Civil Guard, followed a few steps later by the Romanesque church of **El Salvador** on your left. This church was built in the eleventh century, and features a typical round apse and slate roof. One of its renovations added the Gothic main portal on the west side, while retaining its Romanesque side columns and capitals. Christ Pantocrator presides in the tympanum of the north doorway on the street side. Inside is a collection of medieval religious paintings that, because of the relative rarity of paintings from the period, deserve to be seen to gain an impression of the style of the work, no matter that they are in no way to be thought of as masterpieces.

There beside the church of El Salvador, take a right turn onto Avenida a la Feria, which leads after three hundred meters or so to the most auspicious of the medieval establishments along the old pilgrim Way through this town – plus the walk provides a noteworthy overlook of the city. Higher up, behind the wall on your left as you begin this short walk, are the remains of the blown up **fortress**.

Our destination is the **Monastery** of the Magdalene, founded in the thirteenth century by a pair of Italian Augustinians as a shelter for pilgrims. The yellow arrows of the pilgrims' route show us the way to the place. While the street ends at the monastery, the Way continues along a dirt tractor path that leads out across the countryside.

The monastic living quarters, completed in 1778, appear first, followed by the buttressed apse, capella mayor and nave with a Renaissance belfry rising above. After the troubles of the nineteenth century closed the monastery temporarily, it was taken over by the Fathers of Mercy. If the church is closed, knock on the door of the second house up the street from and on the same side as the monastery. We found a gentleman there with a key. He escorted us through the church (and offered to stamp our pilgrim passports).

The **cloister** has a pleasant though rather shadowy atmosphere that combines elements of Romanesque (upper galleries, dating from the sixteenth century) with Gothic (below, fourteenth century).

The pavement of the lower gallery is made of small, rounded river stones such as we have often seen used for paving on this trip. Here the effect was notably different in that the stones were selected for size and color and arranged attractively in geometric patterns.

In one corner of the lower gallery is perhaps the oldest structure of the place: a thirteenth century portal into the **capella del Cristo**, which itself is the oldest part of the church. The chapel was originally Romanesque but was modified during the Renaissance.

The fourteenth-century church has a decor marked with the flamboyant Gothic that presaged Isabelline Plateresque. The capella mayor was rebuilt through the donation of a prominent churchman and scholar, Nuño Alvarez de Guitán, in 1485. When that gentleman died he was entombed here, and you find him on the right side of the church. Over his tomb is a statue of the man, garbed in his best clerical vestments and with book in hand as testimony to his scholarly reputation. In the side apse is a Romanesque **blind arch** decorated with high relief reflecting the transition into Gothic sculptural preferences and techniques. The retable is odd in that it reflects the work of artists from several different periods: Gothic, Renaissance and Baroque. The **Madonna** is known as the Virgen de la Merced, redeemer of captives and prisoners of the Moors.

In the presence of that influential Lady we conclude our explorations for today.

JOURNEY'S END

Today we continue west as usual, but with a difference. Our destination tonight is Santiago de Compostela and the end of our journey in the company of Santiago el Peregrino. For a pilgrim, the Pearly Gates are almost within reach.

The high mountains are behind us as we depart Sarria for Portomarín on route C533. The road courses through a broad, lush valley humped by rolling green hills, beneficiary of the fact that the rain in Spain does not fall mainly on the plain. The rain here on the hilly terrain of Galicia is responsible not only for the preponderance of greenery but also for the dankness of some of the old buildings such as the knight's church that we will visit at Vilar la Doñas later this morning.

The modern highway avoids the original pilgrim route and most of the hamlets along the way for the first half of the twenty kilometers to Portomarín. Thus, after about three kilometers, we must take a side road leading to the village of Sierra and beyond to reach the hamlet of Barbadelo, which lies astride the old pilgrim track.

Barbadelo

Not only church buffs ought to make the detour to the church of Santiago de Barbadelo. It is situated in open countryside full of well-tended farms, many of them with modern homes containing all the latest conveniences. They stand in stark contrast to the twelfth-century church and the ancient house and barns next door to it, which constitute what is left of a monastery founded in the ninth century by a colony of monks from Samos. In its last centuries it survived as a Benedictine chapter until dissolved during the troubles of the nineteenth century.

You may be taken aback initially by the discovery that the

church is flanked, just a few paces from its north and east sides, by a modern mausoleum containing four tiers of crypts, many freshly decorated with flowers and garlands of ribbon. What that tells you is that this eight hundred year-old edifice continues to serve as the parish church for the farm families hereabouts.

The church is single aisled with a wood-beam ceiling and a bell tower. It has all the attributes of a fortress and speaks of the era of its founding. The treasure we came to see here is the time-worn pre-Romanesque carving around its doorways and windows, notably the primitive style of the tympanum and the extraordinary display of mythical beasts decorating the capitals.

On the facade of the church, just above the portal, note the corbels that once supported a porch roof to protect pilgrims and parishioners from the weather. Also remarkable is the roof on the barn that one may look down upon across the tractor path next to the church. It is roofed with broad, ragged-edged sheets of slate, some of them two and three square meters in expanse.

Portomarín

Portomarín is unique amongst all the places we have seen on this highway to Heaven. Ancient as its historic landmarks appear, in fact they and everything else that has the look of antiquity in the town are reconstructions erected in the latter half of the twentieth century. The historic buildings in this town were carefully dismantled, moved, then rebuilt at their present location when Portomarín was transferred from its millennium-old site on the banks of the Rio Miño.

The move to higher ground was necessitated when the Embalse de Belesar was constructed and filled, drowning the original townsite. In the Fall, when the reservoir's water level has been drawn down, the ruin of the old town, including the town's bridge that carried pilgrims across the Miño, can still be seen. Best **view** of it is from the road by the chapel of Santa

María of the Snows. That tiny and undistinguished chapel is located beside the highway high above the modern reservoir and a kilometer past the first of two modern bridges that now cross the Miño. The Madonna in this chapel, while of no particular artistic merit, is much revered by people of the district.

The new town, situated beyond the second bridge and on the hillside above the reservoir, contains the rebuilt thirteenth-century church of San Juan, the seventeenth-century palace of the Berbetoros and the sixteenth-century Casa de Condes, all presented for your inspection on or near the Plaza Mayor. Also displayed as a sort of triumphal arch is the triple-arched doorway on the **Casa do Concello** (town hall) that was salvaged from the former church of San Pedro, dating from 1182. The arcades of its narrow main street, the overhead supported by stout stone pillars, are a further survival from the former town. Beneath them we found the local version of a deli where we purchased the makings of a picnic lunch, enjoyed later on the road west.

San Juan was a **fortified church** serving the Knights of St. John of Jerusalem. Romanesque in style, this oddly square structure is crenellated all around and has a single, semi-circular apse containing window slits beneath its Romanesque arches. These formidable walls betray their religious function only by the rose window on its west side.

The church is known best for the **carvings** around its three doors, particularly the west portal where Christ in His Majesty has the company of the twenty four musicians of the apocalypse. Mateo, the master sculptor who did the famous Pórtico de la Gloria at the Santiago Cathedral, is believed to have been the author of these portals. Other carvings include floral and bestial figures on the north and south doors. The north portal also contains the Annunciation in its tympanum plus capitals displaying mythical beasts and monstrosities. Most notable interior features are the Romanesque **frescoes**, restored at the time of the move, along the walls of the single nave church.

Leave Portomarín on route C535 in the direction of Castro Mayor and Palas de Rey. Castro Mayor takes it name from a one-time Roman camp nearby. The village of Hospital is named for the former Hospital of St. Stephen, last mentioned in the seventeenth century and not seen since. Ventas de Narón was the site of a crucial battle between Christians and Moors in 820. The Christians won.

Vilar de Doñas

Near Lestedo make another brief detour off the highway, taking a road north for about three kilometers to Vilar de Doñas. Our objective is the monastic church of San Salvador, originally part of a convent founded early in the twelfth century by two ladies of the Arias de Monterroso family. From these ladies the monastery gained the name of Vilar de Doñas.

The monastic order appears to have failed, for in 1184 the establishment was taken over by the Knights of Saint James as their headquarters for suppression of banditry along the pilgrim Way as it approached Santiago de Compostela. In later days the place may have became an "old knights home," for we will find a number of their tomb markers and sarcophagi within its walls.

You find the church site on your right, with the church set back behind a low stonewall. Park along the street, which also serves several farm houses which belong to the nearby village that shares the name of the monastery. Approach the church through a small covered courtyard reached through sturdy Gothic archways that extend from the front of the church to the roadside wall. If closed, inquire at the nearby home for a key.

The church of **El Salvador** dates from the thirteenth century and remains active as the parish church for the local farm families. While there have been recent renovations, such as the addition of the roof over the courtyard, the church itself has been spared radical attempts at remodeling. It looks every bit its age and offers an unspoiled mix of Romanesque and

331

transitional Gothic forms except for a late Gothic, almost Baroque belfry.

Small as the structure is, it lacked the wall thickness to display the ostentatious elegance of its Romanesque main portal. Thus you find that a kind of porch-like structure was added to the **facade** to provide the depth of masonry necessary to contain the traditionally-styled doorway. A Cistercian Gothic cornice decorates the edge of the resulting ledge above the grandly carved Romanesque portal. When first visited researching this book, a trio of statues stood atop that narrow ledge. They were of St. Bartholomew, St. Michael with his sword handy, and the Madonna and Child. When the courtyard was roofed, they apparently were removed.

The carved **portal** deserves close attention. It displays a classic example of the Cistercian transformation of Romanesque forms. Of the five arches within the structure of the Romanesque portal, the outer pair of archivolts contain conventional Romanesque florals. In the middle arch you find the Cistercian trademark, the sawtooth design. The inner pair of arches then contain geometric forms, including a pendative hanging above the doorway.

In the capitals above the smooth-faced engaged columns beside the portal, the carving tends towards high relief Gothic but the material presented is late Romanesque: a mix of saints and monstrosities. Inside, the **nave** is single aisled beneath a timbered ceiling with a narrow Romanesque arch leading to the crossing and a triple apse. The crossing is Gothic arched. Transepts and apses are barrel vaulted in traditional Romanesque style.

Tomb markers of knights line the walls. In the semicircular central apse is a display of fifteenth (some say fourteenth) century frescoes that experts consider to be the best surviving example of Galician art at the time. Portrayed are Jeremiah and Daniel, the Annunciation and the Resurrection, plus portraits of several women, believed to memorialize the Doñas of Vilar de Doñas. Unfortunately much of the lower frescoes are badly time damaged.

The main **altar** is remarkable because of the small and thus unobtrusive granite retable with a rectangular cleft at its center that formerly contained a fourteenth century painting of the dead Christ prepared for the tomb. Scenes carved in the retable depict, on the right, a Pieta of Mary, holding the body of Christ after it was lowered from the cross; and, on the left, Christ risen triumphant next to the cross that was to have been His earthly end. Recently the retable was moved to a side altar, allowing the priest to face the congregation while celebrating the Mass.

Palas de Rey to Mount Joy

Return to the highway and resume the drive west through a series of villages and hamlets leading to the town of Palas de Rey. The name commemorates the tradition that the Visigothic King Witza, predecessor of King Roderick, maintained a residence in the town. The town today offers little to expand upon our explorations.

At Palas de Rey our journey finds us back upon a better highway, C547, that from here follows the old pilgrim track all the way into Santiago de Compostela. Less than fifteen kilometers past Palas de Rey is the town of Melide. Follow the road onward into the center of town and the main square, the Plaza del Convento. It takes its name from the former monastery and hospital of the Holy Spirit, now vanished but for its church, which today serves the local parish.

The church of Sancti Spiritus, which you find on the right, was founded in 1375, but its Baroque doorway and facade date from the seventeenth century. Inside, the nave is Gothic and is part of the original structure. Note the profusion of old tombs in the place.

The towns along the road now come virtually one after the other, but fortunately the highway finds its way around many of them. For our interests none of these places retain more than shadows of their old importance as way stations along El

Camino de Santiago.

After the village of Amenal, on the left, is Compostela's modern airport. Just beyond that is the Rio Labacolla (River Wash Your Behind), where pilgrims traditionally stripped and washed themselves and their clothes so as to have a proper appearance as they entered Compostela and presented themselves at the shrine of Santiago to receive their blessing. We decided to heed the example of the pilgrims of old, but not by following them to the river. We found comfortable quarters at one of the hotels along the highway between the airport and the city, freshened up, obtained a map of the city and continued on along the path of the pilgrims toward Santiago.

The villages come fast and furious now, modern constructions running the old towns together along both sides of the highway. Only San Marcos deserves a stop. This historic site is notable for its hill, 368 meters in altitude and about that same distance to the left of the highway. A sign, **Monte do Gozo**, directs a left turn off the highway and leads to the hilltop. It doesn't look like much as hills go, but it rises above the low, rolling countryside dead ahead., and is more than 100 meters higher than the central city of Santiago. Just four kilometers from their destination, this hill granted pilgrims their first view of Santiago de Compostela and the cathedral towers. Pilgrims called the place the Hill of Jubilation, or Mount Joy.

Atop the hill in a park-like setting is a tiny and undistinguished **chapel** dedicated to St. Mark. Alongside is a small parking area. Further afield are the pilgrims' hostal and facilities for a so-called Holiday City development. Nearby is an ugly, incongruous modernistic **monument** commemorating the pilgrimages of St. Francis and Pope Paul II. Given the pilgrim's mood set from Roncesvalles to Rio Labacolla, and his anticipation of what lies so near ahead, the designer of this monument obviously had no notion of what the pilgrimage along El Camino de Santiago is all about.

Don't expect to share the old-time pilgrim's view. From this distance, modern buildings, nearby trees and other obstacles stand in the way, but just a little further along the highway the spires of the cathedral do come into view.

Santiago de Compostela even today is not a particularly large city, and high rise business and residential developments are not a prominent part of the landscape; at least, not yet. Because of that, the towers and tremendous bulk of the cathedral complex still dominate the city seen from any aspect. Pilgrims, with their destination now close at hand and guided by sight of the towers, invariably made a bee-line dash for the cathedral and all that it promised in fulfillment of months of hardship spent along the Way of St. James. After all, this was to be their ticket to Heaven.

We may be as anxious as them to see the place, but we decided not to follow the lead of the pilgrims. Not yet. The vicinity of the cathedral, you see, is now largely restricted to pedestrians. Even where automobiles are allowed, this thoroughly time-warped old city is a maze of narrow, one-way streets not conducive to maintaining the good temper of a driver unfamiliar with the twists and turns of its thoroughfares. But there is time this afternoon to enjoy one of the most unusual sights of the entire journey, the church of Santa María del Sar.

Santa María del Sar

Where C547 intersects Avenida de Lugo, turn left toward the railway station. The avenida is part of the north-south highway that bypasses city center. Our intent for the moment is to become familiar with a route into the city, have a general look around its eastern outskirts, and stretch our legs with a short walk few meters off Avenida de Lugo to a remarkable sight: the twelfth century church of **Santa María del Sar**. Architectural scholars deem to be, after the cathedral itself, the most interesting edifice in Santiago (open 10-1, 4-6; later in Summer).

Our destination is near where Avenida de Lugo overpasses

Calle del Sar, about a half kilometer this side of the railway station. The street is named for the Sar River, located some two hundred meters south. Park along Avenida de Lugo in front of a row of business establishments just beyond the overpass. Walk the few steps back to the overpass and descend the stairs to Calle del Sar. Turn right beneath the overpass and walk about fifty meters down the street to a spacious plaza off to the right. The church can be seen on the far side to the left.

What is most interesting about Santa María del Sar is the peculiarity of its interior construction (which we will describe in a moment) and the fact that it is one of the few medieval structures in Compostela that later architects have virtually left alone in its original Romanesque purity and not bastardized with various Baroque or other later alterations. They left it alone no doubt because they were too frightened by the construct of the place to lay a hand on it.

The church originally was associated with a monastery. Now it is a parish church, serving as such since 1851. It was consecrated in 1136 by Archbishop Gelmírez, who also was the moving spirit behind construction of the cathedral. The existing church is the product of a further rebuilding some forty years later. The building next to it holds the Collegiate Museum of Sacred Art. Exhibits also include archeological items and documents related to the history of the church.

The **exterior** is a plain Romanesque with the unusual feature of stout flying buttresses against its walls. These were added in the seventeenth century to counteract the weakening effects of an earthquake. In fact, if you stand to gain a surveyor's view of the wall facing you, you will see that it leans at least twenty five centimeters out of plumb, base to top cornice. Once inside, however, you will understand even better why later architects feared to lay a finger on the interior of the place.

Still viewing the exterior, the apse is decorated by ornately carved **modillions** and capitals, displaying a variety of monstrosities as well as conventional Romanesque florals. Around on the far side of the apse is an entrance to the church and its cloister, with the north gallery of the latter becoming the first thing the visitor sees.

The **cloister** as originally designed and built has mostly vanished. Only one original gallery is left, but it is worth the time to study it in detail, according to the experts. Some say that first cloister was the brainchild of the famous master architect and sculptor, Mateo. Most authorities regard its artistic merit as second only to Master Mateo's Pórtico de la Gloria at the cathedral, which we will see on the morrow. In any event, there is consensus that the double arches of this Romanesque construction rest upon column capitals attributable to Mateo. Dominating the work are exquisite floral designs in capitals and archivolts. Immediately contrast this north gallery with the others. They are an unimaginative and ponderous Romanesque overall, yet you can make out scraps of capitals and other pieces obviously salvaged from the ruins of Mateo's work and perhaps from other local edifices as well.

We have seen other work attributed to Mateo elsewhere on our journey. As usual, we find the experts comparing it only to his own masterpiece, the Pórtico de la Gloria, rather than to the work of anyone else. In effect, his work set the Spanish standard of excellence for Romanesque sculptural adornment, and here he offers us another aesthetic nibble anticipating discovery of the greatness of his talent and inspiration when we visit Compostela's cathedral.

The **interior** of this landmark structure is revealed as a three-aisled, three-apsed church with a barrel-vaulted ceiling coming to rest upon stout piers with Romanesque arches between. And, yes, your eyes are not deceiving you. Also, yes, you may feel a disturbance of your equilibrium, even to the point of vertigo for some people. The columns supporting the roof do slant outward, while the weight of the vaulted superstructure forever threatens to pressure the exterior walls in the same direction. That hasn't happened in nearly nine hundred years, even during earthquakes, so you are safe enough. Yet you can understand the worry that led to addition of the external flying buttresses after the earthquake several hundred years ago.

Some say the slanted piers are the result of ground subsidence. If so, others argue, corresponding distortions of the barrel vaults above would also be perceptible. Since the ceiling is not misshapen, and since pilgrim diaries mention this peculiarity of the place virtually from the time of building, they believe that the original architect, either from whimsy or to prove that God would lend His support to the structure, actually designed the church to stand with piers awry, just as you see it. For that reason students of architecture are literally awestruck by what they observe here.

As for us, we can judge the truth of the matter for ourselves by making a simple observation. At the rear of the nave where your view is not obstructed by the pews, sight in on the **plinths** (bases) on which the rearmost columns are set. You will see that the plinths stand true. Only the columns are askew. The slant, you now clearly observe, is built into the columns from the very first course of the stone from which they were constructed.

Another point: No matter how whimsical the founding architect may appear to have been, the fact remains that his construction has survived earthquakes that have destroyed more conventional buildings that apparently received less in the way of Divine support. More, his audacity has discouraged later architects from tampering with what he accomplished. For that we may be thankful.

The double tier of blind Romanesque arches encircling the central apse, with the **rose window** glowing like a gigantic Host above the arched opening into the apse, is an elegant view from the nave. Note that the altar, relatively plain and dignified, stands open and free without the dominating encumbrance of a Renaissance retable such as we typically find in churches along the Way. The niche in the upper tier of arches behind the altar holds Santa María del Sar and her Christ Child. Several tombs, all exceptionally well preserved, date from the thirteenth to the sixteenth centuries.

Finally, returning to your car on Avenida de Lugo and

338

before heading back to your hotel, take a few minutes to scout the route to where, on the morrow, you will find a place to park while exploring the old city of Santiago. The best choice for easy access, and the most convenient downtown parking location, is in the underground galleries beneath the Plaza de Galicia. Easiest way to get there is to continue along Avenida de Lugo to the railway station. There turn right on the Rua Horreo, which in about a half kilometer dead-ends at the Plaza de Galicia. The plaza has rotary traffic around it. Keep left, circling the center of the plaza to where, on the west side of the hub, is the ramp descending into the parking galleries.

Now you are set for quick access to your tour on the morrow.

SANTIAGO

A traveler in Santiago de Compostela may be there for no other reason than to rubber-neck; or he might have the more serious motive: to share the experience of countless pilgrims, each with staff in hand, plodding along St. James' Highway to Heaven as has been done by the faithful for more than a thousand years.

We have followed the track of "los peregrinos" as it crossed eight hundred kilometers of Spanish countryside and what seemed like innumerable villages and towns. We joined them afoot at times, better to see the sights and gain something of the flavor of the pilgrims' holy ordeal. Some of us even accounted for the hundred kilometers on shoeleather that qualifies a traveler as a pilgrim. Thus one joins the ranks of those who in good Faith approach the shrine of St. James seeking deliverance from sin and the reward of everlasting peace in the sight of God.

Whatever we call ourselves, traveler or pilgrim, we now abandon our wheels to find our way through the narrow, medieval streets of Santiago. As a traveler this becomes an unforgettable exploratory walk through Spain's most holy city. For pilgrims afoot it is the glorious fruition of months of hardship, danger and suffering on El Camino de Santiago. Here, now but a few steps from the shrine of St. James, jubilation swells in every breast in awareness that the end of their shortcut to Heaven is at hand.

Overflowing with joy at the achievement, full of wonderful anticipations, no one should expect a pilgrim even today to do other than dash at top speed to the shrine of the saint. There the pilgrim offers a heartfelt prayer of thanksgiving, praising the Lord Who granted success to his sacred enterprise. Only then may a pilgrim be ready to turn aside from fulfillment of his quest and explore the city so as to take stock of sights that even in this more sophisticated age are downright impressive and often spellbinding.

During most of the millennium of pilgrimage the social, political and economic character of Europe was characterized by rural communities. Cities were few and far between. Village and town predominated, with the town serving as a regional marketplace for districts that essentially were self sufficient. Thought processes seldom ventured beyond district issues and problems, even for the aristocracy. Given the medieval mindset and the primitive milieu experienced by pilgrims of the time, historical accounts of their introduction to Compostela liken them to the American hayseed of the Thirties suddenly thrust into the previously unimaginable canyons of New York City.

The old city of Santiago, most of its landmarks huddled within protective walls, was not very large by modern standards. Indeed, it was no more than an inconsequential village in Roman times and later. Compostela gained importance and a burgeoning population only after the ninth century discovery of St. James' tomb. In the Middle Ages it was the capital of Galicia and became the royal seat when the Kingdoms of Galicia, Asturias and León were divided among princely heirs according to the custom of the time. Even today the population of Compostela stands at about one hundred thousand, hardly more than half the size of such places as Pamplona and Oviedo, and smaller even than Logroño.

In the modern era La Coruña became the chief city and capital of Galicia. La Coruña is a busy seaport some seventy kilometers north of here. Compostela, economically and politically playing second fiddle, nonetheless persists as the cultural and spiritual heart of the region. It is the seat of an archbishopric and the site of one of Spain's most important universities. Meanwhile its paramount importance in the Spanish mind still stems from the tomb of St. James.

One might say that other than the university, Santiago has but a single industry: the Shrine of St. James. Its airport and railway station, as well as its highways, are busy year around wheeling visitors to and from the relics of Santiago. Most of these visitors are Spaniards.

Now, as for more than a thousand years, the saint still commands special reverence among the Spanish people. They find their spiritual center here with the relics of their patron, a saint who rallied divine powers to their cause, delivering Spain from slavery and oppression by an alien race. Thus the great majority of Spanish visitors come here to reinvigorate or indulge the religious sense so long central to the character of the nation and to being Spanish.

Peculiarly, perhaps, some Spaniards who journey here are not particularly religious. They may even be atheists. Yet they also come to the shrine of St. James for serious personal reasons, although not for indulgences and favors that might speed them to Heaven. For them the saint's shrine commemorates something other than the life of a holy man and the long history of miraculous events worked in his name. For them the shrine symbolizes the spirit of a nation. The legend of St. James, in effect, is secularly that of patriots as well as of a patron saint. For that even a Spanish atheist finds it in his heart to pay his respects to the cultural memory of a spiritual force that lay at the hearts of men and made possible the Reconquest and unification of all the Spains.

Traveler or pilgrim, believer or atheist, after our long journey along El Camino de Santiago, we begin our explorations of Compostela with respectful recognition of the role the legend played in the creation of modern Spain. We start by rejoining the pilgrims at the one-time city gate at which El Camino de Santiago pierced the stout walls of old Santiago.

Our walk begins at the **Plaza de Galicia.** It is probably the landmark nearest to your hotel, or where you have parked your car in the galleries below street level.

The plaza once was the location of the Puerta de Mazzrelas, the southernmost gate in the walls of Compostela. Proceed northeast along Fonte de Santo Antonio, which follows the circuit of the former city walls, now dismantled to make way for this and associated thoroughfares that divert traffic around the ancient center of town.

Further on, take the ramp-like street bearing up on the left. It leads past the main administration building of the **university**. The institution was founded in 1501 and is respected for the wealth of its library as well as for the quality of its schools. As we discover while we walk, Compostela is a university town virtually from end to end, with its various faculties scattered from one side of the old town to the other. During the day you encounter students with books on their way to class, or hanging out on their favorite plazas. At night there will be groups of revelers going bar-hopping or meandering the streets between dance clubs.

These particular buildings of the university date from the late eighteenth century, with extensive alterations and expansion at the turn into the twentieth century.

Beyond the university, take the first right and then the first left. On the right about a hundred meters apart, with the principal city marketplace in between, are two churches: San Fiz (St. Felix) and San Augustín, the latter associated with an active convent.

San Fiz de Solovio is the more interesting of the pair. It was constructed in the twelfth century. The Romanesque front portal comes from that time but, as is obvious to the eye, the eighteenth century saw a complete and not particularly noteworthy rebuilding of the place, including addition of a Baroque tower. Indeed, my impression of the tower found a sort of Chinese flavor to it.

Most significant architecturally is the twelfth century Romanesque portal. Note the Mozarabic cusps in the arch above the doorway, while the florals and geometric figures on the capitals of the side columns are pure Romanesque. The tympanum features Mary and the Christ child receiving the adoration of the Magi and shepherds.

The **marketplace** consists of long, covered aisleways within a ponderous granite structure that is centuries old. Each aisle is devoted to a special display of foodstuffs shown by competing vendors: vegetables, fish, meats. Select at least one aisle to walk along to get an idea of the prices and quality of the offerings.

343

Beyond the market is the Convent of St. Augustine, which we allow but a glance. Instead, we turn right immediately on the near side of St. Augustine, following that street back to the "circulare" thoroughfare on which we started. The latter now has had a name change to Rua da Virxe Circa (Calle Virgen de la Cerca), which approaches the **Puerta del Camino.**

The medieval gate exists now in name only. The site remains as the place where the main highway and the pilgrim route meet the central city. Once the walls were torn down the gateway was turned into a small, open square, the Plaza del Camino. To your left is Calle de las Casas Reales, which the pilgrims follow on their way to the cathedral. On the right, beyond the plaza and the now-vanished walls and gate, is the Convento de Santo Domingo Bonaval. It once stood just outside the walls and offered shelter to pilgrims arriving after the city gates were shut for the night. And since it was one of the first things a pilgrim encountered as they arrived at the city, we follow their example.

The **convent** was founded by Santo Domingo de Guzmán in 1219. The original Romanesque-Gothic church structure was rebuilt in the fourteenth to sixteenth centuries, then largely remodeled in the eighteenth century, and looks it. The associated monastic buildings date from the seventeenth and eighteenth centuries. What makes it a special place to visit is its **Museo do Pobo Galego** (Museum of the Galician People) (open 10-1; 4-7). Since 1976 it has been located in buildings off the cloister of the abandoned monastery.

This museum is unique among our experiences in Northern Spain. Its exhibits reveal the life styles and implements, traditional habitations and apparel, arts and sciences of the Galicians throughout the centuries. It is organized into sections covering different aspects of life and the crafts that made life possible on the sea, the farm, and in the cities.

Architectural students especially must visit the cloister to see Domingo de Andrade's fabulous triple-spiral **staircase**, built in 1700. It is a miracle of engineering as well as an aesthetic delight. It consists of three separate granite stairways, interlaced and without visible support, rising to several different floors in a single tower. At the very top is a balcony providing an excellent view across the rooftops of the city to where the cathedral rises tall in the distance.

Andrade also designed the cloister which, compared to cloisters seen on this journey, is not all that special.

The **church** is a big barn of a place and no more inspiring. It has a Latin cross design with three naves, transept and polygonal apses. Despite its many reconstructions, it remains an excellent architectural example of the Cistercian transition from Romanesque to Gothic. The capella mayor contains a Baroque retable above the altar, with tombs of knights and their ladies roundabout. The place simply lacks the emotional flavor of sanctity that is usually so pervasive in Cistercian designs.

In a spacious chapel to the left is the Pantheon of Illustrious Gallegans. Entombed here are scholars and patriots, poets and politicians. The chapel originally was dedicated to the Virgin Visitation. No matter the intent of the pantheon, it suffers from the general sense of divine abandonment that marks the cavernous place.

Returning to the Plaza del Camino, head west along Calle de las Casas Reales, following the pilgrim route. After about fifty meters, on the left, is the church of **Santa María del Camino**. It is one of nearly fifty churches that adorn the city, along with so many convents, monasteries, religious institutions, palaces and vestiges of what have you, that a student of architecture, Spanish church history or of the several arts, could spend months researching the city and still not have delved deeper than the most obvious of its secrets.

What that means to tell you is that Santa María del Camino, no matter its long history in the service of pilgrims and townspeople alike, and no matter how deserving it may be for detailed inspection by a specialist, for us requires not much more than a mention and a quick look. The same is true for many of the other minor landmarks in the city. Only after we have gained close familiarity with the cathedral and its immediate environs ought we devote whatever time we have left to explorations further afield.

A few steps further along Calle de las Casas Reales, on the right this time, is the **Capilla de las Animas**. This is another modern reconstruction, dating from the late years of the eighteenth century. The original design was a work of Ferro Caaveiro with later work by Ventura Rodríguez and López Freire. The facade with its grand columns is more ponderous than majestic, yet its imaginative representation of souls in the flames of purgatory, praying for release into Heaven, is remarkable. It reminds a pilgrim of what would be in store for him but for the indulgence won by his pilgrimage. The church interior holds a respected Crucifixion by Juan Pernas and Manuel de Prado, the latter a local boy made good as an artist.

Another fifty meters further, bear left into the Plaza de Cervantes (Plaza del Campo). To your left on the near side of the square is the Church of **San Benito del Campo**, one of the oldest churches in Santiago. Its tenth century origins predate the cathedral and just about everything else, including the destruction of the city by Al Mansur at the end of the tenth century. As you might expect by now, it also has been rudely redone and its present face dates from the eighteenth century. Just to the left of the entrance, inside, is a Romanesque tympanum salvaged from the church built after the Moors knocked things down, and a Gothic relief from still a later remodeling.

Bear right out of Cervantes Square on Calle de la Azabachería, named for artisans who made azabache (jet jewelry) in shops along this street. The current version of those shops occupies buildings on both sides, displaying jet jewelry in the windows.

Soon the street leads into the **Plaza de la Immaculada** (Plaza de Azabachería). Here you gain your first unobstructed and close-up view of the cathedral, rising toward Heaven on your left. The entrance to the north transept of the cathedral is now usually closed, but formerly provided direct access for pilgrims to the cathedral's interior and its hallowed shrine.

Because of that, this was sometimes called Paradise Square, since the promise of Heaven lay just beyond those doors, known to Pilgrims as Puerta del Paradiso. The portal you now see is an eighteenth century monstrosity of Baroque and Neo-Classical half-thoughts designed by Ferro Caaveiro y de Mariño.

The square was a busy place, full of vendors peddling goods to pilgrims. North of the square once stood a pair of pilgrims' hospitals, staffed by monks who greeted the poorest pilgrims and provided them with a decent meal, clean clothes and a bath to make them presentable to the saint across the street. Beyond the hospitals was (and is today) the monastery of San Martín Pinario.

The **monastery**, now a seminary, was founded by the Benedictines in the late ninth century, soon after they were given custody of the tomb of St. James. In the fifteenth century the monastery demolished the hospitals and expanded southward to the square, on which it now presents its grandiose Neo-Classical facade. The design was by Gabriel Casas and his famous pupil, Fernando Casas y Nóvoa, in the early eighteenth century.

The facade has a pair of gigantic round columns astraddle its Neo-Classical portal. Above it is a life size figure of San Martín. Atop the gable is Santiago Matamoros industriously engaged in moorslaying. The entrance door leads through into the seventeenth century Cloister de la Portería, but since the place is an active seminary, it is closed to visitors. However, we gained entrance by a polite plea with the porter in his office in the hallway by the door. There wasn't all that much to see, although the cloister is the most grandiose of three cloisters incorporated into this gigantic monastic complex.

From Paradise Square, take the covered Pasaje Gelmírez which leads between the cathedral and the adjoining bishop's palace into the vast expanse of the **Plaza del Obradoiro** (Square of the Goldwork), also known as the Plaza d'España. Walk to the center of the square and take a slow, full turn around to gain full appreciation of the remarkable character of the place. It presents one of the most fascinating architectural displays in all of Europe.

On the north flank is the former **Hospital Real**, now a posh Parador, once a pilgrims' sanctuary built during the fifteenth to eighteenth centuries. Despite its Plateresque main entry, it presents a remarkably staid face to the square, given its history and royal patronage. To the west is the Palacio de Rajoy with ground floor arcades and Neo-Classical pediments upon which you see an equestrian St. James running rampant over the Moors at Clavijo.

Built in 1757 by the French architect Charles Lemaur as a seminary, the **Rajoy Palace** is now administrative seat of the government of Galicia and the City Hall for Compostela. The west wall of the old city ran along the backside of the building, which gives you an idea of just how tiny the medieval city was.

To the south is the Institute of Galician Studies and the administrative offices for the University of Santiago de Compostela, occupying the one-time **College of San Jeronimo**. This is Romanesque in style, and the plainest as well as the smallest building on the square.

On the east side, elevated on a higher level approached by a double staircase (1606) of stone with an ironwork decorative grille, is the **cathedral**. Its Baroque facade and wedding-cake towers dominate everything. Left of it is the **Palacio de Gelmírez,** the bishop's palace, named for the bishop whose dreams encompassed construction not only of the cathedral but this palace and much else that we have seen or will see during our explorations of the city. The palace dates from the same time as the eleventh century Romanesque cathedral structure that lies behind the gaudy Baroque facade. To the right of the cathedral is the wall protecting the cloister from the mundane affairs of life in the square.

The present cathedral had its origins after the depredations of Al Mansur a thousand years ago. The original church on the site was centuries older.

While approaching Logroño we described the semi-legendary events that led to discovery of the sepulcher of St.

James and founding of the shrine that has been maintained here ever since. For a millennium, then, that shrine has been enclosed within the walls of a cathedral, but it is worth a moment to imagine how things came to be the way they are.

Compostela remains situated on uneven ground, even after the leveling effects of a thousand years of urban habitation. In the ninth century the cathedral site was open land on a hillside near a hamlet probably located a few hundred meters southwest of here. A Roman-era cemetery, long abandoned, occupied the hillside. It was used by neighboring shepherds for grazing their flocks.

After the tomb was discovered and the local bishop's vision proclaimed it to hold the remains of St. James, Alfonso II commissioned construction of a small chapel above it. A few decades later, when St. James won fame in his role of Santiago Matamoros at Clavijo, that fame, coupled with stories of a host of other miraculous events, started a rush of pilgrims to the site. A town, and then this city, grew up around the sepulcher to serve the pilgrims and the religious orders that established monasteries and other facilities nearby. Even today there are about three-dozen different religious orders represented in the city.

Alfonso III, The Great, directed construction of the first cathedral, consecrated in 899, helping the city to continue to grow and prosper. After the death of Alfonso III and division of his realm among his sons, Galicia became an independent kingdom with Compostela the royal capital. Then came Al Mansur, the Scourge of God, who in 997 turned Compostela into a wasteland – but left Santiago's tomb untouched. According to Islamic sources, the Moors were by then too fearful of St. James to evoke his fury by desecrating his remains. Nevertheless, the cathedral was razed around the tomb. Christians who had not fled were killed or enslaved except for one elderly monk who stayed to protect the tomb of the saint. For that heroic gesture of loyalty Al Mansur decreed that the old man should neither be slain nor enslaved.

The city, destroyed and depopulated, was slow to rebuild.

Although the Moors abandoned Galicia after devastating the region, they did reoccupy León and the northern Meseta. The wealth and energies of the Christian realm thus were devoted to recapture of León and its rebuilding and fortification during the years leading up to the era of El Cid. Seventy five years thus passed before work began on a new cathedral in Compostela.

Work even then progressed slowly until about 1100, when Compostela was elevated from being the seat of a mere bishop to that of an archbishop. The man named to the new position was Diego Gelmírez. Young, dynamic, a visionary who was politically astute and royally favored, Diego's forty-year reign at Compostela produced what can only be described as a golden age. He did for Compostela what Pericles did for Athens, although on a scale somewhat less grandiose. Still, the effect was the same. He left his permanent mark upon the city, not the least sign of which is the cathedral that stands before us now.

The master builders who engineered its construction are believed to have been a pair of Frenchmen named Bernard and Robert. Their work was initially consecrated in 1105. Choir and transept were finished in 1112, and a viable nave was ready in 1128. Work continued, however, including the building of the west end of the nave, plus the original facade which included the world renowned masterpiece of Master Mateo, the Pórtico de la Gloria.

The complete cathedral was not consecrated until 1211. Its style was Romanesque, one of the largest of that genre ever built. Given the structural limitations of Romanesque design, limitations we described earlier on this journey, you will appreciate how the construction of this cathedral pushed the design techniques to their engineering extremes. The material used is the local grayish-brown granite that everything in the city is made of, from street pavements on up to the tips of the tallest towers. It is a strong, tough stone well suited to bear the pressures of heavy Romanesque walls and ceiling vaults.

Later modifications added a host of interior chapels, the clock tower in 1325, the dome in 1448, and the cloister and a second west tower early in the sixteenth century. Surpassing all that is the fantastic Baroque **facade** here on the west face of the cathedral. In effect, it became an extension of the original structure, a facade built in front of a facade. Considered to be the architectural masterpiece of Fernando Casas y Nóvoa, it was built between 1738 and 1747 in a sumptuous Baroque the like of which you have never seen before. It is the most famous such construct in Spain, where one learns that the Baroque of other lands never quite ascends to the fabulous complexity and richness that Spanish architects achieved.

The **towers**, seventy-six meters tall, already were in place when Fernando began his work. The Torre de la Carica (rattle, which summons the faithful to prayer) dates from the seventeenth century; while the bell tower on the right was part of the original eleventh-century construction, with modifications in later centuries. Fernando changed their faces to match the Baroque of the retable-like structure he erected between them. The result is an integrated architectural presentation concocted in a grand style, an achievement that no other architect ever has been able to match so effectively in the Baroque. It is a work demanding recognition as a masterpiece even by philistines like myself who ordinarily are disenchanted by the symbolic nonsense – symbol for the sake of symbol – and overdone profusion of decor for which the style is noted. Here, for once, I admire what I see.

The central gable features a statue of St. James in pilgrim garb with walking staff, beneath a gingerbread canopy surrounded by all sorts of poetic nonsense including a couple of pairs of putti sprouting wings. If that sounds disparaging, it is because while I am fascinated by the whole, the elements of the detail – rich though they are – simply put me off. There are pilasters and columns and ornately carved capitals galore, with garlands and balustrades and statues of saints, cornices of all fashions, arches blind and open, and pinnacles large and small capping everything. The detail is as exhausting to study as to tell about, so take my hint and view it overall for impression. You will remember what you see more favorably for doing

351

that.

The doorway into the earth between the staircases up to the cathedral leads into a spacious crypt called the **Old Cathedral**. Old it may be; the cathedral it never was. The vaulted chamber was constructed simply to support the forward face and nave of the cathedral where the ground fell away too fast on the hillside that lay beneath everything you see. The crypt was built late in the eleventh century as a first step in construction of the edifice above. The crypt thus provides an excellent example of early Romanesque architectural sophistication developing here in the hinterlands of Europe out of the local beginnings we saw in Oviedo and Leyre. The sophistication of the vaulting, and the carving of the capitals and bosses, here speak of just how far the skills and techniques of Spanish architects and artisans had advanced in the three hundred years since the birth of the Reconquista. Appropriately, the crypt now is used to display materials selected from the cathedral's museum.

The pair of main cathedral doors date from 1610 and were reused by Fernando in his new facade more than a century later. They open onto the famed Pórtico de la Gloria, which is part of the facade behind the facade, which opens into the original Romanesque church. We will return to that portico later for a detailed examination. For now we move south along the west face of the cloister to reach the door to the **museum**, situated in rooms off the cloister. The museum includes the library, chapter house (Sala capitular) and a host of additional rooms.

The library displays old religious books and hymnals, plus the gigantic censer known as the Botafumiero, which we will discuss later when viewing the interior of the cathedral. The chapterhouse contains a collection of tapestries and a colorful stucco ceiling and small shrine with a statue of St. James the Pilgrim. On the remainder of the lower floor are archeological displays of stone and wooden artifacts that reflect the history of the cathedral, plus old drawings of the construction. On the upper floor is the tapestry museum, regarded by experts as one of the finest in the world. Its four rooms feature priceless

Flemish tapestries, plus work from the famed Real Fábrica de Madrid, manufactured from sketches prepared by such luminaries as Goya, Rubens, Bayeu and Teniers.

From the upper floor of the museum, nearby the tapestry collection, a doorway leads onto an outer gallery, situated high above the Plaza de Obradoiro. It provides an excellent view of the plaza and its surroundings. Spend a moment taking in the sight of things.

Exit from the museum places you in the northwest corner of the **cloister,** one of the largest in Spain. Its design is a mixture of late-Gothic and Plateresque. Among those participating in its sixteenth century design and construction were Rodrigo Gil de Hontañón, Juan de Alava, Juan de Herrera and José de Arce. The arcades and vaults are Gothic, while the balustrade with its intricate workings is Plateresque.

In the lower south gallery is a tympanum in a Romanesque arch beneath a tenth century gable. Portrayed there is St. James at the Battle of Clavijo, believed to be the oldest surviving such representation of the Moorkiller at work. These are believed to be remnants of the cathedral built here by Alfonso III, and of the Romanesque cloister built by Master Mateo. More fragments of Mateo's original cloister are found in the archeological museum.

Stored in the cloister are the famous bells that once tolled from the tower of the cathedral built by Alfonso III. When Al Mansur tore the building down, he salvaged the gigantic bells, then had them hauled off to Córdoba quite literally on the backs of hundreds of Christian slaves. At Córdoba he had the bells placed, upside down, in the great mosque of that city. Filled with oil, they served as lamps for illumination of the mosque until 1236 when Ferdinand the Saint had them dragged back here on the backs of Arab prisoners.

Returning to the Plaza d'España, continue our study of the cathedral exterior by walking around to your right, circling the cloister to reach the **Plaza de las Platerías** (silversmiths).

Each southern corner of the cloister has a prominent tower. The one on the west is known as the Torre de la Corona

(Crown); while to the east is Domingo de Andrade's seventeenth century Torre del Tesoro (Treasury), which looks down on the Plaza de las Platerías. And so you enter that plaza, which has an ornately Baroque nineteenth century fountain in its center. It is called the fountain of Los Caballos, obviously because of the four prancing equines spewing water.

The square is bounded on two sides by arcades where silversmiths have traditionally displayed their work. Its eastern extreme merges into the adjacent (up the stairs) Plaza de los Literários. The eighteenth century Dean's House, another Baroque construction, is on the south side of the square along with the Casa de Cabildo (1758). Most impressive of all, bounding both squares but its arcade facing onto the Plaza de los Literários, is the **Casa de Canónigos**, the former residence of the canons of the cathedral, built in the seventeenth and eighteenth centuries. The far east side is occupied by the Benedictine Convento de San Pelayo. While the convent's origins are traced to the ninth century reign of Alfonso II, the face it presents to the square is of seventeenth century vintage.

At this point, let me confirm your impression of things. What we have seen of Compostela tells us that while the creation of the city was a continuous effort from the time of initial reconstruction after the depredations of Al Mansur, two distinct periods of unusual activity can be discerned. Each related to a specific era of Spanish political expansion and economic prosperity.

The first era was in the twelfth and thirteenth centuries, when the kings of León and Castile came to dominate the taifa kings of the south, capturing the wealth of the defeated states and demanding rich tribute from those that remained unconquered. The cathedral and the bishop's palace are the primary reminders of that time.

The second period came during the sixteenth and seventeenth centuries, when Spain was flooded by riches from the New World and used (better to say, often squandered by incompetent rulers, much as has happened to the European Union, United States and Russia in our day) to make Spain the superpower of Europe. The observable results in Compostela are the Baroque and Neo-Classical veneer overlaid on just about everything that already stood above ground, plus the construction of much more in what can only be described as a frenzy of activity that "made" the careers of a host of architects and artists, many of them obviously second rate as both creative minds and technicians.

Here we observe evidence of the second of those surges of building activity along the south and east sides of the plaza. On the north side is evidence of the initial surge, the south transept of the cathedral. The face it presents to the plaza is notable as the oldest exposed exterior of the Romanesque construction that proceeded out of the earlier period of building activity. In short, if you want to imagine what the entire cathedral looked like in its original form, picture it as more of what you see from here.

The doorway leading into the transept is called the Puerta de las Platerías. The approach to it is flanked on the right by a clock tower as tall and even more elaborately Baroque than those adorning the west facade.

Before leaving this square, look south to the Rua de Vilar. The Office of the Pilgrims is (when we visited) located through the first door on the left on that street, which begins just south of the horse fountain. If a pilgrim, visit that office for information on completion of your pilgrimage.

Now stride up the steps for a closer view of the twin arched **Puerta de las Platerías.** It was the first of the cathedral's doorways, although its decoration continued throughout the twelfth and thirteenth centuries. In the double tympana are depicted a host of Biblical scenes in a sort of abbreviated caricature. They include the Nativity, Adoration of the Magi, and the Temptation. Over the arches is Christ, accompanied by St. James and Moses. But that only describes the highlights of a riot of sculpture that literally covers every inch of the archways and the surroundings of the doorway, including a trio of large cats ready to pounce down upon us. On the left of the doorway are the famous representations of King David and his violin, and the adulteress, condemned by her husband to kiss her lover's skull every day. Anywhere else on this journey this fabulous display would be regarded as the highlight experience of the day – but the best here is yet to come.

A pair of arched porches above the portal are nicely decorated with floral carvings. Beside the portal on the right, as mentioned a moment ago, is the clock tower (Torre del Reloj), also known as the Torre de la Trinidad. First constructed in the fourteenth century, it was rebuilt in the early eighteenth century into a functioning clock tower, unquestionably Baroque, by Domingo de Andrade. It has a bell two and a half meters in diameter.

Continuing around the cathedral, we move into the Plaza de la Quintana, sometimes called the **Plaza de los Literários** in honor of a battalion of university students who marched off to fight the French during the Peninsular War. Here the plaza flanks the apse of the cathedral, which contains a series of chapels entered off the ambulatory. Externally, it was extensively remodeled in the seventeenth century by the addition of new walls set against the plain face of the original Romanesque. The new walls, of a Neo-Classical temper, have balustrades and other decor more amenable to the thought processes and aesthetic sense of late Renaissance architects.

A segment of that seventeenth century reconstruction is the famed **Puerta Santa**, which incorporates two dozen Romanesque carvings into a Neo-Classical "frame." Above it is superimposed a trio of statues featuring St. James in the center niche. He is clothed in flowing robe and broad-brimmed hat, and given a walking staff to complete his costume as a pilgrim. At his side are his disciples, Athanasius (on the left) and Theodore. St. James the Pilgrim and his disciples are another work of the Portuguese sculptor, Pedro do Campo, done in 1694.

The carved figures on the wall around the door below, which represent the apostles, prophets and church fathers, were saved when the cathedral's Romanesque choir was replaced by a later version. The door of the portal, protected by an iron grille, is opened only during a Holy Year, celebrated when the July 25 feast day of St. James falls on Sunday. From that custom the portal gained its name. On such years the door is ceremonially opened on New Year's Eve.

Finally, on the north of the square is the broad flight of stairs that lead back to where our viewing of the cathedral began in the Plaza de la Immaculada. That completes our circuit of the place, and has readied us for exploration of its inner spaces. For that we return to the Puerta de las Platerías.

What you discover inside is the original Romanesque church. The magnificence of its design is immediately apparent as you step into the south transept. Here in the **cathedral** of St. James, Romanesque achieved its most spacious and highflying interiors, aided by a design that made maximum use of the triforium above the nave and introduced the ambulatory around the apse. This interior reveals a cathedral that ranks among the dozen or so greatest in the world. The Baroque bric-a-brac in which it was later encased is merely frosting on the sturdy granite Romanesque that forms the core of the thing. It constituted the epitome of the style in Spain, and its design compares favorably with the few grand Romanesque cathedrals of France that survived the vogue of Gothic.

Certainly there have been changes over the centuries. The lantern above the crossing was added in the fourteenth century. We have already mentioned the removal of the original choir from its position forward in the nave. Chapels have been added and remodeled over and over. The original cloister of Master Mateo was replaced by a late-Gothic version in the sixteenth century. The Capella Mayor is dominated by an eighteenth century altar piece; and so on. Despite all that, the pervasive feel and look of the place is plain, sturdy, religiously centered and conservative Romanesque.

Walk along to the **crossing** and consider a few statistics. The dome above the crossing rises thirty-three meters; the nave is ninety-four meters end to end. As you see, the cathedral is a basilican Latin cross, three-aisled design. The apse is a spacious semicircle radiating a series of chapels alongside the ambulatory around the capella mayor. The nave is unusual for a Spanish cathedral in that there is a clear, unobstructed pavement from its main entrance, the famed Pórtico de la Gloria, to the capella mayor.

Hidden in the recesses of the place are nearly a score of chapels, large and small. Add to them the chapterhouse and library, treasury and museum, tower rooms and salons, crypt of the saint and sacristy, plus uncounted nooks and crannies full of saints, angels and fathers of the church. From that you begin to appreciate the immensity of it all. Nor is all of it accessible. Special permission is required to ascend to the galleries of the triforium, or to descend into the chambers beneath the church created when archaeologists in 1946 excavated beneath the nave and transept and discovered the old Roman graveyard surrounding the tomb of St. James. That enterprise even found the tomb of Bishop Theodomir, whose investigation of the strange lights in the old Roman graveyard, and later vision, revealed the sepulcher of St. James and led to all we have seen and experienced these past weeks along El Camino de Santiago.

There is no way we can describe all that you will see here. That would require a book as large again as this one. Yet we can lead you through the place, calling attention to the highlights and allow you to study individual details to any depth that suits your fancy.

We begin with a stroll up the **south aisle** from the south transept. The first room on the left is the sacristy, followed by the treasury, vestibule, and the Capilla de las Reliquias. The treasury is also known as the Capilla de San Fernando, named for the royal saint, Ferdinand III, and featuring a polychrome life sized statue of the man. The treasury also displays rich vestments, plate and other treasures of the church.

The Capilla de las Reliquias contains tombs of assorted kings and queens of the twelfth through the fifteenth centuries, including that of Ferdinand II, king of León during the latter part of the twelfth century and sponsor of many of the finishing touches on the church. It was he who commissioned creation of the Pórtico de la Gloria by Master Mateo, a Spanish master builder and sculptor who worked in Northwest Spain during the twelfth century.

Fernando died the same year, 1188, that Master Mateo completed twenty years of work on the west end of the church, including his masterpiece, the Pórtico de la Gloria, that was the main entrance to the original Romanesque cathedral. Ferdinand's recumbent figure is believed to be an accurate portrayal of the king, taken from life.

And so we arrive at Master **Mateo's masterpiece**, El Pórtico de la Gloria, which stands just inside the west doorway of the cathedral. It is centermost of three portals created by Mateo, all now hidden behind Fernando's Baroque facade.

The Pórtico de la Gloria is another of those creations that truly defy description. The experts regard it as the epitome of Romanesque sculpture, the apex towards which all other artists aspired, but only Master Mateo achieved.

The portico never had doors. It was an open entrance for two hundred years until civil troubles in the town and the massive flow of pilgrims (who turned the cathedral into a sort of flop house) necessitated that the edifice no longer be left open to all comers at all times. So a sort of vestibule was added, containing doors that protected the interior from rowdies and rude-mannered pilgrims.

The Baroque facade with its recycled doors took the place of the vestibule, so now we find that Mateo's portico has become part of a facade inside a facade. While that situation limits the breadth of one's view of the thing, no doubt the portico thus has been largely saved from the adverse effects of natural erosion and the vandalism of man as the centuries rolled. The hint of color on Mateo's work, by the way, is no trick of light on stone. The colors remain from an eighteenth century touch-up of the original paint. In past ages painting was thought to make the monochrome surfaces of mere stone more vital in representation of living figures.

What Mateo constructed, as we have seen elsewhere on Romanesque churches, was a fancy portal on an otherwise plain face. But this portal was something special. More than fifteen meters long and nearly twenty high, it had a depth of nearly four meters from outer to inner face. Yet size here is secondary to the ornate magnificence of the thing. Its main feature, naturally, is its central portico. That consists of a double doorway with a flat lintel (on which the master scribed his signature) supported at the center by clustered columns on the fore of which we find a seated St. James, scroll and staff in hand.

The saint wears a bejeweled halo and a rather a surprised look on his face. He looks poised to hop down from his perch above an elegantly carved column that rests upon a pair of roaring lions with the head of Hercules between. Hercules, the once unconquerable hero, lies crushed in painful defeat, symbolically representing the pagan religions overcome by Christianity.

The carved column represents the Tree of Jesse, out of which Jesus sprang. Note the worn-smooth surface of the lower part of the column. The carving was worn flat by the hands and lips of millions of pilgrims who marked the end of their pilgrimage by the ritual of kneeling to touch and kiss the bottom of the column. Most probably you will find pilgrims lined up to participate in the ritual even as you watch. Accepted practice is to insert thumb and fingers into the five indentations near the base of the column. Pilgrims among you are invited to join those of centuries past and participate in the sacred exercise.

On the inner side of the central cluster of columns is a kneeling figure that tradition says is a self-portrait of Master Mateo himself. Another tradition among pilgrims is to rest one's head for a moment on the brow of the kneeling Mateo. The notion behind the gesture is that, through contact with the stone fashioned by the inspired hands of the artist, one captures for one's self some of Mateo's proven genius.

Above the lintel a gentle, composed image of Christ reigns in the tympanum. His four Evangelists are by his side and eight angels stand solemnly on the wings holding symbols of the

Passion and Crucifixion. The tiny figures in the tympanum above the angels represent souls redeemed by Christ. Splayed across the archivolt are the twenty-four Elders of the Apocalypse with their musical instruments, all set to serenade the Heavenly Hosts assembled here by Mateo.

The pillars alongside the entryway are nests of columns rising on the backs of reclining lions. Perched on each column is a Biblical figure. On the left are Jeremiah, Daniel (barefaced and grinning), Isaiah, and Moses with his tablets of the Law; on the right are Peter with his keys, Paul with a book, James the Lesser, and John the Divine (left to right on both sides). An interesting feature of the portrayal is that all are posed as if the respective pairs were caught in conversation with each other, rather than merely staring off into Heavenly infinity.

It is that strikingly "human" character of Mateo's work that sets it apart from church art of practically all ages. His people have an everyday quality that anyone can relate to. I believe that the characteristic humanistic realism of his work, combined with the artistic elegance of the whole, is what makes this the world famous masterpiece that it is. His work is like the missing link between the classical serenity of Greek and Roman sculpture and the robust idealization of humanity in a Michelangelo. Indeed, there are features of his work which remind one more of an Auguste Rodin than they are mere hints toward a Michelangelo.

The **side portals** are not as elaborately decorated, but anywhere other than at this cathedral they would be outstanding works in their own right. Here they become rather an anticlimax of artistry. Each side portal has its own pairs of apostles and prophets on columns to the side, but neither portal has a tympanum. In the archivolts of the left portal's triple arch are represented the relationships of Christ with the Jews. The inner arch depicts Adam, Abraham, Isaac, Jacob, Judah, Moses, Eve, Aaron, David and Solomon. The central arch displays the figures of an even ten "rebellious" Jews. With them are a pair of children holding a scroll representing the New Testament. The moral suggested is that the Jews need

361

merely accept the New Testament and they, too, shall be saved.

Straddling the left portico are Joel and Obadiah on your left, and Hosea and Amos on the right.

The right hand portal has Christ in Judgment portrayed on the center of each arch, with damned sinners pursued by monsters in Hell while souls of the saved cavort happily in Heaven on the other side. Observe the angel sounding the horn to herald Judgment Day. The figures to the side of the portico are Matthew and Andrew on your left, and Thomas and Bartholomew opposite.

Note that Fernando, when he constructed his Baroque facade, could not leave well enough alone on the inner face fronting Mateo's magnificent doorways. Fernando there presents us with the Apostles Matthew, Luke and John the Baptist along with Old Testament characters Job, Judith and Esther. No matter, stand with your back near Fernando's facade and take time to contemplate the fullest possible view of Mateo's masterpiece. Revel in your impression of the thing. You may never pass by this way again.

Now, from the Pórtico de la Gloria, look forward down the barrel-vaulted central **nave**. In the distance, at the crossing, a generous flow of light cascades down from the lantern. Above, along the sides, a somber glow passes down through the Romanesque arcades of the triforium. It gently overflows into the nave, illuminating long files of pillars and archways framing your view beyond the crossing to the majestic capella mayor, the gaudiness of its features muted by the hundred-meter distance. There is quiet harmony here that the excesses of Gothic and Baroque can never achieve. In this calm simplicity of line we have discovered an archetype of churchness. It escapes all the bric-a-brac of the chapels and treasuries and leaves you alone with the plain majesty of Godliness cast into the harmonies of stone and space. Pause a moment here for further contemplation of the spiritual nature inherent in what those medieval builders wrought. The mood lends clarity to first and last things, and to much in between.

The nave, compared with later structures done with the

advantages of Gothic, is remarkably narrow. Yet compared to other Romanesque structures it is like a broad avenue to Heaven. In height it rises more than twenty four meters, pavement to vault. The impression is that it pushes Romanesque design techniques to the limit.

Walk a ways down the nave, enjoying the ambience, then bear left into the north aisle and to the **Capilla del Cristo** de Burgos. It was built by the Archbishop Carillo y Acuña, who is entombed there. The altar is Churrigueresque.

Forward of that is the **Capilla de la Communion** (Capilla del Sagrado Corazón). Round, with a classical dome, it was built in 1471 in Neo-Classical style and contains the tombs of a pair of archbishops, Rajoy and Lope de Mendoza. It sees daily use for celebration of the Mass. Note the glass doors installed to block out the noisy distraction of pilgrims and tourists as they circulate through the cathedral.

Arriving at the north transept, turn left. In the niche to the left is a triumphant Santiago Matamoros, trampling across a field of felled Moors. The first chapel is the **Capilla de Santa Catalina**, dedicated to the Virgin of Lourdes. Saint Teresa is shown kneeling at the Lady's feet. At the north end of the transept is the Puerta de las Azabachería, outside of which we had our first encounter with this cathedral. Forward of that is a whole nest of chapels: those of San Fructoso, San Andrés (1674) and de la Corticella, in that order, proceeding to the rear. The latter chapel originally was the parish church that predated construction of the cathedral, and was not enveloped by the cathedral until centuries later. Its Romanesque portal displays the Adoration of the Magi in its tympanum. In a niche to the left is a statue of the Virgin and, adjacent, a kneeling Nuestra Señor del Huerto, much revered by pilgrims, who leave prayer notes and tokens said to gain favorable intercession of the hand of God.

Nestled between the Capilla de la Corticella and the main apse of the cathedral is the **Capilla del Espiritu Santo**, created in the thirteenth century by Pedro Vidal of Burgos. Remodeled several times since, its altarpiece is seventeenth century and the choir is by Domingo de Andrade, also seventeenth century. Several of the tombs are very well done.

Now walk back through the north transept to the crossing beneath the dome of the lantern. This tall structure was added in 1445. Later, in 1604, the ironwork device high above your head was added to support the gigantic silver censer, called the **Botafumiero,** which you saw at rest in the library. On major feast days it is hung by ropes from the contraption above your head, so that the censor reaches almost to the floor. From there it is swung by a team of eight men such that at the top of each arc the smoking Botafumiero extends to the far reaches of the transepts and nearly touches the vaulted ceiling. To watch the tremendous swing of the giant device, spewing clouds of incense all the way, is a fascinating sight. It is accompanied by music played by an organist who times his music to the pendulum action of the Botafumeiro, rising to a crescendo when the censer is in full swing, and muting as the pendulum motion slows to a halt and the Botafumiero is removed.

Concerning the **organ**, it is a double instrument built in the early eighteenth century by Miguel de Romay. As a glance up at its maze of pipes confirms, it is unashamedly Baroque, with dozens of putti flitting and dancing about at every turn of the pipes, plus the usual decorative nonsense that a Baroque designer inevitably assigns to everything in sight.

Now look forward to the capilla mayor. The choir stalls are the work of Juan de la Vila, completed in 1606. The gigantic gilded **baldachin** is a seventeenth century Churrigueresque piece supported by four of the largest angels you will ever see. Above the four corners of the structure are the Virtues (by Pedro del Valle) while the center supports an equestrian statue of St. James in his role as the Moorslayer (by Mateo del Prado).

The altar is located directly above the tomb of St. James in the crypt below. The **altar** was made by Figuera in 1715, backed by an earlier (1665) retable made of alabaster highly decorated with jasper and silver. In its center above the tabernacle is a thirteenth century painted statue of a seated St.

James, again with a wide-eyed look of surprise at all the fuss made over him. About 1700 the statue was adorned with precious stones, gold and silver, including a diamond-studded silver shawl.

Above the saint is a group by Pedro del Valle, dating from 1657, portraying St. James the pilgrim and a company of kings.

If you think you see people moving behind the statue of the seated saint you are not mistaken. When the altarpiece was erected in 1665 a stairway was built in back of it so that pilgrims could step up and embrace the statue from behind and kiss the Apostle's cloak. That gesture marks the true end of the pilgrimage, some say.

Others maintain that the final goal of the pilgrimage is in the **crypt** beneath the altar. Reach it via the stairs located off the ambulatory on the left as you face the altar. In the crypt you find a nineteenth century silver casket that contains the collective remains of St. James and his two disciples, Theodore and Athanasius.

Exiting the crypt, you find yourself at the south side of the ambulatory. Nearby is the entrance to the way up behind the image of Santiago behind the main altar. Go up and give the saint a hug or a pat on the back, after which you find yourself on the north side of the ambulatory once again. We will work our way around the ambulatory, left to right.

As mentioned earlier, an **array of chapels** radiates outward from the ambulatory. First on your left, opposite the door from which you exited after visiting Santiago, is the Capilla de la Concepción. Originally Romanesque, its entryway is Plateresque and the altar is Churrigueresque. Central feature (on the left) is the tomb of Canon Rodríguez de Augustín, the work of a Dutchman, Cornelis de Holanda. It is worth mentioning here that the fact we have seen so much work by Dutch artists illustrates the position of Spain as a world power that, among other things, controlled Holland during much of the Renaissance and early modern period.

Next on the left is the Chapel of St. Bartholomew, which is pure Romanesque and one of the oldest here off the ambulatory. It dates from the twelfth century. Beyond are the chapels of San Juan, Nuestra Señora Blanca, and el Salvador. The latter is also known as the chapel of the King of France. It was endowed by that worthy in 1380.

Another entry off the right side of the ambulatory provides access to the inner face of the **Puerta Santa**, which is not that remarkable compared to all else we have been viewing. Other chapels include the tiny Capilla de San Pedro, featured piece in which is the tomb of Doña Mencia de Andrade by J. B. Celma, done in 1571. Lastly, we find the Capilla de Mondragon, designed by Jácome García with an interesting grille by Guillén Bourse. The terracotta reliefs on the altar are by Miguel Ramón. A nice touch in the design is the Gothic balcony and vaulting.

With that we have concluded our examination of the cathedral. If your schedule permits, take a final tour of the nave, and another look down its extent to the altar in the distance. Of everything to be seen here, in a spiritual sense, this view down the nave is the finest and most meaningful experience of all. It was worth these weeks on El Camino de Santiago just to share this view as enjoyed by a thousand years of pilgrim eyes.

As described at the outset of our journey, if you have come all this way as a pilgrim, and have obtained your certificate from the secretary of the cathedral, your privileged status entitles you to a free meal at the famous hostel. This has been the right of pilgrims for half a millennium. However, what you will get is something less than the fixed-price tourist meal at one of the restaurants over in the old town. Also, your seating will be outside the pale of the dining rooms reserved for paying guests. So, if it is lunch time and you favor eating among the aristocrats of the travel fraternity, best advice is to keep your certificate in your pocket, pay the tariff expected in such elegant surroundings, and enjoy yourself.

The **Hostal** de los Reyes Católicos was originally founded as a pilgrim hospital by Ferdinand and Isabella in 1489. Further building, remodeling and renovation have continued unabated into the past century. Enrique de Egas was its principal architect, working between 1501 and 1509. It actually operated as a hospital up until the 1950s when it was converted into a national Parador in 1958.

From the plaza you see the south wing that runs the length of the square. That **facade** is relatively plain but for the grandiose Plateresque entryway midway along that front. The decor around that portal rises all the way from the ground to the eaves. It was originally constructed in 1678 by a pair of French architects, Martín de Blas and Guillén Colás.

The contrast between the Gothic-Plateresque design of this portico and Master Mateo's masterpiece convincingly illustrates the innovative nature of Mateo's mind and the artistry of his hand. Specifically relate the dozen main figures here on the portico of the hotel to the figures carved by Mateo on the Pórtico de la Gloria. These are stilted mannequins where Mateo's apostles and prophets appeared ready to step down from their perches and join us in a stroll down the nave. Here there is mere geometry to the design. Mateo's was a masterpiece of free composition adjusted to the demands of structure. Nonetheless, this portal is notable in its own right as a piece of art history, and suffers mostly from too close comparison with Mateo's masterpiece.

The pair of medallions astraddle the archway above the door depict their Catholic Majesties, while the cast of minor characters is just too extensive to list.

The plainness of the rest of the facade is somewhat overcome by the seventeenth century ironwork balconies extending from each side of the central facade, and the ornate framing around the few doorways opening onto the balconies. As for the interior, it is stocked with antique furnishings (real or copied) amidst tall spaces that lend a nice aristocratic atmosphere to a five-star hotel. Its Sala Real contains murals by Arias Varela, plus portraits of the founders, Ferdinand and Isabella. Also present is a less than flattering painting of Charles V by Goya.

A view of the interior of the parador is possible only when

in charge of an "official guide." One may be found loitering near the front of the cathedral. If you cannot locate one who speaks English, let me tell you about the general features of the place.

The ground plan is best described as a cross within a hollow square. This creates four separate courtyards separated by the cross. Each courtyard is not only architecturally different but is landscaped to exalt those differences. The pair of courtyards on the south date from Enrique Egas' original early sixteenth century construction, while the rearmost courtyards were a product of the eighteenth century. Where the arms of the cross meet is a small but exquisite Gothic chapel with a handsome domed lantern. The chapel is now used for exhibitions and receptions. Its most spectacular feature is a grille, dating from 1556, that separates the nave from the crossing.

Outside on the plaza once more, our attention turns to the bishop's palace, known as the **Palacio Gelmírez** (open 10 to 1:30, 4 to 7) in honor of its founder. Built originally in the early twelfth century, it was completed in its present form in 1266.

Its facade was remodeled during the Renaissance and the interior has experienced a dozen renovations during the passage of the centuries. A tour of its apartments is recommended, because you discover modes of secular architecture from various periods, Romanesque to Neo-Classical, that elsewhere are poorly preserved or not at all.

Spectacular is the thirty-meter long **Synod Hall** with vaulting supported by capitals richly carved in typical Romanesque florals. On the upper floor is another large hall, known as the **Salon de Fiestas**. It was a banquet room with floral-carved vaulting dating from the turn into the thirteenth century. The carved corbels beneath the ribs were the work of sculptors from the school of Master Mateo. They show scenes from the wedding of Alfonso IX, crowned in 1188 as King of León. He married Princess Belangeria of Castile, which led to reunification of León and Castile in the hands of their son, Ferdinand III, the Saint. Interesting in these carvings is that they show scenes depicting everyday tasks, as well as dining implements such as plates and goblets, along with musical instruments. Observe the cusped arches on the north end of the salon, a sure touch of the Mozarab immigrés.

Exiting the bishop's palace, walk south across the Plaza d'España to San Jerónimo, which now hosts the administrative offices of the University of Santiago de Compostela. The **portal** is a beautiful and pure Romanesque. Mary and the Christ Child reign in the tympanum, flanked by their royal majesties of León. Above is a phalanx of nuns escorted by a pair of bishops. The saints to the sides include Santiago, closest to the door at the left, with his shell insignia pinned on his turned up hat and a scrip dangling at his side. Beyond the portal is a pleasant inner courtyard.

Continuing south along the Calle de Franco, on the right is the **Colegio de Fonseca**, which houses the Faculty of Pharmacy and the central library of the university. One wing is also used by the regional government as a meeting place for the Galician parliament. Built in 1544, the college is named for a "dynasty" of bishops of the Fonseca family, who during the Renaissance were as instrumental in furthering the fortunes of Compostela as Diego Gelmírez had been three hundred years earlier. Inside is a pleasant, two storey, cloister-like courtyard containing well-tended lawn and shrubs. It is a favorite hangout for students studying between classes, where they gather on benches set along the lower galleries.

At the next intersection, turn left for a couple of blocks to the Rua del Villar, which was the main street of the old city. The Rua del Villar, and the Rua Nueva a block further on, continue to be busy shopping streets and the center of activity in Compostela today. The narrow streets are pleasantly arcaded and dotted with restaurants and bars, as well as ordinary shops and tradesmen's emporiums.

If you walk directly across the city from the Colegio de Fonseca via the Plaza de Platerías to Rua Nueva, you reach the latter street at its north end, some fifty meters from the church of **Santa María Salomé**. Situated on the east side of the street,

Santa María is a twelfth century church that retains much of its Romanesque facade. Above the portal are the Virgin and Child, but on the left doorpost is the Virgin again, this time depicted about nine months pregnant. How better to convince an untutored congregation of the virgin birth? Seeing is believing.

The corbels and capitals feature assorted monstrosities. Above it all is an eighteenth century Baroque tower built by José Crespo. The interior is rather ordinary, but does have an eighteenth century retable by Miguel Romay that the experts find interesting (yes, those angels are wearing eye-glasses), plus a Calvary (at the left rear) from the same period by Bartolomé Fernández.

Here by the church of Santa María Salomé you are but a couple of hundred meters from where we began our walk at the Plaza de Galicia. If you are in a mood for shopping, the opportunity now presents itself, for this is the center of the principal shopping district of Compostela. Couple that with an exploration of the nooks and crannies of the old city surrounding you.

Another alternative is to walk south on Rua Nueva to its intersection with Calle de los Huérfanas, then bear right through the **Plaza de Toral**. The plaza is dominated by the palace of the Marquises de Bendaña, which sports a statue of Atlas busy at his chore of supporting the world. The plaza is also a noted hangout for artists and students.

From there continue west to the Avenida Figueroa. On the other side of that avenue is the **Paseo de la Herradura**. The Paseo is situated in a pleasant park with a hill that offers a grand view back over the city. Some say the sight of the cathedral from this vantage point is the best view of it there is. Best time of day to see it: Late in the afternoon when everything begins taking on the colors of sunset and the shadows grow long. In the park is still another church, **Santa Susana**, a tiny edifice begun in 1105. From the park there are but a couple of hundred meters to walk along Calle General Mola to where we started at the Plaza de Galicia.

There is still much more to see in Compostela.

One short walk takes us north of the cathedral, through the Plaza de la Immaculada, for a closer look at the monastery of San Martín Pinario and things beyond. We described the facade outside the monastery's cloister as we passed through the plaza on our way to the cathedral. We also mentioned that the monastery was founded in the late ninth century by the Benedictines when they were awarded responsibility for care of the Apostle's tomb.

The first major building on the site dated from 912, when an oratory was built for the monks, only to have it destroyed along with everything else when Al Mansur leveled the city. Bishop Gelmírez included the monastery in his rebuilding program during the twelfth century. Later the entire complex was completely redone in the sixteenth, seventeenth and eighteenth centuries when the Fonsecas were in charge. The place is now a seminary, an appropriate function in this university town dominated by its grand cathedral.

Proceed along the narrow street to the right around the monastery, which leads to the Plaza de San Martín. There, to the left, is the entrance to the **monastic church** of the same name. Built by Mateo López, a Portuguese architect, in 1590, its decor later was placed in the hands of a succession of architects, including Peña de Toro, Melchor de Velasco and Domingo de Andrade.

The main portal of the church opens onto the Plaza San Martín. Note that it is below street level, so the entranceway and the stairway down are surrounded by balustrades. The tri-level facade above the doorway is peculiarly bayed-out on each side of the portal, with engaged columns – fluted on the lower levels, copiously carved above – topped by Corinthian capitals. Statues of various saints stand on carved corbels betwixt the columns.

In the gable is an equestrian figure that reminds one of Don Quixote accompanied by his faithful Sancho, but a more saintly personage is intended. It is San Martín sharing his cloak with a poor pilgrim. What that memorializes is the traditional service of the monks who staffed the medieval monastery. They

371

provided poor pilgrims, some of whom reached here in rags and virtually naked, with more serviceable clothing and a cleansing bath in the fountain that stood nearby in the square between the monastery and the cathedral. Thus the pilgrims were able to meet the relics of the saint in properly presentable fashion so as to make their peace with God through the intercession of Santiago.

In contrast with this lavish facade, we discover an austere, barrel-vaulted interior. Its decor and furnishing were turned over to Casas y Nóvoa and Miguel de Romay who, among other things, created the ornate retable by the main altar. The latter work is regarded as one of the best examples of the local Galician Baroque.

The equestrian figures are Santiago and San Millán, the sainted moorslayers, shown running roughshod over a field of defeated Moors. The **choir stalls** are the work of Mateo de Prado, executed between 1644 and 1647. The choir sits beneath a coffered barrel vault gaily colored in reds, greens and blues, offering quite a different atmosphere than usual for such a place.

Principal side chapel in the church, on the north side near the front, is the **Capilla del Socorro,** the work of Casas y Nóvoa. It includes another of his fascinating gilt retables. Next to it is the Sacristy, designed by the same artist, but much different in decor. Here he devised an elegant room in the form of a Greek cross, where his usual Baroque flamboyance is suppressed.

A hundred meters north of the Plaza San Martín is the intersection with Calle Cuesta Vieja (Costa Vella). A hundred meters to the right is the Hospital de San Roque, which is not particularly noteworthy despite its ancient lineage. So we proceed left along Calle Cuesta Vieja for a hundred meters and down the long staircase that descends the steep hill to where, on the right, stands the **Convento de San Francisco.**

This monastery is said to have been founded by St. Francis in 1214 when he came to Compostela as a pilgrim. It has been rebuilt several times since, mainly in the seventeenth and eighteenth centuries. The associated church, built by Simón Rodriguez in 1742, has a pair of towers and remnants of a Gothic cloister. The facade was built in 1779 and contains a statue of St. Francis by Ferreiro.

Most interesting to us was the monumental **statue** of the saint that stands in front of the church. It is the work of a local sculptor, Francisco Asdrey, erected in 1926. St. Francis is depicted preaching, arms outstretched, standing at the foot of the Crucified Christ, with the Virgin Mary and the others standing by. It is artistically well formed and aesthetically effective as modern church art seldom is.

Most notable inside the church is the tomb of Cotolay, a disciple of the saint, who stayed behind to build the monastery while Saint Francis went elsewhere to tend his business of saving souls.

Note that the former monastic building to the left of the church has been turned into a three-star hotel.

From the monastery proceed south on Calle San Francisco to the Plaza de Obradoiro. On the right is the Faculty of Medicine, followed by the Hostal de los Reyes Católicos and the square.

We leave you here on the magnificent Plaza de Obradoiro. By now you know the route back to your car or hotel through the arcaded streets of the old city, so we refrain from providing further directions. Our task is done. So are our travels with St James.

Perhaps you owe the saint another visit to his cathedral across the way. He might even reward you with a miracle all your own. Such things have happened. If not today, maybe tomorrow. An old pilgrim adage had it that St. James never lets a prayer go unanswered. He just takes his own good time about the doing of it.

SUGGESTED ITINERARY

This itinerary follows the travel plan covered in the pages of the book. It is intended for the working person taking a three-week vacation using a rental car. It is designed to make the most of the opportunity, and treats time and see-worthiness as the essential factors for planning purposes.

Would a longer trip be worthwhile? Are there other things to see? You bet.

At Pamplona the schedule is relaxed, designed to ease recovery from the flight and drive to the city. After that, this itinerary is fast paced. You may choose to slow it down. We put you on the street or highway early each morning in order that one sequence of sights can be seen before siesta time, then we schedule further explorations when things open up after siesta. There is a minimum of "free" time for shopping or just plain lazing about. Nor does this itinerary generally allow for "sleeping in" mornings, or quitting early for any of a score of reasons. But you can have it your own way all the way.

The point is: for the more leisurely traveler there are plenty of opportunities to lay over in pleasant places, or for side trips to sites outside the scope or theme of the junket we describe. What else? A stop over for at least a couple of days in Madrid is recommended for anyone new to the Spanish experience. An angler can wet his line with the shades of Ernest Hemingway and his cronies in Burguete, or in the swift mountain streams of Asturias. A rock climber will be in Seventh Heaven among the crags of the Picos de Europa. Lovers can enjoy a score of romantic hideaways. Bicyclists will meet a host of fellow cycling enthusiasts along the Way, and gain a more intimate feel for the countryside and towns to boot. There is something here for everyone.

Important advisory: Never stray too far, driving on the road or walking in the larger cities, without a good map in hand. The better auto rental agents provide a top-notch road map of Spain and Madrid when you pick up your car. Your agent may also have maps on hand for the major cities along your route. In any event, at your hotel, or at the tourist office in each city or town, you will be able to obtain a local map (plano) on which the major sightseeing attractions, public offices, and traveler's facilities are shown.

Whatever your travel plans, recognize one fact: There are specific visiting days and hours for many places you will want to see. If a place is open mornings only, and closed Mondays, plan accordingly.

Itinerary Details

Day		**Activity**
1	Sat	By air to Madrid.
2	Sun	Arrive Madrid. Rent car. Drive to Pamplona. About a five-hour drive via Soria and Agreda. Hotel at Pamplona.
3	Mon	Roncesvalles and the Navarran Way
4	Tues	Pamplona
5	Wed	Aragonese Way, Leyre to Eunate. Hotel at Puente de la Reina
6	Thurs	The cities of the bridges. Hotel at Estella.
7	Fri	To Logroño and Nájera. Hotel at Nájera.
8	Sat	Morning: San Millán de Cogolla. Afternoon: Santa María la Real
9	Sun	To Burgos. Hotel in Burgos convenient to our walking plan.
10	Mon	Lesmes to cathedral, then cross river to museums.
11	Tues	Burgos cathedral. Afternoon free if desirable.
12	Wed	To Carrion de los Condes and take hotel there.
13	Thurs	To Sahagún, then Cangas de Onís, and take hotel there.

14	Fri	To Oviedo, see Cathedral and environs. Hotel in Oviedo.
15	Sat	Monte Narranco and Santullano in Oviedo.
16	Sun	To Leon with side trips. Hotel in Leon.
17	Mon	Leon
18	Tues	To Ponferrada. Hotel in Ponferrada.
19	Wed	To Sarria. Hotel in Sarria.
20	Thurs	To Santiago. Hotel in Santiago.
21	Fri	Santiago.
22	Sat	Santiago, with optional drive to Madrid in afternoon.
23	Sun	Fly home from Santiago or Madrid.

How to make a two-week vacation do the job:

Do Roncesvalles and Pamplona in one day, skip the Aragonese Road and go directly to the cities of the bridges. Arriving in Burgos, see the Cartuja de Miraflores that late afternoon, do the central sights and cathedral the next day, and move on the day after. Go from Sahagun to Leon, skipping the digression North to Asturias. Do Santiago in one day. Days saved: 7.

GLOSSARY

Almohades "The Unitarians." Twelfth century Moorish dynasty with ascetic Islamic beliefs. Overthrew Almoravides and ruled all North Africa and Moorish Spain. Defeated by Christian alliance at Las Navas de Tolosa in 1212; disappeared from Spain within another decade.

Almoravides "The Hermits." Eleventh-Century Moslem fundamentalist dynasty of Northwest Africa and Spain. Sought to unify Moorish kingdoms of Spain. Defeated Alfonso VI in 1086; defeated by El Cid at Valencia.

Archivolt The inner curve of an arch

Artesonado Describing a wood ceiling with carved, often inlaid panels

Asturian art A pre-Romanesque style based on classical Roman and Visigothic influences; found mainly in a tiny region in the vicinity of Oviedo in Asturias in the late eighth and ninth centuries. In architecture it combines Visigothic barrel vaults with Roman round arches. Double and triple-arched windows are used. Sculpture styled after the Visigothic-Byzantine; painting shows Byzantine influence. Best example: Monte Naranco in Oviedo.

Churrigueresque A Spanish baroque style named after José Churriguera (1665-1725), noted for being extremely ornate. Example: the work of Domingo de Andrade (a choir at Santiago de Compostela) and Fernando Casas y Novoa (west facade of cathedral at Santiago de Compostela 1738) during the eighteenth century.

Cistercian In architecture: Severely simple style originating in the late twelfth century, utilizing the Gothic pointed arch and similarly vaulted transept as a style transitional from the Romanesque toward the Gothic. Notable are the Monastery of Las Huelgas in Burgos and the convent at Gradefes.

Corbel A projecting block (stone or wood), usually carved, often used as a support for something else; e.g., base of an ornamental arch, a carved figure, etc.

Gothic In architecture and art, a style imported from France and notably used at Roncesvalles, Burgos and Leon in the thirteenth century and later. Late Spanish Gothic is marked by Baroque-like flamboyance stemming from German, French and Moslem influences. The dominant effect of Gothic is that of vast space within tall elevations achieved by the pointed arch and ribbed vaults, with the central nave the dominant space, with narrow, usually tall side aisles. Use of interior buttressing led to use of the space between the buttresses as side chapels. The clerestory was either eliminated or minimized, and lighter wall structures were opened to contain stained glass within stone traceries, particularly in grand rose windows and in the altar area. In exterior design, emphasis is on massive flanking towers, flying buttresses, and central lanterns above the crossing of nave and transept, while portals contain richly carved Gothic pointed arches, often triple arched. Ribbing the vaults allowed them to become lighter, reducing the thickness demanded of walls, and allowing them to be perforated by broad apertures containing lightweight stone traceries and stained-glass windows. During the fourteenth and fifteenth centuries the design grew much richer in carved decor, with window tracery changing from geometric to curvilinear, and increased flamboyance of external and internal decorations less related to basic structure than to expression. Thus flying arches became a construct of light semi-arches decorated with spires, canopies, statues and bric-a-brac, increasing the appearance of structural lightness compared to the ponderous heaviness of

Romanesque. Examples: Burgos cathedral (1230) with its spires (1442-58), choir (1497-1512), and lantern (completed 1568) and the Capilla del Condestable; León cathedral with its fabulous display of stained glass.

Gothic sculpture Outstanding at Puerta del Sarmental, Burgos; Tympanum at center door and the Virgen Blanca, Cathedral of León; retable of the Cartuja of Miraflores at Burgos.

Groin vaulting The meeting of two vaults ordinarily rising from equidistant (square) points

Modillion An ornamental block beneath a cornice

Mozarabs Christian subjects of Arab kings

Mozarabic art Christian migrants from southern Spain from the ninth to eleventh centuries brought Moorish art and architectural traditions with them, including the horseshoe arch, and melded it with pre-Romanesque Asturian styles. Best example: San Miguel de la Calzada.

Mudéjar From the twelfth to fifteen century, Moslem architects and artisans working for Christians in the reconquered territories, built Christian edifices with marked Islamic character.

Mudéjar In Arabic, one who stays behind.

Plateresque A flamboyant style developed in the late fifteenth and early sixteenth centuries from Italian and Mudéjar influences, with a baroque richness laid atop Gothic fundamental structures, but with emphasis on pure decor having little relationship to those structures. The term is derived from "platero," a silversmith. Developed in Segovia by Lorenzo Vázquez. In the north of Spain it became pervasive only in Castile, and elsewhere is observed only in isolated features such as the facade on the Hostal de los Reyes Católicos in Santiago.

Retable Originally a shelf behind an altar; became a highly decorated wall-like or partition-like structure rising behind an altar and often filling the width of the sanctuary in front of the apse. Also a similar structure raised against a wall around a doorway, etc.

Romanesque Romanesque architecture is based on the building concepts of the Romans, particularly on the use of the round arch and barrel vault. In Spain it was the dominant form of church construction in the Christian kingdoms of the eleventh and twelfth centuries; influenced by the monastery at Cluny and the Benedictine monks, using the T-cross design (nave and transept) of the early Christian Roman basilica-style church, with the choir at the top much more elongated than in the early Christian plan. Plain and simple lines dominate. Sculpture became prominent as wall decoration, but it was concentrated at doors, etc., rather than being profusely applied everywhere. The form of the sculpture was flat, little elevated from the mass of the stone, as contrasted with the high relief of the Gothic style. Greatest example: The Pórtico de la Gloria at Cathedral of Santiago, by Maestro Mateo (fl 1168-1188.) The supporting structure for the arches and vaults is dominated by piers instead of columns, because of the heavy weight of the vaulting. Early Romanesque still used the Roman wooden roof, at least over the central nave. Stone vaulting came later and, as at Santiago de Compostela, required heavy buttressing of the piers at the exterior wall. Most significant example is the original cathedral at Santiago de Compostela (1075-1130). It was the first church in Spain to have an apse surrounded by a vaulted ambulatory aisle and many offshooting and vaulted side chapels. Others: San Martín of Fromista (1066); San Isidoro at León (1054-67), the latter noted especially for Romanesque sculpture.

Visigothic In art: Little remains; architecture marked by the horseshoe arch and barrel vaulting. Sculptural reliefs quite primitive and showing distinct Byzantine influence. Best examples of the influence: the church of San Miguel de Liño in Oviedo, and Suso at San Millán de Cogolla.

A Traveler's Highway to Heaven

A Traveler's Highway to Heaven